Issues and Trends in Technology and Human Interaction

Bernd Carsten Stahl
De Montfort University, UK

IRM Press
Publisher of innovative scholarly and professional
information technology titles in the cyberage

Hershey • London • Melbourne • Singapore

Acquisition Editor: Kristin Klinger
Senior Managing Editor: Jennifer Neidig
Managing Editor: Sara Reed
Assistant Managing Editor: Sharon Berger
Development Editor: Kristin Roth
Copy Editor: Amanda Appicello
Typesetter: Amanda Appicello
Cover Design: Lisa Tosheff
Printed at: Integrated Book Technology

Published in the United States of America by
          IRM Press (an imprint of Idea Group Inc.)
          701 E. Chocolate Avenue, Suite 200
          Hershey PA 17033-1240
          Tel: 717-533-8845
          Fax: 717-533-8661
          E-mail: cust@idea-group.com
          Web site: http://www.irm-press.com

and in the United Kingdom by
          IRM Press (an imprint of Idea Group Inc.)
          3 Henrietta Street
          Covent Garden
          London WC2E 8LU
          Tel: 44 20 7240 0856
          Fax: 44 20 7379 0609
          Web site: http://www.eurospanonline.com

Library of Congress Cataloging-in-Publication Data

Issues and trends in technology and human interaction / Bernd Carsten Stahl, editor.
    p. cm.
  Summary: "This book provides a wide range of interesting and novel approaches to the relationship between technology and humans. It can be used for teaching as well as for research purposes; it contains insights that are of relevance for social and organizational use of information and communications technology"--Provided by publisher.
  Includes bibliographical references and index.
  ISBN 1-59904-268-1 (hardcover) -- ISBN 1-59904-269-X (softcover) -- ISBN 1-59904-270-3 (ebook)
  1. Information technology--Social aspects. 2. Communication--Technological innovations. 3. Human beings.
I. Stahl, Bernd Carsten, 1968-
  T58.5.I79 2006
  303.48'33--dc22
                    2006027718

British Cataloguing in Publication Data
A Cataloguing in Publication record for this book is available from the British Library.

All work contributed to this book is new, previously-unpublished material. The views expressed in this book are those of the authors, but not necessarily of the publisher.

Advances in Technology and Human Interaction Series

Bernd Carsten Stahl, Editor-in-Chief

Issues and Trends in Technology and Human Interaction
h/c 1-59904-268-1 • s/c 1-59904-269-X
copyright 2007

Advances in Technology and Human Interaction provides a platform for leading research that addresses issues of human and technology interaction. These disciplines range from more technical ones such as computer science, engineering, or information systems to non-technical descriptions of technology and human interaction from the point of view of sociology or philosophy. Apart from aiming to be interdisciplinary this series aspires to provide a publication outlet for research questions and approaches that are novel and may find it difficult to be published in established journals following a rigid and exclusive structure. It is open to all research paradigms, be they empirical or conceptual, but requires that they be accessible and reflected.

For more information, visit www.idea-group.com.

Issues and Trends in Technology and Human Interaction

Table of Contents

Preface

Technology would not exist without human beings. It is created by humans for the purposes of humans. It often has unintended and unexpected effects on humans and can be used for purposes other than originally planned. While technology cannot exist without humans, one can equally well argue that humans cannot exist without technology. This relationship touches on many fundamental questions of anthropology, ontology, and epistemology. Due to the complexity of the field of technology and human interaction, we cannot hope to do it justice in a single volume. The chapters in this current book are therefore focused on a sub-sector, namely the area of information and communication technology. They discuss different topics and angles on the way in which humans interact with ICT. The book reflects a variety of approaches and problems that researchers have investigated in this area. It is meant to be multi-disciplinary and demonstrate the richness of these studies. The reference disciplines that the authors draw upon reflect this multi- and trans-disciplinary nature. They include information systems, computer science, sociology, philosophy, gender studies, and even theology.

This book will provide the reader with a wide range of interesting and novel approaches to the relationship between technology and humans. It can be used for teaching as well as for research purposes, and it will contain insights that are of relevance for social and organisational use of ICT.

Chapter I, *Conducting Feminist Gender Research in the Information Systems Field* by Eileen M. Trauth, Lynette Kvasny, and Anita Greenhill, explores the methodological and epistemological implications of conducting feminist, gender research in the information systems field. These implications revolve around four core themes: (1) feminist research is situated in the margins; (2) current gender and IS research is not adequately problematized; (3) feminist research questions the legitimacy and appropriateness of positivist research; and (4) reflection on the personal characteristics of the researcher such as race, gender, sexuality, and class can inform feminist research. They propose four criteria for conducting feminist IS research:

(1) engaging in researcher reflexivity; (2) challenging the hegemonic dominance, legitimacy, and appropriateness of positivist epistemologies; (3) theorizing from the margins; and (4) problematizing gender.

Chapter II, *A Taxonomy of Stakeholders: Human Roles in System Development* by Ian F. Alexander, explores the question, "Who are the humans interacting with technology?" Systems engineers have often paid too little attention to the nature of the so-called "users" of products under development. They are better called stakeholders, as many roles are involved, and few of those are in direct contact with the developed products. A simple and robust conceptual framework for classifying development stakeholders—a taxonomy—is proposed. The taxonomy is product-centric, with concentric "circles" denoting broad categories of stakeholder. Within these, generic "slots" describe typical classes of a stakeholder; these are subdivided into "roles," which are expected to vary at least in name with the domain. Examples are given, and a popular template is re-analysed using the framework. The taxonomy has immediate value in identifying and validating stakeholder roles in requirements' elicitation. This helps to ensure that key viewpoints on requirements are not missed. That, in turn, reduces the risk of instability and failure during development.

Chapter III, *21st Century Religious Communities* by Susan E. George, takes a very different approach and investigates the relationship of ICT and religion. This chapter examines the development of 21st century virtual communities, focusing upon those communities which have emerged for virtual religion. It aims to: (1) raise awareness of the way in which technology is being used for religious purposes; (2) explain the ways that human interaction in religious communities is influenced by technology, in both supporting traditional modes of interaction and in enabling new, and the main, criticisms; and (3) provide evidence to support the benefit of such communities to religious bodies themselves by turning to the question of technological determinism and the crucial question of just how humanity is influenced by technology.

Chapter IV, *Protecting One's Privacy: Insights into the Views and Nature of the Early Adopters of Privacy Services* by Sarah Spiekermann, addresses one of the central concerns many users have when interacting with ICT, namely privacy. Using privacy and security technology becomes increasingly important in many application areas, for companies as well as for consumers. However, the market for privacy enhancing technologies (PETs) is still small, especially in the private consumer segment. Due to the nature of the technology per se, little is known and can be learned about the views and motivation of those who carefully protect their transactions on the Internet. Are they a niche group? Or do they hold views and have traits that promise a wider-spread adoption of PETs in the long run? This chapter describes a large-scale survey of users of a German anonymity service and provides PET users' demographic and psychographic traits as well as an insight into the thoughts, feelings, and motivations of PET users.

Chapter V, *A Practitioner-Centred Assessment of a User-Experience Framework* by Peter Wright, John McCarthy, and Lisa Meekison, touches on a central issue of the commercial use of ICT. The chapter outlines a practitioner-oriented framework for analysing user experience. The framework depicts experience as compositional, emotional, spatio-temporal, and sensual, and as intimately bound up with a number of processes which allow us to make sense of experience. It was developed and assessed as part of a participative action research project involving interested practitioners. They report how these practitioners used the framework, what aspects of experience they felt it missed, and how useful they found it as a tool for evaluating Internet shopping experiences. A thematic content analysis of participants' reflections on their use of the framework as a tool to evaluate Internet shopping experiences revealed some strengths and some weaknesses. The framework also captured aspects of experience that relate to both the sequential structure of the activity and its subjective aspects.

Chapter VI, *Impacts of Behavior Modeling in Online Asynchronous Learning Environments* by Charlie C. Chen, Albert L. Harris, and Lorne Olfman, addresses another pivotal area where humans and technology interact, namely education, teaching, and learning. The continued and increasing use of online asynchronous learning (OAL) environments for training raises the question of whether behavior modeling, the most effective training method in live instruction, will prove to be effective in OAL environments. If it is, to what extent will it be effective? In this study, behavior modeling training was delivered in three modes: face-to-face, videotaped, and scripted. Each behavior modeling mode expresses social presence to a different degree and, therefore, could impact both learning performance and the willingness of students to take online asynchronous training. This study reports on the effect of behavior modeling modes on three variables in an OAL environment— perceived usefulness, near-knowledge, and far-knowledge transfer—when learning a software application. This research found that the face-to-face environment is not significantly more effective than an OAL environment. The impacts of social presence seem to be higher in face-to-face OAL environments. Although videotaped instruction and scripted instruction were lower than face-to-face instruction, they deliver the same degrees of social presence and lead to a similar satisfaction level.

Chapter VII, *The Sociotechnical Nature of Mobile Computing Work: Evidence from a Study of Policing in the United States* by Steve Sawyer and Andrea Tapia, uses the sociotechnical lens to investigate the use of ICT at work. This chapter discusses the sociotechnical nature of mobile computing as used by three policing agencies within the United States. Mobile devices, access, and service were provided via a third generation wireless network to a focal application, Pennsylvania's Justice NETwork (JNET), a secure Web-based portal connecting authorized users to a set of 23 federated criminal justice and law enforcement databases via a query-based interface. In this study, the authors conceptualize mobility and policing as a sociotechnical ensemble which builds on the social-shaping of technology perspective and the tradition of sociotechnical theorizing focusing on the co-design of work practices and technologies to support work. Drawing from the social informatics tradition, the authors turn a critical, empirical, and contextual lens on the practices of mobility and work. Their analysis of the data leads them to find that the social and the technical are still separate in this mobile work context. This simple view of social and technical as related but distinct often leads to problems with collecting and interpreting evidence of ICT-based system's design and use. The authors further note this over-simplification of sociotechnical action is likely to continue unless more viable analytic approaches are developed and the assumptions of the current techno-determinist approaches are challenged more explicitly.

Chapter VIII, *Rhetoric, Practice, and Context-Sensitivity in Sociotechnical Action: The Compass Case* by Giuseppina Pellegrino, uses a similar theoretical outlook as the preceding one to shed light on a different case. Sociotechnical action, as interpreted in this chapter, comprises a wide array of elements that shape technological artefacts as socio-material and linguistic devices. Concepts grounded in different theoretical streams are used to account for the ambiguous and multiple process of technology construction. Categories of "interpretative flexibility," "inscription," "work-around," "misunderstanding," are reviewed and used in this account. Starting from the implementation of an intranet-based knowledge management system in a 100-staff British firm, different courses of action in technology implementation and appropriation are analysed. Interpretations performed by different actors can raise misunderstanding, failure, and innovation in processes of negotiation and are strongly oriented by power issues. The gap between rhetoric of public discourse and practice situated in specific organizational contexts is argued to be crucial in framing expectations and patterns of sociotechnical action. Ambiguity and multiplicity of the knowledge management system studied (the Compass) illustrate how the mutual constitution of the social and the technical makes technology a "context-sensitive" artefact.

Chapter IX, *The Socio-Pragmatics of IT Artefacts: Reconciling the Pragmatic, Social, Semiotic, and Technical* by Göran Goldkuhl and Pär J. Ågerfalk, uses the sociotechnical lens to discuss issues of system failure. There are many attempts to explain success and failure in information systems. Many of these refer to a purported sociotechnical gap. In this chapter, the authors develop an alternative approach that does not impose such a strong dichotomy, but regards social and technical rather as dimensions along which to study work practices. The developed theory involves not only the "social" and "technical" constructs but also other generic ones, namely "instrumental," "semiotic," and "pragmatic." They call this theory socio-instrumental pragmatism. To illustrate the theoretical concepts introduced, the authors use an example brought from an extensive action research study including the development of an information system in eldercare, developed through a participatory design approach.

Chapter X, *Sociotechnical Spaces—Guiding Politics, Staging Design* by Christian Clausen and Yutaka Yoshinaka, is the fourth chapter to concentrate on the socio-technical approaches. This chapter addresses how insights from the social shaping tradition and political process theory may contribute to an understanding of the sociotechnical design and implementation of change. This idea is pursued through the notion of "sociotechnical spaces" and its delineation, with respect to the analysis of two distinct cases, namely, business process reengineering (BPR) and magnetic resonance imaging (MRI) in the light of "film-less" radiological practice, respectively. The chapter elaborates on sociotechnical space as being an occasioning as well as a result of sociotechnical choices and processes, and points to how socio-material and discursive practices may render such spaces open to problematization and action. It is suggested that the notion of sociotechnical spaces helps generate a sensitising guide for researchers and practitioners, and thus may serve as a constructive means with which to localise potential political concerns in processes of change. This chapter tentatively points to some analytical implications and also to challenges and possibilities for the "bridging" between spaces, which may otherwise be rendered analytically distinct.

Chapter XI, *Concerns with "Mutual Constitution": A Critical Realist Commentary* by Alistair Mutch, is the final chapter among those dealing with the sociotechnical approach, and it extends a critical realist perspective to it. The case for "analytical dualism" as a means of approaching sociotechnical action is presented as an alternative to accounts which tend to conflate agency, structure, and technology. This is based on the work of Margaret Archer, whose work is, in turn, located in the traditions of critical realism. Her commitment to analytical dualism, which stresses both the importance of time in analysis and the emergent properties of structure, is argued to give a firmer purchase on the notion of context than the alternatives based on, for example, the work of Giddens and Latour.

Chapter XII, *A Framework for Monitoring User Involvement and Participation in ERP Implementation Projects* by José Esteves, Joan Pastor, and Josep Casanovas, returns to another central issue in the relationship between technology and humans: the participations of users in the design of the technology. In this chapter, a framework for monitoring user involvement and participation within ERP implementation projects is proposed by using the goals/questions/metrics method. The results of this work are threefold. First, a literature review is presented on the topic of user involvement and participation as related with ERP implementation projects. Second, a framework for monitoring user involvement and participation in ERP implementation projects is proposed. And third, a goals/questions/metrics preliminary plan is proposed to monitor and control user involvement and participation within ERP implementation projects.

Chapter XIII, *Investigating the Interdependence of Organisations and Information Systems* by Laurence Brooks, Christopher J. Davis, and Mark Lycett, explores the interdependence of organisations and information systems using the personal construct theory (PCT) as an underlying conceptual frame. Changing business models and information technologies were investigated in two distinct work settings: in each case, the technique contributed substantial insight into the role of information systems in that context. The analysis shows that the techniques have matured to a stage where they provide a basis for improved understanding of the organisational complexities related to information technologies. The techniques focus on the social construction of meaning by articulating and interpreting the discourse that surrounds the development, implementation, and use of information technology in organisations. This chapter concludes by drawing out the idea of the development of a conceptual model to act as a framework for the analysis of cognitive schema and shared understanding. In developing and participating in this shared understanding, both organisational and technological communities could increase their awareness of each other's issues and concerns, thereby enabling them to improve the conceptual agility of the organisation.

Chapter XIV, *USE IT to Create Patient Relation Management for Multiple Sclerosis Patients* by Margreet B. Michel-Verkerke, Roel W. Schuring, and Ton A. M. Spil, is the only one in the current volume to deal with another problem area of central importance for the interaction between technology and humans—the area of ICT in healthcare. Patients with Multiple Sclerosis (MS) visit various healthcare providers during the course of their disease. It was suggested that information and communication technology (ICT) might help to orchestrate their care provision. The authors have applied the USE IT-tool to get insight in the relevant problems, solutions, and constraints of the MS-care both in the organisational and the information technological area. There is hardly a chain of healthcare, but rather, a network in which informal communication plays an important role. This informal network worked reasonably effective but inefficient and slow. The MS patients-count is only small for most care providers. Patients thought that lack of experience caused their major problems: insufficient and inadequate care. To improve care, the authors proposed a solution that combines an "MS-protocol," the introduction of a central coordinator of care, and a patient relation management (PRM) system. This is a simple Web-based application based on an agreement by the caregivers which will support routing, tracking, and tracing of an MS patient and supply the caregivers with professional guidelines.

Chapter XV, *Contextual Characteristics of Creativity: Effects on IT-Supported Organisational Brainstorming* by Dick Stenmark, looks at the effects technology has on human creativity. As a much needed quality in today's businesses, creativity is an important area of research. Creativity is a complex and multi-faceted concept and can thus be studied from a variety of perspectives. In this chapter, the author describes an attempt to support organisational creativity with information technology, in this case an electronic brainstorming device. While implementing and evaluating this prototype, it was noticed that the sheer presence of technology guarantees neither usage nor success. Contextual factors such as organisational culture and attitudes seem to have an equally important role, and this observation calls for a more focused analysis of the motivational aspects of creativity management. Based on the empirical data from the electronic brainstorming system evaluation and literature on organisational creativity, three general pieces of managerial advice to promote corporate creativity are suggested: (1) reconsider the use of extrinsic rewards; (2) recognise creative initiatives; and (3) allow redundancy.

These 15 chapters show the breadth of research pertaining to the interaction of technology and human beings. The approaches taken and the phenomena observed differ vastly, but they are combined by a desire to better understand how humans and technology interact. Some of the findings are of direct managerial relevance whereas others are of more interest in other areas, be it not-for-profit organisations or public administration. What they have in common is that they will help us understand how humans use technology and what influence technology can have on humans. Such knowledge is of pivotal importance if we are to successfully address the challenges of the 21st century technical civilisation.

Chapter I

Conducting Feminist Gender Research in the Information Systems Field

Eileen M. Trauth
The Pennsylvania State University, USA

Lynette Kvasny
The Pennsylvania State University, USA

Anita Greenhill
University of Manchester Institute of Science and Technology, UK

Abstract

In this chapter,[1] we explore the methodological and epistemological implications of conducting feminist, gender research in the information systems field. These implications revolve around four core themes: (1) that feminist research is situated in the margins; (2) that current gender and IS research is not adequately problematized; (3) that feminist research questions the legitimacy and appropriateness of positivist research; and (4) that reflection on the personal characteristics of the researcher such as race, gender, sexuality, and class can inform feminist research. We propose four criteria for conducting feminist IS research: (1) engaging in researcher reflexivity; (2) challenging the hegemonic dominance, legitimacy, and appropriateness of positivist epistemologies; (3) theorizing from the margins; and (4) problematizing gender.

Introduction

The research area of gender and information technology (IT) is focused on un-covering, understanding, explaining, and predicting the influence of gender and biological sex on one's engagement with IT. A number of disciplines conduct this research including: information systems, human computer interaction, information sciences, telecommunications, computer supported cooperative work, and science, technology and society. In this chapter, we focus on the discipline of information systems (IS). By IS research, we mean those studies that examine the arrangement of equipment, resources, and procedures, often computerized, that are required to collect, process, and distribute data for use in (typically) managerial decision mak-ing in business organizations. We concentrate on IS because this field examines IT in business contexts in which managerial perspectives are privileged. Moreover, IT is often used to intensify and expand the exercise of managerial power. To the degree that women adopt managerial values and beliefs as their own, women may achieve some measure of success (by the majority definition). We argue, however, that what is woefully underrepresented in gender and IS research is a critical, femi-nist perspective on gender.

IS researchers typically examine the ways in which sex-based differences in IT use shape and are shaped by numerous practices such as the conceptualization and use of IT (Gefen & Straub, 1997; Star, 1995), the design of IT artifacts (MacKenzie & Wajcman, 1999; Woodfield, 2002), and the persistence of students in science, math, engineering, and technology-related disciplines (Camp, 1997; McGrath Cohoon, 2001). Sex-based disparities also occur in the mundane and the overt ways in which power and performance are enacted in organizational settings (Adam, Emms, Green, & Owen, 1994; Eriksson, Kitchenham, & Tijdens, 1991; Von Hellens, Nielsen, & Trauth, 2001), in societal and cultural influences on IT careers choices (Nielsen, von Hellens, Pringle, & Greenhill, 1999; Trauth, 2002), and in the continued under-representation of women in the IT workforce (Freeman & Aspray, 1999).

While this research provides many insights into the relationship between gender and IT, the resultant picture is highly fragmented, patchy in its coverage, and inconsis-tent in its depth of theorizing on gender in order to provide a basis for explanation and prediction. In our view, the topic of gender and IT is under theorized in three ways. First, gender is seldom considered as an independent factor in sociotech-nical studies of IS in context (Wajcman, 2001). Instead of viewing gender as a socially-constructed category, researchers seek to understand gender by fixating on differences between biological sexes. Second, much of the published research focuses on data analysis rather than theoretical implications that relate to the existing body of gender, and gender and IT literature (Adam, Howcroft, & Richardson, 2001). Third, there exists an insufficient understanding of the underlying causes of sex-based underrepresentation in the IT profession that would inform educational policies and workplace human resource strategies to attract and retain more women (Tapia, Kvasny, & Trauth, 2004).

Given this critique, the issue arises as to how to study the role of sex and gender in engagement with IT in ways that overcome these shortcomings. We believe the answer is to produce a stream of gender research in the information systems field that is also feminist research. Thus, essential to our discussion of feminist gender research in IS is the recognition of a fundamental difference between feminist gender research and nonfeminist gender research. Whereas the term *gender research* refers to any research project that is concerned with gender and IT use, the term *feminist gender research* refers to research projects that study gender and IT use from the vantage point of particular methodological and epistemological positions. In this chapter, we discuss these methodological and epistemological implications of conducting feminist gender research in the information systems field. We organize our discussion around four criteria for characterizing gender and IT research as feminist research. First, it is conducted from the standpoint of researcher reflexivity. Second, it challenges the hegemonic dominance, legitimacy, and appropriateness of positivist epistemologies as the sole approach to gender and IS research. Third, it adopts a position of theorizing from and understanding of the margins. Finally, it problematizes the concept of gender.

The State of Gender Research in IS

As a prelude to our discussion of feminist gender research, we consider the current state of gender and IS research. Gender studies have traditionally existed at the periphery of IS research.[2] One measure of this is the extent to which gender is perceived to be a relevant component of IT personnel research. For example, a review of the papers presented at the ACM SIGMIS Computer Personnel Research Conference—where the focus of research is IT personnel—over the past 44 years that the conference has been held revealed that, of the 862 conference papers presented, only 29 were found to focus on gender and the IT workforce or gender and IT education (Trauth, Quesenberry, & Huang, 2006). Further, 23 of these have been presented since 2000. Finally, 10 of these gender papers were presented in 2003 when the conference theme was diversity in IT workforce (Trauth, 2003).

Another measure is where gender studies are published. Hence, we conducted an analysis of IS journals. We began by searching the Proquest—ABI/INFORM® Global database using the subject keywords "information systems and gender." This search returned eight scholarly journal articles. A search on "information technology and gender" returned 31 scholarly journal articles across a number of domains including women's studies, American history, education, sociology, and IS. To gain closer insights into the publication of gender research conducted by IS scholars, we searched for gender-related articles in five premiere IS journals. The journal rankings were obtained by a published study which summarized the responses of approximately 1,000 IS researchers around the world (Mylonopolous & Theoharakis, 2001). We selected five of the top 50 IS journals from this ranked list. Next, using the subject keyword "gender," we searched the citations and abstracts of each publication. The start and end dates are the dates for which Proquest provides full text coverage. The results of our analysis are included in Table 1.

Looking at the highest ranking journals in the field, we note that gender-related studies are represented unevenly. In terms of methodology, nearly all of the papers published in *Management Science, MISQ*, and *JMIS* were positivist in their epistemological origins and utilized quantitative methods to measure gender differences on factors such as computer usage in the workplace (Venkatesh & Morris, 2000), perceptions about and usage of e-mail (Gefen & Straub, 1997), job performance and career advancements (Igbaria & Baroudi, 1995), pay disparity (Truman & Baroudi, 1994), and computer playfulness (Webster & Martocchio, 1992). The theoretical perspective informing these studies is essentialism: that women and men are different, and these differences can be teased out by measuring a few key constructs. Positivist survey research and hypothesis testing is the dominant research approach. We expand upon the limitations of positivist methods for feminist research in the second section of this chapter.

A second observation is the range in the number of articles published. On the one hand, the *CACM* has published 14 articles while, on the other hand, ISR has not published any articles that focus explicitly on gender. Three of the *CACM* papers were published in a special issue in January 1995. The *CACM* has published rela-

Table 1. Gender research in leading IS journals

Journal	Rank	Dates	Number of citations
Management Information Systems Quarterly (MISQ)	1	1987-2005	7
Communications of the ACM (CACM)	2	1991-2005	14
Information Systems Research (ISR)	3	1999-2005	0
Journal of Management Information Systems (JMIS)	4	1992-2001	3
Management Science	5	1987-2005	2

tively more papers that have taken an interpretivist epistemology and used qualitative methods.

A third observation is that the highest ranking journal (according to Mylonopolous and Theoharakis) has, to date, only published seven papers that take gender as a central construct. The studies typically use "gender as a variable" to distinguish male and female survey respondents. Feminist methods and theories are not present in this work. Given the historical underrepresentation of women in the field, the relative paucity of feminist research and the dominance of positivist epistemologies in premier IS journals are not altogether surprising. Calvert and Ramsey (1996) contend that dominant group members such as American males of European descent along with diverse peoples with colonized minds often cannot see their own class privilege, power, and dominance. What is lost is inclusion of the critical, radical, and problem-posing nature of feminist theory and practice as an anti-paternalistic discourse. Gender as operationalized in "mainstream" IS escapes intensive probing and questioning; it is simply taken as a given dimension for determining differences between men and women. It remains a challenge to get those who conduct gender research to move from the center, the place of safety which excludes the lives, identities and experience of the "Other." Consequently, the most privileged discourse community, the premiere academic journals, has not, to date, contended with feminist projects in IS.

Contemporary feminist theory provides guidance for reflecting on the "politics of location" and using marginalized spaces as sites for resistance and social change. Specifically, this means making the politics of location situated in the power and privilege of male domination problematic and questioning the ideological weight of essentialist understanding of gender. We believe that a radical form of border crossing is needed in order to reconstruct gender and technology as the rich socio-cultural and political constructs that they are. But border crossing requires a productive dialog in order to create a space where power relations, ideologies, and unfair practices must be challenged and overcome. The margins become this place for transformation and critique.

Gender continues to resist becoming an object of interrogation in IS research. However, as hooks (1989) comments, we need to interrogate systems of privilege that enable dominant groups to ignore the ways that their actions support and affirm the very structures of domination and oppression that they profess to wish to see dismantled. Anger, as a form of disagreement, holds some potential as a feminist methodology (hooks, 1984). Lorde (1984) defends the use of anger by focusing on it as a powerful source of energy serving progress and change. There is a positive potential for anger in shaping feminist research. We, researchers who embrace feminist methods, can use our anger constructively as a way of being heard, as a way to combat stereotypes.

Conducting Feminist Gender Research

One outlet for our anger is to channel it towards constructing alternative ways of theorizing and conceptualizing gender in IS research. We do so by offering guidance as to how to conduct feminist gender research. We organize our discussion around four key components of feminist research.

Reflexivity in Feminist Gender and IS Research

All research is guided by a set of beliefs and feelings about the world and how it should be understood. It represents a worldview that defines, for its holder, the nature of the world, the individual's place in it, and the range of possible relationships to that world and its parts. These are basic beliefs in the sense that they must be taken on faith; there is no way to establish their ultimate truthfulness. (Guba & Lincoln, 1998)

As Guba and Lincoln point out, all research is informed, consciously or unconsciously, by the philosophical assumptions of the researcher. These assumptions concern the ways that the researcher understands the nature of reality, knowledge, human nature and methodology, and consequently the interpretations of the research site. As feminist researchers, our philosophical lens is primarily informed by interpretive and critical epistemologies. We take an interpretive approach but are also critical in order to allow in-depth examination and subsequent presentation of how women engage with technology (Walsham, 1995).

From an interpretive perspective, we assume "that people create and associate their own subjective and intersubjective meanings as they interact with the world around them" (Chua, 1986). This is indicative of a subjectivity in which multiple truth and knowledge claims exist through interlocking contextual understandings, and where reality itself is also a subjective state. In this manner, feminist research for us is an exploration of how these multiple truths and knowledge claims can be found in the boundaries that are socially constructed. The social construction of these truths and knowledge claims inform the practices of both the subjects and the researchers.

From a critical perspective, we believe that our main task as researchers is one of social critique, whereby the restrictive and alienating conditions of the status quo are brought to light. Critical research seeks to be emancipatory in that it aims to help eliminate the causes of unwarranted alienation and domination and thereby enhance the opportunities for realizing human potential (Klein & Myers, 1999). While people can consciously act to change their social and economic conditions, critical theorists recognize that human ability to improve their own conditions is constrained by various forms of social, cultural, and political domination as well as natural laws and resource limitations. Whereas traditional researchers see their task as the description and interpretation of a slice of "reality," critical researchers often regard their work as a first step toward forms of political action that can redress the injustices found in the field site or constructed in the very act of research itself (Kincheloe & McLaren, 1998). Chua (1986) explains that critical studies aim to critique the status quo through the exposure of what are believed to be deep-seated, structural contradictions within social systems and, thereby, to transform these alienating and restrictive social conditions.

Thus, the first component of our depiction of feminist gender research is reflexivity. That is, the life experiences and the characteristics of the researcher such as (but not limited to) race, gender, sexuality, marital and parenthood status, and class are recognized as informing one's feminist research. Thus, we assume that the situated knowledge of feminist researchers is used to produce and implement feminist theory (Collins, 1990).

We come from different social origins, live on different continents, occupy both junior and senior academic positions, and enjoy different lifestyles. We are spouses, mothers, mentors, teachers, and advisors. We conduct our fieldwork with a wide variety of women such as employees in the IT workforce, university students in computer-related disciplines, working class women who use IT indirectly in their work, and underemployed and unemployed women just learning about IT. Our feminist projects have included the intersectionality of race, gender, and class in shaping women's standpoints on computers and the digital divide (Kvasny, 2003a, 2003b, forthcoming), gender and telework (Greenhill & Wilson, 2005; Wilson & Greenhill, 2004), socio-cultural factors that motivate and inhibit women's persistence in IT-related careers (Trauth, 1995; Trauth, Nielsen, & von Hellens, 2003; Von Hellens, Nielsen, & Trauth, 2001), development of a theory of individual differences to explain women's participation in the IT field (Trauth, 2002, 2006; Trauth & Quesenberry, 2005, 2007; Trauth, Quesenberry, & Morgan, 2004), student's perceptions of IT careers (Nielsen, von Hellens, Pringle, & Greenhill, 1999), and coping mechanisms that women and minorities enact as they deal with IT in the home and workplace (Kvasny & Trauth, 2002).

Nevertheless, we share a common commitment to feminist research. Our collective body of research focuses upon the situated and localized nature of knowledge that finds its basis in women's lived experiences. This work also demonstrates a variety of methodological practices which are significantly motivated by our desire to hear the voices of diverse women.

Through reflexive analysis, we hope to participate in and contribute to the broader discourse about the feminist method. Using Bourdieu's (Bourdieu & Waquant, 1992) notion of reflexivity, we examine three ways in which reflexivity influences the practice of research. The first, and perhaps the most, obvious factor is the individual researcher's social origins and coordinates (i.e., class, gender, sexuality, marital status, ethnicity, nationality). These characteristics influence the choice of research topic and our ability to conduct feminist research (Collins, 1998). They also influence the questions that we ask as well as the questions that we fail to ask (Allen, 1996; Nkomo, 1992). The second factor is the position that the researcher occupies within her academic field. Bourdieu notes that the points of view adopted by researchers always owe something to their situation in a field where all define themselves in part in relational terms (Bourdieu & Waquant, 1992). The third factor is the researcher's intellectual relationship with the subjects of their research. Bourdieu speaks of an intellectualist bias which may entice us to see gender as spectacle to be interpreted rather than as a concrete reality to be understood. The implication of the intellectualist bias is that researchers should not impose their theoretical logic onto the practical logic of the women in the field. In what follows, we reflect upon the ways in which our individual identities, positions within our academic fields, and our relationships to the women who allow us into their lives are in support of our research.

Social Identity and Coordinates

How does who we are influence what we do as researchers? The first author, a white American female, has used her social coordinates to inform her theory development regarding gender and IT. She grew up as one of seven sisters with no brothers and lives as adult in a same-sex household. Because of these experiences, she has learned to reject gender categorization; instead, she has learned to look to variation across individuals within sex-based groups. She has incorporated into her theory development her own experience of receiving guidance from role models and mentors (from her older sisters) and her experience of influencing other women (her younger sisters). Growing up in a middle-class family where expectations were high—that each daughter would exceed the educational level and employment horizons of their parents and be able to take care of herself—what was "normal" for her was to pursue advanced education. Consequently, a fundamental aspect of her theoretical work regarding women and IT has become the notion that certain career and educational options need to be considered "normal" for women in order to address the gender gap in the IT profession (Trauth, 2002).

Another fundamental component of her theoretical work—that what is considered "normal" for males versus females needs to be deconstructed—comes from living in same-sex households. It has taught her that much of what is considered "male" or "female" behavior is merely a social construction. What she brings into her research is the experiential knowledge that interests and abilities, with respect to IT or any other profession, are influenced by individual differences; they are not fixed by biology.

The second author, an African-American female, spent most of her youth in the areas of metro New York City and Jersey City, the "inner cities" as middle-class people like to say. She could meet the demands of higher education and corporate America only by suppressing many of her primary experiences and cultural acquisitions such as black vernacular speech, afro-centric clothing and hairstyles. Research on African-American women and technology has allowed her to reconcile herself with her primary experiences, to assume them without losing anything she subsequently acquired.

Reading black feminist writers such as Audre Lorde, bell hooks, and Patricia Hill Collins, she found that this feeling of being the "Sister Outsider" is common among black women in the academy who are rooted in working-class communities. She feels that she never quite fits in at the university, she has no tenured black women in her field to call on for guidance, and yet she cannot easily return to her place of origin because she no longer fits in there either. The research with working-class African-American women is culturally nourishing but tastes bitter sweet. On the one hand, it helps her to stay grounded and to discover more about her history and her culture. On the other hand, it is a painful reminder of how far she has moved away from her roots and of how IT is further marginalizing her people. She often thinks about her social trajectory and the ways that it has caused her to cross through varied social milieus.

Border-crossing gives you a sort of objective and subjective externality—an otherness. You experience the subtle and not-so-subtle forms of gender, class, and racial inequality that cannot but make you perceptive. You see and feel things that others cannot recognize. Yet, you are constantly reminded of your otherness. But this nurtures a vigilance that you are going to research your people's issues, and you are going to be successful in this endeavor. While traveling across these social milieus, she has taken a whole series of photographs that exist in her mind. She processes these mental images as she tries to explicate the experiences of black women appropriating technology. The research questions and theories that inform her research agenda originate from these snapshots. It is research that attempts to get at the social suffering that lies underneath and behind the debates on the "digital divide." It is research that attempts to convey how black women see IT as a vehicle that will help move them to a promised land. It is research that demonstrates how people in a position to deliver on these hopes and aspirations often refuse to hear these yearnings and continue to impose IT in ways that foster digital inequalities. Feminist scholars argue that those who have experienced marginalization themselves are particularly suited to conduct interpretive and critical feminist IT research (Harding, 1997; Hartsock, 1997; hooks, 2000).

The third author began her academic studies after many years in low-paid, low-status employment. She had a turbulent upbringing that resulted in living on and with many people that mainstream Australians would consider marginal if not altogether undesirable. These experiences have inspired strong political opinions regarding equality and social inclusion. She actively engages in research that critically challenges dominant and exploitative practices in management and information systems development. These concerns about equity set her apart from her colleagues. During a gender and IT research project, for instance, fellow researchers did not share the emancipatory ideals and motivations that typify critical researchers. This resulted in an editorial censorship of her concerns regarding computers and society and the significance of this topic to the field of information systems.

In addition to these strong political beliefs, these experiences have helped her to be proud of her sexuality. However, there is a price to be paid for this identification. The stigma associated with expressing sexuality is the stereotypical consequence and automatic prejudgment of being considered the dumb blonde. She is regularly perceived of as the "professor's secretary" or the "mature-age student" and rarely as a legitimate and knowledgeable academic. Regardless of these stereotypes, she feels that the libratory lifestyle that academia provides, combined with her broader life experiences, enable opportunities to challenge the stereotypes and superficial association of physical attributes with intelligence. This is an opportunity to rearticulate, explore, and contribute to the empowerment of women and our demands for equal consideration and equality.

Researchers' Positions

One of the passions that led these authors to study gender is the ethical belief that we cannot let institutions such as the educational system and business organizations continue to systematically exclude girls and women from IT careers. We could not let people in positions of power continue to act in ways that reproduce their privilege and unwittingly perpetuate systemic inequality for women and other marginalized groups. It is also not fair to continually call upon marginalized peoples to enlighten those in positions of power.

While fully acknowledging our limitations as researchers whose power is primarily derived from our ability to express critical thoughts and insights, we feel that it would be unethical for us as female researchers not to intervene. It is our hope that our research can fulfill both scientific and political functions. We trust that it will remind readers of the injustice that occurs when women are being systematically turned away from our profession and not given an opportunity to utilize IT as a mechanism for improving their life chances. It is their personal stories of perseverance, of conformity, and of self-exclusion that we wish to tell because this is what routine surveys that conceptualize gender as a dichotomous variable block from our view. Unfortunately, gender is often treated in this way in our field.

The first author brings to her feminist IT research a considerable body of work related to socio-cultural influences on the development of an IT labor force. This work has informed her theory development about gender and IT. Her work in different cultures has taught her that what is considered acceptable "women's work" in one culture might be restricted to "men's work" in another. She is, therefore, able to connect her feminist gender research to broader issues of cultural diversity and IT (Trauth, Huang, Morgan, Quesenberry, & Yeo, 2006; Trauth, Huang, Quesenberry, & Morgan, forthcoming), cross-cultural effects of IT, and economic development motivations for the creation of an information economy. Both her publication record and her funding record give her feminist research "legitimacy" in the wider IS community. In this regard, she considers herself to be in a privileged position. She has encountered a number of women academics who have encouraged her feminist research because they did not feel that as untenured women they could do that research. As a tenured, full professor, this author occupies a space that enables her to pursue such research. She can work to extend the boundaries of what is considered to be mainstream IS research. Thus, she has come to view her feminist research as something she does, not only because she wants to, but because she can.

The second author is an untenured assistant professor studying the relationships among race, gender, class, and IT. On the one hand, this research is risky in the sense that most IS colleagues would not see this as mainstream research. On the other hand, this research is a safe haven in the sense that it affords an intellectual space that enables her to cope with the stresses that come with being an African-American female working toward tenure at a majority, research-oriented, American university. This intellectual space is created by reading broadly outside of information systems and incorporating theoretical insights from diverse fields such as philosophy, urban studies, women's studies, sociology, and African-American studies. It also comes from cultural practices such as listening to hip-hop, rhythm and blues, and jazz music, and reading the fiction of Toni Morrison, Maya Angelou, Alice Walker, and Terri MacMillan. This intellectual space provides a position from which to critique the status quo and to envision liberating alternatives for harnessing IT to empower women.

The third author, as with many female academics, maintains two distinct and sometimes intersecting research areas. The first concerns the development of information systems, an area that is centrally situated within the IS field. The second concerns women's experiences with IT, an area that is on the margins of the field. Although she describes her main research as information systems development, she acknowledges that the research carried out in relation to gender and IT has provided more financial benefits, greater emotional support, as well as additional personal satisfaction and disappointments. She has been, and continues to be, described by her colleagues as being a woman with opinions. Women with opinions are judged in universities as women who have not yet learned their place or as troublemakers. The political and professional consequence of holding and expressing opinions accelerated her resignation from one academic post as she witnessed women who similarly had opinions being openly bullied and discriminated against.

Intellectual Relationships with Women in the Field

For us, the women with whom we engage with in the field are more than individuals to be studied. They are mothers, sisters, spouses, partners, and daughters. They are human beings to be understood. Because of this view, we cannot get on with the work of understanding if we remain distant, "objective," and "impartial" observers. There is an enormous difference between measuring gender differences and trying to understand gender relations with IT as a strategy so as to improve your own chances of success in the field. We are invested in the same interests and struggles as the women we interview, and we try to understand these relations so as to theorize about them. As female researchers who study IT, we have also lived the subject we are studying. Therefore, we have a practical stake in our research. Because of this, we are in a poised stance to go beyond the positivist paradigm. Our lived experiences give us the tools to engage in interpretive and critical research. Our awareness comes from both reflecting upon our own research practices and from the observed limitations of extant literature that fails to adequately theorize gender.

The first author has conducted in-depth interviews with women IT professionals in several countries. In these interviews, she asks women to relate their educational and employment histories, to speak about influential people and events, to reflect upon the course of their lives. She is asking women to go deep inside themselves, to call up often long suppressed memories and feelings. She believes this cannot be a unidirectional event. Consequently, she has shared similar aspects of her own career and life story. She draws upon her own experience of personal marginalization, a gendered workplace, and challenges to her research in order to connect to her research participants. She also encounters the ethical responsibility of responding to the effects of inviting her participants to open the doors of their memories. In one field study, she and her graduate assistant encountered a woman whose life reflection brought back unpleasant memories and tears that flowed an hour beyond the 90-minute interview slot. Such is the responsibility of those engaged in feminist gender research in IS.

To challenge the unspoken but harshly felt notion of who counts as a subject worthy of research, the second author chooses to work with working-class African-American women in urban milieus in the U.S. in order to bring to light their representation of IT and how they might appropriate IT as part of a strategy for improving their collective life chances. Because she is concerned about the distortions and censorship that emerge from the social asymmetry that exists in relationships between researcher and informant, she establishes a rapport over time before engaging in an informal interview process. She also engages in active listening which entails opening oneself up to questioning and, at some level, adopting the interviewee's language, views, and feelings. During analysis, she tries to read in their words the structure of historically-constituted power relations in order to uncover the complexity of their knowledge and practices. This same disposition governs the translation of the analysis into academic writing.

The third author feels that there is a direct connection between the understanding of information systems in organizations and the impact that this has upon workers—and in particular women workers. She feels that, in acknowledging her life experiences and through observing technological practices with techniques learned in the fields of anthropology and sociology, she can contribute to the ongoing body of knowledge relating to the changing contexts of gender and IT. For her, utilizing quantitative techniques tends to result in a less satisfactory research outcome that provides fewer opportunities to convey ideas and opinions about gender and IT studies. Therefore, she prefers to use qualitative techniques alone or a combination with quantitative techniques to gather data. Accessing women's narratives enables a richer platform from which a story can then be told. In this way, the most successful research outcomes are those that are interesting and express opinions. It is necessary to engage the reader and writer in a joint experience relating to the topic being explored. For the third author, gender and IT is a topic of passion and emotion where opinion is closely entangled with the desire to conduct research. Her work on gender and equity in this way develops, utilizes, and extends the theoretical applications of post-modern feminist thought as an analytical approach to study gender within IS research.

Challenging the Hegemony of Positivism in Gender and IS Research

The second component of our characterization of feminist gender research in IS is that the epistemology challenges positivist hegemony. This derives from our contention that the "what" of the theory drives the "how" of the methodological approach in feminist research. In her discussion of the choice of qualitative methods for IS research, Trauth (2001) considers five influencing factors: (1) the research problem, (2) the epistemological lens, (3) the degree of uncertainty surrounding the phenomenon, (4) the researcher's skills in the use of a particular method, and (5) academic politics. We believe that factors 1 and 2 are particularly salient in the case of feminist gender and IS research. The first factor relates to the distinction between feminist gender and IS research, and non-feminist gender and IS research. We believe that what is to be studied in feminist research is not so much that women are observed to behave differently than men around a particular technology in a particular setting, but rather that the complex factors within and around a woman influence her relationship to technology and technical work. Thus, the research problem and the associated epistemology underlying the research problem are different.

When conducting feminist research, interpretive and critical orientations may be more appropriate than positivist approaches. We believe that methods deriving from interpretive and critical epistemologies are often better suited to feminist projects because they provide insights that differ from those gleaned from positivist research. This argument is based upon our contention that the entire subject of investigation—both the conceptualization of "the problem" and the results that are analyzed—shifts when the epistemological lens is changed. This was born out in Trauth and Jessup's (2000) investigation of the use of a particular IT (group decision support systems) to discuss a high threat topic. The positivist analysis of the sessions concluded that effective group behavior directed toward consensus around alternative solution scenarios had occurred. In sharp contrast, the interpretive analysis uncovered the absence of shared consciousness about the issue and imbalanced participation in the discussion sessions. In addition, the interpretive analysis showed evidence of multiple, rich types of information being shared (cognitive, affective, and behavioral). When comparing the results of both epistemologies, it becomes clear that the interpretive analysis provided a different understanding of the same evidence and new information not found in the positivist analysis. Such research not only demonstrates the epistemological implications of the choice of a research method, it also calls into question the legitimacy of dominant approaches such as positivism for certain research projects.

This same theme is taken up by Howcroft and Trauth (2004) and Trauth and Howcroft (forthcoming) in their argument for greater use of critical methods in IS research. They show how the project changes when the lens shifts from positivist to interpretive to critical. They point out that with respect to research about gender and IT, positivist research is directed simply at discovering whether and where there are gender differences in technology acceptance or participation in the IT professions. Theorizing about these observations is unproblematically left in the lap of essentialism, if it is considered at all. In contrast, interpretive research seeks to understand how gender differences among IT users have come about using established theories such as social construction and emergent theories such as individual differences. The objective is not to revert to biological differences to explain discrimination; this research seeks to better understand underlying social influences. Finally, critical research advocates a position as to why gender inequality exists. Drawing from critical social theory, postmodernism, feminist theory, and Marxism, for example, the goal of this research is to challenge power relations that reproduce inequality.

We recognize that the dichotomy between positivism and feminism tends to be overdrawn. However, we do find limitations of positivism at three interrelated levels: philosophical, moral, and practical (Gorelick, 1991). At a philosophical level, we argue against the pretense of value-free science and the presumption of objectivity conceived of as a set of research procedures and statistical methods. On a moral level, we oppose the extreme forms of positivism that objectify human beings as social facts to be studied. On a practical level, we contest the way in which the hierarchical relationship between the researcher and the researched is unexplored, and the impact of this power differential on the truthfulness of the data provided by respondents.

Theorizing at the Margins

Our third component of feminist gender research in IS is theorizing gender from the margins. By employing researcher reflexivity and recognizing the central place of critical and interpretive epistemologies, feminist gender researchers are encouraged to stand at the periphery and critique the dominant discourses that essentialize womanhood and leave power hierarchies unchallenged. hooks (1989) offers a radical black feminist standpoint for using the margins as a site for resistance and social change. This oppositional worldview exists not only in opposition to dominant discourses about gender and IT, but also as a movement that enables self-actualization. For hooks, it is not enough to oppose and react to patriarchal values and concerns. We must also create counter-hegemonic theories that valorize the knowledge and experiences of women and suggest oppositional directions and possibilities. While there have been several pleas for more research on feminist-inspired IS research (Adam, 2000; Adam et al., 1994; Adam, Howcroft, & Richardson, 2001; Bratteteig & Verne, 1997; Kvasny, forthcoming), feminist research in IS, nevertheless, remains at the periphery.

The periphery, however, may in fact provide an appropriate location for re-envisioning gender and IT. The most visionary feminist research emerges from people who are familiar with both the margins and the center (hooks, 1984). As female researchers studying women's appropriation of IT, we can use our unique position of living both in the center and in the margins to create spaces where women and men can dialog about feminist projects without violating or silencing one another's work. This dialog can only occur by de-centering the dominating male standpoint and moving towards a discourse that valorizes women's lived experiences and situated knowledge and moves the field from gender to feminist studies of IT. Feminist research methods offer a mechanism for breaking through these master narratives about gender and IT. It is not simply a matter of getting women into IT positions because organizations tend to socialize the diversity out of out-group members (hooks, 1994). We need to redefine the conceptualization of gender and IT in ways that reclaim the subjectivity and legitimacy of women. We further believe that a monolithic understanding of womanhood emerges when the existing social constructions of gender ignore or deny the daily lived experiences of women. Such understandings are problematic because they can give rise to alienating and restrictive conditions for the women as users of IT and as IT workers.

For instance, Kvasny has used the feminist standpoint theory to examine how and why the situated knowledge and lived experiences of working-class African-American women shape their perceptions about IT. Using the Biblical metaphor of the Exodus and narratives of ascent, these women viewed IT access and training as part of a strategy for escaping poverty and despair. Whereas most of the extant gender and IS research provides rich insights into the marginalization of women, the women in this study felt empowered by IT. This contradictory outcome is used to make a case for why IS researchers must consider the multiple identities such as gender, race, ethnicity, socio-economic status, and sexuality that shape and are shaped by women's engagement with IT.

Theorizing Gender

This leads to our final component of feminist gender research: problematizing gender. Feminist perspectives are not just for research; they are a modus operandi for life. Therefore, both male and female feminist scholars must not only critique but also offer novel theories for understanding and predicting women's relationships with IT. A central debate in the fields of women's, feminist, gender, and queer studies has centered on the categorization of people based upon the "sameness" of women by virtue of sexual characteristics. The foundation of this sameness perspective within feminist writings stems from the position that the biologically-based category of woman is treated as an all-inclusive category. According to the essentialist theory, the physical differences between males and females account for the participation levels of women in IT, implying that women are somehow physically or mentally unsuited for an IT profession that is socially constructed as masculine (Wajcman, 1991). In this form of knowing, woman, as the essential problem, is perpetuated by the ascription of observable social practices to either men or women (Grosz, 1995; Stasz Stoll, 1978). For instance, the most quoted emblem for this theoretical domain is found in women's capacity to bear children. Sameness feminist positions stress that women have a collection of essential and shared qualities that bind them together. The notion of difference is not considered. Everyone is expected to conform to some norm which typically privileges those in positions of power, and this unwittingly reinforces power relations (Calvert & Ramsey, 1996). For instance, the universal "woman" establishes a role of assumed inferiority with respect to men. It also ignores the diversity that exists within the massive category of woman. Emphasizing an imagined unity can hide from analysis the power relations that exist between men and women and within the category of women.

In contrast to sameness feminism, "difference" feminism offers an alternative way of theorizing that overcomes the essentialist arguments. Difference feminism acknowledges an individual's position and the qualities that have traditionally been allocated to men and women. To possess female biology is not, in and of itself, sufficient to automatically secure acceptance into the conventional understandings of woman-ness. Difference feminism considers gendered roles as social constructions and emphasizes the variety of ways in which women can be constituted as "Other." Being "Other" is not solely about possessing woman-ness, although this is clearly one of its parameters. Individually, woman can be multiple and simultaneous "Others." "Other" exists in difference to being mainstream and, hence, dominant.

For example, the dominant position or stereotypical representation of technology is associated with masculinity. The social construction of women as techno-phobes disinterested in computers reinforces the stereotypical image of women being guided by the skills of a male techno-wizard (Greenhill, 1998). Even though women are just as capable as men are, it is the complexity of each individual's life situation and the consequences of continued social reinforcements that enable inequality to continue. Critical reflection is necessary for looking beyond existing inequality and stereotype notions of what it means to engage with a computer and for giving voice within the computing culture to radical resistance. This voice of resistance may emerge through the influence of a growing voice of feminist writers who are questioning the traditional positions of sameness (see Collins, 1998; hooks, 1981; Kvasny, forthcoming), and those who are critiquing the relation between women and technology (see Adam, Howcroft, & Richardson, 2001; Trauth, 2002; Wilson, 2002; Wilson & Greenhill, 2004).

For instance, Trauth has proposed the Individual Differences Theory of Gender and IT to explain the participation rate of women in IT based on a range of gender studies in several countries (Kwan, Trauth, & Driehaus, 1985; Mitroff, Jacob, & Trauth, 1977; Morgan, Quesenberry, & Trauth, 2004; Quesenberry, Morgan, & Trauth, 2004; Quesenberry & Trauth, 2005; Quesenberry, Trauth, & Morgan, 2006; Trauth, 1995, 2002, 2006; Trauth, Nielsen, & von Hellens, 2003; Trauth & Quesenberry, 2005; Trauth, Quesenberry, & Huang, 2006; Trauth, Quesenberry, & Morgan, 2004; Trauth, Quesenberry, & Yeo, 2005; von Hellens, Nielsen, & Trauth, 2001). According to this theoretical perspective, the participation of women in IT can best be explained by examining the particular identity characteristics of a woman, the varied influences each woman experiences, and the individual ways in which each woman responds to common socio-cultural messages. Wider applications of this theory to race as well as gender have recently been undertaken (Kvasny & Trauth, 2002).

Conclusion

In this chapter, we explain our conception of feminist gender research in IS. Underlying this conception is a fundamental distinction that we make between gender in IS research and feminist gender research in IS. We describe four components of feminist gender research: (1) researcher reflexivity; (2) challenging the hegemonic dominance, legitimacy, and appropriateness of positivist epistemologies; (3) theorizing from the margins; and (4) problematizing gender. We have developed these components from our collective reflection upon our own praxis as female researchers examining issues of gender, equity, and IT. We consider this chapter to be part of a growing body of work on feminist research, in general (Järviluoma, Moisala, & Vilkko, 2003; Ramazanoğlu & Holland, 2003; Warren & Hackney, 2000), and feminist gender research in IS, in particular.

References

Adam, A. (2000, June 8-11). Information systems. In E. Balka, & R. Smith (Eds.), *Woman, work and computerization: Charting a course to the future. IFIP TC9/WG9.1 Seventh International Conference on Woman, Work and Computerization,* Vancouver, British Columbia, Canada (pp. 102-110).

Adam, A., Emms, J., Green, E., & Owen, J. (1994). *Women, work and computerization: Breaking old boundaries—building new forms.* Boston: Kluwer Academic Publishers.

Adam, A., Howcroft, D., & Richardson, H. (2001). Absent friends? The gender dimension in IS research. In N. Russo, B. Fitzgerald, & J. DeGross (Eds.), *Realigning research and practice in information systems development: The social and organizational perspective* (pp. 333-352). Boston: Kluwer Academic Publishers.

Allen, B. (1996). Feminist standpoint theory: A black woman's (re)view of organizational socialization. *Communication Studies, 47*(4), 257-271.

Bourdieu, P., & Waquant, L. (1992). *An invitation to reflexive sociology.* Chicago: University of Chicago Press.

Bratteteig, T., & Verne, G. (1997, January 17-19). Feminist, or merely critical? In search of gender perspectives in informatics. In I. Moser, & G. H. Aas (Eds.), *Technology and democracy: Gender, technology and politics in transition. TMV Conference,* Oslo (pp. 59-74).

Calvert, L., & Ramsey, V. (1996). Speaking as white and female: A non-dominant/dominant group standpoint. *Organization, 3*(4), 468-485.

Camp, T. (1997). The incredible shrinking pipeline. *Communications of the ACM, 40*(10), 103-110.

Chua, W. (1986). Theoretical constructions of and by the real. *Accounting, Organizations and Society,* 583-598.

Collins, P. H. (1990). *Black feminist thought: Knowledge, consciousness and the politics of empowerment*. New York: Routledge.

Collins, P. H. (1998). *Fighting words: Black women and the search for justice*. Minneapolis: University of Minnesota.

Eriksson, I., Kitchenham, B., & Tijdens, K. (1991). *Women, work and computerization: Understanding and overcoming bias in work and education*. Amsterdam: North Holland.

Freeman, P., & Aspray, W. (1999). *The supply of information technology workers in the United States*. Washington, DC: Computing Research Association.

Gefen, D., & Straub, D. (1997). Gender differences in the perception and use of e-mail: An extension to the technology acceptance model. *MIS Quarterly, 21*(4), 389-400.

Gorelick, S. (1991). Contradictions of feminist methodology. *Gender and Society, 5*(4), 459-477.

Greenhill, A. (1998, September 19-20). *Starving women's studies*. Paper read at New Directions of Sociology 5 Post Graduate Conference, Sydney, Australia.

Greenhill, A., & Wilson, M. (2005). Flexibility, freedom and women's emancipation: A Marxist critique of at-home telework. In D. Howcroft, & E. Trauth (Eds.), *A handbook of critical research in information systems: Theory and application* (pp. 152-173). Cheltenham, UK: Edward Elgar.

Grosz, E. (1995). *Space, time and perversions*. St. Leonards: Allen & Unwin.

Guba, E., & Lincoln, Y. (1998). Competing paradigms in qualitative research. In Y. Lincoln (Ed.), *The landscape of qualitative research* (pp. 195-220). Thousand Oaks, CA: Sage Publications.

Harding, S. (1997). Comment on Heckman's "Truth and method: Feminist standpoint theory revisited." *Signs: Journal in Culture and Society, 22*(2), 375-381.

Hartsock, N. (1997). Comment on Heckman's "Truth and method: Feminist standpoint theory revisited." *Truth or Justice? Signs, 22*(2), 367-374.

hooks, b. (1981). *Ain't I a woman: Black women and feminism*. Cambridge: South End Press.

hooks, b. (1984). *Feminist theory: From margin to center*. Cambridge: South End Books.

hooks, b. (1989). *Talking back: Thinking feminist, thinking black*. Cambridge: South End Press.

hooks, b. (1994). *Outlaw culture: Resisting representations*. New York: Routledge.

hooks, b. (2000). *Feminism is for everybody*. Boston: South End Press.

Howcroft, D., & Trauth, E. M. (2004). The choice of critical IS research. In B. Kaplan, D. P. Truex, D. Wastell, A. T. Wood-Harper, & J. I. DeGross (Eds.), *Relevant theory and informed practice—looking forward from a 20 year perspective on IS research* (pp. 195-211). Boston: Kluwer Academic Publishers.

Igbaria, M., & Baroudi, J. (1995). The impact of job performance evaluations on career advancement. *MIS Quarterly, 19*(1), 107.

Järviluoma, H., Moisala, P., & Vilkko, A. (2003). *Gender and qualitative methods.* London: Sage Publications, Inc.

Kincheloe, J., & McLaren, P. (1998). Rethinking critical theory and qualitative research. In N. Denzin, & Y. Lincoln (Eds.), *The landscape of qualitative research* (pp. 260-299). Thousand Oaks, CA: Sage.

Klein, H., & Myers, M. (1999). A set of principles for conducting and evaluating interpretive field studies in information systems research. *MIS Quarterly, 23*(1), 67-93.

Kvasny, L. (forthcoming). *Let the sisters speak: Understanding information technology from the standpoint of the "Other."* The Data Base for Advances in Information Systems.

Kvasny, L. (2003a, May 18-21). Liberation or domination: Understanding the digital divide from the standpoint of the "Other." In M. Khosrow-Pour (Ed.), *Proceedings of the Information Resources Management Association Conference,* Philadelphia (pp. 877-879). Hershey, PA: Idea Group Publishing.

Kvasny, L. (2003b, April 10-12). Triple jeopardy: Race, gender and class politics of women in technology. In E. Trauth (Ed.), *Proceedings of the 2003 ACM SIGMIS CPR Conference on Computer Personnel Research,* Philadelphia (pp. 112-116). New York: ACM Press.

Kvasny, L., Greenhill, A., & Trauth, E. M. (2005). Giving voice to feminist projects in management information systems research. *International Journal of Technology and Human Interaction, 1*(1), 1-18.

Kvasny, L., & Trauth, E. M. (2002). The "digital divide" at work and home: The discourse about power and underrepresented groups in the information society. In E. Whitley & E. Winn (Eds.), *Global and organizational discourse about information technology* (pp. 273-294). New York: Kluwer Academic Publishers.

Kwan, S. K., Trauth, E. M., & Driehaus, K. (1985). Gender differences and computing: Students' assessment of societal influences. *Education and Computing, 1*(3), 187-194.

Lorde, A. (1984). *Sister outsider: Essays and speeches.* Freedom, CA: The Crossing Press.

MacKenzie, D., & Wajcman, J. (1999). *The social shaping of technology*. Buck-ingham: Open University Press.

McGrath Cohoon, J. (2001). Toward improving female retention in the computer science major. *Communications of the ACM, 44*(5), 108-114.

Mitroff, I. I., Jacob, T., & Trauth, E. M. (1977). On the shoulders of the spouses of scientists. *Social Studies of Science, 7*(3), 303-327.

Morgan, A. J., Quesenberry, A. J., & Trauth, E. M. (2004, August 7-11). Exploring the importance of social networks in the IT workforce: Experiences with the "Boy's Club." In E. Stohr & C. Bullen (Eds.), *Proceedings of the 10ᵗʰ Americas Conference on Information Systems*, New York (pp. 1313-1320).

Mylonopolous, N., & Theoharakis, V. (2001). Global perceptions of IS journals. *Communications of the ACM, 44*(10), 29-33.

Nielsen, S., von Hellens, L., Pringle, R., & Greenhill, A. (1999). Students' perceptions of information technology careers: Conceptualising the influence of cultural and gender factors for IT education. *GATES, 5*(1), 30-38.

Nkomo, S. (1992). The emperor has no clothes: Rewriting "race in organizations." *Academy of Management Review, 17*(3), 487-513.

Quesenberry, J. L., Morgan, A. J., & Trauth, E. M. (2004, May 23-26). Understand-ing the 'mommy tracks': A framework for analyzing work-family issues in the IT workforce. In M. Khosrow-Pour (Ed.), *Proceedings of the Information Resources Management Association Conference*, New Orleans, LA (pp. 135-138). Hershey, PA: Idea Group Publishing.

Quesenberry, J. L., & Trauth, E. M. (2005). The role of ubiquitous computing in maintaining work-life balance: Perspectives from women in the IT workforce. In C. Sorensen, Y. Youngjin, K. Lyytinen, & J. I. DeGross (Eds.), *Designing ubiquitous information environments: Socio-Technical issues and challenges* (pp. 43-55). New York: Springer.

Quesenberry, J., Trauth, E. M., & Morgan, A. (2006). Understanding the 'mommy tracks': A framework for analyzing work-family issues in the IT workforce. *Information Resources Management Journal, 19*(2), 37-53.

Ramazanoğlu, C. with Holland, J. (2003). *Feminist methodology: Challenges and choices*. London: Sage Publications.

Star, S. L. (1995). *The cultures of computing*. Oxford: Blackwell Publishers.

Stasz Stoll, C. (1978). *Female and male*. Dubuque, Iowa: William. C. Brown Company Publishers.

Tapia, A., Kvasny, L., & Trauth, E. M. (2004). Is there a retention gap for women and minorities? The case for moving in vs. moving up. In C. Shayo & M. Ig-baria (Eds.), *Strategies for managing IS/IT personnel* (pp. 143-164). Hershey, PA: Idea Group Publishing.

Trauth, E. M. (1995). Women in Ireland's information industry: Voices from inside. *Eire-Ireland, 30*(3), 133-150.

Trauth, E. M. (2001). The choice of qualitative methods in IS research. In E. M. Trauth (Ed.), *Qualitative research in information systems: Issues and trends*. Hershey, PA: Idea Group Publishing.

Trauth, E. M. (2002). Odd girl out: An individual differences perspective on women in the IT profession. *Information Technology & People, 15*(2), 98-118.

Trauth, E. M. (Ed.). (2003, April 10-12). Freedom in Philadelphia: Leveraging differences and diversity in the IT workforce. In *Proceedings of the ACM SIGMIS CPR Conference on Computer Personnel Research*, Philadelphia. New York: ACM Press.

Trauth, E. M. (Ed.). (2006). *Encyclopedia of gender and IT*. Hershey, PA: Idea Group Publishing.

Trauth, E. M. (2006). Theorizing gender and information technology research using the individual differences theory of gender and IT. In E. M. Trauth (Ed.), *Encyclopedia of gender and information technology* (pp. 1154-1159). Hershey, PA: Idea Group Reference.

Trauth, E. M., & Howcroft, D. (forthcoming). Critical empirical research in IS: An example of gender and IT. *Information Technology and People, Special Issue on Critical Research in Information Systems*.

Trauth, E. M., Huang, H., Morgan, A., Quesenberry, J., & Yeo, B. J. K. (2006). Investigating the existence and value of diversity in the global IT workforce: An analytical framework. In F. Niederman & T. Ferratt (Eds.), *IT workers: Human capital issues in a knowledge-based environment* (pp. 331-360). Greenwich, CT: Information Age Publishing.

Trauth, E. M., Huang, H., Quesenberry, J., & Morgan, A. (forthcoming). Leveraging diversity in information systems and technology education in the global workplace. In G. Lowry & R. Turner (Eds.), *Information systems and technology education: From the university to the workplace*. Hershey, PA: Idea Group Publishing.

Trauth, E. M., & Jessup, L. (2000). Understanding computer-mediated discussions: Positivist and interpretive analyses of group support system use. *MIS Quarterly, Special Issue on Intensive Research, 24*(1), 43-79.

Trauth, E. M., Nielsen, S., & von Hellens, L. (2003). Explaining the IT gender gap: Australian stories for the new millennium. *Journal of Research and Practice in IT, 35*(1), 7-20.

Trauth, E. M., & Quesenberry, J. L. (2005, June 23-24). Individual inequality: Women's responses in the IT profession. In G. Whitehouse (Ed.), *Proceedings of the Women, Work and IT Forum*, Brisbane, Queensland, Australia.

Trauth, E. M., & Quesenberry, J. L. (2007). Gender and the information technology workforce: Issues of theory and practice. In P. Yoong & S. Huff (Eds.), *Managing IT professionals in the Internet age* (pp. 18-36). Hershey, PA: Idea Group Publishing.

Trauth, E. M., Quesenberry, J. & Huang, H. (2006, April). Cross-cultural influences on women in the IT workforce. In *Proceedings of the ACM SIGMIS Computer Personnel Research Conference,* Claremont, CA.

Trauth, E. M., Quesenberry, J. L., & Morgan, A. J. (2004, April 22-24). Understanding the under representation of women in IT: Toward a theory of individual differences. In M. Tanniru & S. Weisband (Eds.), *Proceedings of the 2004 ACM SIGMIS Conference on Computer Personnel Research*, Tucson, AZ (pp. 114-119). New York: ACM Press.

Trauth, E. M., Quesenberry, J. L., & Yeo, B. (2005, April 14-16). The influence of environmental context on women in the IT workforce. In M. Gallivan, J. E. Moore, & S. Yager (Eds.), *Proceedings of the 2005 ACM SIGMIS CPR Conference on Computer Personnel Research*, Atlanta, GA (pp. 24-31). New York: ACM Press.

Truman, G. E., & Baroudi, J. (1994). Gender differences in the information systems managerial ranks: An assessment of potential discriminatory practices. *MIS Quarterly, 18*(2), 129-141.

Venkatesh, V., & Morris, M. G. (2000). Why don't men ever stop to ask for directions? Gender, social influence, and their role in technology acceptance and usage behavior. *MIS Quarterly, 24*(1), 115-139.

von Hellens, L. A., Nielsen, S., & Trauth, E. M. (2001, April 19-21). Breaking and entering the male domain. Women in the IT industry. In M. Serva (Ed.), *Proceedings of the 2001 ACM SIGCPR Conference on Computer Personnel Research*, San Diego, CA (pp. 116-120). New York: ACM Press.

Wajcman, J. (1991). *Feminism confronts technology*. University Park: Pennsylvania State University Press.

Wajcman, J. (2001). Reflections on gender and technology studies: In what state is the art? *Social Studies of Science, 30*(3), 447-464.

Walsham, G. (1995). Interpretive case studies in IS research: Nature and method. *European Journal of Information Systems, 4*, 74-81.

Warren, C. A. B., & Hackney, J. K. (2000). *Gender issues in ethnography* (2nd ed.). Thousand Oaks, CA: Sage Publications, Inc.

Webster, J., & Martocchio, J. (1992). Microcomputer playfulness: Development of a measure with workplace implications. *MIS Quarterly, 16*(2), 201-226.

Wilson, M. (2002). Making nursing visible? Gender, technology and the care plan as script. *Information Technology & People, 15*(2), 139-148.

Wilson , M., & Greenhill, A. (2004, June 14-16). Gender and teleworking identities: Reconstructing the research agenda. In *Proceedings of the 13th European Conference on Information Systems, The European IS Profession in the Global Networking Environment, ECIS 2004*, Turku, Finland.

Woodfield, R. (2002). Woman and information systems development: Not just a pretty (inter)face? *Information Technology & People, 15*(2), 119-138.

Endnotes

[1]   This chapter is an expanded version of Kvasny, Greenhill, and Trauth (2005)

[2]   This situation is being rectified through such publications as the *Encyclopedia of Gender and IT* (Trauth, 2006).

Chapter II

A Taxonomy of Stakeholders:

Human Roles in System Development

Ian F. Alexander

Scenario Plus Ltd. & City University, UK

Abstract

Systems engineers have often paid too little attention to the nature of the so-called "users" of products under development. These are better called stakeholders, as many roles are involved, and few of those are in direct contact with the developed products. A simple and robust conceptual framework for classifying development stakeholders—a taxonomy—is proposed. The taxonomy is product-centric, with concentric "circles" denoting broad categories of the stakeholder. Within these, generic "slots" describe typical classes of the stakeholder; these are subdivided into "roles," which are expected to vary at least in name with the domain. Examples are given, and a popular template is re-analysed using the framework. The taxonomy has immediate value in identifying and validating stakeholder roles in requirements' elicitation. This helps to ensure that key viewpoints on requirements are not missed. That, in turn, reduces the risk of instability and failure during development.

Introduction

Motivation

The structure of stakeholder roles and their relationships, such as surrogacy, have only slightly been investigated in the requirements' world (although much more extensively in the political, ethical, and information systems' worlds: one reason for believing that an attempt at an interdisciplinary look at stakeholders may be worthwhile). Requirements' work almost inevitably involves dealing with stakeholders of widely-varying kinds and hence demands a commensurately wide range of elicitation techniques. The first step in identifying which techniques should be applied is, therefore, to identify the stakeholder composition for a new project; and this, in turn, demands a suitable taxonomy of stakeholders.

Too many projects focus their attention too closely on the product—perhaps especially when that is software—to the exclusion of non-operational roles and often even of secondary operational roles such as maintenance. I suspect this is due to "inside-out thinking," where the "system" is seen as important and the "user" as secondary. Such thinking is a hangover from the past. When I was at the university, an IBM 360 mainframe occupied the only air-conditioned tower on the campus. Students were permitted to approach the card-reader with a deck of punched cards; only trained operators were allowed upstairs to see the computer itself. This was truly a priestly hierarchy (Greek *hieros* = holy, *arches* = ruler) of operator roles. As Christopher Locke writes, "Even the word 'users' is an artefact of the [command-and-control] mentality" (Levine, Locke, Searls, & Weinberger, 2000). It is time to move on from treating "the user as a computer peripheral" (in Julian Hilton's words). The system is made for man, not man for the system.

Many industrial development problems seem in practice to be caused not so much by a failure to write requirements as by a failure to perceive that specific stakeholders' viewpoints were relevant. That failure causes whole groups of requirements, typically those related to scenarios involving the missing stakeholders, to be missed.

A similarly unhappy result is obtained when one stakeholder, for example, a software developer, assumes one scope for a product, while another stakeholder, for example, a purchaser, assumes another. For instance, when a developer assumes that it will be sufficient to design, code, and test a piece of software, but the purchaser hopes to have everything set up and the operators trained, then the points of view of the installer, the trainer, and to some extent that of the operators have not been adequately considered and made explicit. Legal disputes and financial losses are then likely.

It seems likely that stakeholder composition is a good predictor of project risk; hence, it should be cost-effective to characterise projects at their initiation according to their likely stakeholder impact (and to other variables, such as safety-relatedness, technological innovation, similarity to previous projects, and so on).

In addition, maintaining a model of stakeholders throughout a development allows changes in stakeholder composition to be modelled explicitly, leading to appropriate changes in requirements.

Stakeholder surrogacy has powerful and paradoxical connotations in requirements' engineering. It is almost a dogma that projects should seek out ever-closer dialogue with stakeholders—consider the current fashion for integrated project teams, facilitated workshops, rapid prototyping, agile development with user stories, and so forth. Yet, all of the time the obvious truth is glossed over: that it is remarkably rare to be able to talk to many stakeholders in the flesh. Every requirements' engineer knows that the basic answer to the client organisation's boss who says, "I know everything that happens in my department, ask me," is "well, sir, that's fine but can I see if the people on the shop floor know of any small issues?" To put it more formally, standardised procedures, no matter how critical[1] and how carefully defined in writing, are always modified when operationalised "on the shop floor." Therefore, it is essential to talk to stakeholders directly—without intermediaries—to find out what actually happens. Yet, requirements' engineers are themselves intermediaries! Stakeholder surrogacy is accordingly discussed at some length in the sub-section, *Surrogacy*.

Worse, many kinds of stakeholder are inaccessible: they may be distant geographically; separated by contractual and procedural barriers; hidden within organisations (with cultural barriers); simply unaffordably expensive to contact given scarce project time and resources; or not yet in existence (for future products).

The naïve "go and talk to the users"—whoever may be meant by that phrase—is therefore far from helpful as advice. This chapter considers what we mean by stakeholder roles on development projects and offers both a theoretical framework for classifying them and some practical suggestions for making use of that knowledge.

It may be that the approach can be applied outside system development, for example, to model political and business stakeholder structures, but that is beyond our scope.

Structure

This chapter is structured as follows:

- *The Proposed Taxonomy*
- *Applying the Taxonomy in Practice*
- *Research Review*

- *Discussion: Features & Limitations of the Taxonomy*
- *Conclusion*

The Proposed Taxonomy

A project's stakeholder sociology can be modelled graphically on an *onion diagram* (Figure 1). This deceptively simple-looking model documents a wealth of information about a project. It presents a view of the project that is centred on its product and serves as an overview of our stakeholder taxonomy.

Figure 1. Onion diagram of product stakeholders

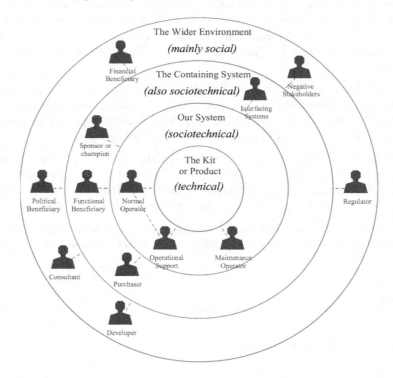

The onion diagram displays a customisable set of named "slots" (silhouette icons), containing stakeholder roles, in three or more "circles" centred on the "kit" or product. For example, "pilot" is a role (not shown) in the "normal Operator" slot in the "our system" circle, where product is an aircraft.

Structure of the Onion Model

This section introduces and defines the terms used in the *onion model* and the associated taxonomy of stakeholders. Terms are highlighted in **boldface** when they are introduced and defined.

The onion model consists by default of a set of three concentric circles. Each circle logically contains the circles drawn inside it. (The term "Annulus" may be used where it is desired to refer to the contents of a circle without those of the circles it contains.) Other circles may be added, most likely by subdividing the default circles.

Hence, a **circle** denotes a subset of entities in the world relevant to a development project. Those entities are slots and circles.

The innermost ring (not strictly a circle) denotes the **kit**, a conveniently short term for the equipment or product under development, whatever its nature, for instance, software or electronics hardware. This could be a one-off piece of custom financial software or a mass-market product, such as a handheld information device. It could equally well be the tangible equipment for a large system, such as a railway line: the system with its many human operators would, of course, be more than just that equipment. The innermost ring thus differs from true circles in not containing stakeholders.

A **slot** is a class of roles that is drawn by default (empty if necessary) in an onion diagram. In effect, it is a prediction or suggestion that roles of a certain kind may be important in a project. For example, "normal operator" is a default slot in the "our system" circle. The existence of the slot is a prediction that, in any system, there will probably be one or more "normal operator" roles. The slot might remain empty in a supposedly "wholly automatic" system, though such a system might still have other human roles such as installer, configurer, and maintainer within the "our system" circle.

A slot is said to be **empty** in an onion model when it contains no roles. For example, take a product like a distress signal flare. This product is fired by a sailor to attract rescuers; whether it succeeds or fails, it is then disposed of. No maintenance work of any kind is carried out on it, so it has no maintenance operator and that slot is empty.

A **role** is a class of stakeholder with a distinct relationship to the product under development. For example, in a passenger aircraft, both the pilot and flight engineer are roles within the "normal operator" slot.

A role is said to be a **surrogate** if it is conducted on behalf of another role, which cannot speak directly for itself. For example, a product manager acts as the purchaser of a new type of product until such time as the product can be sold on the mass market; then the consumers buy instances of the product (or not) for themselves. As another example, the regulator acts as a government-sponsored voice on behalf of the public to ensure safety, and so forth. Surrogacy is discussed in more detail in following sections.

A role is said to be **negative** if it is associated with viewpoints opposed to the successful completion of the product's development, its coming into service, or its successful operation. Viewpoints do not appear in the onion model as such, but can be documented briefly as text attributes of role objects in an associated database (Figure 2), or in full as sets of requirements (not shown) linked to role objects. It may be useful to document generalized viewpoints as attributes of slot objects, summarizing a group of more specific role viewpoints. Tool support is discussed in the sub-section, *Tool & Template Support*.

A **stakeholder** is an individual person or other legal entity able to act like a person (e.g., a limited company, an industry regulator, a registered charity) playing one or more roles. Note however that in accordance with common usage, we loosely describe both slots and roles as "stakeholders" when the class/instance distinction is not of immediate concern.

It would also be possible to limit the definition to "individual person;" this would have the advantage of avoiding possible confusion between "Company XYZ" as a stakeholder and "The Company XYZ Containing System" as a circle. Further, while a suitably-placed individual (e.g., the chairman, the press relations officer) can legitimately represent the voice of a company as a corporate legal entity, that individual cannot legitimately claim to speak for each of the many roles within the company as far as their viewpoints and requirements are concerned. There are thus some dangers associated with treating legal entities as stakeholders; but, there are obvious advantages. For instance, if a conservation body chooses to oppose a development, its negative stakeholding can reasonably be treated as a single voice in accordance with its legal status.

Figure 2. Viewpoints as attributes of traceable slot and role objects

ID	Stakeholder Slots and Roles		Brief Summary of Viewpoint	Polar Angle
SH-37	**2.1 The Wider Environment**			
SH-55	**2.1.1 Consultant**	▶	gives advice	150
SH-56	**2.1.1.1 Tools and Techniques**		advises on efficient use of technology	
SH-65	**2.1.1.2 Environmental Impact**		advises on likely impact of product on the environment	
SH-39	**2.1.2 Financial Beneficiary**	▶	stands to profit from system	240

In this example, "consultant" is a slot in the "wider environment" circle, containing two currently-defined roles. Other attributes include "viewpoint" text (here with very brief examples); "Polar Angle" (proposed by the tool) specifies where icons should appear on the diagram, and so on. Traceability links (indicated by triangles) can be inserted between stakeholder roles and detailed viewpoint requirements, and so forth.

Circles

The four default circles used in the onion model are:

1. **The Product** or **The Kit:** The item under development (e.g., a software program, a consumer electronics device, an aircraft, a communications network).

2. **Our System:** "The Product" plus its human operators and the standard operating procedures or rules governing its operation (e.g., an aircraft with its crew, operating manuals and aviation rules, etc.).

3. **The Containing System:** "Our System" plus any human beneficiaries of our system (whether they are involved in operations or not).

4. **The Wider Environment:** "The Containing System" plus any other stakeholders.

Other circles may be introduced as necessary. For example, an additional circle might be created outside "the containing system" to divide stakeholders relatively closely involved with the project from those more distantly involved in the "wider environment." That might be helpful when a product forms a component of a subsystem within a larger system. That is, when our product is a control box for a train (the containing system), we might wish to consider a "wider system" circle, namely a railway line with stakeholder roles such as line controller, and a "system environment" circle, namely a complete railway network with roles such as network timetable scheduler—as distinct from the "wider environment," which might include stakeholder roles such as the general public and the government.

The kit or product circle is considered to be the part of our system that can be sold, so it does not contain humans. All of the other circles contain stakeholders. This raises an apparent problem of consistency: since it is a purely relative matter which system in the real world we consider to be "our system," it is perfectly possible for somebody else to treat our system as a component part of their product. What is happening here, however, is that they are focussing attention only on the machine (non-human) aspects of our system for the purposes of product development. The stakeholders do not disappear, but they will either be treated as insignificant from the (larger) viewpoint, or they will be promoted to the rank of stakeholder in the larger product.

For example, if the larger product is a train, its normal operator is a driver. Our component product, the train's control box, is also operated by the driver, who only appears once in the model—outside the product, the train, as one would expect. The fact that the driver also operates a sub-product of the train (the control box) does not make the driver a part of the product. Thus, at the level of detail of the larger viewpoint, there is no need to consider separate sub-product stakeholders. In general, therefore, as long as one considers just one "our system" at a time, there is no problem of consistency. A shift of viewpoint—to consider a larger or smaller product—rightly causes a change in the perspective of the onion model.

One might ask whether distance from "the product" means less influence on the requirements for it: this would be a simple application of the spatial metaphor of the onion diagram. (See the sub-section, *Visual Metaphors*, for a more in-depth discussion of a visual metaphor.) However, there seems no reason to believe this. On the contrary, the approach here emphasises that stakeholders who never see the product may be crucially important to a development project. As Coakes and Elliman (1999) say of their stakeholder Web diagrams:

> *The diagram is not intended to depict stakeholders from some judgmental position such as degrees of power, influence, or interest. In particular, care must be taken not to interpret distance from the central [Product] as an indication of importance. Some of the most influential stakeholders may be remote from the organisation.* (p. 11)

A well-known example is the occasion where English Heritage stopped a rail res-ignalling project the day before it was to launch as an attractive red-brick Victorian railway viaduct would have been demolished. No knowledge of signalling or interest in it was necessary. It may be that different stakeholder "slots" come with presumptions about their likely (default) importance, but that is a weaker claim.

The Slots of the Onion Model

The onion diagram by default displays the following "slot" icons in the named circles. Other slots may be added as necessary. In each case, they are defined, based broadly on the framework of Sharp, Finkelstein, and Galal (1999):

- the nature of the roles in the slot with respect to the kit;
- the most likely interactions with stakeholders in other slots;
- the stage(s) in development that the slot is most likely to be relevant; and
- the likely priority (relative importance) of stakeholders in the slot.

Note that the following are what are considered to be the bare minimum of slots, not an exhaustive taxonomy.

Our System

- **Normal operator:** Roles that involve giving routine commands and monitoring outputs from the product, whether these are via a human-computer interface or not.

Normal operators interact directly with the product, with other operators (e.g., maintenance, operational support) and with functional beneficiaries (e.g., providing them with processed information and receiving instructions from them).

Operator requirements are relevant throughout development, but especially during user interface design.

Operability requirements are always important, perhaps especially so for mass-market products (where operability is a selling-point) and for control systems (where safety is involved).

- **Maintenance operator:** Roles that involve maintaining the product, such as servicing hardware and diagnosing and fixing faults. (So-called maintenance of software involves changing the design of the product, and is the responsibility of our developer slot; it is not maintenance in our sense.)

Maintenance operators interact with the product and with normal operators.

It is worth noting that now that outsourcing is in fashion, maintenance people may be contractors. If so, there is a contractual boundary that crosses the "our system" circle (and others outside it). This can easily act as a "geological fault-line," impeding communications and possibly rupturing if anything goes wrong. For example, some organisations outsource their computer and network administration (maintenance operations), while retaining normal operation of the equipment in-house. This typically creates bureaucratic delay and difficulty, which in turn creates tension between the two roles. It may be helpful to draw contractual or other boundaries on the onion diagram and to annotate these with their significance for the project.

Maintenance is often not considered until late in projects; however, maintainability needs to be designed-in, whether as built-in test and diagnostics, internationalised error messages, accessibility of equipment, or spares holdings. Requirements for these need to be in place early in a development.

Maintenance requirements are often more important than they seem. The whole-life cost of many products—from cars to jet engines—depends much more on the cost of maintenance than may be realised. Similarly, maintainability requirements such as the time to repair or replace components can significantly affect quality of service.

- **Operational support:** Roles that involve advising normal operators of a product about how to operate it. These roles are very close to operations but support rather than conduct productive use of the product itself. We have chosen to include them in "our system" for two reasons:

  1.   they behave as operational staff in their daily work; and

  2.   like maintenance operators, they help to keep the system fully operational (enabling the normal operators to continue working effectively).

Operational support people such as "help desk" staff and trainers interact mainly with normal operators. They are "maintenance" for the humans involved, rather than just for the product. The comments on outsourcing under "maintenance operator" can also apply here.

The priority of support probably deserves to be higher than it is on many projects. As with maintenance, good support raises operational effectiveness and availability. Clearly, it is secondary to other slots such as normal operator and functional beneficiary.

Support needs to be considered when preparing manuals and training materials, that is, relatively late in the project; however, supportability may also need to be evaluated earlier, for example, when designing software to yield intelligible error messages, and so forth.

Containing System

- **Functional beneficiary:** Roles that benefit from the results or outputs created by the product. For example, an astronomer benefits from the astronomic data captured by a space telescope though he or she cannot operate the instrument directly. Since products are or should be designed to produce results, this is an important slot.

They interact with operators, giving them instructions and receiving information and any other benefits that "our system" is designed to provide.

Functional requirements form the centrepiece of most specifications. They need to be available early and are used throughout development, for example, in design and for specifying functional tests. They are of the highest importance.

- (Responsible for) **interfacing system:** Roles responsible for neighbouring systems that have electronic or other interfaces to and from the product. Such systems behave much like human operators in terms of demanding specific capabilities from the product, but, naturally, the interfaces are precisely defined as protocols, and so forth.

They interact with operators and/or the product; any other interactions they may have are most likely but not necessarily outside our scope.

Interface requirements form a crucial part of the definition of many developments. They are required from the start. Shifting interfaces and scope are serious risks to projects.

- **Purchaser:** Roles responsible for having the product developed. There are certainly several of these, ranging from product manager (with knowledge of what can be sold) to procurement (responsible for obtaining a contract with a supplier). In the case of a mass-market product, the purchaser is a product manager—a surrogate role, acting on behalf of millions of consumers who will if all goes well ultimately buy the product. Purchasers interact with developers and consultants, and (to obtain requirements) with beneficiaries and marketing also.

The purchaser's input is required from the start, is critical in getting development started and in ensuring that funding for it is not withdrawn. It always has high priority (possibly more than it deserves, but that is out of the control of those working on a project).

- **Product champion** (a.k.a., **sponsor**): Role responsible for initiating development of the product, for obtaining funding for it, and for protecting the development from "political" pressures and funding cuts. The role requires positional power within the purchasing organisation (e.g., the company creating a mass-market product). The product champion is perhaps the best person for the requirements' engineer to meet with first; an effective champion can indicate the scope and purpose of the development, the opportunities and threats, and can suggest who the key stakeholders are. All of this helps to cut the risk to the project.

A product champion's effectiveness is clearly related to the ability to interact with other stakeholders, especially beneficiaries and negative stakeholders (including those within the organisation).

The product champion is critical from before the start of a development and remains important throughout. The role does not necessarily or even desirably contribute to product requirements: it functions mainly at a political rather than a technical level.

Wider Environment

- **Negative stakeholder:** Any role that could be harmed by the product physically, financially or in any other way that might be found justifiable by the authorities (e.g., a court of law, a regulator), or conversely that could attempt to harm the product (for example, householders living close to the route of a planned railway; a nature conservation body with interest in land threatened by such a route; activists opposed to pollution that might be caused by a product under development; employees finding their decision-making abilities reduced by 'intelligent' software; employees that perceive their tasks being oversimplified or made too complex; groups feeling that collaboration or communication were made more difficult).

- A special kind of negative stakeholder (and possibly a distinct slot) is the **hostile agent:** Any role that actively seeks to hinder or harm the development and operation of the system. "Actively" means using some degree of intelligence and creativity to oppose the system. Examples include military enemies, political and commercial spies, hackers, spammers, virus writers, thieves, and fraudsters. Clearly, the degree of harm intended by such agents varies widely, and new subtypes of the hostile agent are constantly emerging. We may distinguish a few subtypes as examples:
  1. **Military enemy:** Intends complete destruction of the product.
  2. **Amateur hacker:** Intends to gain malicious pleasure from unauthorised access.
  3. **Thief:** Intends to steal assets (with essentially unintended harm to those deprived of the assets as a side-effect).

Negative stakeholders may interact with regulators, with beneficiaries, and with any roles in the wider environment able to wield influence, for example, the press, politicians, and other pressure groups.

Hostile roles can be treated as a kind of negative stakeholder or may perhaps be promoted to a slot in their own right. Hackers and virus writers are obvious hostile roles. Competitors, too, could be considered: their relationship could be anything from passive victim to active threat. In the case of military systems, the enemy's expected behaviour and capabilities are naturally a primary consideration.

Negative roles are important from before the start of a development, and then whenever issues like security, marketability, and environmental impact are considered. These affect requirements and design. Security may demand special effort in system testing.

- **Political beneficiary:** Any role in public office or private business that can benefit in terms of power, influence, and prestige through the success of the product. For example, a space agency's management could benefit "politically" from a successful space mission.

Interaction with other roles is usually infrequent and is typically indirect, for example via senior management (purchaser, functional beneficiary, etc.).

Political forces within an organisation can also be negative (see the discussion of product champion in the previous sub-section, *Containing System*). It might be worth representing a "political opponent" although such explicitness can be dangerous, as Checkland mentions (Checkland & Scholes, 1990): "There is an unavoidable political dimension .. to any human affairs which entail taking deliberate action" (p. 50); "delicate judgements are usually required" (p. 51); "if the results (of political analysis) are all bluntly made public, then those results can themselves easily become a potent commodity of power in the 'real' politics of the situation. There is potentially an infinite regress here in which the politics of the situation forever escapes open analysis" (p. 51).

Political roles are important (see "sponsor" in the previous sub-section, *Containing System*) throughout a development and indeed from before it begins.

- **Financial beneficiary:** Any role that can benefit financially from the success of a product (for example, shareholders and directors in a company making a mass-market product).

They often interact weakly with other roles, except perhaps with the product champion and other senior beneficiaries.

Development staff perhaps needs to consider financial beneficiaries directly only rarely; project and programme management may be more concerned. Perhaps the most usual situation is that financial beneficiaries are represented by surrogate roles such as line management. Conversely, financial beneficiaries are likely to take a direct interest only in the largest of developments. They are important at the main "gates" in a development.

- **Regulator:** Any role responsible for regulating the quality, safety, cost, or other aspects of the product (for example, aviation authorities, health and safety executives, rail regulators, radio regulators, financial service authorities).

The regulator is most likely to interact with senior developers. Regulators act as surrogates for the public, interacting with the developer and beneficiary roles as necessary; for example, the aviation authorities certify components on receipt of a satisfactory safety case supported by evidence from the development organisation's safety officer.

In the case of a software product, we could view standards organisations like ISO as non-statutory (voluntary, not enforcing) regulators.

Regulators impose requirements which act as qualities and constraints (rarely as functions). These are important in defining the requirements for a product and again for acceptance and certification. In the case of safety-related products, they are of crucial importance.

- **Developer:** Any of the many roles (requirements engineer, analyst, designer, programmer, tester, safety engineer, security engineer, electronics engineer, metallurgist, human factors engineer, project manager, etc.) involved directly in product development. Note that none of these roles are operational unless tied into operations via a maintenance contract—in which case the affected people have hybrid developer/maintenance roles.

Developers interact mainly with each other (often adopting surrogate "customer" roles in the process—see the following discussion), but also contractually with purchasers. Ideally, developers in the form of requirements' engineers and analysts would interact with *all* other roles, but this is rare and often impossible for reasons of, for example, time and restrictions on access.

Developer roles are mainly involved once development has started; it may be helpful to involve a development opinion (a consultancy role) before that and to keep developers involved (via maintenance) during operations. Clearly, the priority of a developer's requirements is secondary to those of the beneficiaries, although manufacturability is an important consideration for mechanical products such as jet engines.

Suzanne Robertson (2004) suggests that it may be helpful to create an extra circle for "development project responsibility." It may be best for this not to be a concentric circle—in a way, development is another world from operational usage. Developers are in the outermost circle from the point of view of the product but intimately involved from the point of view of development. Hence, it may be an over-simplification to try to force the two taxonomies into one. However, as she says, drawing a development circle "highlights the necessity to have adequate representation of the ongoing maintenance operator and operational support roles and [to] separates real maintenance from new development."

- **Consultant:** Any of the many roles (marketing expert, software expert, business analyst, management specialist, etc.) involved in supporting some aspect of product development, characteristically from outside the development organisation. Internal consultancy is possible but problematic, as it is hard to speak out in the face of "political" pressure within the organisation (except with the help of a "sponsor" [see the previous sub-section, *Containing System*]).

Consultants may interact mainly with the product champion, with purchasers, or with developers, depending on when they were hired, by whom, and for what purpose. For priority and timing, see the comments on developer.

- Another possible slot is **supplier:** A role involved in the manufacture and provision of components, whether custom or commoditized, for the product. In the case of custom components, this is close to a developer role initially. During system operations, both custom and commodity component suppliers have a role closer to maintenance, supplying whatever is needed to keep the system operational.

Suppliers are important in product manufacture, in maintenance, and sometimes in development. In extreme examples, such as the manufacture of a jet engine's intercasing (a complex 3-dimensional casting), the supplier is critical to development as the lead time for the manufacture of the component is comparable to the lead time for the entire engine development. Hence, suppliers may need to be involved very early in a project, possibly even before it begins.

Applying the Taxonomy in Practice

Requirements Elicitation

The simplest and most essential use of a taxonomy of stakeholders is as a guide to the likely kinds of people to interview, observe, and invite to workshops to help gather the requirements for a project. As stakeholders are successively identified and brought into the project, an onion model and associated database can be used to document their roles, contact details, viewpoints, and ultimately requirements. The onion model then gives a direct visual report on the progress of stakeholder discovery and provides pointers to slots that require further investigation.

Characterising the Project

The nature of the stakeholder taxonomy for an individual project determines the kind of stakeholder involvement that will be necessary during the life of the project. One application of the taxonomy is, therefore, to characterise the project in terms of the requirements' elicitation approach and the degree of stakeholder participation that should be selected. This is one of several characterisation dimensions, each of which can help to reduce risk. Other dimensions include whether and how far safety is involved, how complex the interfaces are, and how new the needed technology is.

Elicitation techniques vary widely, from interviewing and workshops through ethnographic fieldwork to market surveys, prototyping, and product trials. Most requirements' textbooks describe a range of such techniques (e.g., Alexander & Stevens, 2002; Kotonya & Sommerville, 1998; Robertson & Robertson, 2006). Textbooks with a user-centred orientation offer a still wider range (e.g., McGraw & Harbison, 1997; Sutcliffe, 2002). The choice of techniques is in practice, however, strongly driven by the stakeholder roles involved. Figure 3 illustrates some common elicitation approaches for operational stakeholders.

Figure 4 similarly illustrates some common elicitation approaches for non-operational stakeholders.

Characterisation can be carried out by assessing which kinds of stakeholders are likely to be most significant in a project and then assigning the most appropriate development life cycle to respond adequately to those stakeholders. For example, if the operational needs are simple but meeting regulatory demands is long and complex

Figure 3. Eliciting from operational roles (outer circles suppressed)

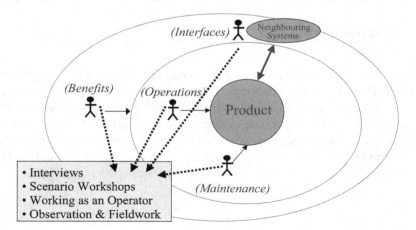

Figure 4. Eliciting from non-operational roles

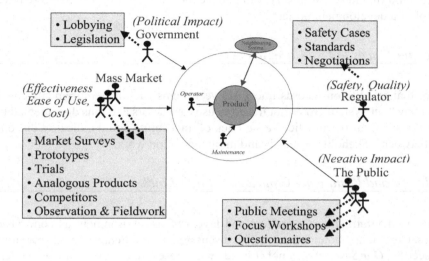

(e.g., for a jet engine) then the life cycle must focus on achieving certification with careful attention to verification and the gathering of evidence for the regulator.

Conversely, if regulation is minimal but operational needs are rigorous (e.g., for a portable consumer product), the life cycle must focus on satisfying users (i.e., hybrid normal operators/functional beneficiaries) so that the product is suitable, through involvement with the development—which will presumably be iterative to permit it to respond to user reactions.

Checking for Stakeholder Problems

Checking for Empty Slots

A tool that records details of slots, roles, and stakeholders can readily detect empty slots. These might indicate forgotten stakeholders or, for example, a missing sponsor, threatening project success.

Checking for Multiple-Filled Slots

Similarly, a tool could readily detect slots populated by more than one role. This is sometimes acceptable, but could indicate sources of conflict. For example, conflict is likely if two departments (e.g., international marketing, product development within a multinational carmaker) both believe they are funding and therefore have control of a development project.

Checking Traces to Use Case Actors

A tool that in addition records traces between items such as requirements could detect any "our system" roles not traced to use case actors and thus documented in operational scenarios, and vice versa. Lack of traceability could indicate a disconnect between stakeholder analysis and implementation work.

Analysing and Visualising Contractual Fault-Lines

An onion diagram shows a product and layers of its environment as concentric circles. Contractual boundaries (see the discussion of Maintenance in the previous sub-section, *Our System*) may not coincide with these circles. A diagram with overlaid boundaries may help stakeholders to visualise the risks inherent in outsourcing or otherwise sharing responsibilities.

For example, Railtrack was the company formed to operate Britain's railway infrastructure of tracks and signalling, while independent franchises operated the trains themselves (along with ticket booking and inquiries). For the system of the railways as a whole, operations were split between Railtrack (the track) and the franchisee (the train). This gave rise to the ironic term "wheel-rail interface," referring not to the problems of friction and wear between iron wheel and iron rail but commercial friction between the occupants of the uncomfortably-split stakeholder slots. The pressure on Railtrack was immense: from shareholders to make money; from the regulator for safety; from franchisees for reliable, low-cost service. Railtrack management responded by letting out contracts for the actual work of maintenance, for example, of keeping the railway in a safe condition. Some notorious accidents followed after a few years. These caused large parts of the rail network to be inspected for cracked rails and then restricted to carrying trains at low speed. These restrictions, in turn, caused severe delays to passengers and large cost penalties to the company. Railtrack folded in a welter of government intervention, blame, and acrimony.

Tool & Template Support

The taxonomy presented here has several practical applications. These do not necessarily require tool support: onion diagrams and hierarchies can be created quite easily in ordinary office software, on paper, or on flipcharts—provided that traceability is not required.

When models must be maintained for extended periods during which a steady trickle of change must be accommodated, tool support with configuration control, and traceability to requirements becomes helpful.

Requirements Database Tool

A tool (Figure 5) supporting some of the earlier-mentioned applications has been implemented in a requirements' traceability tool environment (Telelogic® DOORS) and is available for free download (Scenario Plus!, 2004). This both demonstrates the feasibility of building such a tool, and allows workers to experiment with uses of the approach in a controlled environment (e.g., with a complete audit trail). Figure 2 incidentally illustrates part of the tool's (very straightforward) data model.

The tool permits the creation and editing of an onion model diagram. As illustrated, the tool also acts as a display of the status of the model, making it apparent which slots are filled and which are empty. The tool manages a conventional document-like data structure (a formal module; see Figure 2) in which each slot, role, and stakeholder is represented as a separate object within a hierarchy. Details of each

Figure 5. "Onion model" tool displaying current status of stakeholder slots

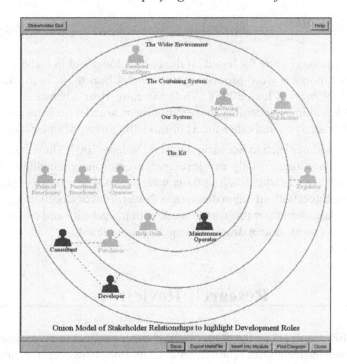

stakeholder are held as a database record within the object; these include name and contact details as well as a text summarizing the stakeholder's viewpoint. Objects can be given (bidirectionally navigable) traceability links to any other objects (e.g., requirements) in the database. Hence, the tool enables the requirements' engineer to provide traces from any number of requirements, use cases, actors, and so forth, directly to stakeholders.

Tools can readily calculate metrics on the status of the onion model. For example, the number of our system slots that are not linked to use case actors gives a measure of the completeness of coverage of known human operators in the use case model.

Clearly, the same information architecture could also serve as the basis for other forms of stakeholder analysis including conflict detection and resolution. These do not necessarily demand tool support, but they do require systematic handling for which a tool can be beneficial. Small projects may instead choose to apply a simple template of likely stakeholder roles, discussed in the next section.

The Scenario Plus! tools could in principle be implemented in any automated software/system development environment that supports traceability between items and provides a suitable application programming interface. The hybrid hierarchical/tabular data structure of DOORS' formal modules was very convenient for implementation, but stakeholder information could certainly be represented without it.

Stakeholder Template

A document template (Figure 6), based on the onion model and in a choice of formats suitable for popular word-processing and spreadsheet tools, is available for free download (Scenario Plus!, 2006). While there are clear advantages for large projects to work within a traceability tool environment, smaller projects can benefit from stakeholder analysis and other forms of modelling using simpler tools.

Customisable templates such as Scenario Plus! and Volere (2004) allow stakeholder analysis to take place in essentially any development environment including indeed those without any specialist modelling tools whatsoever. The analysis could take place in Word or Excel with an onion diagram in PowerPoint or CorelDraw. Clearly, there are advantages for larger projects to work with traceability and configuration management tools so as to keep track of changes more reliably.

Research Review

The focus of this chapter is on the place of stakeholder analysis in system development and perhaps especially in requirements' elicitation. However, the subject of

Figure 6. Fragment of the stakeholder template

The Scenario Plus Stakeholder Template	Word-Processing Version

3.   Stakeholder Roles

3.1   **Beneficiary**

3.1.1   **Functional Beneficiary**

Stakeholder:	Viewpoint:
John Smith	*wants to see accurate weekly & monthly sales figures and forecasts*

3.1.2   **Financial Beneficiary**

Stakeholder:	Viewpoint:

stakeholders is far wider than that. This section, therefore, attempts to set the current work in its system engineering context and also briefly in the wider onion-circles of information systems research and business studies. These literatures are voluminous, so references are confined to key papers on each topic.

This research review section is organised by topic as follows:

- *Stakeholder Analysis*
- *Onion Models*
- *Taxonomies and Hierarchies*
- *Goals and Viewpoints*
- *Human Aspects of System Development*
- *Surrogacy*

The logic of this should become apparent, but in essence the information systems and other literatures on stakeholders are briefly introduced; the background to the paper's use of onion models and a taxonomy of stakeholders is sketched; existing work related to stakeholder classification in the requirements' engineering and usability fields is examined; and finally, since stakeholder surrogacy seems to be significant in system development, research on surrogacy is explored.

Stakeholder Analysis

Mason and Mitroff (1981) helped to introduce stakeholder analysis to business practice. Their definition is: "Stakeholders are all those claimants inside and outside the firm who have a vested interest in the problem and its solution" (p. 43) and "[they] are the concrete entities that affect and in turn are affected by a policy" (p. 95). They suggested ways of identifying stakeholders including: considering standard demographic groups (age, sex, etc.) for relevance; asking people who they consider to be the key stakeholders; and studying accounts of ethnographic fieldwork to discover who seems to have a valid interest.

An authoritative account of business stakeholders can be found in Donaldson and Preston (1995). The paper describes a corporation "as a constellation of co-operative and competitive interests possessing intrinsic value" (p. 66). It states that the stakeholder theory is descriptive of the corporation, instrumental in helping people to examine stakeholder management practices, normative in establishing that stakeholders deserve attention, and managerial in recommending attitudes, structures, and practices. However, it considers the corporation as the system of interest and does not look at software or product development.

Pouloudi (1999) examines the concept of stakeholder and its use in information systems development. The paper is an excellent introduction to the extensive information systems literature on stakeholders, and it analyses some of the weaknesses of the concept (including being "almost a cliché," quoting from D. Willets). For our purposes here, one key point is that it does not make sense to treat human and non-human actors symmetrically: they are simply different. Pouloudi notes the discomfort of Vidgen and McMaster "about assigning anthropomorphic properties to non-human resources" and states that

> *I do not subscribe to the symmetrical treatment of humans and non-humans or the treatment of non-humans as stakeholders, although it is interesting and indeed necessary to consider the way in which non-humans—including .. information systems—"inscribe, represent, and speak for" the interests of stakeholders.* (p. 13)

In the taxonomy presented here, all stakeholders are human; interfacing systems are represented by humans responsible for them, that is, in accordance with Pouloudi's approach. Pouloudi has studied stakeholder identification but in a medical context (Pouloudi & Whitley, 1997). This is very different from system development, but the paper is of interest for its clear thinking and practical approach.

Sharp et al. (1999) suggests a simple recursive procedure, starting from an initial contact person and asking each interviewed person who might be worth speaking to. The procedure terminates when no new names arise or when the new names are found not to be relevant. The paper describes a simple method for identifying stakeholders starting from the initial point of contact (which might typically be the project sponsor). This is one of the few papers to address the issue directly, and its suggestion is sensible. However, it is not a substitute for a template (based on a taxonomy); the method could be time-consuming, and it is likely to reveal only the stakeholders that everybody knows already. To be fair, the method of asking each interviewee who else might be relevant is almost an obvious good practice during requirements' elicitation. The paper also points out that stakeholder classes (slots) should be characterised by their relationships to the system, to other stakeholders, and by the priority to be given to each stakeholder's view. These dimensions are used here (along with the stages where each slot might be relevant), although they are rough guides at best.

Robertson and Robertson (2006, pp. 356-358) distinguish clients, customer, and other stakeholders, including subject matter experts, marketing people, product managers, and so on, and attempts to prioritise them:

the principal stakeholders are the users, clients, and customers (p. 35).

However, the general effect is of a flat unstructured list of many interested parties. The Volere template (by the same authors) similarly proposes a flat list of roles, as one axis of a matrix to organise which kind of stakeholder to consult for which "class of knowledge" (Volere, 2004). The taxonomy proposed in this chapter offers a richer and more explanatory structure and suggests the significance of key roles and their interactions. The Volere template has been updated in the light of the criticism presented here (Alexander, 2005), but its 2004 version remains of interest in showing the difficulties even experienced consultants face in identifying stakeholders. That version is analysed next in the sub-section, *Developer- or Requirement-Centric Taxonomy*.

Alexander and Stevens (2002) includes a chapter on identifying stakeholders (pp. 19-26). It also distinguishes "users" from clients, suppliers, managers "who are concerned for the system to succeed" (and by implication other people with that concern), and regulators, and it briefly discusses the role of people in the development organization (p. 7). The variety of roles is illustrated with a cartoon of stakeholders in a space telescope project (p. 20), which shows an astronaut carrying out maintenance, a ground station engineer operating the spacecraft, an astronomer discussing the data produced by the telescope, and a politician gaining political benefit from the system (Figure 7). The discussion of these roles makes clear that these represent different viewpoints not necessarily conflicting. This was a sensible and pragmatic position, but the proposed taxonomy looks far more deeply at the structure and possible conflicts between stakeholders.

There is much pragmatic wisdom on dealing with stakeholders in Peter Checkland's many writings (for example, Checkland & Scholes, 1990). He does not on the whole focus on the development of products or services, and indeed he seems to believe that that is the easy part of the problem! For example:

Figure 7. Space telescope stakeholders (from Alexander & Stevens, 2002)

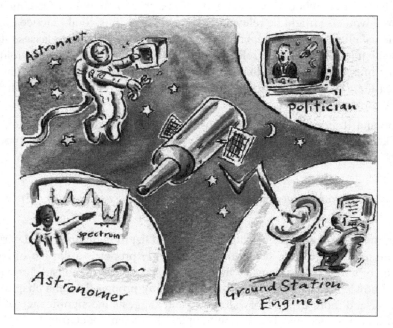

> *It now seems that, in the future, the computer project managed through a 'project life cycle' will increasingly become the occasional special case in which some uncontentious and relatively mechanical administrative procedures are computerized. Where perceptions and meanings, and hence tasks, are more problematical, the 'project' approach needs to be complemented by a process for the continuous rethinking of organizational tasks and processes... .* (Checkland & Scholes, 1990, p. 312)

While we may readily agree with Checkland's emphasis on process rather than project, and take his advice on (human) "perceptions and meanings" and "rethinking" as a hint to keep up to date with our stakeholder analysis, we do not think that software only implements uncontentious mechanical procedures. Indeed, major products such as enterprise resource planning tools can have a powerful and sometimes deleterious impact on organisations (note that we consider the customisation of such COTS tools for an organisation to be a kind of development project).

Another worker—both researcher and practitioner—who helped to pioneer socio-technical design is Enid Mumford. In her long career and her many writings (e.g., Mumford, 1996), she emphasised a humanistic and ethical approach to the people whose work was affected by process redesign and automation. She talks more often about specific people, individuals, clerks, groups, staff, and so on, rather than using generalities like "stakeholders." However, much of her work was precisely about paying more attention to the different groups of people involved in or affected by a project. For example:

> At these meetings a large number of organizational problems emerged and she [Mumford] suggested to the clerks that they should think about how these might be solved.

> She then forgot about this request and fed-back the results of the survey to the members of the technical design group. They subsequently designed what they thought was an excellent socio-technical system, called a meeting of all the clerks, described their proposed system and sat back and waited for the applause. To their astonishment there was silence. Then one of the senior clerks stood up... He then produced an excellent blue-print for a work structure that solved most of the office's efficiency and job satisfaction problems.

> ... The author learnt a very important lesson from this experience... This is never to underestimate a group's abilities. (Mumford, 1996, p. 87)

Onion Models

> Peer: (Pulls off several layers at once.)
>> What an enormous number of swathings!
>> Isn't the kernel soon coming to light?
> (Pulls the whole onion to pieces.)
>> I'm blest if it is! To the innermost centre,
>> it's nothing but swathings-each smaller and smaller.
>> - Nature is witty!
> (Throws the fragments away.)
>> Peer Gynt, Act 5, Scene 5, by Henrik Ibsen (1867)

Onion models have been used for centuries to indicate hierarchical spheres of influence. Alexandre Koyré's wonderful *From the Closed World to the Infinite Universe* (Koyré, 1957) uses the beautiful 11-layered onion diagram of Peter Apian's 1539 *Cosmographia*, a pre-Copernican model of the universe, on its cover (Figure 8). Apian has the imperfect and changeable Earth at the centre, and *Coelum Empireum*

Figure 8. Apian's onion diagram of the universe (from Koyré, 1957)

Habitaculum Dei et Omnium Electorum (i.e., The Empyrean heavens, the dwelling place of God and all the Elect) as the outermost, perfectly unchangeable layer.

This implied a fixed frame of reference for each class of beings in the Great Chain (Lovejoy, 1936), very far from the dynamic situation-dependent stakeholder Webs of Coakes and Elliman (1999), who describe the role of stakeholders in managing change. Their term "stakeholder Webs" has entered popular currency, perhaps by association with fashionable terms like World Wide Web and semantic Web, and may have done much to get people thinking about stakeholders in software development.

Their Webs are drawn as cobwebs with radial lines and concentric ellipses. This makes them look something like onion models, but:

> *The importance of the Web is not in the exact labelling of sectors and boundaries but in seeing the web as a continuum. The sectors and labels shown in [a Figure] are not a prescriptive or a priori model for all webs but ... the groupings that emerged from the case study.* (p. 9)

Thus, the Coakes and Elliman stakeholder Web is expected to be different for each examined system: there is no recognisable taxonomic pattern common to different

Figure 9. A stakeholder Web (from Coakes & Elliman, 1999)

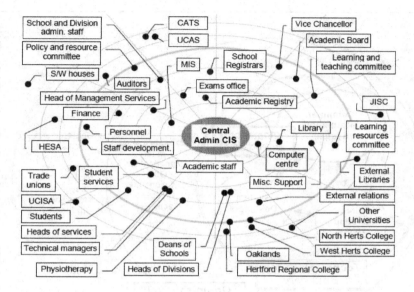

developments. Somewhat in contradiction to this, Figure 1 of their paper illustrates the choice of the system boundary based on Midgley (1992), which shows concentric circles labelled the technical system boundary, the organisational boundary outside that, and finally the human or total system boundary on the outside (Figure 10). Within the technical system boundary are three items linked by bidirectional arrows: computer information system, whose boundary is labelled automation boundary; direct system users; and system designers. Within the organisational boundary is a text label "executive and wider management, other divisions and business activities." Within the human or total system boundary is a text label "shareholders, clients, government, and other stakeholders, beyond the organisational boundary" (p. 6).

This is clearly a rudimentary onion model. We can make the following assignments:

- Computer Information System = (an example of) our "the kit" or product;

- Direct System Users = our normal operators (but see criticism of the term "users" later in this chapter);

- System Designers = our developers, who seem oddly placed within the technical system, given that they may have no part in the system's daily operations. It looks as if the operational boundary is here confounded with the boundary of all matters engineering and technical. The figure is criticised by both Midgley and Coakes and Elliman, who argue that the "critical setting of

Figure 10. Midgley's onion (from Coakes & Elliman, 1999)

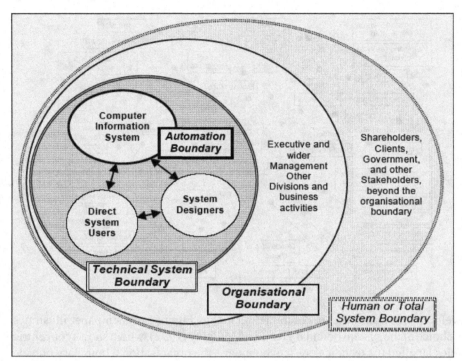

the system boundary" needs to be "determined by examining the viewpoints of stakeholder groups ... rather than technical issues" (p. 6). However, the automation boundary remains important as a contractual and developmental reality; while the figure is clearly defective as regards the technical system boundary, it can be corrected by removing the system designers from it, and inserting any other types of operator that may be needed, as is argued later in this chapter.

- Similarly, executives and management may loosely correspond to our functional, financial, or political beneficiaries, but there is no reason why the organisational boundary should fit neatly within the total system boundary if this is taken to mean our wider environment with respect to a specific kit or product: some parts of the organisation's management may be involved, others not. Simply because some dead-wood paper-pushers are within the organisation does not make them valid stakeholders: that way madness lies.

- Again, Midgley's shareholders, clients, government can reasonably be equated with our financial beneficiaries, purchaser (perhaps—client is a slippery term), and political beneficiary (or perhaps regulator, depending on the situation).

Coakes and Elliman (1999) are probably right, therefore, to reject the Midgley (1992) onion model, but a more carefully-considered model may overcome their objections. Designers and developers do not belong inside the "technical system" boundary—in any case, since it contains people, it must be sociotechnical. The organisational boundary is the wrong one to choose (unless, of course, it is the organisation rather than a product or development which is your focus); and the "human or total system" boundary does seem rather vague. On the other hand, there is usually a containing system (in our terms, see sub-section, *Structure of the Onion Model*) that makes use of the results or outputs of the (sociotechnical) system that we are developing—otherwise, why would anyone pay to develop it—and there are indeed stakeholders such as shareholders and government who may have an interest in aspects of the system, while not themselves playing any part in its development or operation. The problem with a stakeholder Web formed afresh for each new system is that it offers little guidance, whereas the engineers working on yet another telemetry system (say) are immediately aware that what they are doing is very similar to what they did on previous projects. Coakes and Elliman throw out the baby with the bathwater.

A modern onion model related to stakeholders can be found in Donaldson and Preston (1995, p. 74).

However their model's circles, starting from the centre, are the normative, instrumental, and descriptive aspects of stakeholder theory (Figure 11). These:

> *are nested within each other ... The external shell of the theory is its descriptive aspect; the theory presents and explains relationships that are observed in the external world. The theory's descriptive accuracy is supported, at the second level, by its instrumental and predictive value; if certain practices are carried out, then certain results will be obtained. The central core of the theory is, however, normative.* (p. 74)

The Donaldson and Preston onion model is thus used to help visualise the structure of the theory, not the relationships of the stakeholders and a product under development.

Hirschheim and Klein (2003) reflect on the state of information systems research in a long and discursive paper. In a nutshell, they wonder whether information systems can effectively mediate social dialogue, and if so how the field would have to be structured. Understanding organisational stakeholders better would form an important part of that programme. The authors refer to "immediate," "external," and "societal" stakeholders, implying something like an onion structure, although not exactly the one described here. "Immediate" roles, for instance, include "a managerial elite and their masters, the shareholders" (p. 271)—although it is not clear if in fact the shareholders are immediate or one jump removed by being the

Figure 11. A wholly different onion model (from Donaldson & Preston, 1995)

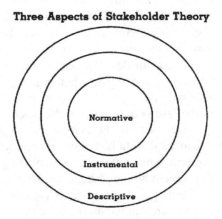

masters of the managerial elite. If the latter, then there might be a reasonable match with the onion model given here: managers = functional beneficiaries, shareholders = financial beneficiaries. However, the focus of the paper is not on products but on information systems professionals themselves.

Taxonomies and Hierarchies

The general subjects of taxonomy and hierarchy are far too broad to be addressed here in any detail. Susan Leigh Star has written engagingly about classification (e.g., Bowker & Leigh Star, 1999). She states that classification systems should exhibit consistent principles, mutually-exclusive categories, and completeness. It is hard to make any such classification of stakeholders; while the roles listed here seem to be usable consistently and are mutually-exclusive, one person can play several roles, and it is impossible to be sure that new roles will not arise, so completeness is unattainable. Any "taxonomy of stakeholders" must be tentative at best.

Under the heading of "hierarchical structure," Jackson (1995, pp. 92-95) wittily makes the point that one taxonomy can only do one job; very often several different hierarchies are needed. Indeed, one of the key principles of Jackson's JSD/JSP methods is to make sure that your representations adequately span the problem. You may need one data structure that understands files: file start—data—file end; and another that understands transactions recorded within those files: start event—more events—end event. Either on its own is insufficient: a transaction might, for instance, span two files. Analysing stakeholders by their relatedness to a product is only part of the story.

Goals and Viewpoints

Two areas of requirements' engineering related to stakeholder analysis are goal modelling and viewpoint analysis.

A **goal** is an intention that a stakeholder has for a development project (or more widely for a business or indeed for a lifetime), for example, that it will make preparing accounts easier. Goals may interact positively or negatively—achieving one goal may make it easier or harder to achieve another. Such interactions can easily be modelled graphically, making conflicts easy to visualise. Hence, modelling goals and their interactions is one way to explore the relationships between stakeholders with different needs. What goal modelling is not designed to do is to identify or classify the stakeholders themselves, though it can explore their social and operational interactions (and even their beliefs). Goal modelling is, therefore, like most other approaches, likely to discover operational ("our system") roles rather than those in the wider circles of the onion model. There is an extensive literature on goals; a good starting point is Yu and Mylopoulos (1998).

Negative interactions can also be intentional and dynamic, in which case they may more directly be modelled as negative scenarios or misuse cases (Alexander, 2002). This approach has the merit of considering threats, risks, and hazards, whether caused intentionally or not, and how to mitigate them. It will, therefore, put the spotlight on negative stakeholders as well as normal operators. However, this approach too tends to direct attention mainly to operational issues.

A **viewpoint** is either the perspective that a given stakeholder has on a development project or its product, for example, that they will continue to have an interesting job and a decent salary, or the projection (for example, of requirements) on to the system from the position of a given stakeholder role, for example, an employee's. Analysing viewpoints helps to discover whole groups of requirements, can indicate possible conflicts, and hence can help to create better and more stable specifications.

A readable introduction to viewpoints is Kotonya and Sommerville (1998). It describes a method of "viewpoint-oriented requirements' development" (VORD), explicitly a stakeholder-centred approach. As well as describing a method for discovering viewpoints and resolving stakeholder conflicts, it presents a simple taxonomy of "abstract viewpoint classes" (p. 219), classifying viewpoints into direct and indirect. These do not correspond exactly to our operational and non-operational. Instead, direct includes "system" (our "interfacing systems"—see sub-section, *Structure of the Onion Model*) and "operator" (our "normal operator"). Indirect is divided into engineering (maintenance and standards: we consider maintenance to be operational, while standards means the regulator), regulatory, organisation (procurer, policy, and training), and environment. A further paper by the same team (Sommerville, Sawyer, & Viller, 1998) describes the PreView approach in which viewpoints are treated as projections on to a system. One stakeholder viewpoint then naturally corresponds to a substantial set of requirements.

Multiview (Avison & Wood-Harper, 1990) is a well-respected approach to system design based on the idea of multiple stakeholders' views on the system and on choosing appropriate tools and techniques according to the problem situation thus defined—as such it owes something to soft systems methodology (Checkland & Scholes, 1990). Both "soft" and "hard" aspects are considered: human exploration and sociotechnical analysis on the soft side; information analysis and specification on the hard side. This is obviously sensible and practical. However, it does not attempt to classify stakeholder roles. Multiview 2 went further in several ways, including a "systemic stakeholder analysis" within its organisational analysis and using ethnography in the sociotechnical analysis (Bennetts & Wood-Harper, 2000). However, it did not attempt a taxonomy of stakeholders.

Human Aspects of System Development

There is an extensive literature on human aspects of system development. It seems, however, to focus quite naturally on the "user" (by which is generally meant our "normal operator") at the expense of all other roles. This is no place for a full literature survey but a good starting point is Sutcliffe (2002), which approaches requirements' engineering from a background in human-computer interaction and has an extensive bibliography.

Sutcliffe distinguishes customers, users, managers, software engineers, system testers, and system maintainers—"Maintenance personnel are rarely consulted in requirements analysis yet they depend on accurate requirements documentation more than most" (p. 17)—and it could be added that they have more to contribute than most, too. These roles are notably concentrated around "our system," but to be fair, they are said to be those that can write requirements. Stakeholders are further classified (p. 56-7) as:

- **Primary:** "Who will actually operate the system" (our "normal operators" [and possibly also our "maintenance operators"]: equivalent to UML "actors").
- **Secondary:** "Users who will not actually operate the system but will consume its output and depend on its operation for successful completion of their work." The astronomer of Alexander and Stevens (2002; see Figure 7) would be an example (our "functional beneficiary"). Note the typical awkwardness and

circumlocution necessitated by overloading the term "users" to mean both operator and beneficiary.

- **Tertiary:** "Senior managers who rarely consume the system output directly but make use of information for planning and strategic control of the business." This seems to denote either our "functional beneficiary" or our "political beneficiary."

Sutcliffe's classification is interesting but limited to thinking about people who receive information outputs. However, the book also describes more general stakeholder analysis methods somewhat surprisingly quoting the ruggedly practical and pioneering (Gause & Weinberg, 1989) rather than the more academic (Kotonya & Sommerville, 1998), which one might have expected.

Surrogacy

Surrogacy has apparently scarcely been researched as a requirements' engineering issue. It is mentioned briefly in some of our own earlier work on stakeholders (Alexander, 2003) and in a practical way on the Scenario Plus! stakeholders template (Scenario Plus!, 2006).

Damian and Zowghi (2002) state that a business management department acted as a surrogate stakeholder:

> *Hence BM became a surrogate customer for the developers in Australia and the need for effective collaboration with DM group emerged as critical in order to meet commitments made to the customers.*

The point is not developed further, but it is clear that in the context of using technology to support RE across sites on different continents (America, Australia, Europe), the issue of who you can actually speak to, and whether they fairly represent who they claim to, is highly significant.

A set of guidelines (Kitapci & Bhuta, 2004) for using the EasyWinWin (requirements' negotiation) tool and approach (Boehm, Grünbacher, & Briggs, 2001) tantalisingly mentions appointing "one of the team members as a surrogate customer if the customer would not be using the EasyWinWin tool." However, the significance of surrogacy is not considered.

Surrogacy is also occasionally mentioned in non-requirements' work on stakeholders (i.e., to do with steady-state business, not with system development). For instance, Wood (1999) writes:

The Chief Executive Officer acts as the surrogate employer of teachers, but it is unclear who is responsible for the teacher relationship.

Similarly, Younkins (2001) expresses the sentiment:

The corporation should be managed for the benefit of its stakeholders and the groups must participate in decisions that affect their welfare. Such participation is indirect with managers having surrogate duty to represent the stakeholders' interests. Managers are said to have a fiduciary relationship to stakeholders and must act in the interests of the stakeholders as their agents.

The focus of such work is however (in both these examples) on the political and social significance of stakeholder responsibilities not on surrogacy as such.

Donaldson and Preston (1995) begin, interestingly, with a quotation from E. Merrick Dodd, Jr., writing in the *Harvard Law Review* of 1932. Dodd does not use the term "stakeholder," but he is plainly thinking of the same concept: "If the unity of the corporate body is real, then there is reality and not simply legal fiction in the proposition that the managers of the unit are fiduciaries for it and not merely for its individual members, that they are … trustees for an institution [with multiple constituents] rather than attorneys for the stockholders." Both the concept of stakeholder and the importance of surrogacy are evident from this early discussion.

Potts (1995) does not explicitly mention surrogacy but does consider the relationship of "customer" and "developer" and some of the misunderstandings that can arise across the gap between them, for example, the contractual interface and hence the supplier/purchaser roles that are created (with inevitable surrogacy). His talk's provocative title also led requirements people to reflect on the nature of the stakeholder/developer "interface."

Discussion:
Features and Limitations of the Taxonomy

"User": A Hybrid Role

One slot that is not provided is "user." We consider this term to be both dangerously overloaded and confusing. It has many loose meanings in colloquial engineering parlance, including:

1. "all stakeholders;"
2. "all stakeholders other than us, the developers" (this meaning verges on the derogatory, and should be avoided);
3. "any stakeholder who gets any benefit from the product;"
4. "any stakeholder who operates the product."

However, perhaps the most widespread meaning is an interesting hybrid of two of our slots: normal operator and functional beneficiary (Figure 12). For example, consumer electronics companies speak of "users." They seem to mean the people who both push the buttons on their products and who enjoy the resulting entertainment (music, video, games, etc.). This user/consumer role seems necessary to combine the roles of operator and functional beneficiary, and, of course, the role of consumer/mass-market product purchaser—not to be confused with the important surrogate role of purchaser adopted by product managers and procurement departments—is not far away either. Indeed, if changing the batteries is considered to be a maintenance operation, then the role is multiple-hybrid.

Popular variant terms such as "end-user" do not clarify the situation. "End-User" seems sometimes to mean "the actual operator of the product, as opposed to the purchasing organisation that is paying for its development," in which case its slot is normal operator. At other times, the implied slot is functional beneficiary, as when

Figure 12. "User" as a hybrid role across 2 or more slots

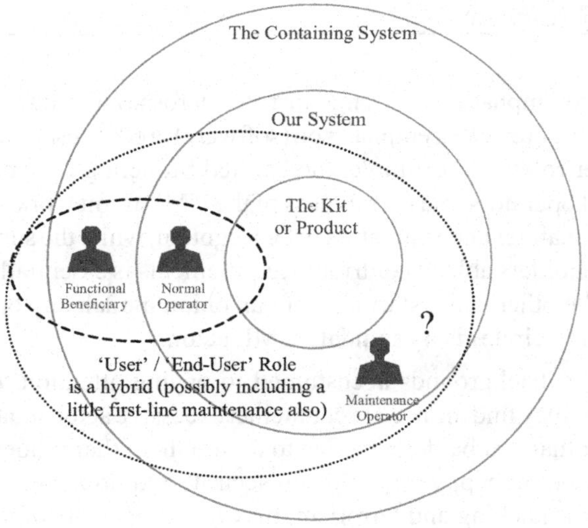

astronomers are called the end-users of a scientific satellite because they make use of the data it collects. In any case, we may ask "the end of what?" with respect to the chain of beneficiaries on the left of the onion model and indeed to the shifting perspectives of the onion models drawn with respect to different products within a system/subsystem hierarchy.

Therefore, the terms "user" and "end-user" have little value, may be harmful in diverting attention away from non-operational stakeholders, and should not be chosen as fundamental taxonomic units.

Overlapping Taxonomies

Clearly, this model is product-centric, although by intention people-focused. It is possible to create process-centric models (around the developer and development activities, the business processes, and system usage), and as argued in the section, *Research Review*, most of the requirements' literature seems to be tightly product-centric to the exclusion of most kinds of stakeholder.

It is unwise to try to make a single taxonomy or hierarchy do too much (Jackson, 1995, pp. 92-95); the aim here is to provide a practical way of discovering and remembering the viewpoints necessary to a development's success. Other models may be needed to cover business processes that stakeholders are involved in. Other hierarchies may be needed to suit other purposes such as defining company responsibilities. More is said on the dangers of reading too much into the model in a following sub-section, *Visual Metaphors*.

Usage-Centric Taxonomy

We have chosen to emphasize the range of roles across onion model circles, as a counterbalance to the prevailing emphasis on (software) product usage to the exclusion of almost all other roles. For example, the Unified Modeling Language's "actors" are chiefly normal operators; the narrowness of the UML framework (Fowler, 2004) often causes even maintenance operators to be forgotten, while the surrounding context of other stakeholders able to contribute requirements is essentially undescribed (Figure 13). On the other hand, starting from an onion model, any operational role (in the "our system" circle) is a candidate UML actor.

Readers from other backgrounds accustomed to paying attention to a myriad of stakeholder groups may find the need to counteract excessive actor-fixation parochial; perhaps, the most that can be done here is to assure them that it does seem to be a problem. The current unhappy emphasis on security requirements, in response to threats as diverse as hacking and terrorism, may however be helpful to make even the most software-fixated developers aware that stakeholders do matter.

Figure 13. UML only explicitly addresses stakeholders inside "our system" with its use case "actors"

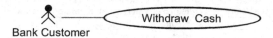

Bank Customer

Developer- or Requirement-Centric Taxonomy

The Volere template (Volere, 2004) contains an interesting and useful list of stake-holders—certainly far more comprehensive than most others in the literature. These are not easy to map into our taxonomy from the stakeholder role names alone: for instance, should "maintenance specialist" be treated as a maintenance operator role or as a consultant role? It could clearly be either. However, the list seems rather developer-oriented: most of the roles appear to fall into the developer and consultant slots (see Table 1).

The numerous "consultant" roles in the Volere list—their names ending in "specialist" or "expert"—make sense if seen from the point of view of a classification of non-functional requirements: perhaps, the thinking ran "here are some usability and some security requirements, we better consult some appropriate specialists about these" (i.e., the knowledge-role-person triangle was the driver for discovering requirement-related knowledge [Robertson, 2004]). Thus, it appears that the

Table 1. Classification of Volere stakeholder roles into the onion model

Onion Model tailored for Volere	All 37 Stakeholder roles defined in Volere.co.uk template	Volere Row No.
The Wider Environment		
Financial Beneficiary	—— none ——	
Negative Stakeholder		
	Opponents of project/product	38
	Public Opinion	41
Developer		
	Packaging Designer	28
	Manufacturer	29
	Project Management	32
	Business Analysts	33
	Requirements Engineers	34
	Technical Designers	35
	Technical Systems Architect	36
	Organisational Architect	37
	Testing Specialists	42
Consultant		
	Business/Subject Experts	11
	Future Ideas Specialists	12
	Current System Specialists	13
	Sales Specialist	17

Table 1. (continued)

Onion Model tailored for Volere	All 37 Stakeholder roles defined in Volere.co.uk template	Volere Row No.
	Marketing Specialist	18
	Aesthetics Specialist	19
	Graphics Specialist	20
	Usability Specialist	21
	Safety Specialist	22
	Security Specialist	23
	Cultural Specialist	24
	Legal Specialist	25
	Environmental Specialist	26
	Standards Specialist	40
	Financial Specialists	44
	Negotiation Specialists	45
Regulator		
	Auditors	43
Political Beneficiary	—— *none* ——	
The Containing System		
Interfacing System	—— *none* ——	
Purchaser		
	Customer	10
Functional Beneficiary		
	Client	9
Champion / Sponsor		
	Protectors of Project/Product	39
Our System		
Maintenance Operator		
	Product Installer	30
	Maintenance Specialist	27
Normal Operator		
	Clerical User	14
	Technical User	15
	Potential User	16
Operational Support		
	Training Staff	31

Volere template is perhaps more specifically requirement-centric than developer-centric. On the other hand, the negative and champion slots are rightly stated to be "project/product"-centric.

The resulting onion diagram (Figure 14) shows that (for all the length of the Volere stakeholders' list) several slots remain unfilled, perhaps surprisingly including the one for stakeholders responsible for interfacing systems.

Several other slots are only weakly represented, for example, "auditors" is the sole (and rather doubtful) role in "regulator."

Volere's "customer" and "client" are slippery terms; in this analysis, they are assumed to correspond roughly to our "purchaser" and "functional beneficiary," respectively; client can, however, also include financial beneficiary.

Figure 14. Onion model of Volere stakeholder roles

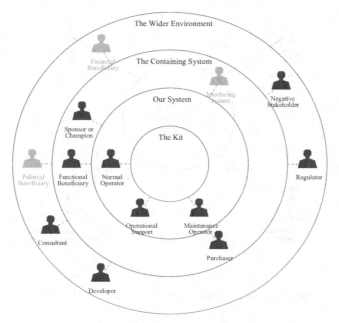

Several slots (greyed-out) remain unfilled. Several other slots (especially consultant, developer) are heavily populated (see Table 1).

Surrogacy

One aspect of stakeholder sociology that is brought out clearly on an onion diagram is **surrogacy**—the representation of one stakeholder's viewpoint by some other person. Surrogacy has (when it has been considered at all) always been seen as a dangerous obstacle to successful requirements work. It is, therefore, remarkable that stakeholder surrogacy (Figure 15) is both central to requirements' engineering (RE) and scarcely discussed in the RE literature (see the section, *Research Review*).

Figure 15 describes some of the surrogacy issues around requirements' engineering as a whole and stakeholder sociology in particular. It is immediately apparent that the different stakeholder-surrogate relationships each have their own advantages and risks. These are briefly analysed in Table 2.

Other forms of surrogacy are also involved, given that both in development projects and in ordinary work (using the developed products) people are usually working on behalf of other people.

Figure 15. Four kinds of stakeholder surrogacy

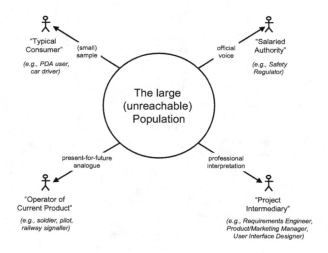

Table 2. Stakeholder-surrogacy relationships

Type of Surrogate Stakeholder	Example	Relationship with Stakeholder Population	Advantages	Risks
'Typical Consumer'	Car drivers paid to give opinion of new models of car	statistical sample	is a real operator/ beneficiary of the product	may not be typical; danger of mis-sampling
'Operator of Current Product'	Soldier helping to define military equipment needs 25 years into the future	present-for-future analogue in the domain	is a real operator of analogous products	analogy may not hold in future environment; obsolescence
'Project Intermediary'	Requirements Engineer writing other people's requirements; Product Manager purchasing development of product on behalf of both consumers and financial beneficiaries (e.g. shareholders)	professional interpretation	familiar with engineering development	misinterpretation through lack of domain knowledge; over-technical focus (bias towards technology); invented requirements (Potts 1995)
'Salaried Authority'	Aviation Authority (Safety Regulator) checking safety on behalf of public	official voice	statutory position; enforcement of requirements enshrined in law	remote from population and product operations; bureaucracy

Combinations and intermediate types can also be identified. For example, environmental pressure groups and "not in my back yard" campaigners may create leaders who, although unofficial and unpaid, may act almost as regulators being invited to meetings and having their (negative) opinion sought.

The history of computing can be seen as a steady retreat from the assumption that we know how to program what we want done in machine language. Languages and tools that are successively more human-oriented (such as assembly language, Fortran, visual programming, databases) have been invented to fill the gap.

The history of requirements can be seen as a steady retreat from the assumption that we know how to say what we want done in atomic "shall" requirements. Documents and diagrams that are successively more stakeholder-oriented (such as user requirements, concepts of operations, use cases, goal models) have been invented to fill the gap.

The roles people play—what they do, and what they want to do—thus seem to be becoming increasingly important to our discipline of RE. Our "machine codes"—individually prioritised and traceable requirements—will not simply disappear. But like hexadecimal, the writing of requirement text is moving steadily into the background as more abstract representations of what people want are invented and adopted in practice.

A "user requirement" has the general form

<named stakeholder role> wants <result>.

If the gold standard for RE is to create requirements like this—claiming that specific stakeholders (we'll pass over the class/instance issue for a moment) want that result, more or less personally for their own work (by which we include leisure uses of consumer products, etc.), then surrogacy is a rampant anomaly. All that surrogate stakeholders can give us are statements of the general form

<named surrogate role> believes that <named role> wants <result>.

In law, statements of this kind are called "hearsay evidence," which is rarely admissible in court. But our surrogates often cannot even claim to have heard anyone else expressing their requirement however distantly. In the clearcut case of the procurement of military equipment on behalf of as yet unborn soldiers, there can be no claim even to hearsay evidence: the requirements are wholly invented.

Surrogacy thus interferes with the core trend and practical process of RE: the move towards gathering requirements directly from real stakeholders. Yet as Figure 15 indicates, surrogacy cannot readily be avoided (even when the "unreachable population" is not especially large). Perhaps, this is one of the fundamental limitations on the engineering of requirements, systems, and software.

Suzanne Robertson comments that it can help to invent a surrogate, for example, Erik the systems analyst. Erik could then be "consulted" on his needs:

> *Whenever we were stuck (should this be in or out, more or less detailed) we went and talked to Erik. Yes really, on our noticeboard we had a photo of him clipped from an SAS airline magazine. He looks like a good journeyman systems analyst, he works for a company that make fruit juices. Medium height, pleasant expression, Scandinavian glasses.* (Robertson, 2004)

Without the surrogate, they'd never have been able to finish the job.

Visual Metaphors

An onion diagram inherently embodies a set of visual metaphors, and these are exploited more or less consciously to give a feeling for stakeholder relationships in a development project. Metaphors inevitably break down at some point, so some caution is required. Attention is drawn to the limitations of the onion model described in the following text.

The most immediate of these visual metaphors is the feeling of successive (indeed recursive) containment of one "onion" within another. As Peter Checkland and others have emphasised, there are always many systems to consider (Checkland & Scholes, 1990). This leads to practical issues of project scope. The scope of a system of people-and-equipment is always larger than the scope of the equipment or product alone, so it is essential to be clear about the existence of the two boundaries (e.g., Robertson & Robertson, 2006).

A circular diagram inevitably announces that something is in the centre of attention, and in a development that is rightly the product; at the same time, it shows that people are "all around" it and have importance. It also suggests the metaphor of closeness for relatedness, and, for example, developers are shown close to purchasers for this reason. Distance could suggest that stakeholders in the outer circles are less important, but this is not intended. Indeed, negative stakeholders, regulators, and political beneficiaries are all able to "stop the show" and must be considered essential.

We also habitually make use of other spatial metaphors; supporting roles seem naturally to find a place below the product, while interfacing systems and regulators can go "off to the side" somewhere.

A cautionary note should be sounded here: a naïve reading of the onion model with the equation: outer = higher in the system or company hierarchy, with regulator in the outermost circle, would imply the equation regulator = responsibility for highest level of system. This is simply wrong. As Michael Jackson cautions (Jackson, 1995, essay entitled "Hierarchical Structure," and see the earlier section *Research Review*), there may be many overlapping hierarchies. Three that are often important in thinking about system development are:

1. The scopes of the product and the systems that contain it: this is the primary and intended meaning of the onion diagram. The operational stakeholders are those inside "the system," as explained next.

2. The organisation (e.g., company) hierarchy, with the workers at the bottom/inside and the managers and directors towards the top/outside. This is not what is intended here. Managers may or may not be stakeholders in a development; non-operational company workers and executives are not automatically assumed to be relevant.

3. The structure of the organisations and stakeholder relationships involved in accepting or rejecting a development, for example, the relationship of the regulator with the developer. This structure is secondarily suggested by the onion diagram, but this does not mean that questions like "Which level of system is the regulator in?" make any sense. The regulator is in a system—that of the political and legal framework of a country or the world—but that is certainly not the same as any onion circle of any ordinary development project.

The onion has its uses in helping people to think about multiple scopes and the need to involve people outside the development team, but it cannot do everything.

Another metaphor that seems quite natural (though perhaps mixing oddly with onions) is that of the chain of command, where a person makes use of a system under their command as an instrument to achieve a "political" goal. They do this by instructing an immediate subordinate—some at the adjacent or immediately contained level—to carry out some operation. That person, in turn, may achieve their goal (a successful operation) by instructing an operator to use a piece of equipment to deliver a specific result. The "chain" metaphor could be represented as a scale from higher to lower if you like the idea of a *Great Chain of Being* from God to man to animals (Lovejoy, 1936); I have chosen to make it the rather more egalitarian left-to-right (with the slight suggestion that actions, like writing, may proceed in that direction).

Conclusion

The trend in system specification away from the machine towards human "users" leads to a natural end-point in modelling and analysing the nature, goals, and viewpoints of human stakeholders. While there has been some academic interest in goal and viewpoint modelling, the stakeholders themselves seem largely to have been overlooked within systems and software engineering (although quite the reverse in soft systems and information systems research).

The "onion model" diagram has an attractive and intuitive simplicity about it, organizing a substantial amount of complexity in analysis of stakeholder sociology and relationships. This is part of a wider interest in and intention to improve the attention that practising engineers pay to stakeholders, including surveys and a reconsideration of development life cycles and project information models (Alexander & Robertson, 2004). The default onion model with three circles and the basic slots is often in itself helpful on projects, but it is readily tailored for more complex situations with additional circles and slots. Ralph Young (2004, pp. 65-67) has adopted the approach, and Suzanne and James Robertson (2004) have similarly done so. Needless to say, it is also pressed into service in Alexander and Maiden (2004).

Tool support is available, but the approach can be applied with nothing more than a hand-drawn diagram and a textual hierarchy of headings for circles, slots, roles, and, if desired, named stakeholders.

The analysis of stakeholders does not presuppose any particular development approach. While it is clearly suitable for an object-oriented worldview with use cases and their actors, it can equally be added to conventional or agile development.

This chapter has presented a simple but it is hoped generally-applicable and readily-customised taxonomy of stakeholders and has suggested some uses for it. If it contributes to encouraging even a few projects to think a little more deeply about who their stakeholders are and what they want, it will have succeeded.

Acknowledgments

I am grateful to Isabel Ramos for her suggestions and encouragement for this paper; to Andrew Farncombe for his clarity on terminology and multiple hierarchies; to Sabina Malfatti for drawing my attention to the onion layers in *Peer Gynt*; and to Suzanne Robertson for her continuing enthusiasm and support. I would also like to thank the anonymous reviewers for their perceptive comments and suggestions, especially on the voluminous information systems literature, and the editor—Bernd Stahl—for his measured criticism and direction.

References

Alexander, I. (2002, September 9-13). Initial industrial experience of misuse cases in trade-off analysis. *IEEE Joint International Requirements Engineering Conference*, Essen, Germany (pp. 61-68). Los Alamitos, CA: IEEE Computer Society.

Alexander, I. (2003, April). Stakeholders—who is your system for? *Computing & Control Engineering, 14*(1), 22-26.

Alexander, I. (2005, January-March). A taxonomy of stakeholders. *International Journal of Technology and Human Interaction, 1*(1), 23-59. (The original form of this chapter, as seen by the Robertsons [Volere, 2004]).

Alexander, I., & Maiden, N. (Eds.) (2004). *Scenarios, stories, use cases through the system development life-cycle.* New York: John Wiley.

Alexander, I., & Robertson, S. (2004, January/February). Understanding project sociology by modeling stakeholders. *IEEE Software, 21*(1), 23-27.

Alexander, I., & Stevens, R. (2002). *Writing better requirements.* London: Addison-Wesley.

Avison, D., & Wood-Harper, A. T. (1990). *Multiview: An exploration in information systems development.* Oxford: Blackwell Scientific Publications.

Bennetts, P. D. C., & Wood-Harper, A. T. (2000). *Software process improvement through the lens of Multiview 2: The development of a contingent factors model.* Presented at the 10th Conference on Business Information Technology, Manchester, UK.

Boehm, B., Grünbacher, P., & Briggs, R. O. (2001, May/June). Developing groupware for requirements negotiation: Lessons learned. *IEEE Software, 18*(3), 46-55.

Bowker, G. C., & Leigh Star, S. (1999). *Sorting things out, classification and its consequences.* Cambridge, MA: MIT Press.

Bush, D. (2003). Personal communication.

Checkland, P., & Scholes, J. (1990). *Soft systems methodology in action.* New York: John Wiley. (New edition with a 30-year retrospective, 1999).

Coakes, E., & Elliman, T. (1999, July). Focus issue on legacy information systems and business process engineering: The role of stakeholders in managing change. *Communications of the AIS, 2*(4).

Damian, D. E., & Zowghi, D. (2002, September). The impact of stakeholders' geographical distribution on managing requirements in a multi-site organization. In *Proceedings of the IEEE Joint International Requirements Engineering Conference,* Essen, Germany (pp. 319-328). Los Alamitos, CA: IEEE Computer Society.

Donaldson, T., & Preston, L. E. (1995). The stakeholder theory of the corporation: Concepts, evidence, and implications. *Academy of Management Review 1995, 20*(1), 65-91.

Fowler, M. (2004). *UML distilled, a brief guide to the standard object modeling language* (3rd ed.). Boston: Addison-Wesley.

Gause, D., & Weinberg, G. (1989). *Exploring requirements, Quality before design.* New York: Dorset House.

Hirschheim, R., & Klein, H. K. (2003). Crisis in the IS field? A critical reflection on the state of the discipline. *Journal of the Association for Information Systems, 4*(5), 237-293.

Ibsen, H. (1867). *Peer Gynt*. Modern English translation: Theatre Communications Group, 1992. (First published in Norwegian, 1867).

Jackson, M. (1995). *Software requirements & specifications, a lexicon of practice, principles and prejudices*. Harlow, UK: Addison-Wesley.

Kitapci, H., & Bhuta, J. (2004). *EasyWinWin negotiations: Guidelines and Easy-WinWin report*. Retrieved January 4, 2006, from http://sunset.usc.edu/classes/cs577a_2003/assignments/Team/ EasyWinWin%20Negotiations.htm

Kotonya, G., & Sommerville, I. (1998). *Requirements engineering: Processes and techniques*. New York: John Wiley.

Koyré, A. (1957). *From the closed world to the infinite universe*. Baltimore; London: The Johns Hopkins University Press. (Reprinted in paperback, 1968).

Levine, R., Locke, C., Searls, D., & Weinberger, D. (2000). *The ClueTrain manifesto, The end of business as usual*. London: FT.com.

Lovejoy, A. O. (1936). *The great chain of being*. Cambridge, MA: Harvard University Press. (Reprinted in paperback, 1990).

Mason, R., & Mitroff, I. (1981). *Challenging strategic planning assumptions: Theory, cases, and techniques*. New York: John Wiley & Sons.

McGraw, K., & Harbison, K. (1997). *User-centered requirements, The scenario-based engineering process*. Mahwah, NJ: Lawrence Erlbaum Associates.

Midgley, G. (1992). The sacred and profane in critical systems thinking. *Systems Practice, 5*(1), 5-16.

Mumford, E. (1996). *Systems design, Ethical tools for ethical change*. Basingstoke, UK: Macmillan.

Potts, C. (1995, March). Invented requirements and imagined customers: Requirements engineering for off-the-shelf software (Invited workshop introduction paper). In *Proceedings: 2nd IEEE International Symposium on Requirements Engineering*, York, England (pp. 128-130). Los Alamitos, CA: IEEE Computer Society Press. Retrieved July 7, 2006, from http://www.cc.gatech.edu/fac/Colin.Potts/pubs/1995/re95/re95InventedReqtsOTS.pdf

Pouloudi, A. (1999, January 5-8). Aspects of the stakeholder concept and their implications for information systems development. In *Proceedings of the 32nd Hawaii International Conference on System Sciences*, Maui, HI (Vol. 7, p. 7030).

Pouloudi, A., & Whitley, E. A. (1997). Stakeholder identification in inter-organizational systems: Gaining insights for drug use management systems. *European Journal of Information Systems, 6*(1), 1-14.

Robertson, S. (2004, March 18). Personal communication.

Robertson, S., & Robertson, J. (2004). *Requirements-led project management.* Boston, MA: Addison-Wesley.

Robertson, S., & Robertson, J. (2006). *Mastering the requirements process* (2nd ed.). Upper Saddle River, NJ: Addison-Wesley.

Scenario Plus! (2006). Scenario Plus! Web site. Retrieved July 7, 2006, from http://www.scenarioplus.org.uk (Onion model tool for Telelogic® DOORS, stakeholders template for Microsoft® Word, etc.).

Sharp, H., Finkelstein, A., & Galal, G. (1999). Stakeholder identification in the requirements engineering process. *DEXA Requirements Engineering Process Workshop* (pp. 387-391).

Sommerville, I., Sawyer, P., & Viller, S. (1998). Viewpoints for requirements elicitation: A practical approach. In *Proceedings of the Third IEEE International Conference on Requirements Engineering.*

Sutcliffe, A. (2002). *User-centred requirements engineering, theory and practice.* London: Springer.

Volere. (2004). *Volere stakeholder analysis template.* Retrieved February 20, 2004 (downloaded for analysis) from http://www.volere.co.uk (It has since been updated in the light of this criticism, but the comments apply to the 2004 version.)

Wood, D. (1999). *Trends in stakeholder management & measurement in the public sector.* Retrieved January 4, 2006, from http://www.navigate.co.nz/newsreti. htm

Young, R. R. (2004). *The requirements engineering handbook.* Boston: Artech House.

Younkins, E. W. (2001, Spring). Morality and character development: The roles of capitalism, commerce, and the corporation. *Journal of Markets & Morality, 4*(1), 94-111. Retrieved January 4, 2006, from http://www.acton.org/publicat/ m_and_m/2001_spring/ pdf/mm-v4n1-younkins.pdf

Yu, E., & Mylopoulos, J. (1998, June 8-9). *Why goal-oriented requirements engineering.* Requirements Engineering Foundation for Software Quality Workshop 1998, Pisa. Retrieved July 7, 2006, from http://www.cs.toronto. edu/pub/eric/REFSQ98.html

Endnote

[1]   For instance, I am assured that this is as true in air traffic control as it is in other domains (Bush, 2003).

Chapter III

21ˢᵗ Century Religious Communities

Susan E. George
University of South Australia, Australia

Abstract

This chapter examines the development of 21ˢᵗ century virtual communities, focus-ing upon those communities that have emerged for virtual religion. It aims to (1) raise awareness of the way that technology is being used for religious purposes; (2) explain the ways that human interaction in religious communities is influenced by technology, in both supporting traditional modes of interaction and in enabling new, and the main, criticisms; and (3) provide evidence to support the benefit of such communities to religious bodies themselves by turning to the question of tech-nological determinism—and the crucial question of just how humanity is influenced by technology.

Introduction

The Internet has created new human communities linking people from geographically, socially, culturally, and otherwise disparate backgrounds. Virtual communities may be defined as "a collection of people sharing common interests, ideas, and feelings over the Internet or other collaborative networks. Web-based virtual communities have been defined as social aggregations that emerge from the Net when enough people carry on public discussions long enough, with sufficient human feeling, to form webs of personal relationships in cyberspace. These communities are becoming increasing important forums for individuals and groups that share a professional interest or share common activities" (Dasgupta, 2006). In his book, *The Virtual Community*, Rheingold (1998) defines virtual communities as social aggregations that emerge from the Internet when enough people carry on public discussions long enough and with sufficient human feeling to form webs of personal relationships in cyberspace.

Virtual communities may be considered an outcome of the recent developments in communications technologies and a natural anthropological consequence for humanity embracing communications technology. While the original computer networks were never designed as a human communication medium, they have come to penetrate society for communication purposes in many ways—from mobile phones to Internet banking, hand-held computers to "intelligent" agents and voice-recognition at human-machine interfaces. The Internet has particularly brought people together from all over the world in various "online communities" and "virtual worlds" in the new "meeting place" of cyberspace. Virtual communities are found in every domain—in realms as diverse as education and health, recreation and science. One of the most important human realms in which virtual communities are found is that of religion.

First, we consider the nature of religion and note that a social and communal expression is vital; and we consider the ways that technology is being used for religious purposes. Second, we consider ways that technology both supports conventional practice and enables new expression, focusing upon Christianity. Third, we consider ways that religion benefits from virtual communities—in spite of some opposition.

Religion: Real and Virtual

Religion has proved very hard to define. Definitions of religion are often too narrow and exclude many of the belief systems which most people will agree are religious, or they are too vague and ambiguous, leading one to conclude that just about any and everything is actually a religion. Some of the more successful attempts identify a set of markers such as practical and ritual, experiential and emotional, narrative and mythical, doctrinal and philosophical, ethical and legal, social and institutional, and the material (Smart, 1992). The more markers present the more "religious-like" the belief system is. Sometimes religion is regarded as subjective, designating the feelings and acts of people which specifically relate to God and is distinguished from theology. From this subjective perspective, religion may be defined by the benefits it offers—the inclusion in a social community, the accompanying "rights" and "responsibilities," personal fulfilment, spiritual and emotional benefits from that and other assets.

One important element of religion is its communal and social expression. In fact, religion is often distinguished from spirituality, which is used to refer to devotional aspects of faith and interior individual experiences (Mc Grath, 2001). In a Christian context, the "body of believers" has a special significance as the "church." The faithful are invited to gather and not cease to meet together—whether that is in a physical church building or other! The synagogue as a Jewish place of worship literally means a "meeting place," where people would come together. For Islam, one of the five pillars entails the giving of alms as if all are "brother and sister" in the same family. For these major world religions, and for many others, the social dimension may be regarded as one of its distinguishing marks and a "meeting together" as a crucial component.

When we coin the term "virtual religion," we are speaking of interactions within cyberspace. Many theorists have divided communications history into three main epochs: the oral tradition, the literary tradition, and the visual tradition (Postman, 1985). Each of these traditions provides "ways of knowing" what is true and what is not. Summitt (1993) suggests that society is entering a fourth tradition, that of interactivity where the locus of interaction is cyberspace. This is where "virtual religion" is happening. The interactivity facilitated by the Internet means that those in geographically or otherwise isolated areas may (in some capacity) participate in corporate expression of religion, cutting across cultural, social, economic, linguistic, and other borders in a way never previously possible. Importantly, there is a two-way communication in the interaction—in the exchange that makes virtual religion so unique and a very real component of life at the start of the 21st century.

At the start of the 21st century, there are many, many religions in existence. Originally, only three religions were recognised: Christianity, Judaism and Paganism (i.e., everybody else). At present time, Judaism, Christianity, Islam, Hinduism, and Buddhism are considered by some to be the big five. The major two are Christianity and Islam. Each of these religions addresses questions of meaning and purpose in life, the way to live, and metaphysical elements of human existence. Each major religion also carries with it some form of "transcendence" of the human condition. In Islam, Christianity, and Orthodox Judaism, this involves "meeting the divine." In Hinduism and Buddhism, this involves reaching a state of "nirvana," which can be found within an individual in this world.

Noble (1977) finds that both religion and technology share one fundamental and underlying theme, which is their drive to transcend natural mortal life—nature, our bodies, humanity, and the world. Most major world religions—with perhaps the exception of secularism—have the concept of "life after death," whether this is "reincarnation" back to this world or a "resurrection" to another. In this idea of "transcending" death, there is the ultimate expression of transcending human limitation through transcending human mortality. The prominence of computer-mediated communication is an example of transcending the distances between people enabling interaction in online communities linking from people all over the world through the Internet.

Brenda Brasher's (2001) book, *Give me that Online Religion*, describes online religious communities and practices in general. The book helps document and analyse the phenomenon of online religion. Brasher argues that online religion will be an integral part of our global future. She presents stories of three separate individuals who are documented as they seek a spiritual goal via the Internet. One person sought more information about the Jewish faith and ended up attending a virtual Seder and converted to Judaism. Another person sought a deeper faith and found it through interaction with the "Christ in the Desert" Web page. He followed his cyber visit with a physical visit to the monastery in New Mexico and physically became involved in off-line religion. The third person had a purely online experience as a neo-pagan, who turned to the Internet for her various liturgical practices rather than meet face-to-face. As Brasher says, "Cyberspace is a medium enabling a new generation of human spirituality to be actualized."

Genevieve Bell (2004) observes in *Technologies of Enlightenment* that new technologies are delivering religious experiences in new mediums and creating new possibilities and opportunities for spiritual and religious life—everything from Cyber Seders, the papal SMS service, Mecca finding mobile phones, Buddhist blessings of the Internet, and the ngonli almanac online. Intel's "Inside Asia" particularly focuses on religion and culture in Asia.[1] Their forum explains some anecdotes of how technology has impacted religious practice, including the following: (a) "It is mid-afternoon in Malaysia. A devout Muslim stops his work, turns toward Mecca and says a prayer, as he is required to do five times a day. Although he is far from a mosque, he knows exactly where to position himself: his cell phone has an embedded compass that points him in the direction of Mecca;" and (b) "The Chinese have a practice of burning paper items, typically paper money, during funeral ceremonies to ensure the dead will have what they need for a good life in the next world. Today, they also burn paper versions of cell phones, laptop computers, and flat-panel televisions."

At the start of the first appearance of Christian entities on the Internet, Ken Bedell (1999) identified that many entities were not actually calling themselves churches. Instead, Bedell called the entities "Internet congregations" and in doing so focused in on one of the main uses of the Internet in creating virtual Christian communities. Bedell categories virtual Christian communities in six ways using "information" or "communication." Cutting across both of these assumptions are three strategies:

support for current institutions, bridge to current institution, and create new forms of institution.

In 2000, Wilson (2000) coined the term "Internet church" in his book of the same title describing how Christianity apprehended the Internet at the turn of the century. Typical resources of the Internet church are a Web site with a bulletin board forum or perhaps an online chat room. There may be an information page related to doctrine and/or some other static resource for the members of the community. But, simply having a Web site does not encompass all that the Internet church is.

The Internet church, virtual church or e-church, is essentially an online community which includes the normal components of church in an electronic forum. There may be archived addresses, liturgies, prayers and meditations, even video and audio recordings of actual gatherings. A bulletin board may be used for prayer or as a discussion forum to enable members to engage with each other. Members may keep in touch with electronic-mailing lists and/or SMS messages and mobile phones. Tools such as discussion boards and blogs may be used for gathering opinions in place of lengthily real-world meetings; and multimedia and computer graphics can produce uplifting "devotionals."

Susan George (2006) categorises various ways that Christianity has apprehended virtual religion in her book, *Religion and Technology in the 21st Century: Faith in the E-World*. George surveys some examples of what may be called an "Internet church," starting with the earliest example of "Internet church" in the First Church of Cyberspace[2] in 1994 to e-church[3] in 2001 and I-church[4] in 2004. Two broad classes of Internet entities are identified categorised by: (1) the technology utilised and (2) the function in church life and mission supported by the technology. To be an Internet church, the entity should not compromise that which is considered to be essential to the "essence" of a church. This calls into question just what is considered to be a "church."

Online Christianity

In the specific context of technology applied to Western Christianity, the section discusses how technology has supported conventional church life and mission. There are excellent study resources, a wealth of electronic aids, and software resources often interactive in nature engaging the learner; worship can also be supported with technology and made relevant to a multimedia experience generation. Such IT systems undoubtedly (at the best of times) benefit church life with improved efficiency, accuracy, ease of communicating information, reliability, and so forth.

In terms of religious dialogue between adherents of various religions, technology is obviously facilitating the dialogue. The "About" forum is just one discussion group (http://forums.about.com) where atheists and agnostics, Islamics, Christians, and many others from all over the world are meeting 24 hours a day, 7 days a week and engaging in the deepest religious and philosophical questions ever asked. The interactions occurring in such online environments may be labelled "virtual religion," just as real as any debate that might take place in the actual world in forums more recognisably identified as "religious."

Virtual religion may be more "accessible" to people including the disabled, or the geographically isolated, and those with other special needs for whom the real-world church could not cater. The Internet shrouds the user in anonymity, making it useful for enquirers to hold detailed communications about elements of religion, without having to reveal their identity and possibly "loose face" if they are enquiring and still sceptical or embarrassed about their ignorance of certain matters. This "anonymity" may be especially important in some cultural instances than others; perhaps where there is overt persecution, it offers the seeker some protection.

Andrew Careaga reports that, "One out of every four Internet users has sought religious or spiritual information at one point or another in their virtual travels, and on a daily basis, more people use the Internet for spiritual purposes than for gambling, banking, finding a date, trading stocks, or buying and selling at Web auction sites like eBay combined."[5] Cyberspace is regarded as a new "market place," where people meet together, are hand-in-hand with everyday business, will discuss politics, religion, and philosophy, and ask those questions that traditional religion has conventionally answered in churches, synagogues, mosques, and other religious meeting places. People are going to the Internet more than they are to any organised religious meeting place.

Some Criticisms

An increase in technology has apparently occurred hand-in-hand with a decrease in religiosity—at least a decline in the participation in organised, traditional religion. Some see that technology breeds a sense of empowerment and self-sufficiency. With appropriate technology, the human can control many facets of the world removing the need for God, at least fostering a reliance on technology rather than anything supernatural. Drawbacks are obvious when the system fails and when IT detracts more subtly from the relational community of a church.

Whether people are any less religious remains a question. The "Closer to Truth" forum discusses this question noting the intriguing paradox that as the world becomes more scientific, extreme religions are gaining ground (The Kuhn Foundation, 2003). Others point out that technology has replaced religion and become a "god" of society (Strong, 1991). Other negatives of technology have been identified from a specifically religious perspective. The education and training accompanying science and technology has been directly linked to a decline in participation or organised religion.

The Catholic Church has faced particular questions relating to its worship and liturgy in light of "virtual" and "remote" communication possibilities. In particular, it has had to address the question of whether sacraments can be administered over the Internet where normally the celebration depends "on the physical presence of the gathered faithful." The ruling of the U.S. Bishops' Secretariat for the Liturgy was that no sacrament can be received by electronic communication. The same ruling was found for the ritual involving "adoration of the cross," which was not permitted to be done via a Web-cam without physically being in the church building.[6] This has implications for all "remote" links—"live" telecast, Internet transmissions, Web-cams and video links—since technology cannot replace the physical presence among gathered people.

Theological rulings are not the only reasons why online communities are not desirable. If people engage solely in online social groups, friendships and other intimates in the real world can be put on hold. The technology can be adopted uncritically without discerning the options and setting appropriate limits. A new sort of addiction can grow among those who have tasted the Internet and replace the real-world interactions with a virtual world. While examples of online communities can be found, some questions that remain are who uses them, how, when, why, and where.

Benefit to Religious Bodies

Spreading the Message in Today's World

One of the main thrusts of Christianity that make the Internet a most appropriate partner is the "evangelistic" nature of the religion. That is, unlike some religions such as Buddhism, there is a definite thrust toward "spreading the message" and evangelism. Just as Christians were charged to "go out into all the world" at the inception of the religion in the 1st century Roman Empire, so the Internet is considered by many to be a "Roman Road" in which Christians are charged to venture in the 21st century. Wilson (2000) describes the Internet church as an opportunity to change the history of Christianity, comparing the "information superhighway" to the Roman Roads built almost two millennia ago that facilitated the spread of Christianity.

In terms of technology benefitting religiosity, George Barna (1998), in his book, *The Second Coming of the Church*, argues that most Christian churches are operating on out-dated models of authority, leadership, and congregational structure failing to meet the needs of a changing culture. He believes that in this decade, "millions of people will never travel physically to a church, but will instead roam the Internet in search of meaningful spiritual experiences." Thus, technology assists the church in its endeavour to foster spirituality and the quest for God. Using a computer for online religious activity could become the dominant form of religion and religious experience. Soukup (2000) also believes that it is vital to understand the media in reaching the culture with natural implications for the religious expression in online communities.

One initiative in the virtual church recognises that younger people are attracted to online communities through games (e.g., http:// www.waltemathe.org/virtkirch/), and a gaming strategy may be the way that inhabitants of cyberspace are drawn into deeper discussions through role playing and other possibilities. The existence of increasingly-sophisticated graphical interfaces and virtual worlds with avatars and other virtual gadgets will increase the appeal of online religion to the generation who is accustomed to such "presentation" in every other area of their life.

Returning to Authenticity of Relationships

People are building virtual communities in reaction to the disintegration of traditional local communities. Religious communities are no different when it comes to their disintegration and institutionalisation. It is perhaps paradoxical that the face-to-face interactions of religious communities are often not as "deep" as those exchanges that are fostered in virtual communities. A whole new dimension of "presence" is opened up when people communicate through text exchanges; personality issues and public speaking skills do not dominate to agenda, and real "social" presence can be fostered in the absence of physical presence.

Levelling Political Influences in Management

The Internet is inherently suited to the post-modern world and its "questioning" of relationships. Hughes (2000) suggests, "The world's industrial and technological societies are organised as states with hierarchical bureaucracies. Yet, the Internet is not organised or controlled by state bureaucracies or industrial corporations. Perhaps, it is a new form of social organisation, with opportunities for structures that are not bound by the hierarchical relationships of the state."

Discussion

Technology to Benefit Human Life

Technology is "science applied to daily life." Technology is expected to influence every aspect of existence—from education to healthcare, recreation to international politics. Many definitions focus particularly upon commerce or industry—"the practical application of science to commerce or industry" (www.cogsci.princeton. edu/cgi-bin/webwn)—or engineering—"the practical application of knowledge, especially in a particular area such as engineering" (www.projectauditors.com/Dictionary/T.html). Technology undeniably touches every facet and excludes none—not even religiosity.

Many definitions see technology as not only the application of science but an application designed to benefit humanity. For example, definitions include "the application of scientific advances to benefit humanity" (sln.fi.edu/franklin/glossary. html) and "the creation of products and processes for the purpose of improving human chances for survival, comfort level, and quality of life" (www.geog.ouc. bc.ca/ conted/ onlinecourses/ enviroglos/ t.html). We may consider how technology has benefitted and served humanity in what many would regard as one of its deepest and most distinguishing capacities, that is, in its capacity for religiosity, for pursuing the ultimate human quest of purpose, meaning, and significance.

Since technology does apply science to daily life, a need is found for monitoring the ethical questions and vital issues of the use of technology—to judge whether it is "good" or "bad." Science in its purist form is not concerned with moral judgement or with "purpose." Groups that do monitor the application of science typically have a religious affiliation. Sometimes, these groups are seen in negative terms, representing people who are resistant to change, reinforcing the false dichotomy of "science" vs. "religion" rather than presenting a body reflecting upon the application of science.

Technology Out of Control?

A key question concerning technology is the extent to which it is "under control." Martin Heidegger (1977) claims that technology is relentlessly overtaking us and believes that humanity's goal is to find a way of living with technology that does not allow it to "warp, confuse, and lay waste our nature." Heidegger puts it that, "Only a god can save us" from the juggernaut of progress. Heidegger sees this juggernaut of progress as unrelentingly carrying humanity on a journey and humanity is an unwitting passenger carried upon a path that may ultimately lead to our own destruction.

The way that technology is increasingly embedded in existing (and already accepted devices) demonstrates the subtle way that it enters into society. Simple devices are becoming smarter and smarter. Washing machines connect to the Internet, and mobile phones alert you to intruders in your home. Cars have onboard guidance systems, and aircrafts fly themselves. The possibilities of technology are almost limitless.

Information and communication technologies, the Internet, mobile phones, wireless networks, blogs, software bots, and many other elements of computer technologies have become part of that "juggernaut" that Heidegger could only have imagined at the end of the 20th century.

Other philosophers such as Borgmann (1993) also see technology (in a modern and post-modern world) to include a waning recognition of the possibility of any substantial spiritual existence. It is as if technology destroys that component of humanity. Dreyfus and Spinosa (1997) ask how can we relate ourselves to technology in a way that not only resists this devastation, but that also gives it a positive role in our lives? This is marked as the key question for our generation.

Summary

The Internet has created new human communities linking people from all over the world in a range of virtual communities from educational to religious, health to gaming. The term "virtual religion" speaks of interactions within cyberspace. Brenda Brasher's (2001) book, *Give Me That Online Religion*, describes online religious communities and practices in general. Genevieve Bell (2004) observes in her book, *Technologies of Enlightenment*, that new technologies are delivering religious experiences in new medium. Ken Bedell (1999) examines Internet congregations and the way that Christianity apprehended the virtual technologies; while Wilson (2000) coined the term "Internet church" at the turn of the century. Simply having a Web site does not encompass all that the Internet church is. A community is vital.

Susan George surveys some examples of what may be called an "Internet church," starting with the earliest example of "Internet church" in the First Church of Cyberspace in 1994, to e-church in 2001, and I-church in 2004. Two broad classes of Internet entities are identified categorised by: (1) the technology utilised and (2) the function in church life and mission supported by the technology. Of course, it is controversial whether virtual communities can theologically call themselves churches—depending upon the criteria for what is a church.

There are many benefits of virtual religion, such as that it may be more "accessible" to people including the disabled and sensory impaired or the geographically isolated. The Internet shrouds the user in anonymity, which is appropriate for some people in some situations. Andrew Careaga reports that many people seek spiritual information in their virtual travels and on a daily basis.

However, there are some criticisms about virtual religion. An increase in technology has apparently occurred hand-in-hand with a decrease in religiosity and a decline in the participation in organised, traditional religion. Some see that technology breeds a sense of empowerment and self-sufficiency, instead of the reliance upon God which most world religions seek for the "transcendence" of the human condition. If people of virtual communities engage solely in online social groups, friendships and other intimates in the real world can be put on hold.

Yet, it remains true that virtual religion has a lot to offer religious bodies, especially Christianity. In terms of evangelism, the Internet is considered by many to be a "Roman Road" in which Christians are charged to venture in the 21st century. Millions of people will never travel physically to a church but will instead roam the Internet in search of meaningful spiritual experiences. In terms of fostering community within the religious body, there are also promising signs that the community is more authentic and that there is a levelling of political influences that is also beneficial to returning to the "real nature" of Christian communities.

The biggest "benefit" of online religion remains the answer it presents to the question of whether technology is a juggernaut of progress running away with humanity or is under our control. The use of technology for religious quests represents humanity making appropriate use of technology, using it as a tool to further the ultimate answer of human identity; rather than being a tool to ultimate destruction, it is a tool to ultimate enlightenment.

References

Barna, G. (1998). *The second coming of the church*. Word Publishing.

Bedell, K. (1999). *Internet congregations in 1999*. Paper presented at the 1999 Meeting of the Religious Research Association, Boston. Retrieved from http://www.religion-research.org/RRAPaper1999.htm

Bell, G. (2004). *Technologies of enlightenment?: Religion and ubiquitous computing at Intel and beyond*.

Borgmann. (1993). *Crossing the postmodern divide*. Chicago: The University of Chicago Press.

Brasher, B. (2001). *Give me that online religion*. New York: John Wiley and Sons.

Dasgupta, S. (2006). *Encyclopaedia of virtual communities and technologies*. Hershey, PA: Idea Group Reference.

Dreyfus, H. L., & Spinosa, C. (1997). *Highway bridges and feasts: Heidegger and Borgmann on how to affirm technology*. Retrieved from http://www.focusing.org/dreyfus.html

George, S. (2006). *Religion and technology in the 21st century: Faith in the e-world*. Hershey, PA: IRM Press.

Heidegger. (1977). Only a God can save us now. Trans. D. Schendler. *Graduate Faculty Philosophy Journal, 6*(1).

Hughes. (2000). *Virtual communities*. Retrieved from http://www2.fhs.usyd.edu.au/bach/pub/community/virtcom.htm

Mc Grath. (2001). *Christian theology an introduction*. Blackwell.

Noble. (1977). *America by design: Science, technology and the rise of corporate capitalism*. New York: Alfred A. Knopf.

Postman. (1985). *Amusing ourselves to death: Public discourse in the age of show business*. New York: Penguin Books.

Rheingold. (1998). *The virtual community*. Retrieved from http://www.rheingold.com/vc/book/intro.html

Smart. (1992). *The world's religions*. Cambridge, MA: Cambridge University Press.

Soukup. (2000). *Media, culture and Catholicism*. Rowman & Littlefield.

Strong. (1991). The promise of technology versus God's promise in Job. *Theology Today, 48*(2). Retrieved from http://theologytoday.ptsem.edu/jul1991/v48-2-article4.htm

Summitt. (1993). *My world and welcome to it: A look at the construction of social reality in virtual reality*. Unpublished manuscript.

The Kuhn Foundation. (2003). *Can religion withstand technology? Closer to truth*. Retrieved from http://www.pbs.org/kcet/closertotruth/explore/show_14.html

Wilson. (2000). *The Internet church*. Word Publishing.

Endnotes

[1]   http://www.intel.com/research/exploratory/papr/inside_asia_lessons.htm

[2]   http://www.godweb.org/index1.html

[3]   http://www.echurch-uk.org/

[4]   http://www.i-church.org/aboutichurch.php

[5]   http://www.e-vangelism.com/e-v_intro.html

[6]   http:// www.monksofadoration.org/webadore.html

Chapter IV

Protecting One's Privacy:

Insights into the Views and Nature of the Early Adopters of Privacy Services

Sarah Spiekermann
Humboldt University Berlin, Germany

Abstract

*Using privacy and security technology becomes increasingly important in many application areas for companies as well as for consumers. However, the market for **privacy enhancing technologies** (PETs) is still small, especially in the private consumer segment. Due to the nature of the technology per se, little is known and can be learned about the views and motivation of those who carefully protect their transactions on the Net. Are they a niche group? Or do they hold views and have traits that promise a wider-spread adoption of PETs in the long run? This chapter gives an insight into the traits and views of 5,037 customers of a popular German anonymity service called JAP (Java Anon Proxy). Due to its high-service reputation and unchanged questions posted on the service's Web site for over 2½ years, insights could be gained on PET users' demographic and psychographic traits. Moreover, 482 free-text comments could be analysed to provide a unique insight into the thoughts, feelings, and motivations of PET users.*

Introduction

When we refer to **anonymity** and **privacy** today, we often refer to a "right." An example is the prominent citation of Warren and Brandeis' (1890) call for "the right to be let alone" or the "right to informational self-determination" as it is found in the German basic constitutional law. However, as electronic communication channels become more ubiquitous, this right is increasingly being undermined. For those who want to protect their privacy right, new tools and services are developed, maintained, and marketed: privacy enhancing technologies (PETs).

One important PET is anonymizing technology. It is offered in such forms as anonymizing proxies, mixes, or onion routing procedures. Little insight has been gained into the **users** of such privacy technology. Even though a myriad of privacy studies have been conducted in past years showing that privacy and anonymity are theoretic concerns across countries and cultures, these studies have not treated the question whether *everybody* wants to be anonymous.[1] Instead, it is always assumed that privacy is such a value in itself that it needs protection. This stands in sharp contrast to the fact that few people seem to act to protect their privacy, that is, on the Internet (Spiekermann, Grossklags, & Berendt, 2001). There is only one study to our current knowledge on a privacy software called "Privacy Bird"® (Cranor, Arjula, & Guduru, 2002) that has looked at *the actual* users of privacy technology. Knowledge on PET *usage reasons* and thus *motivation* to protect oneself in an electronic communication environment thus seems to be sparse as of today. Besides the psychological investigations into the general desire for seclusion or self-disclosure (Cozby, 1973), no insight exists into the subject.

Consequently, more information needs to be discovered about those who use (and buy) PETs. It should be investigated whether these early adopters are the forerunners of a bigger market. Are they different from the average Internet user and citizen? In what respect? And what reasons do anonymous surfers give for actively seeking protection? The current article sheds some light onto these questions. It does so by presenting results from a questionnaire-based study which was conducted over a timespan of 2½ years with 5,037 users of a mix-based anonymity service called AN.ON.

Method

From July 4, 2001, to October 13, 2003, an online questionnaire was posted in German and English on the Web site of an anonymity-service called AN.ON (http://anon.inf.tu-dresden.de). AN.ON is a free anonymity service with a client application called JAP. The service allows people to anonymously surf the Internet.

This means that neither Web servers nor a person's access provider or a malicious hacker can observe from whom and to whom Web page requests are being routed. AN.ON/JAP is technologically based on a mix infrastructure, operated mainly at public universities and institutions in Germany and the U.S. (New York). Currently, around 2,000 users are permanently online with the software, and more than 20,000 people have downloaded the client application.

The Web-based questionnaire was answered by 5,604 service users from around the world during these 2½ years. For the current analysis, 4,896 answers originating from the German-speaking territories and 141 answers from the U.S. were taken into account. For the German-speaking territories, more precisely, 4,492 are from Germany, 194 from Austria, and 189 from Switzerland. The analysis presented in this chapter focuses on and combines all German-speaking respondents and treats them as one answering pool. American statistics are reported on separately in order to be able to compare potential differences that may be due to cultural differences (Hofstede, 1984). Five hundred and sixty-seven questionnaires were not included in the analysis due to the widely-distributed national heritages and small samples per nationality.

The number of questionnaires filled in suggests that around 25% of those who have come in touch with the software participated in the survey. This participation rate is high given that privacy technology *per se* may attract people with rather little willingness to reveal information.[2] Probably, high acceptance and service recognition are required over a long time to win the trust of users; to a degree, that is the case for the AN.ON/JAP service. We, therefore, believe that the reason for so many people participating in the survey is due to the fact that AN.ON/JAP is seen as a university project. As such, it has some inherent right to carry out a survey given that the service is provided free of charge and in a non-commercial environment. Also, the questionnaire remained unchanged on the Net for years (it still is); it was completely anonymous and required a very little time investment. We, therefore, believe that a potential self-selection bias is relatively small. The reliability of our data is further supported by the fact that a majority of demographic findings corresponds to the Privacy Bird® user study.

Users of Anonymity

In order to structure the analysis of the service users, **segmentation** analysis was adopted from marketing, using demographic and psychographic variables to describe PET user groups. The demographic approach divides people on the basis of demographic variables such as age, gender, income, and so forth. It is the most popular form of distinguishing user groups because it is easy to measure and gives insight into target market size and the preferred media for reaching a segment. Psychographic analysis on the other hand groups buyers on the basis of their social class, lifestyle, and/or personality. Here, it is argued that the goods people consume express their lifestyle (e.g., manly woman vs. fashionable woman).

Five subsequent time periods of four to five months between 2001 and 2003 have been distinguished for all respondents from the German-speaking territories in order to test for a change in answering patterns over time. Each time period has an equal number of 979 users. If no extra information is provided hereafter, numbers and percentages relate to respondents from the German-speaking territories only. U.S. numbers are commented on separately.

Demographic Insights

AN.ON/JAP users in the German-speaking territories are mostly male. Ninety-four point eight percent of the respondents are male while only 3.5% are female, and 1.7% did not provide an answer to the gender question. Over the five time periods, this uneven male-female distribution among users did not change significantly. In contrast, 55-60% of Internet users today are male in the German-speaking countries while about 40-45% are female.[3] This suggests that a disproportionately high number of males are using the anonymity service compared to those who use the Internet. Among the 141 American JAP users, a similar trend could be observed: 92.2% were male, 5% female, and 2.8% did not answer the question. When comparing the heavy male base of the AN.ON/JAP users with those who participated in the P3P Privacy Bird® user study, the trend is confirmed. Here, 84% of the users were male. It can thus be concluded that privacy technology so far seems to be more important to men.

In terms of age, AN.ON/JAP users show a wide distribution. Still, with 56.2% under the age of 30, a disproportionately high number of younger people use the service. The common demographics of German Internet users see only 36% in this age group.[4] People over 50 on the other side are less well represented. While, in 2002, they represented about 20% of the German online population,[5] AN.ON/JAP users in this age group only account for a mere 4.3%. Surprisingly, this trend is reversed in the U.S. AN.ON/JAP user community. Around double the number of users are older than 40 years of age in comparison to their European counterparts (see Table 1).

This U.S. trend is supported in an extreme form by the findings of Cranor et al. (2002) on the Privacy Bird®. In their study, even 45% of the users are seniors (over 50).

Concerning the professional background of AN.ON/JAP, almost 25% of users are students, and 22.9% hold jobs which require a university degree (referred to as academic background). Here, it must be noted that the definition of academic versus non-academic background has been drawn along the lines of the qualifica-

Table 1. Age groups of users by region

Age Group	AN.ON/JAP Users in DE/AU/CH	AN.ON/JAP Users in the U.S.
Up to 20	16.7%	9.2%
21-30	39.5%	31.9%
31-40	26.2%	27.7%
41-50	10.9%	20.6%
51+	4.3%	7.1%
No information	2.5%	3.5%

tion *needed* for a job. Thus, if people indicated that they are Net-administrators or Web-designers, they were not counted among those with an academic background or university degree. At the same time, technical directors or software engineers have been considered as academics due to the challenging nature of their professional roles (even though some of them may not hold a university degree). For U.S. respondents, this measure could not be deducted. Still, results obtained by Cranor et al. (2002) are along these lines. They note that 31% of Privacy Bird® users have a post-graduate education, and 91% have some college education. Overall, the results seem to suggest that the majority of the PET users have a high educational background.

Among non-academic AN.ON/JAP users, we additionally analysed what types of jobs they precisely hold. We did not see many craftsmen, housewives, or waiters here, but more people with a technical orientation in their jobs. In fact, it turned out that 44.2% of the non-academic users indicated to have a job that is IT-related. Fifty-five point eight percent of the non-academics users are from the diverse backgrounds that have no link with information technology.

Psychographic Insights

For psychographic analysis, it has first been analysed what operating system AN.ON/JAP users are using and how long and frequently they are online with the AN.ON/JAP anonymity service.

It turned out that the majority of AN.ON/JAP users is online daily (67.6%) or at least several times a week (13%), and also stays online with 74.6% stating to be online several hours a day. This "online-lifestyle" as it may be termed has not changed significantly among the respondents over the five investigated time periods. And U.S. AN.ON/JAP users are very similar to their European counterparts: 63% state to be online daily with the AN.ON/JAP service, over 60% for several hours. Tables 2a and 2b give an overview of service usage frequency and intensity. The findings of Cranor et al. (2002) go into the same direction but are even stronger: 91% of their respondents have been online daily.

Table 2. (a) Frequency of usage, (b) intensity of usage

Frequency of Service Usage (How Often?)	AN.ON/JAP Users in DE/AU/CH	AN.ON/JAP Users in the U.S.
Sporadic (1- 2 week)	15.7%	11.3%
Normal (3 days/week)	13.0%	13.5%
Heavy User (daily)	67.6%	63.2%
Missing	3.7%	12.1%

(a)

Usage Intensity (How Long?)	AN.ON/JAP Users in DE/AU/CH	AN.ON/JAP Users in the U.S.
Ad hoc, max 1 hour	19.8%	15.6%
Intensive (1-5 hours)	15.6%	8.5%
Always on (5-8 hours +)	59.0%	62.3%
Missing	5.7%	13.5%

(b)

Even though Microsoft® Windows was said to be in use by over 83% of the respondents, it turned out that also 11.7% of the respondents are using the Linux® OS. This is a very high proportion of users given that Linux® is said to generally account for 2-3% market share in desktop environments.[6] Among the U.S. AN.ON/JAP user respondents, the share is similarly high: 12.8 % are Linux® users.

Why People Want to be Anonymous:
Usage Reasons Observed

In addition to knowing more about the characteristics of AN.ON/JAP users, their usage reasons are of great importance for service design as well as for the public debate. In the current study, respondents had multiple answering options as to why they actually use an anonymity service. These answers include profiling fears, free speech, censorship, protection against access providers, and against the state as well as against hacking (see Table 2).

Looking at the answers given, a user's fear to be profiled clearly dominates all usage reasons. Ninety-six percent of the respondents to the questionnaire said that they either wanted to avoid profiling or being tracked by Web servers. This implies that despite privacy statements published on most Web sites today, a lack of trust exists between Web site owners and users. The second reason for JAP/AN.ON usage (named by 66% of the respondents) was said to be protection from surveillance by the ISP.

Surprisingly, the third rank of usage reasons is the desire to protect oneself against the state. Fifty-three point seven percent of those who answered marked that they either seek protection against governmental secret service or against the police or both. One may deduct that an important share of anonymity service users is marked by a deep distrust in the state. This is surprising because Germans are said to highly trust in the state, police, and jurisdiction. This is reflected in studies continuously conducted for the European Commission—the Eurobarometer. Here, 75% of German respondents rate the police as the institution enjoying the highest level of trust (in Austria—73%).[7] This means that those critical of the state are disproportionately represented in the JAP user group.

Looking into the age distribution for these different usage reasons, it can be observed that all age groups equally seek protection against profiling practices. In contrast, when it comes to protection against the access provider, strong differences are apparent between the age groups. While more than 71% of those under 30 wish to be protected against the access provider, only 47% of those above 50 share this view. Equally, mistrust in the state is much more prominent with those below 20 where

Table 3. Reasons for usage in German-speaking territories

% of respondents	Reason for AN.ON/JAP usage
96%	Protection against profiling practices
66%	Protection against access provider
54%	Protection against the government
35%	Free speech
11%	Circumvention of filters
5%	Hacking

Table 4. U.S. reasons for usage

U.S. User Reasons for AN.ON/JAP Usage	Detailed Reasons	% of Respondents Who Picked "True"
Protection against profiling practices	Protection against Web servers	76.6%
	Protection against profiling	84.4%
Protection against access provider	Protection against access provider	75.9%
Protection against the government	Protection against secret service	50.4%
	Protection against police	34.8%
Free speech	Free speech	54.6%
Circumvention of filters	Circumvention of filters	16.3%
Hacking	Hacking	4.3%

again 71% state distrust as opposed to 38% in the group above 60. This finding may imply that younger people are more critical of surveillance than elderly are.

For U.S. JAP users, the *ranking* of usage reasons is similar. Ten percent more respondents from the U.S. consider protection from their access provider important. And almost 20% more respondents value free speech opportunities higher than their European counterparts. Also, circumvention on filters bears equal importance. Protection against government is at a comparable level. Fear to be profiled though is lower in the U.S. and than in Europe.[8] Table 4 gives an overview.

Users Free Text Comments: Speaking Their Minds About Privacy

Besides multiple answering options to specify the reasons for anonymity, one text-field in the questionnaire gave respondents the opportunity to freely describe other drivers to use the service. Interestingly enough, this field was used by 482 AN.ON/ JAP respondents in the German-speaking territories. It thus became a rich source of insight into why people want to be anonymous. Based on a content analysis of these 482 comments, 16 different reasons for JAP usage could be discerned. **Content analysis** is a qualitative means to analyse text (Früh, 2001). For the current purpose, key words and phrases that are related to the same "threat notion" were combined to form one group. Table 5 gives an overview of the ten most important reasons provided by 424 people. Fifty-eight comments were excluded from the table because they were only mentioned by a few participants. They related to personal paranoia, protection against commercial entities, desire for free speech, support of the AN.ON project, protection from spam, and professional use.

The most prominent reason mentioned in the comments was that people regard anonymity as a fundamental part of their life. People said that they wished to be anonymous "on principle," "simply," "fundamentally." We called these people "the general conscious." Their remarks were typically framed neutrally. In contrast, a group we call the "Freedomers" displayed strong emotion with respect to their wish for privacy. Some stated their wish to be let alone with an aggressive connotation in the sense that "it is nobody's business to know what I do." Others wrote their comments in capital letters and with exclamation marks. Usually these people directly referred to themselves ("I," "My"). Some used the word "free" or "freedom."

In contrast to the group of "the general conscience," we could distinguish another group which we called "the political conscience." Their comments contained more "political" cues. These people explicitly talked about their "right" to privacy referring to political institutions and laws. They expressed their insistence on established democratic norms and argued out of a strong political consciousness. Some said that they want to "protest" against current developments or "set signs" for others.

Table 5. Categorisation of free comments

Rank	Users of Anonymity	Comment—Reasons Given for Seeking Anonymity on the Net	No. of answers	%	Cul. %
1	The General Conscience	These people say that they want to be anonymous "on principle," "simply," "fundamentally." The position is as a middle ground between a personal desire for freedom and political consciousness.	63	16%	16%
2	Freedomers	These people display strong emotions when commenting the service usage, sometimes writing their comment in capital letters and with explanation marks. Usually these people directly refer to themselves ("I," "My"). Some use the word "free" or "freedom." Some state their wish to be let alone with an aggressive connotation in the sense that "it is nobody's business to know what I do."	53	13%	29%
3	Orwellians	These people state a deep lack of trust in the government. They refer to George Orwell, Big Brother, or to countries and political institutions that may survey them (U.S., Echelon, state police, etc.). Here *personal protection* activities *against* the state are stressed rather than a *right in relation to* the state. Fear and anger about surveying practices of the state are inherent in the comments. More moderate voices refer to recent legislation that implies state surveillance.	45	11%	40%
4	The Curios	These people say that they want to try out the new technology, are curious, or just want to test.	36	9%	49%
5	People with Secrets	These people admit that they use anonymity to pursue activities judged as undesirable by others (incl. music related file sharing, visiting sex-sites, gaming, hacking etc.)	35	9%	57%
6	The Political Conscience	These people explicitly talk about their "right" to privacy referring to political institutions, to law or norms. They express their insistence on anonymity as fundamental for democracy and argue out of strong political consciousness. Some say that they want to "protest" against current developments or set signs for others.	35	9%	66%
7	Filter Counterers	These people say that they want to circumvent filters.	26	6%	72%
8	Sniffer Avoider	These people fear that others (including administrators, access providers, fellow students, or their bosses) read their e-mail or have a look at their log files that they have access to.	19	5%	77%
9	Free Neters	These people explicitly refer to "Internet" or "WWW" and the way they see the medium and want to maintain its original "free" nature.	18	4%	81%
10	Hacker Avoider	These people fear hackers and a potential misuse of their IP.	17	4%	86%

Finally, analogous to the multiple choice part, protection against the state was also found in the comments. It was the third most prominent group of comments made. Reference was made to George Orwell, Big Brother, or countries and political institutions that may survey citizens (e.g., U.S. secret service, Echelon, state police, etc.). Here *personal protection* activities *against* the state were stressed rather than a *right in relation to* the state. Fear and anger about surveying-practices were inherent in the comments. More moderate voices referred to recent legislation implying more state surveillance.

A brief analysis of the age and background of those who provided comments showed that there was no significant difference between those who provided comments and those who did not. Also, it was not possible to differentiate a significant relationship between age or background and the type of comment given. A slight tendency could be observed that younger people (below 20) insisted more on their "freedom" while this type of comment was less present with older respondents. In contrast, older people (over 50) were strongly present among those expressing "general consciousness." In terms of academic background, those with no academic background wished the least to be protected against the state while students figured strongest in this type of comment.

All in all, answers obtained on usage reasons allow us to conclude that profiling fears and monitoring by access providers and companies seem to be major drivers behind the wish to be anonymous. However, a conscious observation of state practices and political developments as well as the commercialisation of the World Wide Web are strongly apparent in peoples' comments. Comments provided by respondents imply that an important number of users are highly emotionally involved with the topic of privacy. Anonymity is considered as a fundamental right by respondents. Distrust in the state is disproportionately present in the user group.

More than 20 AN.ON/JAP users from the U.S. gave verbal comments that distributed similarly to their European counterparts across the reasons presented in Table 5. However, their number is too small to make a similar analysis.

Conclusion

The investigation of 4,896 users of the anonymity service AN.ON/JAP over 2½ years has generated a good first insight into who the people are that actively seek privacy on the Net today. All in all, the demographic and psychographic data suggest that the anonymity service is used by a group of people that is not representative for the current Internet user population. Looking at the fact that young males with an IT background, an "always-on" and Linux®-friendly mentality dominate service usage, it could be argued that, potentially, PETs today are in an "early-adopter" market phase. Moreover, this market is marked not only by a critical reflection on common profiling practices and potential ISP logging, but also by conscious observation of state practices and political developments.

The drawback of the study presented here is that the data is based only on the users of one particular anonymity service. Even though we observed demographic and psychographic similarities with the users of AT&T's P3P Privacy Bird®, we cannot exclude that users of software, such as cookie protection software or simpler proxy-based anonymity services, may be different in some respects. The same is true for consumers who physically buy privacy software packages and bundles containing other product categories, for example, anti-virus software. More remains to be done, thus, to understand the whole breadth of "privacy consumers."

References

Cozby, P. (1973). Self disclosure: A literature review. *Psychological Bulleting.* *79*(2).

Cranor, L. F., Arjula, M., & Guduru, P. (2002). Use of P3P user agent by early adopters. In *Proceedings of the ACM Workshop on Privacy in the Electronic Society.*

Früh, W. (2001). *Inhaltsanalyse—Theorie und Praxis.* Konstanz: UVK Verlagsgesellschaft

Hofstede, G. (1984). *Culture's consequences—international differences in work-related values.* London: Sage Publications.

Spiekermann, S., Grossklags, J., & Berendt, B. (2001). E-privacy in 2nd generation e-commerce. In *Proceedings of ACM EC'01 on Electronic Commerce,* Tampa, FL.

Warren, S., & Brandeis, L. (1890). The right to privacy. *Harvard Law Review,* *4*(5).

Endnotes

[1]   International studies on privacy perception and erosion through electronic media include, for example, the "IBM Multi-National Consumer Privacy Survey" (October 1999), the Eurobarometer 46.1 report entitled, "Information Technology and Data Privacy," as well as the Pew Internet & American Life Project's report, "Trust and Privacy Online: Why Americans Want to Rewrite the Rules" (August 2000)

[2]   In comparison, the survey conducted by AT&T Research on the Privacy Bird® had 4,000 people confirm that they would be willing to participate in a survey on the Privacy Bird®. Despite this first round in collecting participants, finally only 16.55% responded.

[3]   Nielsen/Netratings, "European Women on the Net," June 24, 2003.

[4]   WWW Benutzeranalyse W3B, May 2001.

[5]   Deutsche Welle: "German seniors take to the Net," October 11, 2002.

[6]   IDC Research cited in: ZDNet, "Microsoft to bump Apple into Sync-hole", December 19, 2002.

[7]   Eurobarometer 59—Public Opinion in the Union, Spring 2003.

[8]   Note though that the two tables cannot be compared directly to each other for 2 reasons: (1) the cultural propensity to give multiple answers may be higher in the U.S. than in Europe, and (2) Table 3 has combined multiple answers for profiling practices and protection against the state.

Chapter V

A Practitioner-Centred Assessment of a User-Experience Framework

Peter Wright
University of York, UK

John McCarthy
University College Cork, Ireland

Lisa Meekison
Anthropologist & Freelance Consultant, Canada

Abstract

In this chapter, we outline a relational approach to experience, which we have used to develop a practitioner-oriented framework for analysing user experience. The framework depicts experience as compositional, emotional, spatio-temporal, and sensual, and as intimately bound up with a number of processes that allow us to make sense of experience. It was developed and assessed as part of a participative action research project involving interested practitioners. We report how these practitioners used the framework, what aspects of experience they felt that it missed, and how useful they found it as a tool for evaluating Internet shopping experiences. A thematic content analysis of participants' reflections on their use of the framework to evaluate Internet shopping experiences revealed some strengths and some weaknesses. For example, certain features of the framework led participants to reflect on aspects of experience that they might not otherwise have considered, for example, the central role of anticipation in experience. The framework also captured aspects of experience that relate to both the sequential structure of the activity and its subjective aspects. However, it seemed to miss out on the intensity of some experiences, and participants sometimes found it difficult to distinguish between some of the sense-making processes, for example, interpreting and reflecting. These results have helped to refine our approach to deploying the framework and have inspired an ongoing programme of research on experience-centred design.

Introduction

As computers migrate from work to leisure and family life, new perspectives and conceptual tools are required to understand human activity and the participation of technologies in activity. Developments, such as the World Wide Web, virtual reality, cyberspace, the penetration of computers into homes, cars, and games, and the integration of information and communications technologies resulting in wireless, mobile, and ubiquitous computing, suggest a revision of how we construe both people and technology. A person's attachment to the mobile phone is not just functional, it is also aesthetic (Katz & Aakhus, 2002; Taylor & Harper, 2002), and their use of the Internet is as much an expression of their sociality as it is a mark of their productivity (Markham, 1998; Turkle, 1995). Interacting with computers is now as much about play, fun, entertainment, community, and personal identity as it is about goals, tasks, and work. It is as much about children playing with cyberpets, teenagers gender swapping, and elderly people socialising on the Net, as it is about the middle-aged executive managing knowledge assets (Blythe, Monk, Overbeeke, & Wright, 2003; Jordan, 2000; Norman, 2004). As Kuutti (2001) characterised it, the user, who started out in the 1970s as a cog in a rational machine and became a social actor in the 1990s, is now a consumer.

The transition that Kuutti described points to the fact that people need to be able to *live* with emerging technologies, not just *use* them. Therefore, the focus for designers has to move beyond usability to *user experience*. The general impact of an emphasis on experience with technology can be seen in the popularity of works such as Turkle's (1995) analysis of "life on the Internet," in which she explored the social meaning of computers, the cultures of computing, and the impact of the Internet on our sense of self. The specific impact can be seen in attempts to understand and act on the concept of *user experience* in consumer arenas such as electronic commerce (see, for example, Lee, Kim, & Moon, 2000; Pu & Faltings, 2000) and more generally in the area of HCI and interaction design (Garrett, 2002; Laurel, 1991; Shedroff, 2001). Recent developments, in particular, have seen several attempts to provide conceptual frameworks for analysing user experience. Jordan (2000), Hassenzahl (2003), Hull and Reid (2003), and Norman (2004), for example, have all developed models of user experience with a broadly cognitive psychological orientation. Others have developed frameworks that take as their starting point a more pragmatist or phenomenological foundation (Davis, 2003; Forlizzi & Battarbee, 2004; Forlizzi & Ford, 2000; McCarthy & Wright, 2004). The diversity of these approaches is perhaps not surprising given the complexity and richness of experience, but common to all of these approaches is a concern to characterise not only the intellectual aspects of experience but also the aesthetic, emotional, and sensual. Many focus on what technology means to people and how technology relates to our sense of self, identity, community, and culture—what McCarthy and Wright (2004) refer to as the "felt life" our interactions with technology.

One of our own contributions to the development of experience-centred design is a conceptual framework inspired by John Dewey's (1934) analysis of *Art as Experience* and the work of the literary scholar and philosopher Mikhail Bakhtin (Morson & Emerson, 1990). An important consideration for any conceptual framework is the extent to which it helps with the practical problem of designing for, and evaluating, user experience. The aim of this chapter then is to report an action research assessment of our framework by design practitioners. Our objective is to assess whether they can use the framework effectively and, if so, to determine what they gain from its use. Before we report the assessment, we will first outline our general approach to experience and then briefly describe the framework.

Conceptualising Experience

Although it is clear that the turn to experience in technology design reflects an attempt to engage with the experience of people using technology, the concept "experience" is elusive and difficult to specify. In dictionaries (see, for example, the Oxford English Dictionary, 1982) and in social scientific discourse, experience has often been defined and used in ways that reduce it to subjective feelings, behaviour, or knowledge (Bruner & Turner, 1986; Dewey, 1925, 1934). In contrast, Dewey's (1925, 1934) pragmatist philosophy was geared towards a clarification that would end the tendency to reduce experience. He argued that experience is the irreducible totality of people acting, sensing, thinking, feeling, and meaning making in a setting, including their perception and sensation of their own actions. Experience, he wrote:

> *.... includes **what** men do and suffer, **what** they strive for, love, believe and*
> *endure, and also **how** men act and are acted upon, the ways in which they*
> *do and suffer, desire and enjoy, see, believe, imagine - in short, processes*
> *of experiencing. ..... It is "double barrelled" in that it recognises in its pri-*
> *mary integrity no division between act and material, subject and object, but*
> *contains them both in an unanalyzed totality.* (Dewey, 1925, p.10/11)

According to Dewey, then, experience is the continuous transaction between people
and their environments, which includes sensations, thoughts, feelings, and values.
Seeing experience as the dynamic interrelationship between people and environment,
or as the continually changing texture of their relationship, effectively makes person
and environment a whole, or as Dewey put it "an unanalyzed totality." This holism
is pivotal to pragmatic conceptualisation of experience, arguing that there is no point
in trying to understand person and environment as separate from one another. In
Dewey's two major works on experience, *Experience and Nature* (1925) and *Art
as Experience* (1934), the starting point is the creature living in an environment;
neither of which could exist in quite the same way without the other. His approach,
which has also been described as natural humanism, sees continuity between human
experience and all other animal experience. This is clearest in the weight he gives
to sensory and affective sense making. For him, the sense we make of our experience has its roots in the feelings of fear, recognition, threat, or joy that accompany
a sound, smell, or sighting. In this context, Dewey (1925) argues that, "Feelings
are no longer just felt. They have and they make sense." In and of themselves,
feelings are the immediate meaning of an event or situation: the feeling of warmth
and friendliness in a friend's house or in a chat room; the feeling of excitement at
meeting a person or trying out a new system for the first time. The weight given by
Dewey to predominantly pre-linguistic sensory and affective sense making has been
borne out in more recent times in the neurosciences and evolutionary psychology
(e.g., Demasio, 1999; Donald, 1991, 2001).

Taking into account the emergence of language, community, and values, Dewey
(1925, 1934) viewed emotion, an elaboration of sensory and affective sense making, as the pivotal moment in human experience—the quality of the dynamic inter-
relationship described earlier. According to Dewey, the paradigmatic experience
is an aesthetic experience in which any sense of alienation from other people and
the environment is overcome and in which the natural human need for a sense of
meaning and value is satisfied. For him, the unity of aesthetic experience is a felt
or emotional unity. Therefore, a central feature of Dewey's approach to experience is the idea of unifying emotion holding experience together and giving it an
aesthetic quality. He argues that emotion "selects what is congruous and dyes what
is selected with its color, thereby giving qualitative unity to materials externally
disparate and dissimilar" (Dewey, 1934, p.42). So even though a day's hill walking
is comprised of many disparate elements and will inevitably have good and not so

good parts, according to Dewey, its emotional quality gives it an experiential unity that shapes our perception of the event as it unfolds and our memory and recounting of it afterwards.

Dewey (1934) identifies a number of conditions necessary for a fulfilling experience. They are:

- A sense of anticipation about the experience and of continuity between that anticipation, the experience as it unfolds, and reflections on it afterwards;

- A sense that each part of the experience accumulates into something meaningful for the person (e.g., planning the walk, driving to the start, the less interesting part through scrubland, the challenge of the climb, the great views from the hill, etc.);

- Some level of tension (e.g., about the difficulty of the climb or whether the views from the top will match expectations); and

- A sense of fulfilment (e.g., on reaching the top finding not only a view, but a view that surpasses all expectations and a feeling that it was a hard-won reward).

These conditions can be seen as an analytic tool to be used when we encounter problems with the unfolding of an experience—what went wrong, why we lost interest, why others got restless, and so forth. As an example, we have referred to aspects of a countryside walk to clarify the conditions for a fulfilling experience. Using these conditions as an analytic tool would facilitate enquiry into the experience of irritation or frustration that might accompany encountering a dead-end midway through the walk. Dewey's conditions suggest that such frustration is due to being unable to complete the walk and fulfil anticipated experiences of the climb or the view from the top, and now anticipating the anti-climax of telling fellow walkers about this frustrated attempt. Often, there is little that can be done about such frustrations on a country walk, and natural or man-made obstacles become part of the discourse of communities of walkers. This should not be the case with interactions with technology that has been designed for use by people. Attention to user experience in design should minimise such occurrences, and Dewey's conditions may help in this regard.

Although the sensory and affective are the starting points of Dewey's conceptualisation of experience, his theory also embraces the sense we make of immediate qualitative experiences in the longer stretch of our life experience and addresses the relationship between the immediate and long-term aspects of experience. And, although the immediate sense of surprise, warmth, sleaze, or comfort that we have when we enter a new situation or when we engage with a new technology is transitory, it can also be vivid or intense. Indeed Hickman (1998), commenting on

Dewey's theory of experience, suggests that it is precisely the impact of something vivid but transitory in a situation that makes us pursue that situation again in the future. For example, for hill walkers the vivid but transitory experience of the view from the top may make them want that experience again. It becomes a project and hill walking becomes an interest pursued in reading and discussion as well as in the actual activity itself. In the process, elements of our experiences and situations become known, not just had. As they become known, they enter into the realms of community and cultural sense making, where we bring the resources of community and culture to bear on our appropriation of experience. Through imagination—for example, imagining how friends might feel about a walk I have just done or indeed about my shopping on the Internet—experience becomes expressive and meaningful in a way that can be shared with others. The meanings appropriated through such imaginative acts can find their way into present interaction, colouring the immediate quality of another experience.

Bakhtin (1986, 1993) provides an account of the relationship between experience and meaning making that is complementary to Dewey's. Bakhtin's work is useful when considering how the immediate quality of experience is made personal. In terms of ongoing experiences of technology, Bakhtin's work shifts our focus from the immediate quality of an experience to the sense we make of an experience in terms of our experience of our selves, our culture, and our lives.

Bakhtin's central contribution in this area is the idea of dialogicality. Dialogically, any account of experience, including a person's own account to themselves of an experience of buying through the Internet, is social, plural, and perspectival. In Bakhtin's terms, it is *interanimated* with the discourses of others. For example, my sense of myself as someone who supports small local bookshops is interanimated by discourses on global capitalism, the importance of choice provided by small specialist booksellers, and the centrality of a personal relationship in choosing which books to buy. These discourses, however, might be accommodating of an Internet bookseller who appears to try to develop a buyer-seller relationship with me based on an understanding of my reading preferences, provides specialist choices, and seems to support small specialist booksellers. If my book-buying activity moves from the small local bookshop to an Internet store that presents itself as engaging meaningfully with some of these discourses and that has other qualities of interest to me also, for example speedy completion of an order, my sense of my self is subtly changed through dialogue with that bookseller.

This relational subjectivity can also be seen in the reflections of filmmakers and writers. Writers and filmmakers practise their craft under the influence of a practical understanding of experience and how they might influence or help create experience. Boorstin (1990), a Hollywood script writer, argues that the filmmaker must be able to experience the film in the way the public will but, in addition, must know what it takes to ensure that the public will construct just that experience. He demonstrates how filmmakers deploy technical knowledge of how an audience responds to different kinds of framing, lighting, rhythm, and character—different combinations of which can make a second very long or short and a relationship warm or claustrophobic—to help the viewer create a particular cinematic experience. He argues that one of the sensibilities of great filmmaking is, having deployed technical knowledge and experience, to see like the audience, always anew and open to surprise.

Our aim in drawing together the writings of philosophers such as Dewey and Bakhtin and reflective practitioners such as Boorstin is to try to understand experience to help designers and evaluators create fulfilling interactive experience. This review has enabled us to conceptualise experience as an irreducible, dynamic interrelationship between person and environment, in which meaning has sensory, affective, and emotional dimensions as well as the cognitive and sociocultural aspects that we are used to dealing with in psychology and the social sciences. We have also seen that it may be useful to distinguish between the immediate experience that a person has and the meaning of that experience as it becomes known and thereby appropriated personally and communally. The dialogical dimension added by Bakhtin's work draws our attention to the ways in which immediate experience is associated with personal, social, and cultural sense-making processes, specifically relational aspects of interpretation and reflection, and communal processes such as telling others of our experiences. Implicit in much of the foregoing is a sense of experience unfolding across time and space. This can be seen in both the transitoriness of the immediate experience and in the spatio-temporal relations between the immediate and the lifelong.

The pragmatist literatures on experience which we have trawled offer a very rich account of experience with some of the characteristics that we have just summarised emphasised more in the work of one writer or another. In order to appropriate these literatures for use in the design and evaluation of rich person-technology experiences, it may be useful to make explicit those aspects of experience that we judge most relevant to the task. To do this, we have constructed a framework, based on the earlier-mentioned work, which pulls together a set of concepts that may be useful as tools to evaluate user experience with emerging technologies. Taking a pragmatic orientation to theories and concepts as tools to be used, the value of this framework can only be assessed in terms of its value in enriching interactive experience. Therefore, in the next section, we describe the framework, and in the following section, we take a first step in using it and, together with a team of e-commerce practitioners, assessing its use.

The End-User Experience Framework

The framework that we present in this section represents an attempt to model experience in a way that designers and analysts of interactive systems would find useful. It is derived from the literatures reviewed in the previous section and the provenance of each element in those literatures has already largely been established. For example, Dewey's concern for a holistic approach and the equal weight he gave to affective and intellectual sense making is manifest in our characterisation of four intertwined threads of experience. Some of Boorstin's perspectivalism is reflected there too. In terms of sense making, Dewey's concepts of anticipation, reflection, and the pre-linguistic sense of meaning are echoed in our account of the sense-making processes. Bakhtin's concern for unity as an active accomplishment is reflected in our characterisation of appropriating, reflecting, and recounting. But more subtly, what we have tried to do in our presentation of these threads and processes is to understand Dewey through Bakhtin's dialogical lens. Thus, self-other relations as continually constructed permeate the framework.

Earlier, when we described Dewey's (1934) conditions for a fulfilling experience, we briefly demonstrated how the conditions could be used as an analytic tool to explain why a particular hill-walking experience might be frustrating. The framework we present here is intended to perform similar work for people's experiences with interactive systems by helping to explain why, for example, particular interactive experiences are satisfying and others frustrating. So, although there may be more elegant ways of describing experience, such as the narrative, analogical approaches used in ethnography (see, for example, Anderson, 1994; Geertz, 1993; Orr, 1990), our hope is that the explicit separation and classification of aspects of experience in the user-experience framework will prove useful in the design and evaluation of

Figure 1. The threads of experience and the sense-making processes

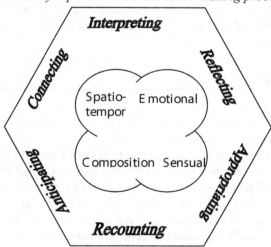

interactive systems without losing too much of the relational, holistic approach to experience from which the framework is derived.

The framework is composed of two simple lists. The first, the four threads of experience, describes the major aspects or components of experience which we draw from the literatures reviewed in the section, *Conceptualising Experience*. The second identifies six sense-making processes associated with meaning in the same pragmatist accounts of experience.

The Four Threads of Experience

Following Dewey and Bakhtin, we propose that the braid of experience is made up of four inter-twined threads: the compositional, the emotional, the spatio-temporal, and the sensual.

The Compositional Thread

The compositional thread is concerned with relationships between the parts and the whole of an experience. Looking at a painting, composition refers to the relations between elements of the painting and their implied agency, and between viewer, painting, and setting. In an unfolding interaction involving self and other, in a novel, play, or technologically-mediated communication, it refers to the narrative structure, action possibility, plausibility, consequences, and explanations of actions. In Internet shopping, the choices that are laid out for us can lead us in a coherent way through "the shop" or can lead us down blind alleys. Attention to the compositional thread evokes questions like: "what is this about?"; "what has happened?"; "where am I?"; "what will happen next?"; "that doesn't make sense?"; "I wonder what would happen if?"

The Sensual Thread

The sensual thread of experience is concerned with our sensory engagement with a situation, which orients us to the concrete, palpable, and visceral character of experience—the things that are grasped pre-reflectively in what Dewey (1934) refers to as the immediate sense of a situation (for example, the look and feel of a mobile phone, the garish colours and grating sounds on a Web site, and the sense of warmth and welcome in a room). Whether or not sensual attraction to an object (e.g., a mobile phone or a Web site) is welcome depends on our needs, desires, and what we value at that particular time. Such attraction could be unwanted and lead to frustration or disgust, or it could complement the emotional content of the experience.

The Emotional Thread

This emotional thread refers to judgments that ascribe to other people and things importance with respect to our needs and desires. Our frustration, anger, joy, and satisfaction acknowledge our need for others or the other in our struggle to achieve emotional unity. We can reflect on our own emotional aspect of an experience, and we can through empathy relate to the emotional aspects of others' experiences. Relating to a character in a movie is an obvious example, but we might also empathise with the artist or designer who creates an artefact even though that person is not materially present in the situation.

We need to distinguish between the sensual and emotional threads since we can engender emotions associated with achievement through the exercise of control over sensations such as attraction, fear, or anxiety. Although I might get an immediate thrill from buying the most beautiful mobile phone in the shop, it may cut against my commitment to not being conned by surface features and advertising. My decision not to buy the most beautiful phone and instead to buy a plainer one that is half the price but just as good may leave me with a strong feeling of self-satisfaction. Here, the sensory and emotional threads interact to shape the experience, the actions chosen, and the sense we make of them.

The Spatio-Temporal Thread

An intense emotional engagement can make our sense of time change. A frustrating experience can leave us perceiving space as confined and closeting. Space and time pervade our language of experience. We talk about needing space to settle an emotional conflict and of giving people time. Time may speed up or slow down, pace may increase or decrease, spaces may open up or close down. Space and time may be connected or disconnected. In our construction of the spatio-temporal aspect of an experience, we might distinguish between public and private space; we may recognise comfort zones and boundaries between self and other, or present and future. Such constructions affect experiential outcomes such as willingness to linger or to re-visit places or our willingness to engage in exchange of information, services, or goods.

Making Sense In- and Of- Experience

According to Dewey's (1925, 1934) and Bakhtin's (1986, 1993) ideas on experience described in the section, *Conceptualising Experience*, people actively construct or make sense of experience. Bakhtin's emphasis of the dialogical in sense making suggests that making sense of experience is reflexive in that we always view experience from a personal perspective, whether it is the first person or the third person, or whether it is by recounting an experience to oneself or for others. This is central to what it means for something to be an experience. For both Dewey and Bakhtin, there can be no experience without self and other, or subject and object, interacting reflexively. As indicated earlier, we have distilled the following six sense-making processes from Dewey and Bakhtin's work as an explication of processes that may be useful for understanding people's experiences with technology. There is no implication of linear or causal relations between these processes. It is conceivable, for example, that in anticipation of some future planned action, we reflect on the consequences of that action engendering a certain sensual response. Or it could be that how we recount our experience to others may change how we reflect on it.

Anticipating

Anticipation or expectation is a continuous process in experience. When visiting the Web site of a well-known company for the first time, we bring expectations, possibilities, and ways of making sense that we associate with prior experience with the brand off-line. Although anticipation suggests something that is prior to the experience, it is important to remember that it is not only prior. The sensual and emotional aspects of anticipation and our expectation of the compositional structure and spatio-temporal fabric of what follows shapes our later experience. It is the relation between our continually revised anticipation and actuality that creates the space of experience.

Connecting

Connecting refers to the immediate, pre-conceptual and pre-linguistic sense of a situation encountered. In the spatio-temporal aspect, this may be an apprehension of speed or confusing movement or openness and stillness, for example. Sensually, connecting may engender an immediate sense of tension or perhaps a thrill of novelty. Emotionally and compositionally, connecting may engender nothing more than a sense of relief or anticipation at something happening.

Interpreting

Interpreting an unfolding experience involves discerning the narrative structure, the agents, and action possibilities, what has happened, and what is likely to happen. The process of interpreting may evoke a sense of the thrill of excitement or the anxiety of not knowing. At an emotional level, we may feel frustration or disappointment at thwarted expectations, or we may regret being in this situation. On the basis of our interpretation falling short of our anticipation, we may reflect on our anticipation and alter it to be more in line with our interpretation. From a spatio-temporal aspect, the questions are: Can we make sense of the experience in space and time?; Do we know where we are, where we've been and where we have to go?

Reflecting

At the same time as interpreting, we may also make judgements about the experience as it unfolds. We may try simply to make sense of the things that are happening and how we feel about them. Or wonder whether there is progress or movement towards completion. From an emotional aspect, we may relate events to motivation and whether we achieved any sense of fulfilment. How does the experience tally with our anticipation, and how do we feel about being in this situation and this time? From a sensual perspective, we wonder why we are anxious or bored. This is like an inner dialogue that helps us to meaningfully recount our experience to others, the anticipation of which may help us to reflect. "I wonder what Tom would think of this?"

Appropriating

By appropriating, we mean making an experience our own by relating it to our sense of self, our personal history, and our anticipated future. If it turns out to be an experience we identify with or want to experience again, the centre of our personal universe may have shifted slightly. Moreover, by imagining the experience in the context of a past and a future, we may give it a meaning that is more personal to us. Does that sensual "white knuckle ride" of the theme park or the unique sense of immersion in undifferentiated colour as a first-time scuba diver descends into "the blue" change who we are, make us rethink how we want to be and want to be seen? Do the compositional aspects of the experience relate positively to our sense of self or not? Do we feel it is morally right or socially acceptable to go shopping at a virtual supermarket? Is the experience of using a video phone one in which new possibilities for action in our everyday life become apparent, or is it yet another concession to an undesirable technological future?

Recounting

Recounting is fundamentally dialogical, as it involves telling others or ourselves about the experience. Like reflecting and appropriating, it takes us beyond the immediate experience to consider it in the context of other experiences. Recounting gives us the opportunity to savour the experience again, to find new possibilities and new meanings in it, and this often leads us to want to repeat the experience. And, as a dialogical process of meaning making, recounting facilitates our accommodation to the valuative responses of others. As we tell the experience, it can change depending on the moment-to-moment response of the other.

In the section, *Conceptualising Experience*, we reviewed literature on experience in an attempt to begin to provide a sound basis for conceptualisations of user experience in people-technology relations. Now, in this section, *The User-Experience Framework*, we have shaped some of the ideas from the earlier section into a framework that we hope will be of use to designers and evaluators of interactive systems who are concerned with the quality of experience people have with their systems. In the next section, we will report an action research assessment of the use of the user-experience framework in a commercial setting, which was designed with some e-commerce practitioners to assess the use of the framework by themselves and their colleagues.

Internet Shopping at Virgin®

An Action Research Study of the Framework in Use

This study was carried out with the support of Siegelgale®, a leading international branding and e-commerce consultancy, and Virgin®. Virgin® was chosen because participants in the study were familiar with the company, already having had Virgin® shopping experiences, and because, at the time, Virgin® had an ideal mix of shops and services for our purposes. For example, they had a strong online presence, including several purely Internet-based offerings, bricks and mortar stores, a WAP service related to Virgin® Radio, and multiple products and services.

The aim of the study was to explore with practitioners, who were involved in evaluating online and off-line shopping experiences, their use of the user-experience framework. The practitioners became involved in this research because they felt that an understanding of user experience would help them in their work. In the spirit of participatory action research (Rapoport, 1970; Wadsworth, 1998), some of the participants were involved in devising the assessment process, and all of them were free to choose a Virgin® shopping activity that was of some interest to them when assessing the framework. Moreover, the research was intended to help authors and participants refine their understanding of user experience and of the usefulness of the framework in their work. Specific research questions were:

1.   What kinds of insights into Internet shopping experiences would the framework elicit?

2.   What aspects of Internet shopping experience would it miss?

3.   How useful would it be as a tool for helping make sense of experience?

Method

The method employed was qualitative action research in which participants were required to have and record "Virgin® experiences." Because it was conceived as an exercise in participatory action research and design (Schuler & Namioka, 1993), in which those who are likely to use a tool participate in its development, participants had the freedom to explore and critique the framework in a setting close to real-world use. Therefore, within the constraints of practicality and availability, they were allowed to select their own Virgin® shopping experiences.

In this study, the user-experience framework was used to guide participants' sense making with a view to understanding the kinds of insights it elicits, the aspects of experience it misses, and the extent to which participants felt it helped them to make sense of their shopping experiences. The user-experience framework suggests two possible starting points for enquiry: the threads of experience and the sense-making processes. We chose the sense-making processes because we thought they provided the more accessible starting point. Each process was unpacked for the participants in the form of a list of questions that suggested what aspects of sense making the process was intended to explicate. The full list of questions is available in the *Appendix*.

The study was designed to collect data at three points:

1.   Baseline data was collected in the initial interview in which participants' impressions of Virgin® and their expectations of what shopping with Virgin® would be like, and the sources of those expectations, were elicited.

2.   Participants made contemporaneous notes on their shopping experiences. It was suggested to them that they use the sense-making processes part of the framework to structure these notes. The resulting notes are the primary source of data on the experience of Internet shopping and on the framework as a resource for making sense of the experience.

3.   After participants handed in their notes, we held individual debriefing sessions with them in which we asked them questions about their experience to elicit an oral recounting of the experience. In the debriefing, participants were also asked to comment on the usefulness of the framework as they had employed it as a tool for eliciting accounts of interactive experiences.

Participants

Seven employees of Siegelgale®, two men and five women aged between mid-twenties and mid-thirties, volunteered to take part in this study. They were all graduates and regular users of a variety of information and communication technologies, particularly Internet and phone-based services. In keeping with the participatory action research approach of this study, they were all also involved in the design and/or evaluation of e-commerce and were, therefore, in a position to judge whether the framework would help them in their work.

Procedure

During the first meeting with all of the participants at their workplace, they were each briefed individually on the aims and objectives of the research and on the idea of making sense in- and of- experience. They were also specifically introduced to the sense-making processes identified in the framework. These processes were explained to them with the aid of a set of questions for each process that expressed what was meant by the particular process. These questions were intended to illuminate each of the processes and to clarify the differences between them. The questions are listed in full in the *Appendix*.

Once the participants felt comfortable with the concepts in the framework, we asked them to choose some Virgin® services that they would like to experience.

Table 1. The shopping experiences that participants chose to attempt

Participant	Virgin Shopping Experiences to be Attempted
1	• Make enquiries at virginmoney.com • Buy books and records at virginmega.com • Buy books and records at a traditional bricks and mortar Virgin® Megastore
2	• Find the price of a flight at virgin-atlantic.com • Make an enquiry at virginmoney.com—how much do I need to save to retire at 60? • Buy a CD at a traditional bricks and mortar Virgin® Megastore
3	• Upgrade phone at virginmega.com • Find out details about phone handsets at a traditional bricks and mortar Virgin® Megastore • Find Virgin® shop locations from Virgin® WAP

Table 1. (continued)

4	• Listen to music and buy a CD from Virgin® WAP • Check music schedules, gigs etc. on Virgin® WAP • Buy a CD at a traditional bricks and mortar Virgin® Megastore
5	• Get information on buying mutual funds at virginmoney.com • Check availability of CDs by a particular group and buy one that I don't have at virginmega.com
6	• Check availability and price of two CDs and possibly buy them at virginmega.com • Make enquiries about mortgage quotation and debt consolidation at virginmoney.com • Buy a CD at a traditional bricks and mortar Virgin® Megastore
7	• Buy books and records at virginmega,com • Buy books and records at a traditional bricks and mortar Virgin® Megastore

Most elected to have three experiences, although some chose two. The full list is in Table 1. We completed this first interview by asking participants what they felt about Virgin®, what they expected their experiences would be like, and how those expectations had formed.

The participants engaged in their respective shopping experiences over a maximum period of four days. They were permitted to approach the experiences in whatever order suited them and to complete them in the time that suited them within the four days, from one sitting to a number of sittings over the full time allowed. They were required to make contemporaneous notes on their experiences and were encouraged to use the framework of the six sense-making processes to structure these notes. Having completed their shopping experiences, they then handed in their notes, and we conducted one-on-one debriefing sessions that gave them the chance to give an oral recounting of their experiences. We also asked them to describe what it was like to use the framework and the methodology to order the events and feelings of their experiences.

Thus, at the conclusion of this research, we had three sets of data to analyse: the initial interviews, the participants' records of their experiences, and the content of the debriefing. The analysis consisted of a thematic content analysis of the records of the initial interview, final debriefing, and of the participants' contemporaneous notes.

Analysis of Data

Initial Interviews: Expectations and Prior Perceptions

In the initial interviews, participants expressed a variety of opinions about what they expected their Virgin® experiences to be like. Participants identified their anticipations as stemming from a number of sources listed in Table 2.

The majority of the participants were well-disposed to Virgin® prior to their participation in the research as can be seen from Table 3 in which the Virgin® attributes they identified are listed.

Table 2. Sources of expectations about Virgin® experiences identified by participants

Prior experiences with the same Virgin® service in the same channel.
Prior experience with the same service in a different channel.
Prior experience with a different service in the same channel.
Prior experience with a different service in a different channel.
Other peoples' narratives about Virgin® experiences.
The name of the service, especially if it appeared descriptive (for example, Virgin® Money).
Advertising.
Experiences with different products and services (for example, the online bank Egg) overlaid with assumptions about Virgin®.

Table 3. Attributes of Virgin® identified by participants in the initial interview

Positive Attributes Identified	User friendly with a "feel good" factor; Entertaining; Funky; Modern; Colourful; Young; Honest; Fun; Informal; Good customer service; Fresh; Provocative; Anti-establishment; Innovative
Negative Attributes Identified	Gimicky; Cheap; Appearance-driven

Contemporaneous Notes: Shopping Experiences

Positive expectations notwithstanding, it was clear from the analysis of the con-temporaneous notes that some participants had had difficulty achieving some of their objectives for their various experiences. Their troubles stemmed from the following causes:

- **Inaccurate expectations of the service:** While this occurred in several instances, there was a particular problem with virginmegastore.com. One participant noted that the site was "not as rewarding experience as I'd hoped for, it was more of an information site as opposed to a interactive site." A number of participants assumed that it would be both an informational and a transactional site but found instead it was a promotional "magazine-like" site. This caused much irritation.
- **The services, be they online or bricks and mortar, had usability problems:** At virginmoney.com, for example, while one participant sailed through the registration process, two others had numerous difficulties resulting in error messages and general confusion. Further, at Virgin® Megastore, one found it took a long time to find a store plan which would inform him where he could find the books' section. Thus, by the time he found the section, he already felt that he had wasted time and was unwilling to spend much time browsing.
- **There was poor localisation, resulting in confusion about the real-world location of online services:** All of the participants read the Virgin® brand as British, and thus expected all of the services linked to the virgin.com site to be UK-based. Those who went from there to virginmegastore.com were perplexed by the fact that they landed on a U.S.-based site with, for example, a U.S. and Canadian store locator, but no information at all about British stores. One participant commented that the site was "not that useful to me as it is very U.S. oriented." Worse, it often took participants a few minutes to figure this out, time they later considered "wasted."
- **There was no clear reason given on the site for participants having to reg-ister—which was a requirement for obtaining information and services:** This was only relevant for virginmoney.com, which demanded registration to access anything more than the most basic information on the site. Participants did not understand why they had to register just to use goals calculators, and so forth, and often chose to leave the site and perform the same tasks else-where, where they would not have to register. One commented as follows in her notes:

Oh! They want me to register now. I'm confused...can't I just look at financial planning stuff? I don't want to register yet. I'm going to leave.

Table 4. Sources of responsibility for failing to achieve objectives identified by participants

---

"Bugs" and/or limitations inherent to the channel (this was especially the case for WAP).

The service in and of itself.

A particular articulation of the service (e.g., the Virgin® Megastore on Oxford Street vs. the one at Piccadilly).

The participants themselves.

Virgin®.

In the context of the foregoing comments, it is worth noting that many aspects of Virgin® sites and services have been changed since this study to improve usability.

Participants assigned responsibility for failing to achieve their objectives to a number of different sources, which are listed in Table 4.

Those participants who started out well-disposed to Virgin® were the most likely to trace the responsibility for their difficulties to a source other than Virgin®. Nevertheless, if these particular participants subsequently had problems achieving their objectives in the course of another Virgin® experience, they were apt to feel particularly let down, as if a trusted friend had betrayed them. Participants blamed themselves in the instances where they realised they had inaccurate expectations of the service to start with and tended to readjust their objectives to what they perceived the service offered. For example, most participants expected virginmegastore.com to be transactional but promptly set themselves other goals when they found that it was not. However, if participants found their new objectives thwarted as well, they tended to shift blame to the service, stating that their expectations were being poorly managed and thus their time wasted. For example, one participant wrote, "The web site visit was so bad that I might relish recounting the experience to friends...."

Although the participants' accounts highlighted where Virgin® is delivering poor or fragmented customer experiences, they also indicated where Virgin® is "getting it right," that is, providing consistent experience, creating and meeting expectations, and even creating the new or wonderful. Particular successes included:

- **Participants generally knew they were in a Virgin® environment:** The consistency of the Virgin® look and feel, the tone of voice, "hip or trendy" design, and the positioning of the logo all contributed to making participants feel that they were in the right place.

- **Some services, such as Virgin® Atlantic, are delivering a consistent service across touch-points, leading to a seamless experience:** For example, one participant reported that, "the va.com site seems to try to make the potentially dull site more fun, with simple perks and design features, much like the airline itself."

- **Even where some Virgin® offerings fail to provide a consistently good experience across touch-points, one may stand out for its excellence and save the experience as a whole:** One participant was attempting to get information on switching to Virgin® and on upgrading to a Nokia tri-band phone. Having found neither the Virgin® shops nor virginmobile.com helpful, she started to despair that Virgin® was "all hype and no substance." However, she then tried the Virgin® Mobile call centre, where she had a remarkably different experience. She did not have to wait for service, and the salesperson was well-informed, friendly, and easy to speak to. Thus her final impression of Virgin® was "cool and upbeat."

- **On occasion, Virgin® was able to elicit strong and positive emotional responses from the participants:** For example, one participant commented that the site:

Made me feel good, happy feeling ... Felt comfortable straight away because felt like I was in a familiar environment—reflects what I know about Virgin®.

Participants' responses to Virgin® point to several conditions that help create these strong feelings:

a. If customers perceive themselves to be in control of the experience, they feel "relaxed and empowered" and are more likely to trust the service provider. Crucially, they may also be more likely to invest time.

b. Beautiful, "fresh" design—be it online or in-store—is affective and thus effective. It also makes a strong first impression and has the power to generate excitement.

c. Innovation, novelty, and humour, which appear to participants as key aspects of the Virgin® brand, can create difference and enchantment. For example, one user was charmed to find "Pardon?" written on the package of the ear plugs supplied by Virgin® Atlantic, and three out of three participants mentioned VirginMoney.com's exhortation to read the small print on the site—"because it came from our lawyers...[and was] expensive."

d. Participants responded warmly to those touch-points that appealed to their curiosity and offered them the chance to play, be it with in-store listening consoles in the Virgin® Megastores or interactive calculators on VirginMoney.com.

Final Debriefing and Interview: Evaluating the Framework

Analysis of data from the debriefing and final interview suggests that the framework was useful for evaluating shopping experiences. There was a general consensus that the framework was useful in both online and off-line settings and that it provided a process for evaluating experience, especially the consistency of experience across multiple channels. The main comments of participants on the value of the framework include the following:

- **It was helpful to address the issue of anticipation at the outset, as what one expects and hopes will happen sets the stage for what does happen:** Indeed, several participants said that this was a subject worthy of investigation in its own right, especially as it pertains to the attempts to create a totality of experience across multiple touch-points.
- **A particular strength of the framework is that it provided the means to capture both factual (e.g.,"this happened, then this happened") and subjective aspects of experience:** In their contemporaneous notes, all participants had included records of events that had happened while shopping and some comments on their feelings about how those events unfolded. In the debriefing, a number of participants commented that the framework had been a useful reminder to attend to both aspects in their notes. One commented that the framework was good at "capturing both factual as well as subjective aspects of experience."
- **The framework dealt with experience in depth:** Some participants said that they felt the framework was embracing enough to cover the full gamut of their thoughts, feelings, and actions during the experience. For example, one participant said that the framework was "good for capturing expectations and emotions, capturing of fact and being conscious of separation". Though, as we shall see later, some also felt that the framework did not always capture the highs and lows of experience.
- **The framework not only provides the means to analyse experience, it could implicitly guide strategists and designers as they create purpose-built user experiences:** By delineating the threads and the sense-making processes of an experience, the framework provides a tool for designers to look at experiences from a user's perspective. This means thinking about not just what users see, but additional factors including other sensory stimuli, location, sense of time, visceral reactions, emotional connections, and the way users may relate a given experience to other experiences.
- **The framework does not always capture the highs and lows of experience:** A weakness of the framework noted by one of the shoppers was its failure to

address the kinds of high points and low points that can become the focus of attention in recounting. This comment seemed to reflect a sense that the framework lacked explicit attention to the intensity of emotions and feelings.

One of the main aims of the case study was to determine if people could work with the framework in order to articulate user experiences. Our participants' experiences with the framework suggest that certain issues need to be resolved for future use. These include:

- While our questions concerning *Anticipating* adequately covered issues such as the perception of the company and the expectations of the channel, some participants felt we overlooked the *feelings* attached to tasks, such as the excitement of arranging air travel, or the trepidation surrounding WAP. Participants found these feelings so significant that, despite the fact that the framework itself inherently accommodates such emotional factors, they suggested that they should be emphasised in the method.

- Some participants were unsure about the separation of some elements such as *Interpreting* and *Reflecting*. This suggests that, while appropriate in the framework itself, it is too strange for users to try to interrupt the flow of experience to gauge such nuances in their own reactions.

- Some participants felt that being primed by knowledge of the sense-making processes in advance helped them to think about what should be noted. One distinguished between the use of the framework to sensitise users to aspects of experience in this way and its possible analytic uses.

Conclusion

In undertaking the study reported in this chapter, we wanted to get a sense of what insights practitioners would get into shopping experiences. We also wanted to know what aspects of experience the framework might miss and how useful participants would find it as the tool for evaluating experience. The thematic content analysis of participants' contemporary notes on their shopping experiences indicated a number of ways in which their shopping experiences were more or less satisfactory. These were summarized in the sub-section, *Contemporaneous Notes: Shopping Experiences*. Discussing these observations with participants suggested a number of issues. They include:

- Expectations are an important factor in shaping a person's experience. It is the relationship between a person's expectations and their actual experience that affects the emotional quality of the interaction leading, for example, to disappointment, surprise, satisfaction, and so on.

- The issue of localisation highlights the fact that people enjoy feeling that they know where they are and that where they are is where they expect to be. For example, links to shops that, without warning, take people from a British site to a North American one can be disorientating.

- People may be reluctant to provide personal information without a clear rationale or an obvious benefit to them. They may, for example, assume the reason is unwanted follow-ups and marketing.

- Poor usability can still be a problem even on professionally-designed sites leading to erosion of trust in the service provider.

- People consider Internet services as part of a broader relationship with a company or organisation and seem to value consistency across touch-points.

- An emotional commitment to an Internet shopping service depends upon among other things: Customers perceiving themselves to be in control of the experience; finding their curiosity and playfulness aroused by the site; and feeling that the site is novel and appealing.

Although not all of these findings are novel, what they suggest is that the framework was successful in allowing the participants to identify and articulate important design factors. We also asked the participants to reflect on the experience of using the framework as a tool for analysis. When reflecting on their use of the framework, participants picked out certain features that led them to think about aspects of experience that they might not otherwise have considered. For example, they had not considered the role that anticipation and expectation plays in how we make intellectual and emotional sense of an experience and how this might be included in an empirical evaluation of experience. In many accounts of user experience, it is assumed that the experience begins when we log on to a site and ends when we press the "confirm" button. The framework helped participants to expand their consideration of experience in both directions—to what goes on before the interaction and to what goes on after it, for example, the way in which through reflection and recounting we may or may not decide to go back to a site for a second or subsequent visit.

The participants valued the way in which the framework helped them relate the affective aspects of interaction to behavioural aspects of the experience such as what they had to do and in what order. The affective aspects allowed them to think about issues such as sense of time, visceral reactions, and emotional connections between different experiences in ways that were more insightful than other approaches. They also felt that the framework provided a "common-sense" account of experience that could be used by other types of practitioners such as designers and business analysts for whom a user perspective is of value.

The participants also had some critical comments on the framework that fell into two categories: ones that pointed up some limitation of the framework as it stood and ones that would have liked the framework to be able to do extra work that it was not originally designed for. For example, some participants had difficulty separating the sense-making processes *Interpreting* and *Reflecting*. Although we still believe that there is a distinction between these two processes that is worth preserving in the framework—between the activity orientation of *interpretation* and the evaluative orientation of *reflection*—it is clear that we shall need to make the difference between them much clearer to future users of the framework. Another comment—that the framework did not capture the highs and lows or intensity of experience—seems to ask the framework to do analytical work that it was not originally intended to do. In response, we would suggest that the emotional thread identified in the framework accommodates aspects of the intensity of experience without, however, attending to its measurement, which was not the intention of the framework but which might be a subject of future research.

Any such critical comment notwithstanding, the most positive outcome from our perspective is that, despite participants finding some aspects of the framework difficult to work with, they were consistently able to generate the kind of data that would allow designers and analysts to understand user experience and to use that understanding in designing better interactive experiences.

While the strength of this study was the participatory action orientation that led us to test the framework with practitioners in a practical setting, it had some limitations, which would need to be addressed in further evaluation of the framework. The main weaknesses relate to the method used to deploy the framework in this study, that is, asking participants to relate their experiences to the six sense-making processes. It required an a priori introduction to a technical element of the framework which might have better been employed to explain experience already had. It may have also implied that more weight should be given to the sense-making processes than to the threads, resulting in a sense that the intensity of experience was underplayed. Another aspect of the method was that it required participants to make contemporary notes on their experiences. It is arguable that this could have contributed to shaping the experiences as more reflective than they might otherwise have been.

Because the framework is open rather than prescriptive, it provides fertile ground on which to develop alternative methods of deployment. These would likely be project dependent, although we do already have some ideas about how to create more elegant and participant-friendly methods. One possibility for this would be to ask participants to focus on describing the "threads" rather than the sense-making processes of experience. Contrary to our original expectations, the threads may be more immediately accessible to participants than the sense-making processes. Another would be to partner with participants during the course of their experiences, asking them the kinds of questions that were used in this study to explain the sense-making processes but freeing them from the burden of contemporaneous note taking. This might create a more natural situation, something akin to a socially-shared experience. A third possibility would be to ask participants to generate a "stream of conscious-ness" narrative of their experience in real time or retrospectively, or even to send text or voice messages to the researcher, and for researchers and participants together to use the framework to explain and evaluate the experiences recounted.

Our experiences of working with Siegelgale® and of developing and assessing the framework in a practitioner-centred way has led us to further action research projects concerned with experience-centred design. In particular, we have begun to explore and develop a range of techniques, tools, and methods to help designers engage with user experience (Wright & McCarthy, 2005). There have been a number of developments in this regard that mark the beginnings of an experience-centred design methodology. For example, we have developed a number of broadly-ethno-graphic approaches to the analysis of user experience (Blythe, Reid, Geelhoed, & Wright, 2006). In their *technology biographies* technique, Blythe, Monk, and Park (2002) analyse people's understandings of- and relationships with- technology in their lives. They asked their informants to tell them stories about their experiences of technology in their homes and their personal lives. These stories provided valuable insights into how the individuals valued technology and how it related to their sense of place and their sense of themselves. Elsewhere, we have presented analyses of experience with technology that resembles Blythe, Monk, and Park's approach. Mc-Carthy and Wright (2004) use personal autobiography to understand online shopping experiences, and Wright and McCarthy (2003) use an individual's personal account of his career as an airline pilot as a starting point for understanding the creative and ethical experience of procedure following in the cockpit. Blythe et al. (2004) have also developed a form of scenario-based design to envisage and explore user experience. In their Pastiche scenarios, well-known characters from novels, film, or TV are pastiched as users of new technology, to explore sensitive and challeng-ing areas of design. They have used the technique effectively to engage users and designers in meaningful design dialogue (Blythe & Wright, 2005; Blythe, Wright, & Monk, 2004). Other researchers are also developing variants of user prototyping to support designing for experience. Buchenau and Suri (2000), for example, employ a range of innovative techniques to give designers an understanding and empathy for user experiences as diverse as piloting remote submersibles and undergoing defibrillation via a wearable pacemaker.

This growth in experience-centred design research and the development of new tools and techniques has the potential to improve design practice. But such improvement requires researchers to work closely not only with users but also with designers and developers in order to analyse the value of such tools and techniques for design practice and their impact on user experience.

Acknowledgments

We would like to thank Siegelgale® and Virgin® for their participation and support. We would also like to acknowledge support from the UK EPSRC in the form of funding a visiting fellowship (GR/S18799/01) which enabled the collaboration between Peter Wright and John McCarthy and also a three-year research project on theory and method for experience-centred design (GR/S70326/01).

References

Anderson, R. J. (1994). Representation and requirements: The value of ethnography in system design. *Human-Computer Interaction, 9*, 151-182.

Bakhtin, M. (1986). *Speech genres and other late essays*. Austin, TX: University of Texas Press.

Bakhtin, M. (1993). *Toward a philosophy of the act*. Austin, TX: University of Texas Press.

Blythe, M., Monk, A., Overbeeke, C., & Wright, P. C. (Eds.) (2003). *Funology: From usability to user enjoyment*. Dordrecht: Kluwer.

Blythe, M., Monk, A., & Park, J. (2002). Technology biographies: Field study techniques for home use product development. In *Proceedings of the ACM Conference on Human Factors in Computing Systems, CHI 2003, Extended Abstracts* (pp. 658-659). New York: ACM Press.

Blythe, M., Reid, J., Geelhoed, E., & Wright, P. (2006). Interdisciplinary criticism: Analysing the experience of *RIOT*!: A location-sensitive digital narrative. *Behaviour and Information Technology, 25*(2), 127-139.

Blythe, M., & Wright, P. C. (2005). Bridget Jones; iPod: Relating macro and micro theories of user experience through pastiche scenarios. In A. Sloane (Ed.), *Home-oriented informatics and telematics* (pp. 291-302). New York: Springer.

Blythe, M., Wright, P. C., & Monk, A. F. (2004). Little brother: Could and should wearable computing technologies be applied to reducing older people's fear of crime? *Personal and Ubiquitous Computing, 8*(6), 412-415.

Boorstin, J. (1990). *Making movies work: Thinking like a filmmaker*. Beverley Hills, CA: Salaman James Press.

Bruner, E. M., & Turner, V. (Eds.) (1986). *The anthropology of experience*. Urbana: University of Illinois Press.

Buchenau, K., & Suri, J. F. (2000, August 17-19). Experience prototyping. In *Proceedings of the ACM Conference on Designing Interactive Systems: Processes,*

Practices, Methods, and Techniques, DIS 2000, New York (pp. 424-433). New York: ACM Press.

Davis, M. (2003, November 7). Theoretical foundations for experiential systems design. *ETP 03,* Berkeley, CA (pp. 45-52). New York: ACM Press.

Demasio, A. (1999). *The feeling of what happens: Body, emotion and the making of consciousness*. London: Vintage.

Dewey, J. (1925). *Experience and nature*. LaSalle, IL: Open Court.

Dewey, J. (1934). *Art as experience*. New York: Perigree.

Donald, M. (1991). *Origins of the modern mind*. Cambridge, MA: Harvard University Press.

Donald, M. (2001). *A mind so rare*. New York: Norton.

Forlizzi, J., & Battarbee, K. (2004, August 1-4). Aesthetics, ephemerality and experience: Understanding experience. In *Proceedings of Designing Interactive Systems (DIS 2004),* Cambridge, MA (pp. 261-268). Cambridge, MA: ACM Press.

Forlizzi, J., & Ford, S. (2000). The building blocks of experience: An early framework for interaction designers. In *Proceedings of the ACM Conference on Design of Interactive Systems, DIS 2000,* New York City, NY, August 17-19 (pp. 419-423). ACM Press.

Garrett, J. J. (2002). *The elements of user experience: User-centred design for the Web*. Indianapolis, IN: New Riders Publishers.

Geertz, C. (1993). *The interpretation of cultures: Selected essay*. London: Fontana Press.

Hassenzahl, M. (2003) The thing and I: Understanding the relationship between user and product. In M. A. Blythe, K. Overbeeke, A. F. Monk, & P. Wright (Eds.), *Funology: From usability to enjoyment* (pp. 32-42). Dordrecht, The Netherlands: Kluwer Academic Publishers.

Hickman, L. A. (1998) (Ed.). *Reading Dewey: Interpretations for a postmodern generation*. Bloomington: Indiana University Press.

Hull, R., & Reid, J. (2003). Designing engaging experiences with children and artists. In M. A. Blythe, K. Overbeeke, A. F. Monk, & P. Wright (Eds.), *Funology: From usability to enjoyment* (pp. 179-188). Dordrecht, The Netherlands: Kluwer Academic Publishers.

Jordan, P. (2000). *Designing pleasurable products: An introduction to the new human factors*. London: Taylor and Francis.

Katz, J. E., & Aakhus, M. (Eds.) (2002). *Perpetual contact: Mobile communication, private talk, public performance*. Cambridge: Cambridge University Press.

Kuutti, K. (2001, April 24). *Hunting for the lost user: From sources of errors to active actors—and beyond.* Paper presented at Cultural Usability Seminar, Media Lab, University of Art and Design, Helsinki. Retrieved April 24, 2002, from http://mlab.uiah.fi/culturalusability/papers/Kuutti_paper.html

Laurel, B. (1991). *Computers as theatre.* Reading, MA: Addison Wesley.

Lee, J., Kim, J., & Moon, J. Y. (2000, April 1-6). What makes Internet users visit cyber stores again? Key design factors for customer loyalty. In *Proceedings of CHI'2000*, The Hague, Amsterdam (pp. 305-312). New York: ACM Press.

Markham, A. (1998). *Life online: Researching real experience in virtual space.* Walnut Creek, CA: AltaMira Press.

McCarthy, J., & Wright, P. (2004). *Technology as experience.* Harvard, MA: MIT Press.

Morson, G. S., & Emerson, C. (1990). *Mikhail Bakhtin: Creation of a prosaics.* Stanford, CA: Stanford University Press.

Norman, D. (2004). *Emotional design: Why we love (or hate) everyday things.* New York: Basic Books.

Orr, J. (1990). Sharing knowledge celebrating identity: War stories and community memory in a service culture. In D. S. Middleton, & D. Edwards (Eds.), *Collective remembering: Memory in society* (pp. 169-189). Beverley Hills, CA: Sage Publications.

Oxford English Dictionary. (1982). *The Concise Oxford English Dictionary.* Oxford: Oxford University Press.

Pu, P., & Faltings, B. (2000, April 1-6). Enriching buyers' experiences: the Smart-Client approach. In *Proceedings of CHI'2000*, The Hague, Amsterdam (pp. 289-296). New York: ACM Press.

Rapoport, R. N. (1970). Three dilemmas in action research. *Human Relations, 23*(4), 499-513.

Schuler, D., & Namioka, A. (Eds.) (1993). *Participatory design: Principles and practices.* Hillsdale, NJ: Erlbaum.

Shedroff, N. (2001). *Experience design.* Indianapolis, IN: New Riders.

Taylor, A. S., & Harper, R. (2002, April 20-25). Age-old practices in the new world: A study of gift-giving between teenage mobile phone users. In *Proceedings of CHI'2002,* Minneapolis, MN (pp. 439-446). New York: ACM Press.

Turkle, S. (1995). *Life on the screen: Identity in the age of the Internet.* London: Phoenix.

Wadsworth, Y. (1998, November). What is participatory action research? *Action Research International.* [Online journal]. Retrieved from http://www.scu.edu.au/schools/gcm/ar/ari/ari-papers.html

Wright, P. C., & McCarthy, J. M. (2003). An analysis of procedure following as concerned work. In E. Hollnagel (Ed.), *Handbook of cognitive task analysis* (pp. 679-700). Mahwah, NJ: Lawrence Erlbaum.

Wright, P. C., & McCarthy, J. (2005). The value of the novel in designing for experience. In A. Pirhonen, H. Isomäki, C. Roast, & P. Saariluoma (Eds.), *Future interaction design* (pp. 9-30). London: Springer.

Appendix

The Questions Supplied to Participants to Help Clarify the Sense-Making Processes

The following questions were devised with two of the participants as a way of clarifying what each of the sense-making processes mean in terms of the user experience framework. For example, the questions listed under *Anticipating* are intended to clarify a variety of aspects of anticipating an experience, specifically in this case and experience of Internet shopping. During the first meeting with the participants in which they were briefed individually on the aims of the research, they were specifically introduced to the sense-making processes in the framework. At this point, the questions listed in this *Appendix* were used to help explain the sense-making processes. During the rest of the study, participants had a list of these questions to refer to. However, they were not expected to answer these questions per se, rather to use them to guide the notes they made on their shopping experiences.

Anticipating

What do you expect will happen?

- What do you think you will be able to do?

- Describe what you imagine will happen as you begin your task.

- Does your sense of who Richard Branson is and/or what he stands for affect your sense of what to expect at all? If so, please explain.

- What expectations do you have based on previous Virgin® experiences with the same service/channel or different service/channel?

- What expectations do you have based on completing the same tasks in the past with different companies or brands (or sites/stores/airlines)?

- What expectations do you have based on something someone else has described about this service, this channel, or Virgin® as a brand?
- What is going on in the environment around you that might affect your anticipation, for example, fighting down Oxford St. and hoping for peace in the Megastore, furtively trying to shop for a mortgage while at work, and so forth?

Connecting

What is your first impression?
- When/how do feel that the experience actually starts?
- What do you first apprehend of the experience?
- Colours, tempo, movement, salespeople, and so forth.
- How do spatio-temporal factors affect this, and why?
- What does this first impression make you feel?
- Tension, thrill of novelty, and so forth.
- Is there anything in particular that immediately engages you or puts you off (e.g., colour, sound, images used, etc.)
- What sensual/sensory and emotional factors of this experience or episode allow a connection with the brand or create a feeling of disconnectedness with your expectations of the brand?

Interpreting

How are you making sense of what you are finding?
- Do you feel that the experience is living up to what you anticipated? Please explain.
- Do you feel that there is a logical and coherent order to what is happening?
- Have you "settled into" a response or feeling about what the experience is offering?
- Do you know where you are, where you've been and where you have to go, for example, do you know what you have to do next? What cues provide this guidance?
- Are there bottlenecks somewhere? Why?
- How aware of time are you? Is it taking a long time to do what you want, or is time racing by?

- Is there a clear end point?
- Could you accomplish your task within a reasonable amount of time?
- How does the composite of these elements affect your interpretation of the brand?

Reflecting

- What are you feeling about the experience?
- Are your feelings about the experience consistent throughout, or do they change?
- Do you feel motivated to continue or frustrated at what's going on? Do you wish you could shorten or prolong the experience? Why?
- Who do you feel is in control—you or Virgin® or someone/something else?
- Do you trust the information or service you're getting? Why/why not? Is anything happening to enhance or undermine that trust? Please explain.
- Do you feel a sense of on-going engagement?
- If this experience is indeed different to what you expected, how do you feel about that? Do you feel inclined to give a little leeway to the service/brand/channel? Why or why not?
- Do you feel that the experience is being directed at you? Why/why not?
- Do you feel a sense of fulfillment or achievement at the conclusion of the experience? Why/why not?
- How is the experience consistent or inconsistent with the values you associate/d with the brand?
- Do you feel the brand is fulfilling its promise?

Appropriating

How are you making sense of this experience within a larger framework of experience, for example, with Virgin® or with the channel?

- Did it fit in with how you like to do things?
- How did it change or deepen your impression of the brand/service/channel?
- Was there any aspect of it that made you feel uneasy? Please explain.
- What aspects did you find particularly rewarding?

- Was there anything that surprised you? If so, what was it and why?
- Did the experience remind you of anything and, if so, what?

Recounting

- How would you describe the overall experience?
- What were the most memorable things about it?
- Do you feel much inclined to describe it to anyone? Does it make a good story?
- Are there any bits you particularly enjoy remembering?
- How do others react to your story?

Chapter VI

Impacts of Behavior Modeling in Online Asynchronous Learning Environments

Charlie C. Chen
Appalachian State University, USA

Albert L. Harris
Appalachian State University, USA

Lorne Olfman
Claremont Graduate University, USA

Abstract

The continued and increasing use of online asynchronous learning (OAL) environments for training raises the question of whether behavior modeling, the most effective training method in live instruction, will prove to be effective in OAL environments. If it is effective, to what extent will it be effective? In this study, behavior modeling training was delivered in three modes: face-to-face, videotaped, and scripted. Each behavior modeling mode expresses social presence to a different degree and, therefore, could impact both learning performance and the willingness of students to take online asynchronous training. This study reports on the effect of behavior modeling modes on three variables in an OAL environment, perceived usefulness, near-knowledge, and far-knowledge transfer, when learning a software application. Nine hypotheses were proposed. Four hypotheses were supported and five were not. This research found that the face-to-face environment is not significantly more effective than an OAL environment. The impacts of social presence seem to be higher in face-to-face OAL environments. Although videotaped instruction and scripted instruction were lower than face-to-face instruction, they deliver same degrees of social presence and lead to similar satisfaction level.

Introduction

International Data Corp. (IDC) projected that the worldwide e-learning market will grow to $21 billion by 2008, with $13.5 billion in the United States (U.S.) (Tucker, 2005). The burgeoning online learning and training markets, and the increasing training budgets of businesses and schools, have provided users of online training and marketing tools with practical reasons to investigate the effectiveness of online asynchronous software training.

Behavior modeling is viewed as the most effective training method in live instruction (Bolt, Killough, & Koh, 2001; Compeau, Olfman, Sein, & Webster, 1995; Simon, Grover, Teng, & Whitcomb, 1996; Yi & Davis, 2003). Three general modes of behavior modeling have been compared experimentally: (1) face-to-face (F2F) instruction, (2) videotaped instruction, and (3) scripted instruction. Since online asynchronous training does not use live instructors, it is possible that the F2F mode may be more effective than the other behavior modeling training modes. This chapter presents the results of a study to compare three modes of software training delivered in a Web-based format. It uses a "live instructor" behavior modeling format as a control.

Simon et al. (1996) categorize general training approaches into instruction-based, exploration-based, and behavior modeling. These three approaches are designed to improve learning outcomes for students with different learning styles in an F2F environment. However, in today's educational environment, the OAL environment may eventually replace the F2F environment for educational and training purposes. It is already the case that a student can study lecturers' prepared slides and notes, browse relevant Web sites, ask for solutions via discussion boards and chat rooms, and employ other means of assistance in the online environment in solving problems. However, in the online environment, the immediacy of an instructor's F2F demonstration is hard to achieve. It is doubtful that behavior modeling methods have yet been adapted fully to the complex and changing OAL environment.

Behavior modeling is based on instructor demonstration. It may be one of the better approaches for F2F instruction, but it may not be equally effective for online asynchronous instruction. For example, in a live training class, the instructor will demonstrate some software processes and ask the students to repeat the activity. However, in an OAL environment, where there is no live instructor, the demonstration may lose some of its benefits. The possibility exists that the behavior modeling approach is not the most effective training method in online training situations. Therefore, the effectiveness of behavior modeling in its different modes should be established in an OAL environment.

From the perspective of research design, "replication can and should mean testing empirical implications of theory—interpreting 'theory' broadly—in similar and dissimilar situations and experimentally and nonexperimentally" (Kerlinger & Lee, 2000, p.570). The OAL environment provides a research opportunity to validate the assertions of Bostrom, Olfman, and Sein (1990) and Simon et al. (1996) and to extend their software training frameworks to the OAL environment.

This study took place in an introductory computer course in two California universities. Face-to-face, videotaped, and scripted instruction, the three modes of behavior modeling training noted earlier, were compared to see which produced the best performance, student satisfaction, and agreement with learning style.

Learning Styles and Online Behavior Modeling

Different studies propose different learning styles (e.g., Myers-Briggs's Type Indicators and Kolb's Learning Style Inventory [LSI]) to serve their needs (Mitchell, 2000). Most of them agree that learning styles are experiential or phenomenological in nature (Kolb, 1984; Lewin, 1951). Students change their learning styles based on their learning experiences (Harris & Scwahn, 1961). Students with different learning styles also show preferences for different teaching methods (Gregorc, 1982) and software training methods (Bostrom et al., 1990).

In the OAL environment, instructors should customize Web-based learning tools for students with different learning styles. Ross and Schulz (1999) suggested that online training tools may need to be tailored for students based on their LSI profiles. The behavior modeling approach has been considered the most effective approach in the F2F environment. Learning style seems to be inconsequential with respect to behavior modeling. It is possible that the behavior modeling approach may still be the most valid method for training in the OAL environment, regardless of the students' learning styles. It is not known which learning medium would be the most effective vehicle for the behavior modeling approach in the OAL environment.

The OAL Environment

Online asynchronous training differs from traditional training in its self-directed and self-paced learning approach (Belanger & Van Slyke, 2000). As a result, it is plausible that individual differences have more influence on learning outcomes in the OAL environment. Many researchers (Davis & Davis, 1990; Palvia, Palvia, & Zigli, 1992; Vessey & Galletta, 1991) have investigated learning preference and its influence on learning outcomes. It is widely believed (even being a tenet of the Kentucky Education Reform Act of 1990) that students learn more effectively if they are taught via their preferred learning styles. Ramsden (1988) affirms that learning styles or orientations of students need to be taken into consideration when a teacher designs the curriculum. The effectiveness of online courses is highly correlated with the interactivity levels of online learning systems (Lavooy & Newlin, 2003). In addition, the length of attention on a particular subject may help users acquire knowledge and retain it in their long-term memory in the online learning environment,

This study limits its focus exclusively to software training in an online asynchronous mode. This choice reflects the reality that most online training delivered across continents is in the online asynchronous mode and that use of that mode is destined to grow incrementally and exponentially. Therefore, this study is intended to develop a more versatile, compatible, and responsive online software training strategy for online asynchronous students in the IT field.

Online Asynchronous Mediums for Behavior Modeling Method

Simon et al. (1996) define the behavior modeling approach as "a combination of the exploration and instruction methods that concentrates on the idea of observing and doing while following a role model" (p. 44). The behavior modeling approach customizes the learning environment for all students making it easier to understand learning materials. Its lecture formats include specific learning points and hands-on experimentation. Imitating the instructor to use a target system encourages the students to participate and experiment using the target system to follow their own paths. Online asynchronous training mediums empower the practice of behavior modeling because users can study lecture slides on one hand, rely on external resources to solve problems, and get feedback from teachers and students. Online asynchronous mediums, such as e-mail, discussion forums, Wikis, and Blogs, provide learners the ability to create and share knowledge through question and answer dialogs. These tools assist users in solving problems and getting feedback from instructors and other learners.

Without the presence of a live instructor, the scripted solution potentially narrows the difference of training approaches (yielding a smaller effect size) that may contribute to the difference of training outcomes. Videotaped or videotaped-based behavior modeling may somewhat resemble the F2F learning environment. Since a live instructor is replaced with a scripted or videotaped demonstration, there is a necessity for students to play a more active role in an OAL environment. Nevertheless, the suitability of delivering behavior modeling in these different modes is unclear. Assessing the relevance and applicability of behavior modeling training method in different modes is the first important step towards discovering an optimal online asynchronous behavior modeling training method.

Social Presence and Information Richness of Online Asynchronous Mediums

Theories of social presence and information richness (SPIR) have strong implications to online learning. For instance, e-mail with social cues can deliver psychological presence while asynchronous conferencing (e.g., Whiteboard™ and chat rooms)

Figure 1. SPIR features of e-learning mediums (based on Chen Olfman, & Harris, 2005; Daft & Lengel, 1986; Fulk, 1993; Zack, 1993)

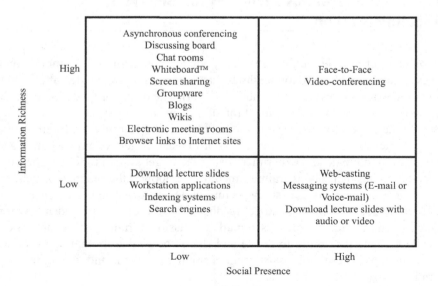

can deliver richer information than downloaded files. Figure 1 shows a taxonomy illustrating the SPIR features of online asynchronous training mediums.

In the F2F environment, exploration-based, instruction-based, and behavior modeling approaches are three useful training methods to teach software use. In an OAL environment, different online mediums can support each traditional training approach. Lecture slides, indexing, FTP, and other access to workstation applications can be used in instruction-based mode for software training. Message systems, conferencing, and browser links to Internet sites, on the other hand, allow students to explore solutions for problems given by instructors.

The effectiveness of behavior modeling is a function of people and the environment (Lewin, 1951). Integrating mediums with differential SPIR degrees into the OAL environment may affect the usefulness of behavior modeling method. Comparing the behavior modeling method in F2F, scripted, and videotaped modes allows students to investigate the impacts of differential social presence on learning effectiveness.

Potential Difference of Training Approaches Between F2F and OAL Environment

The literature indicates that incorporating the three general training approaches (instruction-based, exploration-based, and behavior modeling) that have long been successfully established in the traditional F2F environment into an OAL environment can be problematic. As a case in point, the success of the exploration-based training approach in the OAL environment is contingent upon: (1) the quality of the course materials, (2) the OAL environment (Web site) design, and (3) the available bandwidth. This differs from the training approach in the F2F environment where quality of course materials is the major determinant. Moreover, generic examples used in the course materials may be relevant to some online asynchronous users and irrelevant to the others. In the OAL environment, the student population is more diversified. An inability to customize course materials based on students' backgrounds may reduce the effectiveness of the exploration-based training approach. Lack of a live instructor is likely to make the situation worse. Students with lower motivation may direct their attention to other matters not relevant to the immediate learning task without the presence of an instructor to provide the necessary discipline to redirect students' attention.

Swan (2002) recommended that social presence and interaction be incorporated into the design of online courses to improve trainee satisfaction and learning outcomes. Through the reiterative communication process, the exploration-based approach in the F2F environment can mitigate any misunderstanding between instructor and students about the goals of the training and course materials. In the OAL environment, an asynchronous communication pattern takes place. Misunderstanding is generally identified after a learning attempt takes place; that is, the instructor and students do not communicate with each other at the same time (asynchronous). This phenomenon may discourage some students with lower self-guidance abilities from keeping pace with the goals. The wealth of Internet information can even distract some students' attention away from the course objective. In the F2F environment, the live instructor can facilitate the process, give timely feedback, and quickly get a discussion back on track. This condition does not exist in the OAL environment. There is a need to make a trade-off between information richness and reach for students who do not have high-bandwidth connections at home or work. An instructor may need to give up some richness of information to reach larger number of students. Without knowing the accessibility of students to the Internet, instructors will have trouble deciding the right trade-off. Class size adds another variable complicating the situation. The greater the class size, the more time an instructor will need to respond to students' questions in both the F2F and OAL environments.

The behavior modeling method is an enhanced mode of instruction-based and exploration-based methods. As a result, the behavior modeling method naturally inherits potential flaws of the other two methods in the OAL environment. In addition, in the OAL environment students may have trouble with the lack of modeling behavior from a live instructor to assist their learning. One alternative that can address this issue is to substitute scripted or videotaped lectures for the instructor's lectures. The interactive presence of the instructor was the key determinant for the success of the behavior modeling approach in the F2F environment. The validity of the claim that using the video replacement for the instructor is the most effective training approach for students of all learning styles in the asynchronous environment may not be supported. Additionally, learning outcomes can be further degraded because the real-time reiterative communication process between instructor and students is lost.

Our literature review found no effective online asynchronous training strategy has been formulated to date. Assessing the relevance and applicability of behavior modeling in an OAL environment is the first important step towards discovering more suitable strategy to deliver it in different modes.

Research Design

The setting for this study was in courses offered by two accredited universities in California. This study applied Simon et al.'s (1996) well-constructed training theory to test experimentally three modes of the behavior modeling approach in an OAL environment. In doing so, we hoped to detect the effects of the independent variables (training method and learning style), as well as their combination, on training outcomes. The study was conducted in a field setting that enabled the study to garner greater external validity than would be the case with a laboratory study. A field experiment methodology has the merits of "testing theory" and "obtaining answers to practical questions" (Kerlinger & Lee, 2000, p.583). The exploratory nature of the study requires that variables (e.g., learning style, training methods, and subject areas of study) under investigation be manipulated.

Regardless of the teaching environment (online or off-line), computer training is intended to instill in users a level of competency in using the system and to improve their satisfaction with the system. A user's competency in using a system is contingent upon his or her knowledge absorption capacity. Ramsden (1988) found that effective teaching needs to align students with situations where they are encouraged to think deeper and more holistically. Kirpatrick (1967) suggests that learning effectiveness needs to be evaluated by students' reaction, learning, and knowledge transfer. Bayman and Mayer (1988) suggest that the levels of knowledge absorbed by students may include syntactic, semantic, schematic, and strategic knowledge. Mennecke, Crossland, and Killingsworth (2000) believe that experts of one particular knowledge domain possess more strategic and semantic knowledge than novices.

Knowledge levels, as Simon et al. (1996) suggest, can be categorized as near-knowledge transfer, far-knowledge transfer, or problem solving. Near-knowledge transfer is necessary to understand software commands and procedures. Far-knowledge transfer is to ensure that a student has the ability to combine two or more near-knowledge transfer tasks to solve more complicated problems.

Both the use of software and the satisfaction levels of using them are useful surrogates to measuring the effectiveness of an information system (Ives, Olson, & Baroudi, 1983). End-user satisfaction levels have been widely adopted as an important factor contributing to the success of end-user software training. Since the study is to replicate Simon et al.'s (1996) research in a dissimilar environment, near-knowledge and far-knowledge transfer, and end-user satisfaction levels were adopted in this study to measure training outcomes.

Participants filled out a questionnaire regarding their experiences with the software and other database applications. This survey was used to check subjects' computer literacy and experiences. To determine the effectiveness of the training treatments, subjects were evaluated immediately after training. Evaluation of retention and transfer of learning included ten multiple-choice questions and one database problem to solve. This study further links scientific investigation and solutions to real-world situations while exploring the possibility of applying key determinants for the success of IT training strategy, found in the traditional training environment, to the online asynchronous training situation.

Pilot Study

A pilot study was performed that solicit opinions of ten users using a prototype online asynchronous training Web site. These users were not participants in the actual study. Based on the feedback received, the online training-related problems were modified before the actual study was conducted.

Subject Recruitment

Subjects were business major undergraduates who needed to learn the software. The subjects received no additional pay or monetary benefits for their participation in the study. Rather, students were notified in advance of their mandatory presence. Students also knew that an additional score of 5 (out of 100) would be credited to their total score of the semester. Subjects were not pre-screened for their participation because of the nature of the study. A total of 115 students registered to participate in the classes and all participants were expected to attend the mandatory class. The students were randomly assigned to one of the three treatments on a class basis: (1) F2F behavior modeling (FBM), (2) scripted behavior modeling (SBM), and (3) videotaped behavior modeling (VBM). Figure 2 shows the allocation of participants among the three treatments.

Training

Students were given 10 minutes to fill out a pre-training questionnaire. Students taking the online software training first attended a five-minute analogical instruction to explain how the e-training system (Blackboard®) worked and how to use the e-training system. After the training session was completed, the students went directly into the software lesson. Students in the face-to-face class did not receive the online software training. The class instructor decided the timeline based on his ability to complete the teaching of the five subjects covered in the study. Since the length of time can affect the learning outcomes, the timeline was standardized at 20 minutes for online training approaches.

Figure 2. Allocation of subjects

Training Approach	Behavior Modeling Modes			Number of Total Subjects
	FBM	VBM	SBM	
Number of Subjects	45	35	35	115

The topic to be taught included five main features and functions: (1) create tables, (2) create forms, (3) input records, (4) create queries, and (5) generate reports. All training sessions were conducted using a single instructor, providing continuity throughout all training sessions. This was to prevent the influences of teaching experiences and skills on learning effectiveness.

In the OAL environment, the instructor's presence is often not an essential factor. The limitation of bandwidth also constrains the use of videotaped teaching materials. The study recognized the limitations of these constraints. Therefore, scripted and videotaped presentations were conducted in a computer lab where a 10/100 Mbps LAN infrastructure was established. The length of time for both online behavior modeling methods was controlled to be the same across all three treatments to avoid the outlier influence of exposure time. Although the compromised solution might not fully capture all of the key elements of each training approach, it adequately reflected the real situations of conducting online asynchronous training. Teaching materials were deliberately designed to reflect the key elements of behavior modeling approach.

Scripted Behavior Modeling

SBM is an enhanced mode of exploration and instruction approaches. The behavior modeling approach includes both inductive and deductive approaches. The treatment was conducted in the same computer classroom as the other online training treatments. Both general concepts and procedural information sections were conducted utilizing Hyperionics' Hypercam™ Version 1.70.06 software screen capturing application. The application allowed the researchers to record all the step-by-step cursor movements of instruction with voice annotation. More importantly, the Hypercam™ application substituted for the live instructor-based delivery. Each scripted demonstration focused on one particular function of the database management topic. At each learning point of a particular function, students were encouraged to experiment by practicing the related exercises.

Videotaped Behavior Modeling

Videotape was employed to deliver the image of a live instructor and his/her voice to students on the OAL environment. Like video-conferencing, videotaped-based training permits psychological presence in addition to using both inductive and deductive approaches. Despite the benefit, the instant interaction between instructor and students are eliminated. Students may have lower satisfaction level of taking the videotaped-based training than the F2F training. Videotaped-based training enlarges the difference between the instruction-based and exploration-based approaches.

This increases the effect size that may have higher impacts on the effectiveness of training.

F2F Behavior Modeling

Without the presence of a live instructor, the scripted solution had the potential of narrowing the differences between training approaches that may contribute to the difference of training outcomes (a small effect size). To properly control the potential problem, a group in which students received the traditional FBM training approach was introduced. The instructor followed the same script as the one designed for the behavior modeling class in the online asynchronous training mode. The length of time allotted to conduct the training was controlled to be the same as the other online training approaches. The traditional behavior modeling group took the same pre- and post-training tests as the three online groups to properly evaluate the contribution of training approaches and learning styles to training outcomes. The training literature recommends that a control group in a training experiment be included (Wexley & Latham, 1991).

Post-Training Evaluation

Treatment and control groups were administered two tests and satisfaction evaluations upon completion of the 20-minute training treatment. The two tests included 10 multiple-choice questions and one problem to solve. The multiple-choice questions were intended to evaluate students' procedural knowledge (near-knowledge transfer) of the commands and features needed to manage a database using the software. Solving a real problem allowed the researcher to evaluate the ability of the students to transfer that knowledge (far-knowledge transfer) to another subject. There were a total of four sub-questions that required more than one command to solve. Five minutes were allocated for the multiple-choice test while 20 minutes were allocated for the problem-solving test. The two tests were graded on a 10-point scale. The multiple-choice test result was based on the number of questions correctly answered. The software problem was assigned a value based on the number of functions successfully completed. The students had 10 minutes to fill out the post-training questionnaire.

Experimental Controls

Training Materials

Training materials were carefully crafted by adopting the non-anonymous Delphi method to reach a consensus of experts. Many rounds of discussion with experts insured that the customized content of training materials could properly capture the key elements of different training approaches. This was to ensure that the effect of size across training treatments was well addressed.

Training Packages

The training packages were designed to maximize the effect size or the difference of three training treatments. All training packages began with the illustration of four examples to manage a database using the software. Two examples are prepared for each major. Subjects were encouraged to use one of the two examples relevant to their major to practice through the training session. Step-by-step instruction was adopted to illustrate each function.

Prior Computer Experience

All participants were classified as "novice" computer users or beginners because of their first exposure to the in-class training. Since it was a challenge to locate novice users or users with absolutely no computer experience, the recruitment of under-graduate business majors from two California universities controlled the potential influence of varying prior computer experiences of participants. Most importantly, the majority of these students had not been exposed to the software. This situation provided an objective baseline from which to assess the real effects of training approaches by managing the outliers of computer experiences.

Motivation

Controlling for motivation insured that all students had the same incentive to participate in the experimental study. Since the students were students who registered for the class, their participation was not voluntary. Upon completion of the training session, students took two exams, a 10 question multiple-choice test, and a software problem to solve. The total scores represented 5% of their aggregate semester grade.

Training Session Time Length

The length of training time is closely correlated with the learning performance of novice students (Wexley & Baldwin, 1986). To mitigate the influence of varying training time, the training time was fixed at 20 minutes based on the class instructor's judgment as to the optimal time in which to complete teaching five features of the topic "Database Management" in the FBM class. While 20 minutes may seem short for a training session, given the well-defined domain of the task, the 20-minute session was deemed appropriate and validated by external sources.

Dependent Variables

For reasons of internal validity, the study uses the same measurable indicators, near-knowledge and far-knowledge transfer, extensively used in training and learning experiments. Near-knowledge transfer is a student's ability to understand syntactic and semantic concepts and procedures after taking an online asynchronous training. Multiple-choice questions are most widely used for this purpose in other studies. In addition, the study was particularly interested in understanding the problem-solving capabilities of students after taking online asynchronous training. Built upon prior studies, the study asked students to actually use the target system to solve a given real problem within a limited time. The software project results were used to measure the far-knowledge transfer.

The study also used Davis and Olson's (1984) perceived usefulness and perceived ease of use instruments to measure end-user satisfaction levels.

Hypotheses

The online behavior modeling approach replaces the live instructor with the video-taped or scripted demonstration. Some key elements of the FBM approach may be lost. Behavior modeling training in the F2F mode may be more effective at improving the learning outcome for a student than the behavior modeling approach in the online asynchronous mode. Researchers have demonstrated that behavior modeling is more effective than instruction-based or exploration-based approaches in the traditional environment. A similar relationship may still be identified in the OAL environment. Proving that the F2F behavior modeling is more or less effective than the online behavior modeling could justify the validity of replicating the same pattern in the OAL environment. Hence, it is only hypothesized that the FBM approach is more effective than the online behavior modeling to improve learning outcomes for students of all learning styles. In the OAL environment, the videotaped-based training may retain more key elements of the online behavior modeling approach, such as the psychological presence of an instructor, than the scripted training approach. Therefore, it is plausible that the videotape-based training is more effective than the scripted training approach.

Perceived Usefulness (PU)

H1a: The FBM is more effective than the VBM approach to improve perceived usefulness for students regardless of learning styles.

H1b: The FBM is more effective than the SBM approach to improve perceived usefulness for students regardless of learning styles.

H1c: The VBM is more effective than the SBM approach to improve perceived usefulness for students regardless of learning styles.

Near-Knowledge Transfer (NKT)

H2a: The FBM is more effective than the VBM approach to improve near-knowledge transfer for students regardless of learning styles.

H2b: The FBM is more effective than the SBM approach to improve near-knowledge transfer for students regardless of learning styles.

H2c: The VBM is more effective than the SBM approach to improve near-knowledge transfer for students regardless of learning styles.

Far-Knowledge Transfer (FKT)

H3a: The FBM is more effective than the VBM approach to improve far-knowledge transfer for students regardless of learning styles.

H3b: The FBM is more effective than the SBM approach to improve far-knowledge transfer for students regardless of learning styles.

H3c: The VBM is more effective than the SBM approach to improve far-knowledge transfer for students regardless of learning styles.

Data Analysis and Results

Ninety-seven students completed the study. Eighteen students did not complete the assignment due to missing data and class absence. Due to the possible interaction effects of attitudes and learning performance (near- and far-knowledge transfer), the assumptions of homoscedasticity (p=0.023) and normality were tested and supported. Table 1 presents mean and standard deviations of dependent variables for the three treatments. Table 2 presents the results from the multivariate tests of significance to investigate the effects of personal factors on dependent variables.

Table 1. Means and standard deviations of dependent variables

Dependent Variables	FBM		VBM		SBM	
	Mean	S.D.	Mean	S.D.	Mean	S.D.
Satisfaction	5.50	1.095	4.11	1.484	4.62	1.382
Near-Knowledge Transfer	7.80	1.44	8.48	1.57	7.83	1.76
Far-Knowledge Transfer	7.70	3.11	8.14	2.29	5.78	3.11

Table 2. Multivariate test of significance

Effect	Wilks' Lambda	F	df	p	Observed Power
BM Modes	0.736	5.081	2; 94	0.000*	0.993
Experience	0.656	1.631	8; 88	0.035*	0.965
Class Year	0.866	2.283	2; 94	0.038*	0.786
GPA	0.751	2.268	4; 92	0.010*	0.915

Table 3. Univariate tests of between-subject effects

Source	Measure	SS	df	MS	F	P	Observed Power
BM Modes	Satisfaction*	15.243	2	15.243	9.085	.000	.972
	NKKT	7.197	2	3.598	1.417	.247	.297
	FKT*	100.147	2	50.073	5.732	.004	.856
Experience	Satisfaction	11.319	4	2.830	1.472	.217	.440
	NKT*	24.449	4	6.112	2.540	.045	.698
	FKT*	93.050	4	23.262	2.584	.042	.707
Class Year	Satisfaction*	20.855	2	10.427	5.857	.004	.864
	NKT	2.552	2	1.276	.493	.612	.129
	FKT	25.616	2	12.808	1.344	.266	.284
GPA	Satisfaction*	21.247	4	5.312	2.927	.025	.767
	NKT	16.772	4	4.193	1.684	.160	.499
	FKT*	101.322	4	25.331	2.842	.029	.753

Testing results indicate the existence of main effects of behavior modeling modes. Database application experiences, class year, and GPA (grade point average) are only three personal factors that have a statistically-significant effect. These findings lead support to the proposition that different behavior modeling modes could have impacts on students' learning performance and attitudes due to their social presence attribute.

Table 3 presents the results of the univariate tests performed to understand the accountability of subject effects. Significantly differential impacts of behavior modeling modes, frequency of using database applications, class year, and GPA were detected across dependent variables. Behavior modeling modes of training and GPA had significant impacts on the end-user satisfaction and far-knowledge transfer capability. In contrast, the frequency of using database applications has little relationship with end-user satisfaction. This may be due to the relative simplicity of the tested subjects for experienced users. The more experienced users tend to score significantly higher than novice users with respect to learning performance.

The post-hoc test (Wilcox, 1987) was analyzed in order to verify the formulated hypotheses. Table 4 presents the post hoc analysis of behavior modeling modes on end-user satisfaction. Table 5 presents the post hoc analysis of behavior modeling modes on far-knowledge transfer effectiveness. The results indicate

Table 4. Post hoc analysis of BM modes on end-user satisfaction

BM Modes		Mean Difference	Significance
FBM	SBM	.8840*	.015
	VBM	1.3949*	.001
SBM	FBM	-.8840*	.015
	VBM	.5109	.360
VBM	FBM	-1.3949*	.001
	SBM	-.5109	.360

* $\sigma = 0.05$

Table 5. Post hoc analysis of BM modes on far-knowledge transfer effectiveness

BM Modes		Mean Difference	Significance
FBM	SBM	1.92*	.021
	VBM	-.44	.857
SBM	FBM	-1.92*	.021
	VBM	-2.37*	.017
VBM	FBM	.44	.857
	SBM	2.37*	.017

* $\sigma = 0.05$

that subjects taking FBM have higher perceived usefulness than the two online asynchronous treatments. This finding supports H1a and H1b. Contrary to these hypotheses, students receiving VBM did not express higher satisfaction level than students receiving SBM. The existence of reversed relationship in the measure of far-knowledge transfer may be due to higher expectation of VBM than SBM. However, its statistical evidence on H1c is not clearly indicated. Technical barriers of retaining the same resolution level as SBM in VBM course materials may not properly meet the expectation of students.

Our findings did not support H2a, H2b, and H2c. First, VBM and SBM groups scored higher than FBM in the measure of near-knowledge transfer. Second, while students receiving VBM scored higher than those receiving SBM, the score differential was not statistically significant. The similar performance in the measure of near-knowledge transfer across three behavior modeling modes indicates that the element of social presence may have no effects on the dependent variable.

H3a is not supported because the VBM group scored higher than FBM, even though there is no significant difference between these two modes. This may indicate that both FBM and VBM modes present a similar degree of social presence to students. The effect size seems to be much bigger between SBM and any other two behavior modeling modes. Both the FBM and VBM groups outperformed the SBM group with statistical difference. H3b and H3c are supported. Our speculation that social presence has impacts on far-knowledge transfer effectiveness is partially supported.

Correlation tests showed that a positive correlation exists between end-user satisfaction and three elements of the social presence attribute—control (0.621, p=0.01), sensory (0.559, p=0.01) and distraction (0.446, p=0.01). Realism (-0.086) is the only social element that is reported as having no correlation with the measure. These findings do confirm with our speculation that the social presence would have impacts on the satisfaction levels of end-users who take online asynchronous training. That is, subjects taking FBM expressed a higher degree of control, realism, sensory, and distraction than VBM. And, subjects taking VBM have a higher degree of social presence than those taking SBM. The same pattern of evidence is also detected on the correlation tests between social presence elements and the other two dependent variables—near- and far-knowledge transfer effectiveness. These evidences further affirm the importance of integrating social presence elements into online asynchronous training.

Discussion

Behavior modeling allows students to imitate the behavior of instructors in the F2F environment while preserving the strength of induction and deduction pedagogy.

Online asynchronous students may not be as receptive to behavior modeling course materials with high social presence because it is harder for students to imitate the behavior of instructors that F2F students can receive. The reality has necessitated the trade-off among different training behavior modeling modes. Therefore, key challenges ahead of us are to understand whether the trade-off is necessary. No significant difference may exist among three behavior modeling modes in terms of their social presence impacts on end-user satisfaction and learning performance. If this is the case, lights may need to be shed on non-technological issues. Otherwise, technological barriers, particular the bandwidth and course materials with a high social presence element, may still be an issue.

This study indicated that students assimilating software knowledge through either VBM or SBM achieved comparable levels of satisfaction. However, most of the students still reported higher satisfaction by taking the FBM than the other two online asynchronous behavior modeling approaches. This result, somewhat consistent with the stated hypotheses, indicates the differential impacts of social presence appear to be much higher between F2F and OAL environment. VBM and SBM deliver the same degree of a social presence element that leads to a similar satisfaction level.

Social presence seems to not be a crucial factor contributing to the effectiveness of transferring near-knowledge. Three behavior modeling modes of training lead to no differential impacts. The step-by-step element of the instruction approach seems to be more important than the social presence element. Three behavior modeling modes of training retain the induction element, thereby allowing students to have the same mastery level of software command and functions.

Counter to the findings, social presence elements did lead to higher performance in far-knowledge transfer effectiveness. FBM and its counterpart VBM preserve a comparable degree of social presence that contributes to higher mean scores than SBM. This evidence confirms our viewpoints that behavior modeling modes with higher social presence would have higher impacts on far-knowledge transfer than behavior modeling modes with lower social presence.

Limitations

Course materials of VBM and SBM were delivered to students through a projector. Technical barriers to have students take advantage of higher levels of student control and flexibility available in OAL environment seem to be the issues which lead to insignificant differences of end-user satisfaction between VBM and SBM. Most of answers towards the open-ended question, "What were missing from or needed to be added to the online training session?" centered on the control issue. One student commented that "sometimes there was confusion and the training went on further and caused some confusion." Another participant stated that she needs "the ability to stop and go back, just in case you missed something." Another way of expressing the lower control level of the course materials includes the control of audio quality and learning pace. Students with varying degrees of experiences and knowledge in database applications expressed dissatisfaction with the play speed of course materials and the frequency of repeating some basic commands. For instance, one student stated, "maybe the sound could be better and a little bit slower pace." While other students suggested that "background noise should be omitted—they were distracting;" "long pauses should be omitted;" and "it may not have been necessary to instruct the users on how to drag and drop when creating the queries (at least not more than once)."

Although the study was not designed to have replay/forward/backward functions, the degree of control seems to be an issue that is here to stay. Given no differential impacts on the end-user satisfaction and near-knowledge transfer, we will not be able to determine whether the control or social presence is a more influential factor. Despite the limitations, we conclude that the control factor is a less important issue than the social presence factor to the effectiveness of far-knowledge transfer. Subjects of the study taking VBM and SBM were given no control of the replay/forward/backward functions. Yet, we can clearly identify the differential impacts of social presence on the measure of far-knowledge transfer. These evidences point out the possibility that the control factor may have impacts on the end-user satisfaction and near-knowledge transfer. The study could not test or quantify this possibility because the technical barriers of having the replay/forward/backward functions enabled for all students could not be overcome. That is why open-ended questions were used to measure participants' opinions about the potential value of such functions. Additionally, the control element of social presence is also measured using a survey. The findings indicate that three modes of behavior modeling training do provide a satisfactory level of control. Future studies to measure end-user satisfaction, near-knowledge transfer, and the degree of control may need to be performed to directly investigate these relative impacts.

A second limitation concerns the existence of potential flaws in recording quality and speed. Although a survey to measure the realism factor of VBM and SBM was conducted, no significant impacts on three dependent variables could be identified. This may result from the varying perceptions of audio and video quality, pace, and so forth, among all participants. A better instrument to measure these perceptions should be used next time to serve as covariates for further analysis.

Because of unequal cell sizes of the three treatments, the assumptions of MANOVA and ANOVA had to be complied with to improve the study's reliability. Most of their assumptions were met, except those of independent observations and equal variance-covariance. Participants receiving FBM treatment are students from one of the universities. Other participants are students from the second university. They received VBM and SBM treatments. The former is a private university while the latter is a state university. Students' demographical background may pose a potential threat to the assumption of the independent observations. Additionally, the assumption of equal variance-covariance may also be endangered. The correlation test indicates that students' self-reported GPA, class year, and frequency of using database application positively correlate with learning outcomes. Interpreting our findings may require the consideration of the correlation effect.

In addition to the potential threats of internal validity, the experimental study is also constrained with the generalizability of its findings to the assimilation of conceptual knowledge. However, we do believe that this would not be an issue because the study was principally rooted in end-user computing field and had a clear objective of improving the learning effectiveness of IT skills, that is, primarily procedural knowledge. Still, researchers can make the generalizability of our findings a less debatable issue by replicating the study with different applications or with different research methodologies.

Conclusion and Implications

While the importance of learning strategy and of degree of a student's control may continue to prevail, the design of course materials with a higher social presence element may need to be properly incorporated in the OAL environment. Doing so allows students to improve their satisfaction level and far-knowledge transfer. There are two options to integrate our findings into the implementation of online asynchronous software training. In the scenario that students are unfamiliar with an OAL system or environment and face-to-face meetings can take place at the beginning of the session, a two-phased hybrid approach could be more effective than a pure online behavior modeling approach. Instructors may want to first conduct FBM approach in the beginning of training sessions before students' familiarize themselves with the training platform. Once the introduction phase is concluded, the VBM mode of training could be assimilated to accommodate the personal schedule of the instructor and students. Based on our findings, the hybrid approach may lead to the same degree of end-user satisfaction and learning performance, particularly in far-knowledge transfer.

In the second scenario, one in which most of students have had experiences of taking online asynchronous training and are familiar with online asynchronous system, VBM could be as useful as FBM in terms of improving end-user satisfaction and far-knowledge transfer. Contingent upon which scenario a instructor is faced with, the two-phased hybrid of FBM and SBM and pure SBM may need to be used interchangeably.

A salient fact is that conducting online asynchronous software training is much more complex than the choice between hybrid and pure behavior modeling modes.

When faced with a more complex learning environment (e.g., subjects with varying cultural and educational backgrounds, IT skills, cognitive ability, and learning platforms), control, interaction, and other factors may have more influential impacts than social presence factors on the learning outcomes (Piccoli, Ahmad, & Ives, 2001). Investigating those factors not within the scope of the study may need to be further probed.

These preliminary results suggest a number of avenues for future research. We found that the degree of control may enhance or relegate the learning outcomes of students. Too much control by an instructor may risk devaluing the merits of personalized and flexible learning experiences. Without a certain degree of control by an instructor, students may risk over-exercising the merits of flexible learning experiences that may lead to distraction and degraded learning productivity. How to balance the degree of control relegated to students and based on what factors may need to be researched.

Our findings also indicate that personal attributes (e.g., experiences with targeted software, class year, or GPA) correlated with learning outcomes. Some students complained that learning materials were not customized for them. Their answers are either "too fast," or "too slow" for certain commands, such as "how to drag and drop when creating the queries." Future research direction may want to focus on the capability of online asynchronous training session to present alternatives for students with varying personal backgrounds. For instance, an instructor may want to distribute to students a package of learning materials with differential control levels. The package may include three modes of behavior modeling approach in VCD format (e.g., .avi file) or video streaming formats for few popular applications (Realplayer™, Windows Media® Player and QuickTime®). This technological design would allow researchers to closely examine the importance of control factor.

The human dimension is far more challenging to an instructor in a pure OAL environment where in-class instruction never takes place. A wide variety of individual characteristics may lead to the incapability of any instructor to individualize programs for all students. This leads to inefficiency of producing online course materials and ineffectiveness of satisfying end-users. The friction between the users' desire for learning flexibility and instructors' scarce resources is "the biggest challenge in online learning" (Cameron, Beam, & Beam, 2000, p. 101). Nonetheless, future research may be able to cope with the challenges by examining the impacts of cognitive styles on the effectiveness of different online asynchronous functions. For instance, researchers who are interested in the "Discussion Forums" function may want to investigate the usefulness of forming forums based on leadership, learning, or creativity styles.

Students with different creativity styles may be receptive to different tasks (Fellers & Bostrom, 1993). The online asynchronous platform could be a fertile environment that can be used to support both explorative and generative tasks. Since the student-centered environment improves the accessibility and availability of information and domain experts (instructors and knowledgeable classmates), it is possible that the production of creativity could be more efficient than the traditional F2F environment (Csikszentmyhalyi, 1990). However, whether the OAL is suitable for any particular creativity style remains an open question.

In conclusion, this study clearly illustrated the differential impacts of three behavior modeling modes of software training, namely FBM, VBM, and SBM, on end-user satisfaction and knowledge transfer effectiveness. In addition, the study reiterated the potential of presenting viable and effective alternatives to exercise different behavior modeling modes of training in the online asynchronous learning environment.

References

Bayman, P., & Mayer, R. E. (1988). Using conceptual models to teach BASIC computer programming. *Journal of Educational Psychology, 80*(3), 291-298.

Belanger, F., & Van Slyke, C. (2000). Information technology learning and performance. *Communications of the ACM, 18*(1), 61-70.

Bolt, M. A., Killough, L. N., & Koh, H. C. (2001). Testing the interaction effects of task complexity in computer training using the social cognitive model. *Decision Sciences, 32*(1), 1-20

Bostrom, R. P., Olfman, L., & Sein, M. K. (1990). The importance of learning style in end-user training. *MIS Quarterly, 14*(1), 101-119.

Cameron, B., Beam, M., & Beam, P. (2000). Creation, costs and management: The measure of full-service online learning. In *Proceedings of IEEE Professional Communication Society International Professional Communication Conference*, Cambridge, MA, and *Proceedings of the 18th Annual ACM International Conference on Computer Documentation: Technology & Teamwork* (pp. 99-109). Piscataway, NJ: IEEE Educational Activities Department.

Chen, C. C., Olfman, L., & Harris, A. L. (2005). Differential impacts of social presence on the behavior modeling approach. *International Journal of Technology and Human Interaction, 1*(2), 64-84.

Compeau, D., Olfman, L., Sein, M., & Webster, J. (1995). End-user training and learning. *Communication of the ACM, 39*(7), 40-48.

Csikszentmyhalyi, M. (1990). *Flow: The psychology of optimal experience*. New York: HarperCollins.

Daft, R. L., & Lengel, R. H. (1986). A proposed integration among organizational information requirements, media richness, and structural design. *Management Science, 32*(4), 554-571.

Davis, D. L., & Davis, D. F. (1990). The effect of training techniques and personal characteristics on training end users of information systems. *Journal of Management Information Systems, 7*(2), 93-110.

Davis, G. B., & Olson, M. H. (1984). *Management information systems: Conceptual foundations, structure, and development.* New York: McGraw-Hill, Inc.

Fellers, J. W. & Bostrom, R. P. (1993). Application of group support systems to promote creativity in information systems organizations. *Proceedings of the Twenty-Sixth Hawaii International Conference on Systems Sciences, '93.*

Fulk, J. (1993). Social construction of communication technology. *Academy of Management Journal, 36*(4), 921-950.

Gregorc, A. F. (1982). *An adult's guide to style.* Columbia, CT: Gregorc Associates.

Harris, T. L., & Scwahn, W. E. (1961). *Selected readings on the learning process.* New York: Oxford University Press.

Ives, B., Olson, M., & Baroudi, S. (1983). The measurement of user information satisfaction. *Communications of the ACM, 26*(10), 785-793.

Kerlinger, F. N., & Lee, H. B. (2000). *Foundations of behavioral research.* New York: Harcourt Brace College Publishers.

Kirpatrick, D. L. (Ed.). (1967). Evaluation of training. *Training and development handbook.* New York: McGraw-Hill.

Kolb, D. A. (1984). *Experimental learning: Experience as the source of learning and development.* Englewood Cliffs, NJ: Prentice-Hall.

Lavooy, M. J., & Newlin, M. H. (2003). Computer mediated communication: On-line instruction and interactivity. *Journal of Interactive Learning Research, 14*(2), 157-165.

Lewin, K. (1951). *Field theory in social science: Selected theoretical papers.* New York: Harper & Row.

Mennecke, B. E., Crossland, M. D., & Killingsworth, B. L. (2000). Is a map more than a picture? The role of SDSS technology, subject characteristics, and problem complexity on map reading and problem solving. *MIS Quarterly, 24*(4), 601-627.

Mitchell, J. L. (2000). *The effect of matching teaching style with learning style on achievement and attitudes for women in a Web-based distance education course.* IN: Indiana State University.

Palvia, S., Palvia, P. C., & Zigli, R. M. (Eds.) (1992). Global information technology environment: Key MIS issues in advanced and less-developed nations. In *The global issues of information technology management.* Hershey, PA: Idea Group Publishing.

Piccoli, G., Ahmad, R., & Ives, B. (2001). Web-based virtual learning environments: A research framework and a preliminary assessment of effectiveness in basic IT skills training. *MIS Quarterly, 25*(4), 401-426.

Ramsden, P. (Ed.). (1988). Context and strategy: Situational influences on learning. *Learning strategies and learning styles.* New York: Plenum Press.

Ross, J. L., & Schultz, R. A. (1999, Fall). Using the World Wide Web to accommodate diverse learning styles. *Journal of Education for Students Placed at Risk (JESPAR), 47*(4), 123-29.

Simon, S. J., Grover, V., Teng, J. T. C., & Whitcomb, K. (1996). The relationship of information system training methods and cognitive ability to end-user satisfaction, comprehension, and skill transfer: A longitudinal field study. *Information Systems Research, 7*(4), 466-490.

Swan, K. (2002). Immediacy, social presence, and asynchronous discussion, In J. Bourne, & J. C. Moore (Eds.), *Elements of quality online education: Volume 3* (pp. 157-172). Needham: Sloan Center for Online Education.

Tucker, M. A. (2005). E-Learning evolves. *HRMagazine, 50*(10), 74-78.

Vessey, I., & Galletta, D. (1991). Cognitive fit: An empirical study of information acquisition. *Information System Research, 2*(1), 63-84.

Wexley, K. N., & Baldwin, T. T. (1986). Post-training strategies for facilitating positive transfer: An empirical exploration. *Academy of Management Journal, 29*(3), 503-520.

Wexley, K. N., & Latham, G. P. (1991). *Developing and training human resources in organizations* (2nd ed.). New York: HarperCollins.

Wilcox, R. R. (1987). *New statistical procedures for the social sciences: Modern solutions to basic problems.* Hillsdale, NJ: Lawrence Erlbaum Associates, Publishers.

Yi, M. Y., & Davis, F. D. (2003). Developing and validating an observational learning model of computer software training and skill acquisition. *Information Systems Research, 14*(2), 146.

Zack, M. H. (1993). Interactivity and communication mode choice in ongoing management groups. *Information Systems Research, 4*(3), 207-239.

Chapter VII

The Sociotechnical Nature of Mobile Computing Work:
Evidence from a Study of Policing in the United States

Steve Sawyer
The Pennsylvania State University, USA

Andrea Tapia
The Pennsylvania State University, USA

Abstract

*In this chapter, we discuss the sociotechnical nature of mobile computing as used by three policing agencies within the United States. Mobile devices, access, and service were provided via a third generation wireless network to a focal application, Pennsylvania's Justice **NET**work (JNET). JNET is a secure Web-based portal connecting authorized users to a set of 23 federated criminal justice and law enforcement databases via a query-based interface. In this study, we conceptualize mobility and policing as a sociotechnical ensemble that builds on the social-shaping of technology perspective and the tradition of sociotechncial theorizing focusing on the co-design of work practices and technologies to support work. Drawing* *from the social informatics tradition, we turn a critical, empirical, and contextual lens on the practices of mobility and work. Our analysis of the data leads us to find that the social and the technical are still separate in this mobile work context. This simple view of social and technical as related, but distinct, often leads to problems with collecting and interpreting evidence of ICT-based system's design and use. We further note this over-simplification of sociotechnical action is likely to continue unless more viable analytic approaches are developed and the assumptions of the current techno-determinist approaches challenged more explicitly.*

Introduction

One of the many alluring possibilities of mobile computing is that people will be able to access computing resources while on the move. In organizational contexts, mobile computing (or mobility as we refer to it here) engenders scenarios of increased productivity through instant access to computing resources at any time from anywhere. Here, we explore the sociotechnical nature of this envisioned future for mobility. In the social informatics tradition, we turn a critical, empirical, and contextual lens on the practices of mobility (Kling, 1999, 2000; Kling, Rosenbaum, & Sawyer, 2005; Sawyer & Eschenfelder, 2002).

We first explain why policing is an appropriate domain in which to explore mobility and work. We then conceptualize mobility as a sociotechnical ensemble. In subsequent sections, we lay out the research, outline our data collection and analysis, then present and discuss seven findings. We conclude by focusing on implications regarding sociotechnical analysis.

Why Focus on Policing?

There are at least three reasons why policing is an appropriate domain for studying mobility. First, police officer's work has always been highly mobile. It is also knowledge-intensive and pervasive (for more on this, see Manning, 2003). Second, there continues to be great interest in using ICT to better support police officer's information needs. For example, Manning (1996), in his study of cellular phone take-up among police, reported on the long-standing disparity between police officer's information needs and the abilities of the ICT used to provide them that information.[1] Third, policing and criminal justice have long been a focus of academic study and that provides us with extensive literatures on police work, the social norms, informal and formal organizational governance mechanisms, and an understanding of their technological basis (see Klockars & Mastrofski, 1991; Manning, 1977, 2003).[2]

Current research findings provide contrary views as to whether the take-up of ICT are driving the organization and structure of police departments or if it is the reverse (Lin, Hu, & Chen, 2004; Manning, 2003; NASCIO, 2003; Taylor, Epper, & Tolman, 1998). Evidence clearly shows that the uptake of new computer-based systems and uses of mobile technologies (beyond the nearly omni-present radio communications suite in most cars and with most police officers in the U.S.) is accelerating in the U.S. (Nunn, 2001). Partly, this attention comes in response to the country's increased attention to Homeland Security (Rudman, Clarke, & Metzel, 2003), although efforts to improve policing through advanced computing pre-date current attention (Northrup, Kraemer, & King, 1995). The limited functionality and advanced age of many criminal justice and police systems further magnifies this attention (Brown, 2001).

Contemporary research also suggests that police are open-minded about new technologies (wireless and otherwise) and generally view favorably the potential of new technologies to change policing (Lin et al., 2004; Nunn & Quinet, 2002). In fact, evidence shows that most police departments across the United States have one-to-three year plans either to implement wireless technology or have already implemented some form of wireless technology (Dunworth, 2000). To support these efforts, both the United States Departments of Homeland Security (DHS) and Justice (DoJ) provide a range of grants to support information technology innovations in police departments throughout the nation. In addition, there is funding by local jurisdictions and a variety of other sources, including internally generated revenue, such as fines, to support technological innovation.

Mobile Computing as a Sociotechnical Ensemble

Sociotechnical perspectives focus both conceptual and analytical attention on three concepts: that which is social, that which is technical and their inter-relations. In our study of mobile access to computing resources for police work, the sociotechnical perspective helps us to highlight that mobility is a complex and interdependent Web of relations among people (workers and managers), their organizational rules and roles, and various computing resources (such as the technical aspects of the mobile infrastructure, devices used, information sources, and applications accessed). Following Orlikowski and Iacono (2001), we conceptualize mobile access to computing resources as an *ensemble* comprising the wireless network, access devices, applications being used, information and data (both structures and content), procedures followed, norms of behavior (relative to events, systems, and others), governance structures, and both institutional and environmental constraints.

Conceptualizing mobility as a sociotechnical ensemble helps highlight the nuanced and multi-faceted inter-dependencies uniting people and what they do with computing resources and how they are designed and used. We further believe that what is social and what is technical are engaged in certain times and places and in certain ways. Thus, we build on the work of policing by focusing on specific events and situate these events in specific times and places. This contextual frame provides us the means to ground the analysis of the sociotechnical interactions.

The particular interactions among these constructs will likely vary by situation. For example, in a routine[3] event such as a traffic stop, these constructs are tied together in a prescribed way. There are policies regarding the use of the car and personal (attached to the officer's uniform) radio, a standard set of practices that guide the set of interactions the officer has with both the police dispatcher and with the driver of the car being stopped, particular rules about the information needed from police resources (such as registration, license plate numbers, car details, and even data on the driver based on the driver's license proffered to the officer), and what data the officer can and should collect. Escalation procedures are proscribed, and these vary based on time of day, assessments of the local situation, and other operational considerations.

For instance, imagine that a sergeant[4] sees a pick-up truck speeding down a breakdown lane to avoid stopped traffic in the travel lanes and gives chase. The driver of the truck sees the police car giving chase and, as is customary in the U.S., pulls over to the side of the road. The sergeant sees that the driver is agitated to the point where he is cursing out the vehicle's window; the truck is shaking from "omni-directional fury," and he calls for back-up from his car radio. While waiting for back-up, the officer puts on black leather gloves (in case they scuffle), unsnaps his weapon's securing strap (in case it goes beyond scuffling), calls in to police dispatch with the vehicle information, and then switches to his body radio, talk-activated. With the radio live (and all other officers on that frequency quiet, and the police dispatcher dispassionately updating time until back-up arrives),[5] the sergeant approaches the upset driver and starts the (relatively-prescribed) process of gathering particular information on the driver's identity as the first step in writing up a traffic citation. The back-up officer arrives while the sergeant is confronting the driver, pulls up diagonally in front of the stopped pickup (to reduce the possibility of a "drive-off") and stands in plain view and direct line of sight to the driver, weapon at the ready.

A more common traffic stop will have less drama for the driver (but perhaps some irritation), may not require back-up, bring out the visible presence of force, and likely does not escalate until the driver receives multiple citations. But, both traffic stops engage the same set of devices, applications, network, common information, and data flows; draw on the same governance structures; follow the same set of procedures (albeit down differing paths, but paths stemming from the same procedural guides); and reflect common and well-developed norms of policing behavior (norms both explicitly taught through extensive training and also learned and reinforced by doing policing).

We acknowledge that there are several active streams of sociotechnical research/ theorizing (see Horton, Davenport, & Wood-Harper, 2005). For example, the European tradition of sociotechnical theorizing (which we build on here) takes a social shaping of technology (SST) perspective. The SST perspective highlights that the material characteristics and actions of any technology are shaped by the social actions of the designers, the specific uses of that technology, and the evolving patterns of use over time. Conceptualizing mobility and policing as a sociotechnical ensemble builds on the social-shaping of technology perspective (SST) (Bijker; 1995; Law & Bijker, 1992; Mackay & Gillespie, 1992; MacKenzie & Wajcman, 1985; Williams & Edge, 1996).

In doing this, we reject both technological determinism and social constructivist approaches in favor of the mutually-constituted view of material technologies as shaping and being shaped by evolving social processes. Both polarized frameworks have problems with agency, in that constructivists give none to technology and the technological determinists attribute none to society. Both are linear, one-dimensional, blackbox the artifact, and only address the outcomes of technological change (Feenberg, 1991; Thomas, 1994).

We draw from the SST perspective because it facilitates the examination of the larger context of technological change, the processes of technological change, and most specifically the content of the technological change itself (Williams & Edge, 1996). Central to the SST framework is the concept of choice, in that technological innovation and development can be represented by a series of choices of one technological path over another through a process of negotiation and sometimes leading to irreversibility and lock-in of certain technologies (Arthur, 1989; Callon, 1993; Collinridge, 1992; Cowan, 1992; Rosenberg, 1994). And, finally, the SST perspective is particularly adept at exposing the governance, control, and polical motivations behind technological choice and development, critically exposing privilege and power (Bijker, 1993; Hard, 1993; Latour, 1988; Winner, 1977, 1980;)

A second, work-studies tradition of sociotechnical theorizing focuses on the co-design of work practices and technologies to support work. This co-design perspective has been taken up in North America and evolved in two ways. The first is a benign neglect of the interaction between what is social and technical, leading to an evocation of the concepts without a concomitant analytical activity (see Scacchi, 2004, for a critical discussion). The SST approach is more recent and reflects social informatics in that the efforts are focused on developing specific analytic approaches that make explicit aspects of the social, the technical, and their interaction (see Kling, McKim, & King, 2001).

Rather than focusing on a specific theoretical approach to examining the sociotechnical action of policing and mobility, we engage Bijker's (1995) principles of sociotechnical change theory to illustrate the generic goals of this approach and to discuss the theoretical tensions that exist in sociotechnical IT research. These tensions provide a range of possibilities for specific sociotechnical research efforts. Here, we use them as orienting principles for our conceptualization of mobility and the consequent design of our research, data collection, and analysis.

Bijker's (1995) four principles of sociotechnical change theory are derived from work in the sociology of technology. These four principles provide a set of goals for any theory that strives to take a sociotechnical perspective: the *seamless web* principle, the principle of *change and continuity*, the *symmetry* principle, and the principle of *action and structure*. The seamless web principle states that any sociotechnical analysis should not *a priori* privilege technological or material explanations ahead of social explanations, and vice versa. The principle of change and continuity argues that sociotechnical analyses must account for both change and continuity, not just one or the other. The symmetry principle states that the successful working of a technology must be explained as a process, rather than assumed to be the outcome of "superior technology." Success and/or failure of a particular technology are explained as a result of socio-technological developments, not as a cause of those developments. Success is in the eye of beholder. The actor and structure principle states that sociotechnical analyses should address both the actor-oriented side of social behavior, with its actor strategies and micro-interactions, and structure-oriented side of social behavior, with its larger collective and institutionalized social processes.

While Bijker's principles provide a set of ideals for sociotechnical research to strive for, in practice they illustrate tensions to be managed in the research process. Given the space limitations, in the analysis to follow, we focus on highlighting findings relative to our concepts and not specifically examining how the four principles guide this work.

Evidence from a Field Trial of Policing, Computing, and Mobility

To explore the sociotechnical perspective on productivity and the effects on work due in part to pervasive access to computing resources, we report on a field study[6] of police officer's uses of an integrated criminal justice system accessed via the public wireless data network from laptops and personal digital assistants (PDA) provided to the participants (see Sawyer & Tapia, 2003, 2004; Tapia & Sawyer, 2005a, 2005b) Each element of our field trial is discussed next.

Mobile Access to Pennsylvania's Justice Network

Mobile access for this trial was done via a third generation (3G) data network. In the U.S., 3G networks are rolling out (typically based on population density) and mirror the cellular phone network in terms of coverage. However, 3G networks use Internet protocols, packet switching (and, thus, digital packets), spread-spectrum transmission (which is inherently more secure than cellular and 2G standards), and can sustain throughput speeds of up to 150 kilobits per second. The 3G data networks in the U.S. are private and multiple providers compete directly in each market. While wireless coverage is extensive, no one carrier provides complete coverage of the geography of the U.S., and there may be gaps in service within covered areas. Moreover, collectively, all providers' coverage does not cover the geography of the U.S., and a service gap in one providers' coverage is not alleviated by the coverage of a second. The major carriers in the U.S. have deployed their 3G networks in different ways and at different rates.[7] Generally, though, they have focused on deploying in areas where they are most populated (cities and suburbs) and most traveled (along major highways). Costs, reliability, and coverage vary greatly in all other areas (Federal Communications Commission, 2002)

The focal application was Pennsylvania's **J**ustice **NET**work (JNET),[8] a secure Web-based portal connecting authorized users to a set of 23 federated criminal justice and law enforcement databases via a query-based interface. The JNET architecture is characterized by four elements. First, and as noted, for the user it acts as a portal to the criminal-justice-related databases of the Commonwealth of PA (and the U.S. federal government). The data are owned by the relevant state or federal agency (for example, PA's Department of Transportation, or PennDOT, maintains driver's license records and a picture database), and JNET provides a query-based access to the driver's license photos. Second, JNET is a secure system. Users are carefully vetted before they get access, their use is tied to specific roles, and these roles grant them varying levels of access to the range of data available. Further, use is tied to secure connectivity (enabled through encryption and virtual private networks), and this requires several forms of identification to be used.[9] Users must also re-authenticate periodically during their sessions in order to assure security during use. And, re-authentication is required when accessing certain specific databases through JNET. Until the field trial we report on here, there was no mobile access: thus, security was done via fixed lines and desktop computers. Third, JNET also provides electronic messaging, e-mail, and reporting functions for users. These functions serve as a common message board across all criminal justice personnel in PA. The e-mail alerts provide a means for people to keep track of activities where they have some interests. For example, it is possible for a parole officer to set up a query on a particular name, social security number, or case number(s). If that name or those numbers come across the message board, he or she will be alerted and can more easily follow-up on their parolee. Fourth, JNET has been operational since early 2000, and it supports thousands of queries each month (and use has grown by nearly 10% per month since inception) (JNET, 2004).[10]

The third part of the mobile access to JNET is the device being used to provide mobile access to JNET (and to the Internet more broadly). This device must have a special 3G modem card and needs to be mobile. Most police cruisers have an integrated laptop, making this seemingly a trivial effort (put in the wireless modem card, load on the security software, and use a browser). However, there were a number of operational and legal issues that made this a non-trivial effort. For example, many of the laptops are not equipped with space to load the modem card. Battery draw on police cruisers is substantial, and this further limits laptop use (and the 3G modem cards draw substantial power to run the antenna and maintain connectivity). Moreover, some cruiser's laptops have other software whose security and operational/licensing requirements precluded additional applications from being added.

For officers not in a cruiser, the mobile device must be carried on their person. Again, this is not a trivial effort considering that almost every square inch of the average police person's body is covered by some piece of gear. Moreover, the combination of current equipment (including communications, weapons, body armor, etc.) is nearly 25 pounds. This means that the mobile device must often displace something the officer already carries. We return to this discussion later in the chapter.

Field Trial Design, Data Collection, and Analysis

The field trial's design focused attention to collecting data on the *wireless network's* use, *device* uses, *JNET*, and other *application's* uses, *information and data sharing*, and changes or alterations to police officer's *work practices* (particularly changes to in-field operations), *social norms* on computing/uses (particularly regarding the value and importance of both mobile access and JNET), and the officer's operational *governance* (particularly the role of dispatch). As we noted at this chapter's onset, in focusing on criminal justice we leverage the extensive knowledge of policing and also partially control the industrial (extra-organizational) factors by staying within one work domain.

The field trial also served as an intervention: mobile workers were provided with either a laptop or a personal digital assistant (PDA) and secure access to the public 3G network. This was done in two phases for pragmatic reasons. The first phase lasted three months, included five participants, and focused on laptop usage. The small number allowed us to refine data collection protocols and ensure that we could meet the technological demands of supporting the access, security, and application use demands of a demanding operational environment. The second phase began directly after the first phase's completion, involved 13 participants, lasted three months, and focused on PDA usage. All five of the participants in the first trial were part of the second trial. This provided us with a subset of users who were engaged in mobile access to JNET for six months. The two-phase trial's six-month duration was guided by practical constraints of user's ability to participate in a trial while doing their normal policing and official duties. The number included in the trial was constrained by the costs of providing devices, connectivity, and support to the officers.

Participants in both trials were police and other criminal justice officers from three organizations (one county-level and two local-level) located within one Pennsylvania county. Two incentives were used to motivate participants. First, we promised that all participants could keep the mobile device(s) they were given to use (late-model laptops and high-end PDAs, both equipped with 3G modem cards, and, in the case of the PDA, an external sleeve and battery pack to support the modem card). Second, we made it clear that the participants' input would be used to drive the design of JNET for criminal justice uses, particularly for mobile access. Participants mentioned that both were important to their deciding to engage. In addition, we worked with the department heads and unit police chiefs to ensure that officers were given official recognition for engaging in the field trial. Participating department heads and unit police chiefs were both enthusiastic and supportive.

We used seven forms of data collection. First, we did pre- and post-interviews (at the beginning and end of each trial period) of all users. In phase one, these were face-to-face, open-ended, and semi-structured interviews that lasted from 60 to 90 minutes. In phase two, we used a more structured, self-administered survey in place of some of the open-ended user interviews and followed-up with a phone-call discussion. Second, we led focus groups of users following the trials. These were voluntary, and only two participants did not participate (for schedule reasons). Third, all users completed a one-week time diary of work behavior during the field trial. Fourth, members of the research team did ride-alongs with users. We chose to ride-along with both police and court officers, and with both supervisors and patrol officers. Fifth, we gathered documents during all interviews, observations, and visits (and did extensive Web and library research to support the field work). Sixth, we engaged in informal weekly interactions (via phone, e-mail and in person) with users. Finally, we gathered data about laptop uses, wireless data transmission, and JNET usage via unobtrusive means (such as browser logs, server logs, and telecom activity logs). Data from the first six sources were either transcribed into digital format or collected at the source in digital format. Data from the usage logs came in digital format.

Our analysis focused on identifying issues with the 3G network's connectivity/reliability, speed and access, uses of JNET (and other sources/applications), information and data access, and the roles of the mobile devices. This was done through analysis of data drawn from the trouble-ticketing log, analysis of time use (drawn from the logs) regarding connection via 3G networks, volume of data transfer and time/usage of JNET, and through a series of topical analyses of the texts created from the six forms of intensive data collection.

Analysis of data regarding information and data sharing, work practices, social norms, and operational governance followed traditional qualitative data analysis approaches (see Miles & Huberman, 1994). In particular, we used three techniques: interim analysis of the data to guide both future data collection and its interpretation, explanatory even matrices, and content analysis of the transcripts, logs, and field notes.

Findings

We present and discuss seven findings. We find that police officer's uses of 3G *wireless networks* is dependent more on coverage and reliability of access than on speed (bandwidth). Certainly, higher throughput speeds are better than lower speeds (particularly when transferring driver's license photos, as we discuss later). However, if coverage is not certain, then officers either forget to access the network or become frustrated and actively choose to NOT access the network. Moreover, if an officer takes the time, cognitive energy, and effort to connect and the access attempt fails (for any number of reasons), it appears they quickly cease trying.

We find that the police officers in our study do not value laptops as access *devices*. They do, however, appreciate these devices for other activities (such as reports and so forth, not connected to wireless access). Police officers valued PDAs to an even greater degree. Again, these *devices* are valued for personal information management and not as connective devices to the 3G network. We did not attempt to trial pen-based or tablet computers: we suspect that these may combine the portability of a PDA with the power and screen size (an important issue for officers) of a laptop.

The mobile access to, and uses of, *JNET* and other *applications* was difficult to assess for two reasons. First, the low reliability of the network coverage made it difficult for officer's to access these applications. The officer had to become very familiar with coverage patterns (that is, where they could and could not gain access) and then be able to adjust their work patterns to accommodate this coverage. Second, authentication and security overhead in access complicated the log on procedures and caused connection drops. The two-factor log on procedures made it difficult for officers in the field to manage both connection and conduct their work. The design of JNET (which asks for updates on passwords and re-authentication as different databases are searched) meant that it was easy for JNET to shut down the session unless the officer devoted considerable attention to managing the interaction. This considerable attention to JNET had to come at the expense of attention to other aspects of the officer's work. In any operational event (such as a traffic stop), the officer would not make this commitment.

Despite this difficulty, officers value JNET for its ability to provide them *information* about drivers, particularly the driver's license photos and driver's records. On this (and limited evidence of this) alone, officers prized mobile access to JNET and found value in mobility. We did not see any changes in *information and data sharing* for at least two reasons. First, the design of JNET for mobile access is to provide it to officers, instead of through police dispatch. Most of all of the other information and data sharing, however, goes through police dispatch (both in a controlled voice-based interaction and via current text-based systems that come to the police cruiser's onboard laptop).

We saw little changes to police officer's *work practices*. Perhaps this is not surprising—the operational environment of policing is harsh and sometimes fatal. Police train extensively, continually, and with great care to develop procedures to take an ambiguous situation and make it less so. Changes in operational procedures are, thus, slow to come, painstakingly thought out, and must be demonstrable improvements. If not, police are unlikely to risk their lives.

The great enthusiasm and interest on the uses of computing to improve policing seems to be one of the strong *social norms* that police carry forward (Manning, 2003). However, when confronted with changes to operational procedures and concerns with the computing system's reliability, the social norms of policing operations such as safety, professionalism, and force projection overwhelm the potential value of mobile access to computing resources that cannot be consistently demonstrated.

The trial of mobile access to JNET and other computing resources amplified the institutional embeddedness of the command and control structures in policing. In particular, the critical social, organizational, and technical roles that the police dispatcher plays came clear during this trial. The design of JNET for individual access does not work well within police officer's operational *governance*. Were JNET to be a dispatch-based access model, however, governance and information sharing would likely change more quickly.

A Sociotechnical Action Perspective

In this section, we reflect on these seven findings and general SST principles, and return to Bijker's (1995) four principles of sociotechnical change theory.

First, the social shaping of technology perspective (SST) lends itself to this analysis in three ways: through a focus on interpretive implementation, sociotechnical ensembles, and the concept of the boundary object.

While many sociotechnical theorists have focused on the innovation stage of technological development, SST allows for a central place for the stage of implementation and stresses the non-linear, transformative, interpretive, and iterative nature of this stage (Williams & Edge, 1996). Fleck (1988) describes this process as "innofusion," a struggle between design, trial, exploration, and use, as spiral, interactive, and complex. Using this lens, we can examine the struggle between the relevant social groups, including the designers of the PDA and laptop devices, the designers of the 3G wireless cards, the developers of the JNET software, the providers of the 3G wireless broadband service, the policing administration of various departments and the officer-users, as entering, perhaps unwittingly, into a collaborative design process for mobile JNET. The struggle that we witnessed between each of these groups trying to make the devices work can be seen as such a process.

The concept of sociotechnical ensembles is also highly useful in this setting. SST stresses that technology and organizations cannot be treated as separate entities. There exists a complex web of mutual dependency between all relevant social groups, devices, expertise, and information. Bijker uses the term *sociotechnical ensemble* to denote this network of objects, infrastructures, and humans and the roles they play (Bijker, 1995). These elements of the ensemble, whether human or technical, must work together to produce a functioning whole. We can clearly see the relationships of dependency within a sociotechnical ensemble in the mobile JNET trial, even more explicitly when the ensemble failed to perform to expectations. In order for this trial to have been labeled a success by all relevant social groups, the devices, service, and software would have needed to perform as promised. However, the wireless coverage was inconsistent and unreliable; the batteries were not sufficiently powerful to sustain required usage; the security protocols were tedious; the officers' tasks and information needs did not match what was offered; and the officers need for administrative and IT training and support was unmet. At each of these points, the ensemble failed to perform in conjunction and never approached harmony.

It is obvious that mobile JNET was defined differently to different relevant social groups. For the officers, mobile JNET was defined as a novelty, a potentially interesting tool to gain information in the field but not reliable, simple, or hands-free enough to use in critical life-or-death moments. For the developers of JNET, mobile JNET was an extension of an already-proven killer desktop application that just needed a few logistical bugs worked out to be a killer mobile application. For the device providers, mobile JNET was an open door into local government market development. For the 3G wireless providers, mobile JNET was a group of unanticipated users who taxed and challenged a system that was not designed for their use. These relevant social groups can also be seen as communities of practice who share a technological device in common, yet who interpret that device very differently. A boundary object is defined as an object that is located in the middle of a group of actors with divergent viewpoints (Bowker & Star, 1999; Star, 1989). The concept of the boundary object implies negotiation of definitions between different communities of practice of a common artifact. This negotiation is also a process infused with elements of competition, protection of one's assets and territory, ownership of the finial definition, and control of the object (Fox, 2000).

The principle of the seamless web is that analysis should not *a priori* privilege the technological explanations ahead of social explanations, and vice versa. The principle of change and continuity means that analysis must account for both change and continuity. The symmetry principle focuses analysis on the temporal processes by which the social and technical interact. The actor and structure principle makes clear that analysis must account for both action and structure. In Table 1, we summarize these principles relative to the seven findings we noted in the previous section, and, in the remainder of the text in this section, we discuss this summary.

Building on Table 1, we make three observations. First, the institutional structures that help to govern the work of policing serve as powerful moderators to both taking

Table 1. Sociotechnical analysis

Findings	Principles	Comments
Coverage and reliability of access more important than speed/ bandwidth	Seamless web	Technological features (bandwidth) were seen as more central than operational needs of officers (operational reliability).
PDA valued for personal use, not for mobile access	Symmetry	Take-up of the device is a social decision, shaped by technical characteristics, and often made for personal needs.
JNET and other *applications* are used when mobile	Change and continuity	The expectation that JNET would be valuable for mobile officers (as it has been for officers via fixed access) was borne out in the study.
Officers value *information* drawn from *JNET*	Change and continuity	The expectation that information received while mobile would be valued was borne out in the study.
No changes in *information and data sharing*	Actor and structure	Social and operational structures seemed to be resilient to new technologies of access and use.
No changes to police officer's *work practices* and *social norms*	Actor and structure	Work practices seemed to be resilient to new technologies of access and use.
No changes to work *governance*	Actor and structure	Governance structures seemed to be resilient to new technologies of access and use.

up and taking advantage of new practices such as having mobile access to computing resources and information. Even when the principles of change and continuity are instantiated with evidence that moving out access to high-value resources (from fixed to mobile connection) is welcomed, the structural pressures constrain action. And, the findings from this study provide more support for the principles of seamless web and symmetry. That is, there are no direct effects of new ICT on outcomes (as seen in the ways that PDAs were taken up and used in this trial). Nor is it possible to make predictions of change based on solely technological properties (as evidenced by the unfounded belief in bandwidth here).

Second, we observe that the current professional practice of evaluating new ICT does not seem to engage sociotechnical principles. For example, the failure to fully engage sociotechnical principles when designing and testing mobile access to JNET reflects a naïve view of sociotechnical action: that social and technical are distinct of one-another (and that change in one leads to change in the other). The findings we noted earlier are unsurprising: current institutional structures in policing were not considered (or, worse, ignored—as was the case with dispatch) when designing new work technologies. And, the technological elements must be considered on par with social elements: had this been more carefully considered, bandwidth would not have been the focus—it would have been reliability.

The field trial design reflects the collaboration between wireless service providers, device manufacturers, local and state police and information technology leaders, and faculty. That the resulting trial underplayed the sociotechnical issues leads us to theorize that organizational decision-makers, users, and technology evaluator's orientation towards problem-solving will make it attractive to focus on matching technical features with work and organizational needs. In doing this, they are not likely to address the systemic interactions or to consider extended interdependencies. In essence, this simplification in analysis comes at the cost of accuracy in implementation.

Sociotechnical approaches currently appear more likely to be applied in *post hoc* analysis. They become a comfortable frame for scholars to use. However, they are at best a weak analytic structure to base proactive action. That is, the principles are useful to frame and interpret evidence but are difficult to use in guiding specific designs. What is missing is the intermediate-level guidance linked to specific technologies or specific social actions. In the absence of this intermediate-level guidance, the principles are difficult to apply proactively.

Building on this, it seems important, if not imperative, that sociotechnical models provide more intermediate guidance. By this, we mean support for constraints and enablers tied to particular social actions or that highlight elements of particular technologies. This intermediate level of sociotechnical knowledge is likely to be represented as contingent or localized models. In doing this, such localized models point academics and practicing professionals more directly to dominant patterns of interactions and consequences and make these findings available in ways that more directly influence ICT/systems' design and organizational decision making.

In the United States, such a localized model might be found in the example of a single police officer in a vehicle. This officer has expectations of reliability in terms of his or her equipment including: the vehicle itself; communication equipment; weapons; connectivity via radio to a central dispatch office and other officers; and fast-arriving back-up sent by dispatch in times of need. This model would fail if the situation changed to a single officer on foot or on a bicycle, to multiple officers in a vehicle, or to officer/non-officer combinations. This intermediate model demands being situated if the sociotechnical ensembles of policing organizations, device designers, and software developers are going to proactively develop technologies for criminal justice institutions that are not destined for some form of failure.

Our final observation from this analysis is the over-simplification of sociotechnical action is likely to continue unless more viable analytic approaches are developed and the assumptions of the current techno-determinist approaches challenged more explicitly. Given this view, it seems likely that organizational decision makers, users, and ICT designers will have trouble making sense of evidence drawn from failed attempts to implement and use ICT based on their simple views of ICT use, cause, and effect. We believe the inability to understand this data is driven by the unsound approach of invoking direct effects of ICT use, not by the measurements taken or instruments used to gather evidence (e.g., Sawyer, Allen, & Lee, 2003).

While the research literature focused on the effects of ICT highlights the indirect and often nuanced relationships among use of ICT and performance, professional practice continues to press for the direct effects model of ICT value. This suggests that more robust, system or contingency, models of ICT effects are needed (e.g., Avgerou, 2002). This is one of the most active areas of scholarship in IT, and this activity needs to enter the texts, teaching cases, and classrooms of the next generation's IT leaders, organizational managers, and technology developers. For example, those who have focused specifically on the roles of mobile and fixed location uses of ICT in policing all note that the operational value derived from using new ICT-centric information systems is minimal if discernable (Ackroyd, Harper, Hughes, Shapiro, & Soothill, 1996; Dunworth, 2000; Meehan, 2000).

What seems important to us is a more focused effort to engage the principles of sociotechnical action in direct comparison to the bases of direct effects models (e.g., Kling & Lamb, 2000). They develop a comparative analysis of tool and Web models of computing relative to organizational activity. In doing this, they highlight both the seamless web principle (privileging neither the social nor the technical) and the principle of action and structure by highlighting the concept of a social actor—one that has agency but constrained by institutional structures (Lamb & Kling, 2003). Building on these two principles in the work reported here, we provide a means of representing the principle of change and continuity by explicitly linking elements of the technical structure of JNET, the institutional structures of police work, and the actions of police.

References

Ackroyd, S., Harper, R., Hughes, J., Shapiro, D., & Soothill, K. (1996). *New technology and police work*. Buckingham: Open University Press.

Arthur, W.B. (1989). Competing technologies, increasing returns and lock-in by historical events. *The Economics Journal*, *99*, 116-131.

Avgerou, C. (2002). *Information systems and global diversity*. Oxford: Oxford University Press.

Bijker, W. (1993). Do not despair: There is life after constructivism. *Science, Technology and Human Values, 18*(4), 113-138.

Bijker, W. (1995). Sociohistorical technology studies. In Jasanoff et al. (Eds.), *Handbook of science and technology studies* (pp. 229-256). London: Sage Publications.

Bijker, W., Hughes, T., & Pinch, T. (Eds.) (1987). *The social construction of technological systems: New directions in the sociology and history of technology*. Cambridge, MA: MIT Press.

Bijker, W., & Law, J. (Eds.) (1992). *Shaping technology/building society: Studies in socio-technical change*. Cambridge, MA: MIT Press.

Bowker, G. C., & Star, S. L. (1999). *Sorting things out: Classification and its consequences*. MIT Press.

Brown, M. M. (2001). The benefits and costs of information technology innovations: An empirical assessment of a local government agency. *Public Performance & Management Review, 24*(4), 351-366.

Callon, M. (1993). Variety and irreversibility in networks of technique conception and adoption. In D. Foray, & C. Freeman (Eds.), *Technology and the wealth of nations: The dynamics of constructed advantage* (pp. 232-268). London: Pinter.

Collinridge, D. (1992). *The management of scale: Big organizations, big decisions, big mistakes*. London: Routledge.

Cowan, R. (1992). High technology and the economics of standardization. In M. Dierkes, & U. Hoffmann (Eds.), *New technology and the outset: Social forces in the shaping of technological innovations* (pp. 279-300). Frankfurt; New York: Campus/Westview.

Dunworth, T. (2000). Criminal justice and the information technology revolution. In Horney (Ed.), *Policies, processes and decisions of the justice system* (Vol. 3, pp. 372-426). Washington, DC: National Institute of Justice/Office of Justice Programs.

Feenberg, A. (1991). *Critical theory of technology*. New York: Oxford University Press.

Fox, S. (2000). Communities of practice, Foucault and actor-network theory. *Journal of Management Studies, 37*(6), 853-867.

Hard, M. (1993). Beyond harmony and consensus: A social conflict approach to technology. *Science, Technology & Human Values, 18*(4), 408-432.

Horton, K., Davenport, E., & Wood-Harper, T. (2005). Exploring sociotechnical interaction with Rob Kling: Five "big" ideas. *Information, Technology and People*.

JNET. (2004). *Usage statistics*. Retrieved from http://www.pajnet.state.pa.us/pajnet/site/default.asp

Kling, R. (1999). What is social informatics, and why does it matter? *D-Lib Magazine, 5*(1). Retrieved from http://www.dlib.org:80/dlib/january99/kling/01kling.html

Kling, R. (2000). Learning about information technologies and social change: The contribution of social informatics. *The Information Society, 16*(3), 217-232.

Kling, R., & Lamb, R. (2000). IT and organizational change in digital economies: A socio-technical approach. In B. Kahin, & E. Brynjolfsson (Eds.), *Understanding the digital economy: Data, tools and research*. Cambridge, MA: MIT Press.

Kling, R., Rosenbaum, H., & Sawyer, S. (2005). *Understanding and communicating social informatics: A framework for studying and teaching the human contexts of information and communication technologies*. Medford, NJ: Information Today.

Klockars, C., & Mastrofski, S. (Eds.). (1991). *Thinking about police: Contemporary readings*. New York: McGraw-Hill.

Lamb, R., & Kling, R. (2003). Reconceptualizing users as social actors in information systems research. *MIS Quarterly, 27*(2), 197-235.

Latour, B. (1988). How to write "The Prince" for machines as well as machinations. In B. Elliott (Ed.), *Technology and social process* (pp. 20-43). Edinburgh: Edinburgh University Press.

Law, J., & Bijker, W. (1992). Technology, stability and social theory. In W. Bijker (Ed.), *Shaping technology/building society* (pp. 32-50). Cambridge, MA: MIT Press.

Lin, C., Hu, P., & Chen, H. (2004). Technology implementation management in law enforcement. *Social Science Computer Review, 22*(1), 24.

Mackay, H., & Gillespie, G. (1992). Extending the social shaping of technology approach: Ideology and appropriation. *Social Studies of Science, 22*(4), 685-716.

MacKenzie, D., & Wajcman, J. (Eds.) (1985). *The social shaping of technology: How the refrigerator got its hum.* Milton Keynes: Open University Press.

Manning, P. (1977). *Police work: The social organization of policing.* Prospect Heights, IL: Waveland Publishing.

Manning, P. (1996). Information technology in the police context: The "sailor" phone. *Information Systems Research, 7*(1), 275-289.

Manning, P. (2003). *Policing contingencies.* Chicago: University of Chicago Press.

Meehan, A. (2000). The transformation of the oral tradition of policing through the introduction of information technology. *Sociology of Crime, Law and Deviance, 2,* 107-132.

NASCIO. (2003). *Concept for operations for integrated justice information sharing version 1.0.* The National Association of State Chief Information Officers. Retrieved from https://www.nascio.org/publications/index.cfm

Northrup, A., Kraemer, K. L., & King, J. L. (1995). Police use of computers. *Journal of Criminal Justice, 23*(3), 259-275.

Nunn, S. (2001). Police information technology: Assessing the effects of computerization on urban police functions. *Public Administration Review, 61*(2), 221-234.

Nunn, S., & Quinet, K. (2002). Evaluating the effects of information technology on problem-oriented-policing: If it doesn't fit, must we quit? *Evaluation Review, 26*(1), 81-108.

Orlikowski, W., &. Iacono, S. (2001). Desperately seeking the "IT" in IT research—A call to theorizing the IT artifact. *Information Systems Research, 12*(2), 121-124.

Rosenbach, W., & Zawacki, R. (1989). Participative work redesign: A field study in the public sector. *Public Administration Quarterly, 43,* 111-127.

Rosenberg, N. (1994). *Exploring the black box: Technology, economics and history.* Cambridge, MA: Cambridge University Press.

Rudman, W., Clarke, R., & Metzel, J. (2003, July 29). *Emergency responders: Drastically underfunded, dangerously unprepared.* Report of an Independent Task Force Sponsored by the Council on Foreign Relations. Retrieved from http://www.cfr.org/pdf/Responders_TF.pdf

Sawyer, S., & Eschenfelder, K. (2002). Social informatics: Perspectives, examples, and trends. In B. Cronin (Ed.), *Annual review of information science and technology* (Vol. 36, pp. 427-465). Medford, NJ: Information Today Inc./ASIST.

Sawyer, S., & Tapia, A. (forthcoming). *Always articulating: Theorizing on mobile and wireless technologies*. The Information Society.

Sawyer, S., Tapia, A., Pesheck, L., & Davenport, J. (2004). Observations on mobility and the first responder. *Communications of the ACM, 47*(2), 62-65.

Sawyer, S., Wigand, R., & Crowston, K. (2005). Redefining access: Uses and roles of information and communications technologies in the residential real estate industry from 1995-2005. *Journal of Information Technology, 20*(4), 3-14.

Star, S. L. (1989). The structure of ill-structured solutions: Boundary objects and heterogeneous distributed problem solving. In *Distributed artificial intelligence, Vol. 2*. London: Pitman.

Tapia, A., & Sawyer, S. (2005a). The sociotechnical nature of mobile computing work: Evidence from a study of policing in the United States. *International Journal of Technology & Human Interaction, 1*(3), 1-14.

Tapia, A., & Sawyer, S. (2005b). Beliefs about computing: Contrary evidence from a study of mobile computing use. In K. Lytinnen, Y. Yoo, & J. DeGross (Eds.), *Designing ubiquitous information environments socio-technical issues and challenges* (pp. 21-40). London: Kluwer.

Taylor, M., Epper, R., & Tolman, T. (1998). *Wireless communications and interoperability among state and local law enforcement agencies* (National Criminal Justice Clearinghouse Rep. No. 168945). Washington, DC.

Thomas, R. J. (1994). Introduction. In *What machines can't do: Politics and technology in the industrial enterprise*. Berkeley: University of California Press.

Williams, R., & Edge, D. (1996). The social shaping of technology. *Research Policy, 25*, 865-899.

Winner, L. (1980). Do artifacts have politics? *Daedalus, 109*, 121-136.

Winner, L. (1993). Upon opening the black box and finding it empty: Social constructivism and the philosophy of technology. *Science, Technology & Human Values, 18*(3), 362-378.

Endnotes

[1]   Manning (1996) focused on the take-up and uses of cellular phones by police. Personal cellular phone ownership and use is now common among criminal justice officers. While the take-up and use of cellular phone is beyond the scope of this article, two attributes are worth noting. First, the officer's use their own (personal) cellular phones and do not consider them as part of their professional equipment. Second, personal use has made officers aware of issues with wireless coverage, reliability, and use.

2   Given the extensive literature on policing, in this chapter, we draw from but do not develop or discuss principle findings. Instead, we refer the interested reader to anthologies of such work (listed in our references and cited here). The interested reader can also find courses in crime, law, and justice offered in most sociology departments and the extensive material on the Web in locations such as the U.S. Department of Justice, the UK Home Office, and the International Association of Chiefs of Police.

3   Perhaps one of the more difficult parts of a police officer's job is to remember that even a seemingly common thing such as stopping a speeding car may lead to armed confrontation. Thus, training is focused on preventing common from becoming routine.

4   Policing in the United States is organized along paramilitary lines. Thus, sergeants are senior/experienced officers, typically with both patrol and supervisory responsibilities.

5   Most police in the United States work alone, which means: (1) they rely on the radio as a link to others and (2) the police dispatcher is a critical node in this linkage. The radio stays on, and no one else speaks so that all can listen for a gunshot or the words "officer down."

6   Our research design here builds on previous public-sector field studies of work (e.g., Rosenbach & Zawacki, 1989).

7   Details of the debate and key issues in wireless network deployment, coverage, access, and use are beyond the scope of this chapter.

8   For more information about JNET, see www.pajnet.state.pa.us.

9   Security in the trial was done via "two-factor" identification. This means having a physical key, called a dangle by the officers, that stores a digital record identifying the owner that is tied to a logical password that must be entered when the physical key is connected (via USB port) to the computer.

10   JNET is one of the earliest and most visible examples of a small and growing number of these integrated criminal justice information systems that are a focus on Homeland Security efforts in the United States. Others include the Capital Area Wireless Integrated Network (CAPWIN, see www.capwin.org), the automated regional justice administration system (ARJIS, see www.arjis.org), and a fast-growing number of municipal efforts, such as systems in Chicago, IL, Montgomery County, MD, and Los Angeles County, CA.

Chapter VIII

Rhetoric, Practice, and Context-Sensitivity in Sociotechnical Action:
The Compass Case

Giuseppina Pellegrino
University of Calabria, Italy

Abstract

Sociotechnical action, as interpreted in this chapter, comprises a wide array of elements which shape technological artefacts as socio-material and linguistic devices. Concepts grounded in different theoretical streams are used to account for the ambiguous and multiple process of technology construction. Categories of "interpretative flexibility," "inscription," "work-around," and "misunderstanding" are reviewed and used in this account. Starting from the implementation of an intranet-based knowledge management system in a 100-staff British firm, different courses of action in technology implementation and appropriation are analysed. Interpretations performed by different actors can raise misunderstanding, failure, and innovation in processes of negotiation and are strongly oriented by power issues. The gap between rhetoric of public discourse and practice situated in specific organisational contexts is argued to be crucial in framing expectations and patterns of sociotechnical action. Ambiguity and multiplicity of the knowledge management system studied (the Compass) illustrate how the mutual constitution of the social and the technical makes technology a "context-sensitive" artefact.

Introduction

The concept of sociotechnical action emerges from a dialogue between different theoretical streams which emphasise the necessity of a non-deterministic approach to technology. Among these "traditions," social informatics (Kling, 1999) and social construction of technology (Bijker, 1995; Bijker & Law, 1992) seem to be especially relevant in providing a rich account of how technology cannot be reduced to either a set of tools driving social change from outside or to a mere outcome of pre-existing social structures.

The horns of this apparent dilemma can be overcome through sociotechnical action as a concept able to account for the multiplicity and complexity of the process from which technology emerges.

Therefore, the core arguments of this contribution aim to understand the constitution of sociotechnical action along the following lines:

- Discursive frames setting up favourable links between technologies and a specific social order (Iacono & Kling, 2001);
- Gaps between rhetoric framed in public discourse and practice embedded in local contexts;
- Misunderstanding and ambiguity in the interpretative flexibility of technology (Bijker, 1995);
- Construction of technology as "success/failure" following narrative patterns (Fincham, 2002);
- Appropriation of technology as based on work-around (Pollock, 2005) performed on the vision inscribed in the artefact (Akrich, 1992);
- Multiple points of view as irreducible resources for sociotechnical action (Horton, Davenport, & Wood-Harper, 2005);
- Power issues which establish multiple institutional regimes of truth in knowledge management (Ekbia & Kling, 2003);
- Eventually, unintended outcomes in technology appropriation and use (e.g., marginalisation and non-use of technological artefacts).

These points will be explored with reference to strategies and dynamics enacted in building up an intranet-based knowledge management system (KMS) in a British company. By underlining constraints and problems actors experienced in such a process, the call for a sociotechnical approach oriented to unpack power, social, and organisational issues will be supported.

To de-construct the path of implementation and early appropriation of the KMS, the lens of misunderstanding will be used. Pragmatic and socio-linguistic studies of misunderstanding (Dascal, 1999; Weigand, 1999) emphasised how "coming to understanding" is a complex process, often constrained by differences in cultural and contextual frames. Such a process will be "evoked" to underline the crucial role of communication and discourse in shaping materialities of what is defined as "new technology." In the terms of sociotechnical action, the equivalent of "coming to understanding" can be found in the mutual constitution of the technical and the social itself as linguistic and material device. The result of such a mutual constitution does not bow to any pre-planned aim as many different worlds can be enacted through language (Berger & Luckmann, 1967). Indeterminacy of technology (cf. Horton et al., 2005) manifests itself through contradictory or competitive worlds, embedded and reflected in the current use and configuration of the technological system analysed.

Interestingly, the concept of misunderstanding emerges from the fieldwork, and in this sense, it may be appropriate to introduce it. Multiple misunderstandings characterised all the stages of construction of the enquired intranet system. The actors also often labelled the results of their multiple negotiations as originating from "misunderstandings." Ambiguity and different interpretations of the system fostered negotiations and conflicts among the actors: the company managers as official policy makers of the process; the clients as partners (at first) and then opponents to the use of an intranet by company consultants working at their sites; the software vendor that designed the system; the joint project team through which the whole project was managed; the system administrator; the office-based staff; and the company consultants. All of these actors at their different levels (individuals, workgroups, other organisations) contributed to shape the construction of what was called KMS or, with the official name, "the Compass" (from now onwards).

The chapter is structured as follows. Literature and public discourse about benefits and characteristics of an intranet as technology dedicated to corporate and business contexts will be presented in light of the concept of interpretative flexibility (Bijker, 1995). The gap between such a literature and critical studies of organisational practice in intranet implementation will be addressed as a key issue shaping sociotechnical action. Through an account of negotiations and misunderstandings centred on the Compass, multiple points of view on the process will be provided. Among them, the concept of knowledge management as supported or embedded in the intranet system will be analysed as imbued with power plays. The conclusive remarks and discussion will emphasise the mutual constitution of the technical and social dimension in technology as context-sensitive artefact, in order to theorise the Compass case and articulate a "sociotechnical action frame."

Flexible Artefacts:
Interpretations Between Rhetoric and Practice

In order to frame the proposed case study in a wider set of assumptions, it is important to depart from the technology in question (intranet).

A central issue here is how the rhetoric of "the intranet" as reliable technology easy to implement is translated into practice and shaped by organisational contexts. Whereas public and popular discourses frame an intranet as a coherent and unique technological array ("the intranet"), the Compass case shows how an intranet is multiple, ambiguous, and linked to misunderstandings.

The way to the sociotechnical drawn in this contribution points to organisational settings as contexts of use of an intranet, framing it as context-sensitive technology (cf. *infra*). It follows that acceptance, performance, and use of an intranet cannot be understood without making reference to the company history, the attitude towards innovation, and the construction of an organisational identity. Rather than emphasising how an intranet changed the organisation, therefore, the stage at which this technology was analysed in the case study calls for a closer analysis of how actors try to make sense of a system, fitting it in the current texture of taken-for-granted practices. This "operation" is bound with multiple constraints which might explain lack of performance and unexpected failures.

Most technical and managerial-oriented literature in the IS field tends to emphasise effectiveness and innovation carried by intranet technology as support to decision-making processes (Sridhar, 1998), strategic component of information management (Curry & Stancich, 2000), and especially knowledge management, with particular emphasis on knowledge sharing and distributed environments (Lai & Mahapatra, 1998; Stoddart, 2001). The objective of this literature is to identify models and stages for an effective development, implementation, and adoption of intranet technology as the last frontier in the management and deployment of complex, Web-based information systems.

Partly in response to this normative literature, a relevant body of empirical research has been carried out starting from interpretive case studies, trying to enquire how and why intranet technology was implemented and adopted in large corporations and institutions (Bansler, Damsgaard, Scheepers, Havn, & Thommesen, 2000; Cecez-Kecmanovic, Moodie, Busuttil, & Plesman, 1999; Damsgaard & Scheepers,

2000). This stream of research, still investigating reasons for failure and success in intranet implementation, is more critically oriented towards issues linked with power relations, organisational practices, and emergent social aspects of technology.

Adhering to such a stream, the concept of interpretative flexibility (Bijker, 1995; Bijker & Law, 1992) constitutes an appropriate point of departure. Interpretative flexibility is defined as the set of meanings, discourses, and interpretations performed by several actors with reference to a specific technological artefact (e.g., an intranet-based KMS).

As a key word in sociotechnical action, *interpretative flexibility* points to the importance of multiple points of view shaping "indeterminacy of technology, [...] to make some sense of the choices in "the garden of forking paths" (Williams & Edge as cited in Horton et al., 2005).

Multiplicity is exactly what fosters and cultivates this garden through a set of rhetoric discourses. In the case of an intranet, they are oriented to depict it as a technology easy to implement, effective and even "revolutionary." In order to contextualise these discursive frames, however, it is necessary to point to relationships between an intranet and previous organisational practices, technologies, and routines. These relationships also have to do with the ambiguity/flexibility of an intranet as both supporting work activities and intervening on communicational issues as a new medium. The analysis will illustrate how these two key dimensions were managed and interpreted in the Compass case.

As argued by the social construction of technology (SCOT) perspective (Bijker, 1995), any technology is socially constructed by relevant social groups interacting around a technological artefact. They interpret the artefact itself, and meanings attributed to it constitute what is called "technology." Far from being a mere description of what technology is, interpretative flexibility is the starting point for a sociological analysis of technology: no interpretation or property of technology is immanent in itself (Bijker, 1995; Bijker & Law, 1992). To understand how people in organisations make sense of technology says many things about how a particular technology is designed, set up, and implemented. Depending on the meanings associated with an intranet, different approaches and constraints will emerge and the technological artefact will be charged with multi-layered functions and interpretations (cf. Hall, 2004). Such meanings or interpretations do not deal with mere technical aspects of the artefact. They instead convey social assets, conceptions of knowledge and interaction, relationships among relevant social groups, as well as practices and organisational arrangements through which technology is deployed.

In this respect, an intranet as interface towards previous information systems, an intranet as support to knowledge management, and an intranet as a publishing or work tool are different interpretations which associate Web-based technologies with business contexts. Such contexts, at the same time, constitute a specific characteristic of intranet technology as "organisationally bounded" (Stenmark, 2003). As a consequence, it is more appropriate to talk of "an" intranet than of "the" intranet: multiple configurations and declinations of this technology are located in specific organisational settings, which constitute it as "context-sensitive."

Public Discourse/Local Practice

Language and discourse are primary resources for sociotechnical action (Flichy, 1996; Iacono & Kling, 2001): a technology *becomes* what we see through the arena constituted by social imagery and public discourse. In other words, technology's interpretative flexibility is affected by public discourse as a device of codification of technology's aim and its inscribed visions.

On the other hand, public discourse plays a crucial role in connecting rhetoric with practice, which constitutes two sides of the same coin: the discourse "on" technology and the discourse "of" technology (Pellegrino, 2003). Any new technology is developed and elaborated at a linguistic, collective level. Discursive frames are constantly set up in order to:

> [...] indicate favorable links between internetworking and a new preferred social order. These frames help to legitimate relatively high levels of investment for many potential adopters and package expectations about how they should use internetworking in their daily routines and about how they should envision a future based on internetworking. (Iacono & Kling, 2001, p. 97)

Intranet and the Compass are not an exception: some "favorable" links can be recognised through the expected advantages of their implementation, as based on universal communication, performance, reliability, cost, speed, standards along with the distinctive feature to make users publishers and effective producers of information (Holtz, 1997). Emphasis on cost cutting and/or cost saving, as well as the ease or immediacy of the implementation process, are among the most recurrent arguments of the discourse "on the intranet" as a single and unambiguous technological architecture. This discourse is frequently summarised through lists of good reasons to adopt an intranet inside organisations. A substitutive vision of this new technology with reference to previous technological systems is another feature of such a discourse. It is typically oriented to think of an intranet as the main tool to create the paperless office or to set up effective knowledge management systems. In the discourse "on the intranet," knowledge and information often constitute a blurred arena where no clear differences are either seen or established. It follows that "information" as synonym of "experience" is expected to be captured and shared through an intranet and other Web-based information systems, neglecting contexts and practices of interaction through which that very experience is accomplished. This is particularly evident with reference to the so-called IT-driven literature on knowledge management. An "epistemology of possession" as opposed to an "epistemology of practice" circumscribes the limits of "a technological fix to knowledge management."

> *If knowledge is deeply embedded within and inseparable from the practices and activities that people undertake, it cannot exist independently of human agents, as knowledge/knowing involves the active agency of people making decisions in light of the specific circumstances that they find themselves in.*
> (Currie & Kerrin, 2004, p.12)

The missing distinction between information and knowledge explains how some implementation processes incur failure and misunderstandings: they are often led by a fashionable imagery where technology is expected to substitute for entire social assets and settings. These assets and settings are not evaluated or considered before implementing technology itself, even if they end with constituting what technology will become and how it will perform. Therefore, a substitutive approach prevails in processes of technology construction. On the other hand, technology-in-practice (Orlikowski, 2000) shows integrative patterns of interaction between old and new as well as complex and inseparable sociotechnical arrangements emerging from this interaction. Therefore, the technological discourse as such shows its limits (Newell, Swan, & Scarbrough, 1999), and an intranet can increase or establish electronic fences inside organisations (Newell, Swan, & Scarbrough, 2001).

Another relevant feature of the discourse "on the intranet" concerns its closeness to the Internet as a "root system" or architecture whose basics would be almost automatically transferred to company and business environments. From the continuity between the Internet and "the intranet," expectations, routines, and evaluation of intranet performance are drawn.

Whereas the Internet represented a central point of reference to both evaluate and design the Compass, its implementation process, representations of the users, and ongoing negotiations showed different discourses from those circulating on the media and especially in business and popular literature on the topic. Problem-solving processes and appropriation of technology by the users often contradict technology's imagery, contributing to the emergence of different sociotechnical arrangements from those "deployed" in the public discourse about technologies.

Misunderstanding at Work:
Multiplicity and Ambiguity in the Compass Case

The research site that is the subject of the enquiry was a 100-staff company whose main administrative and managing headquarters was located in the Northwest of England. In addition, regional locations and client sites were widespread throughout the UK. About 80% of the company workforce consisted of consultants working at client sites whereas about 20 people worked at the company headquarters dealing with administrative tasks and support services (e.g., marketing, R&D, and so forth). The company mission was defined as providing "a range of IT services and solutions that are focused on helping medium to large organisations build and deploy high quality integrated e-business systems." However, the company history indicated that there was more of a focus on testing than integration of information systems in various industries and particularly in the banking and finance sector.

In early 2001, the project to buy an intranet-based KMS started. Notwithstanding the fact that the company's skills and mission were focused on e-business and systems integration, the process concerning the Compass was partly externalised. Two different providers were contacted and their respective proposals were taken into consideration.

To review the proposals, a joint project team was set up, comprised of company consultants, the system administrator who worked for the company, and representatives from the software provider company. The presence of this project team was crucial in orienting courses of sociotechnical action.

The research was conducted with an ethnographic approach using participant observation, semi- and unstructured interviews, as well as analysis of company documentation concerning all of the stages of the process. The ethnographic study was carried out from October to December 2002, subsequent to the second release of the system. However, the access to the company covered a longer time: the first contacts started in October 2001 through e-mail. Documentation concerning the company, the Compass implementation, and the research agenda were exchanged with the managing directors and the sales administrator. The first visit to the company headquarters dated May 2002. Continuous presence in the headquarters for three months allowed the following of all of the actors involved in the process in their everyday interaction. In addition, some of the early implementation negotiations codified in various company documents were reconstructed and analysed.

Ambiguities and misunderstandings which characterised the whole construction of the Compass are summarised effectively through the process of naming the system itself. A consultant said that:

> *Some people call it KMS, some people call it Compass and I just think of it an intranet. Perhaps this system has an 'identity crisis' too? I think the concept of an intranet is good, but that the implementation is not so good.*

A clear distinction is drawn here between the concept and the implementation of a specific technology. KMS was the acronym of both "knowledge management system" and the system provider name. Its use revealed, in this way, the perception of the system as something not belonging to the organisation. Moreover, the same concept of an intranet as "the internal Internet" was in question since "It was an intranet at the beginning but it's really an extranet because consultants aren't within company and Compass was designed around consultants, not for office based staff" (Consultant). It is thus clear that one source of misunderstanding arose due to the consultants being workers employed outside of company headquarters. Furthermore, consultants often considered themselves as "native(s) of the client company they work at" (Managing Director; Consultant). Company managers as a result wanted to both support the consultants' identity and offer an added value to clients. These two groups of actors constituted the key targets of the whole process, to the extent that the KMS was designed "around consultants." But unforeseen client reactions—driven by power issues—impeded the fulfilment of such a two-fold plan. Consultants could not access the Compass from the client sites they worked at. Undervalued security issues and power plays made the negotiations between the company and the clients less smooth than expected. This inter-organisational constraint contributed to the "marginalisation" of the consultants as main users of the Compass, obliging them to bypass the system through e-mail and "older" communication media. But such an obligation also inspired many strategies of work-around and appropriation (cf. infra).

The following interview excerpt expresses a typical consultant's position towards the Compass:

> *I think the main problem is I can't access it during the day, so I think if it was there, I could access the system [...] because I could doing a service look at how it was done before, and if not I could raise a question to the community and hope so to come back with an answer that will help me. So I think it would be a lot better, I would use it a lot more I think if I could access it during the day. Whereas using it in the evening I use it more for admin work [...].* (Consultant)

As a consequence of clients':

[...] very strict policy about not to use the Internet and e-mail [...] consultants have to access Compass from home or a hotel room [...]. So there are ways around it [Compass], for example for posting documents we use e-mail. (Board Member)

Because of this double constraint (clients preventing consultants from using the Compass and resilience of "older" media), both consultants and clients were not involved in the process as the company managers expected. Therefore, not only inter-organisational relationships modified the expected uses of the system as framed in the early negotiation stages, but they also constrained potential or alternative uses of the system by the consultants. As a result, they were marginalised as main users of the system, and the Compass was more used by administrative staff in the main office than at the client sites. Clients' policies about the Compass show how negotiations concerning security and innovation raised misunderstandings due to undervalued power issues: clients did not want to "disclose" their organisational information systems to consultants. The Compass added valued was not perceived as such. This strategy comprised not only a discursive practice but was also translated into a socio-material array (clients' strict control on their own networks). Both the aspects shaped and oriented sociotechnical action in the Compass case.

Another source of misunderstanding and inter-organisational constraint came from the presence of an external software provider. It affected implementation dynamics and shaped negotiations at multiple levels. For example, there was a back and forth learning process based on joint meetings, presentation events, and many documents circulating in the two companies. As summarised by some of the actors, such a process was punctuated by many misunderstandings in communicating and defining features of the system:

After drawing this document [KMS Business Requirements], we received Design Specifications and we looked at that, made comments and they turned it back with a few changes and then these documents were back many times because we didn't agree about some things. Anyway final specifications don't match how it works at the minute. (Compass Administrator)

The process was apparently participatory: "[...] What we did was we sent out requests to all the staff if they had ideas about how to change the system, new ideas or improvements. We had got lots of suggestions" (Compass Administrator) so that "all the enhancements we classed priority one have been incorporated into the upgrade" ("Compass Upgrade—July 3, 2003").

The software provider was the main actor who raised very high expectations on the system performance, potential, and reliability (cf. Currie & Kerrin, 2004), whereas its implementation and upgrade were also affected by specific forms of power, like visions inscribed in the system (Akrich, 1992); user representations (Akrich, 1995; Suchman, 2002); implicit distinctions between people and technology, along with (failed) attempts to make the Compass an obligatory passage point (Callon, 1986). It was not only the software provider to exert this power over the company, but also the reverse: whereas the software provider was proposing a very open, Google™-like searching system ("a big pot"), the company moved the product in a different direction:

> We wanted something they had not thought. An engine to learn things—previously it was used for help-desk and things like that and they were very excited to help us since we move their product in a direction they didn't know. (Consultant, member of the project team)

The way these ongoing changes were pursued came through inscribing specific routines or courses of action (e.g., "an engine to learn things" rather than "a big pot") in the Compass as technological artefact. The process of inscription (Akrich, 1992; Callon, 1986; Hanseth & Monteiro, 1997) involves converting an appropriate constituency in the organisation to someone's point of view. In this instance, managers attempted to achieve it by blocking an open search approach, contradicting the assumption that the system was aimed at sharing knowledge. This indirectly encouraged people to hoard knowledge (Currie & Kerrin, 2004).

> We didn't like that, everybody accessing the system and getting into it [...]. At the beginning they [the software provider] didn't understand that we wanted different areas and permissions and access [...]. We came across the problem half the way down, we realised that we misunderstood each other. (Compass Administrator)

In the current configuration, therefore, a very hierarchical writable/readable system of permission and access substituted for the original search engine proposed by the vendor. In this respect, the change of the system indicates a problem-solving approach oriented to exert control and limitations over modalities of knowledge sharing and transfer, narrowing them to knowledge as object easy to codify and formalise.

Given that concerns with power constrained the system development, it is of the greatest importance to underline the strategies actors enacted by actors to work-around the system, exerting in turn a form of power. The concept of work-around is closely connected with practices of conflict and negotiation in system development and use (Pollock, 2005).

Work-Around Knowledge (Management):
Power, Narratives of Failure, and Non-Use

The gap between rhetoric and practice of technology implementation and the interplay of discursive and material practices allow to follow and critically interpret the various courses of action around the Compass. Courses emerge as narratives of failure and non-use.

The point about failure and non-use provides an account of how things happen so to "theorise" events rather than simply documenting them (Kling, 1999). In this respect, the concept of work-around is a bridge between theory and practice.

Quoting Gasser, Pollock defined a work-around as: "[...] intentionally using computing in ways for which it was not designed" or avoiding a computer's use and "[...] relying on an alternative means of accomplishing work" (as cited in Pollock, 2005, p. 497).

At the discursive level, work-around is represented by definitions of failure and success deployed in narrative patterns. These very narratives are shaped by the context and by the discursive and material practices that constitute it.

As the Compass was deployed through different releases, variations in the system performance and its interpretation emerged during the process: technical improvements were perceived, but also lack of performance, disappointing transitions, and non-use (mis-use, unsatisfactory use, and unexpected use). Explanations of non-use can be retrieved in actors' statements about the system, as in the following interview excerpts:

> *[...] Actually it doesn't work as well as it could do [...] I think it has a lot to do with the way we use it. There are technical limitations but I think it's more the way we use it [...] I think there was a kind of expectation and it was very high. But actually it doesn't work as well as it could do.* (Marketing Manager)

> *My feeling is we haven't met or delivered what they expected. That's an impression I got for quite a few reasons. First of all documents and design specifications. Reading through documents and what've got there are lots of differences. I think there were expectations and requirements. Lots of things don't exist in what we currently have.* (Quality Manager)

What emerges from these descriptions is a gap between expectations framed in the documents about specifications of the system and its current configuration. Such a gap can be interpreted as a local occurrence of the gap between rhetoric and practice (cf. *supra*). Furthermore, it manifests itself as a narrative of failure, constituting the Compass case as a failure story, in which narratives (Fincham, 2002) have a crucial role in identifying limits of the system itself. Courses of action concerning the Compass are contextualised by actors as "failures in delivering what we wanted" (Board Member) and by attributing such failures to "others" (the clients forbidding consultants to access the Compass from their sites; the software vendor that did not deliver on its promises). By failure, actors usually meant a gap between expectations/plans and the current use of the system. Authors of the narrative often coincide with the relevant groups involved in the process, especially managers and consultants. Different themes of failure can be identified: one of the most interesting is centred on the collaboration tool of the Compass as electronic community of consultants. The collaboration tool was an off-line communication system part of the Compass. Its objective was to build up specialised communities to share knowledge about similar projects run by consultants at different client sites. This tool was constantly worked-around and bypassed by consultants in their daily routine due to multiple reasons. Among the most frequently cited, there were the following: company size, off-line performance, difficulties in accessing the Compass, excess of formalisation required by the system when compared with more familiar or consolidated communicational routines. As stated by one of the managing directors:

> *Nobody seems to ask questions. They don't use collaboration tool: it might be they don't understand it; it might be it takes too much time; it might be they don't like typing a question onto a machine; it might be they prefer to ring the people; it might be there is no sense in having off-line components in an intranet; it might be everybody knows who the experts are and their phone numbers [...].*

Such an analysis of the non-use of the collaboration tool denotes both a missing consideration of social assets which constitutes technology and the emerging awareness that these assets can enable or, reversely, constrain technology. Lack of consideration of contextual constraints (e.g., client security policies, company size, knowledge accumulation, and transfer in practice) made the design of the system, apparently participatory, fit a "design from nowhere" position (Suchman, 2002). As Horton et al. (2005, p. 58) highlighted:

> *the marginalization (by problematization) of the user allows engineering and operations research formulations of work to prevail—as a consequence, the systems that are built impose formal constraints on work processes that exclude details of the local practice and reinforce the processes of manipulation and alienation of the user. Decisions about which engineer*

(or vendor) and what project technique (often proprietary) to select are deeply political, as are, by implication, the systems analysis and design methods that underlie such choices.

In the Compass case, ongoing changes as well as back and forth learning processes were imbued with deeply political decisions, which ended with replicating a Windows®-like file system, a very structured "file cabinet" without any added value:

> *We've already got an expensive file system [...] Search engine was the real power, otherwise we would spend a lot of money just to replace or replicate something we already have. It's like: I'm looking for car benefit scheme and I have to go through a long list of documents, I have to put on my glasses and look... .* (Service Delivery Manager)

This transformation can be read as both a narrative of failure and a work-around to bypass the vision originally inscribed in the Compass. Furthermore, such a work-around is not "innocent" as the attempt to control and filter access to the system played a crucial role in this change.

On the other hand, when identifying the "real power" of the system, the discourse on an intranet was shaped again by the comparison with the Internet. Such a discourse, in fact, constitutes an unavoidable term to evaluate use and performance of the Compass as emerging from multiple relations of power and communication.

Other competing narratives concerned the idea that knowledge sharing is centred on and enabled by "new technologies" whereas, in other stories elicited, it emerges a clear perception of technology as a constraint to a more informal knowledge sharing. In such a way, the story also reveals how an "odd couple" (Alvesson & Kärreman, 2001), namely knowledge and management, could not be delegated easily to the sociotechnical array called "the Compass."

As stated in an official document:

> *the company required a knowledge management solution to deliver five elements: information capture, addition of context, information retrieval, proactive information push, and learning capabilities.* (From "Sales Overview")

This description of the system both summarises the company expectations and evokes some of the most popular topics in the managerial-oriented literature about knowledge management. In this respect, it reflects a certain "managerialist ideology" which assumes that knowledge will be freely and voluntarily shared inside organisations (Currie & Kerrin, 2004). Again, this brings to undervalue the limits of a technological discourse (cf. Newell et al., 1999; Walsham, 2001) which tends to depict technology as the best support and ultimate innovation to share and transfer knowledge. Such a discourse contrasts with a relevant body of research in which the situated, practice-based nature of knowledge and learning is emphasised (Gherardi, 2000, 2001; Lave & Wenger, 1991; Wenger, 1998).

In their critique of knowledge management, Ekbia and Kling (2003) invoked a more central role of power issues in order to frame knowledge management strategies. Introducing the Foucauldian concept of "institutional regime of truth," they argue that the very concept of knowledge management relies on multiple systems through which statements about the world are formulated and believed as true. These systems are imbued with power and proposed as an alternative explanation to organisational culture to make sense of knowledge management contradictions.

Therefore, power issues shape the ambiguous nature of knowledge and learning, as well as the role played by technology. This is confirmed in the Compass case. In fact, interpretative flexibility manifested itself through contradictory and opposite conceptions of how to embed knowledge in the system. A regional manager summarised these conceptions in the following way:

> *I think the aspect of searching, of having a big pot to store everything [...] I think this was the original idea [...] You put information in, you get information out, you don't care where information lies. While in Compass we had the information stored, we found that for practical use it's actually easier to make sense of that having a structure, giving it a structure, a file cabinet.*

This ambiguity concerning the concepts of knowledge and technology (structured and unstructured visions were competing with each other) was another source of misunderstanding among actors.

But domesticating the big pot into a file cabinet is inextricably connected to the need of controlling and filtering the access to the system. Again, as stated by the system administrator, "not everybody could access everything."

Whereas "learning capabilities" were attributed to and searched through the technological system, the Compass implementation had its origins in difficulties with processes more centred on information sharing among different company locations:

> *[...] there was difficulty in sharing information from the main office to the others [...] lots of operation problems and consistency problems.* (Managing Director)

However, these problems became even more complex as soon as the process of implementation started. The point resembles Currie and Kerrin (2004, p.18) case, where:

> *[...] epistemological problems significantly inhibited effective utilisation of the intranet. The main problem was that of relevance. That knowledge is embedded in practice meant anything posted on the intranet by one individual or group was insufficiently contextualised for others to use [...].*

Discussion: Theorizing the Compass Case in a Sociotechnical Action Frame

Some reflections and conclusive remarks may be drawn from the Compass case study as an attempt to "theorise" it in light of a "sociotechnical action frame." In ultimate analysis, it appears to be constituted by the following "pillars":

- **Flexible artefacts:** Are shaped by multiplicity and ambiguity, acting through the gap between rhetoric and practice. Their flexibility resides in a broad set of material and linguistic practices fostered by public discourse and local practice.
- **Power and politics of inscription:** Orient courses of sociotechnical action and affect success and failure of technology appropriation. They also reduce indeterminacy of technology and stem its flexibility.
- **Artefacts are context-sensitive:** Contexts are both (re)constructed in accounting/appropriating technology and "deleted" in its design/implementation. Such a contradiction, which makes the context relevant and invisible at once, constitutes the artefacts as context-sensitive.

Flexible Artefacts

The first point of the frame refers to interpretative flexibility. In the Compass case, multiple interpretations were performed and supported by the social groups involved in the process of implementation and appropriation. In this respect, an intranet system was interpreted, at the same time, as the Compass (namely, a knowledge management system); as an arena to set up a controlled community (making consultants feel closer to the organisation); last but not least, as a tool of service to newcomers in the company. As stated by the Compass Administrator:

it would work for people joining the company in the near future or having joined recently rather than people working here for a long time. If you've been working here for years [...] you will know who's able to answer your question about Load Testing anyway.

These competing and concurrent interpretations configure the studied technology as multiplicity rather than singularity, confirming that multiple points of view are an irreducible resource in sociotechnical interaction (Horton et al., 2005). A primary source which feeds flexibility of technological artefacts is public discourse and expectations about their performance expressed by key groups (e.g., media agencies, collective movements, specialised communities, vendors, and also company managers). They act in a global rhetorical arena where "multiple institutional regimes of truth" (Ekbia & Kling, 2003) are established, shaping especially the status of knowledge and its relationships with power, organisations, and artefacts.

However, these utopian and often de-contextualised discursive frames both foster and contradict the mutual action which couples social groups with artefacts. Such an action is linguistic and material, so that the artefact comes to inscribe certain courses of action rather than others (e.g., Google™-like vs Windows®-like structure).

A sociotechnical approach, therefore, has to take into consideration that linguistic and discursive practices can be as obdurate as other types of practices. It means that linguistic interaction and negotiation of meanings are always translated into other types of action. For example, starting from the Internet as a "matrix" to evaluate the Compass performance, the process ended with transforming the Google™-like search engine into a file cabinet. No guarantee of matching between linguistic and material dimensions is given in the process due to the intervention of misunderstanding as a driving force in producing unintended outcomes. But, both the dimensions are involved in shaping the mutual constitution of the social and the technical. The Compass case provides an example of this mutual relationship between discourses/negotiations around the artefact and their material configuration. The case also represents a local version of the global rhetoric on knowledge management as driven by intranet and Web technologies.

Power and Politics of Inscription

The second point of the frame concerns power, politics, and strategies of inscription aimed at reducing or changing technology's interpretative flexibility. They play a crucial role in defining the current configurations of technological systems. The Compass implementation as based on outsourcing and intervention of actors external to the company (the software vendor and the clients) brought about multiple translations over the system and increased misunderstandings around it (e.g., the role of consultants as main users of the Compass was not recognised by clients; the open search approach proposed by the vendor was rejected by the company management and so forth). These actors affected visions to be inscribed in the Compass.

Inscriptions also fix meanings—and in this way constitute an exertion of power (cf. Bijker, 1995)—through enforced routines. Processes of inscription, therefore, frame the users' ordinary, everyday action in coping with these systems. Non-use, work-around (Pollock, 2005) and bypassing of the system through older media/technologies emerge as practices coupled with narratives of failure/success of technology situated in organisational settings. They also represent patterns of (inter)action between technological systems defined as "new" and previous sociotechnical assets. In this respect, the Compass case reflects the lack and the need of "located accountability" (Suchman, 2002) in design and implementation. Located accountability is grounded in the awareness that "the only possibility for the creation of effective objects is through collective knowledge of the particular and multiple locations of their production and use" (p. 96).

Such a lack of knowledge about particularity and multiplicity is even more prominent when the technology in question intervenes on information and communication and is expected to substitute for face-to-face contexts of knowledge sharing and transfer (e.g., the Compass). Expectations oriented to substitution more than integration between old and new, therefore, undervalue how much technologies, when dis-embedded or detached from contexts of use, can formalise and complicate the process of communication they aim to mediate (Brown & Duguid, 1998).

On the other hand, power issues often constrain utopian visions of technology, revealing attempts of "normative control" performed reducing knowledge to a set of formal repositories (Currie & Kerrin, 2004).

Artefacts are Context-Sensitive

The third and last point of the proposed frame is that sociotechnical action is embodied in contexts of use which are arenas of negotiation and temporary agreement on technology's interpretative flexibility. However, detachment from those contexts to adhere to a public rhetoric which takes technology's potential for granted is an ongoing "temptation" and a pattern of action. It reinforces disappearance and invisibility of contexts in the process of implementation due to deeply political choices which inform design and implementation of complex technological systems (cf. Horton et al., 2005). Anyway, this visibility/invisibility makes technological artefacts highly sensitive to contexts. Such a sensitivity is a complementary dimension to indeterminacy of technology: as technology does not have any immanent property that shapes its constitution, it is very sensitive to contexts. The point relates to both Kling and Scacchi's Web computing model and Kling's conceptualisation of sociotechnical interaction network (as cited in Horton et al., 2005).

This implies that understanding the thickness of practice and historical path dependence in processes of technology construction is crucial to cope with circumstances of material and symbolic interaction which shape the artefacts. By path dependence it is meant to be the accumulation of technology, knowledge base, and routines, which can lead firms to increasing positive returns (Coombs & Hull, 1998), but also end with "competence traps" (Levitt & March, 1996), preventing organisations from innovation. Such an ambiguity embedded in the path can be managed differently and result in different artefacts. The Compass case, for example, solved this ambiguity by adapting an intranet to a well-known model (Windows®-like approach), bringing the organisation into a "competence trap."

Then failure and success of technologies are context-sensitive rather than based on the "bad" or "good" exploitation of a mere technical potential. Here, context-sensitivity means recognizing that the mutual constitution of linguistic and material elements contributes to make a specific technology what it becomes: contexts provide many cues to interpret the artefact, but they also shape it.

It can be claimed any technology emerges as a set of temporary configurations resulting from local consensus (or dissent) around interpretations of social assets that can be associated with it. Failure cases like the Compass might provide both social scientists and practitioners with indications about how to unpack complex processes involving multiple points of view. Failure cases, even more than success, show the role played by multiplicity in shaping sociotechnical action.

To conclude, the gap between rhetoric and practice represents a starting point to situate patterns of sociotechnical action in locations of technology production and reproduction. These discursive and material locations are the settings that constitute technology as an array appropriated by users. Unintended outcomes of this constitution assume a crucial role "in the garden of forking paths": indeterminacy of technology is deployed through complex interactions that lead to specific paths/artefacts. Walking through them means to rely on rhetoric, practice, and context-sensitivity as "compasses" orienting sociotechnical action.

References

Akrich, M. (1992). The de-scription of technical objects. In W. E. Bijker, & J. Law (Eds.), *Shaping technology/building society. Studies in sociotechnical change* (pp. 205-212). Cambridge, MA: The MIT Press.

Akrich, M. (1995). User representations: Practices, methods and sociology. In A. Rip, T. J. Misa, & T. J. Schot (Eds.), *Managing technology in society. The approach of constructive technology assessment* (pp. 167-184). London: Pinter.

Alvesson, M., & Kärreman, D. (2001). Odd Couple: Making sense of the curious concept of Knowledge Management. *Journal of Management Studies, 38*(7), 996-1018.

Bansler, J. P., Damsgaard, J., Scheepers, R., Havn, E., & Thommesen, J. (2000). Corporate intranet implementation: Managing emergent technologies and organizational practices. *Journal of the Association of Information Systems, 1,* Article 10, 40 pages.

Berger, P., & Luckmann, T. (1967). *The social construction of reality.* New York: Doubleday.

Bijker, W. E. (1995). *Of bycicles, bakelites and bulbs.* Cambridge, MA: The MIT Press.

Bijker, W. E., & Law, J. (1992). *Shaping technology/building society. Studies in sociotechnical change.* Cambridge, MA: The MIT Press.

Brown. J. S., & Duguid, P. (1998). Organizing knowledge. *California Management Review, 40*(3), 90-111.

Callon, M. (1986). Some elements of a sociology of translation: Domestication of the scallops and the fishermen of St. Brieuc Bay. In J. Law (Ed.), *Power, action and belief. A new sociology of knowledge?* (pp. 196-229). London: Routledge.

Cecez-Kecmanovic, D., Moodie, D., Busuttil, A., & Plesman, F. (1999). Organisational change mediated by e-mail and Intranet. An ethnographic study. *Information Technology & People, 12*(1), 9-26.

Coombs, R., & Hull, R. (1998). Knowledge management practices and path-dependency in innovation. *Research Policy, 27,* 237-253.

Currie, G., & Kerrin, M. (2004). The limits of a technological fix to knowledge management. Epistemological, political and cultural issues in the case of intranet implementation. *Management Learning, 35*(1), 9-29

Curry, A., & Stancich, L. (2000). The intranet—an intrinsic component of strategic information management? *International Journal of Information Management, 20*(4), 249-268.

Damsgaard, J., & Scheepers, R. (2000). Managing the crises in intranet implementation: A stage model. *Information Systems Journal, 10,* 131-149.

Dascal, M. (1999). Introduction: Some question about misunderstanding. *Journal of Pragmatics, 31,* 753-762

Ekbia, H., & Kling, R. (2003). Power issues in knowledge management. *CSI working chapter WP-03-02* (p. 26). Retrieved December 16, 2005, from www.slis.indiana.edu/CSI/WP/WP03-02B.html

Fincham, R. (2002). Narratives of success and failure in systems. *British Journal of Management, 13*(1), 1-14.

Flichy, P. (1996). *L'innovazione tecnologica. [The Technological Innovation].* Milan: Feltrinelli (Italian ed.).

Gherardi, S. (2000). Practice-based theorizing on learning and knowing in organizations. *Organization, 7*(2), 211-223.

Gherardi, S. (2001). From organizational learning to practice-based knowing. *Human Relations, 54*(1), 131-139.

Hall, H. (2004, June 3-4). The intranet as actor: The role of the intranet in knowledge sharing. In K. Horton, & E. Davenport (Eds.), Understanding sociotechnical action. In *Proceedings of USTA04 Workshop*, Napier University, Edinburgh, UK (pp. 109-111).

Hanseth, O., & Monteiro, E. (1997). Inscribing behaviour in information infrastructure standards. *Accounting, Management and Information Technologies, 7*(4), 183-211.

Holtz, S. (1997). *The intranet advantage.* Emeryville, CA: Ziff-Davis Press.

Horton, K., Davenport, E., & Wood-Harper, T. (2005). Exploring sociotechnical interaction with Rob Kling: Five "big" ideas. *Information Technology & People, 18(1),* 50-67.

Iacono, S., & Kling, R. (2001). Computerization movements. The rise of the Internet and distant forms of work. In J. Yates, & J. Van Maanen (Eds.), *Information technology and organizational transformation. History, rhetoric and practice* (pp. 93-135). Thousand Oaks, CA: Sage Publications.

Kling, R. (1999). What is social informatics and why does it matter? *D-Lib Magazine, 5*(1). Retrieved November 28, 2005, from www.dlib.org:80/dlib/january99/kling/01kling.html

Lai, V. S., & Mahapatra, R. K. (1998). Evaluating intranets in a distributed environment. *Decision Support Systems,* (23), 347-357.

Lave, J., & Wenger, E. (1991). *Situated learning. Legitimate peripheral participation.* Cambridge: Cambridge University Press.

Levitt, B., & March, J. (1996). Organizational learning. In M. D. Cohen, & L. Sproull (Eds.), *Organizational learning* (pp. 516-540). Thousand Oaks, CA: Sage Publications.

Newell, S., Swan, J., & Scarbrough, H. (1999, July 14-16). *Intranets and knowledge management: De-centred technologies and the limits of technological discourse.* Paper presented at the Critical Management Conference, UMIST, Manchester School of Management, Manchester, UK.

Newell, S., Swan, J., & Scarbrough, H. (2001). From global knowledge management to internal electronic fences: Contradictory outcomes of intranet development. *British Journal of Management, 12*(2), 97-112.

Orlikowski, W.J. (2000). Using technology and constituting structures: A practice lens for studying technology in organizations. *Organization Science, 11*(4), 404-428.

Pellegrino, G. (2003, July 7-9). Calling technology: Discourses on/of the intranet in a comparative case-study. In M. Brigham, A. Contu, & C. Brown (Eds.), Critique and inclusivity. In *Proceedings of the 3rd Critical Management Studies Conference*, Lancaster University Management School, Lancaster University, UK [CD-ROM, 13 pages].

Pollock, N. (2005). When is a work-around? Conflict and negotiation in computer systems development. *Science, Technology, & Human Values, 30(*4), 496-514.

Sridhar, S. (1998). Decision support using the intranet. *Decision Support Systems*, (23), 19-28.

Stenmark, D. (2003). Knowledge creation and the Web: Factors indicating why some intranets succeed where others fail. *Knowledge and Process Management, 10*(3), 207-216.

Stoddart, L. (2001). Managing intranets to encourage knowledge sharing. Opportunities and constraints. *Online Information Review, 25*(1), 19-28.

Suchman, L. (2002). Located accountabilities in technology production. *Scandinavian Journal of Information Systems, 14*(2), 91-105.

Walsham, G. (2001). Knowledge management: The benefits and limitations of computer systems. *European Management Journal, 19*(6), 599-608.

Weigand, E. (1999). Misunderstanding: The standard case. *Journal of Pragmatics, 31*, 763-785.

Wenger, E. (1998). *Communities of practice. Learning, meaning and identity*. Cambridge: Cambridge University Press.

Chapter IX

The Socio-Pragmatics of IT Artefacts:

Reconciling the Pragmatic, Social, Semiotic, and Technical

Göran Goldkuhl
Linköping University & Jönköping International Business School, Sweden

Pär J. Ågerfalk
University of Limerick, Ireland, & Örebro University, Sweden

Abstract

There are many attempts to explain success and failure in information systems. Many of these refer to a purported sociotechnical gap. In this chapter, we develop an alternative approach that does not impose such a strong dichotomy, but regards social and technical rather as dimensions along which to study work practices. The developed theory involves not only the "social" and "technical" constructs but also other generic ones, namely "instrumental," "semiotic," and "pragmatic." We call this theory "socio-instrumental pragmatism." To illustrate the theoretical concepts introduced, we use an example brought from an extensive action research study, including the development of an information system in eldercare, developed through a participatory design approach.

Introduction

Development and implementation of an information system (IS) is a very demanding task, and many times the expectations from such endeavours are not met. Unexpected negative effects often arise while anticipated positive effects fail to appear. There are many attempts to explain IS failure (and, indeed, success) in general terms. Some of them refer to a sociotechnical gap—a gap between what is socially required and what is technically feasible (e.g., Ackerman, 2000). Such explanations tend to make a sharp differentiation between the social and the technical. For example in the sociotechnical tradition represented by Mumford and Weir (1979), there are discussions about balancing the technical system and the social system. This is built upon a view that computerised information systems are technical systems with social and organisational effects—a view that seems almost entirely to permeate mainstream IS research (see, for example, DeLone & McLean, 1992, 2003; Benbasat & Zmud, 2003). This is also in-line with the soft systems' view that there is a "serving system" to support a "system to be served" (Champion & Stowell, 2002). There are criticisms towards such a conceptualisation. For example, Nurminen (1988, p. 82) writes "by removing the social dimension from the systems entity, we imply that the technical system is basically non-social." In the same spirit, Goldkuhl and Lyytinen (1982) suggest that the traditional view of information systems as "technical systems with social implications" should be inverted to "social systems, only technically implemented." What are the grounds for such a view? An IS is not only a technical object; it is a technical object carrying information. Information—in order to be externalised and technically mediated through an IS—must be expressed in a language. From this follows that an IS, besides being technical, is also a kind of linguistic system (ibid; Winograd & Flores, 1986). Language is not only used for describing the world, it is also a part in constituting parts of the world, as pointed out by Mead (1934): "Language does not simply symbolise a situation or object which is already there in advance—it makes possible the existence or appearance of that situation or object, for it is part of the mechanism whereby that situation or object is created." Since every IS uses language for purposes of communication and understanding, what Mead claims about language also counts for information systems.

Instead of a separation into a social realm (humans acting in the IS environment) and technical realm (the IS), another approach is proposed here—using "social" and "technical" as dimensions along which to study work practices. The theoretical way to proceed is to articulate a common theory for both the IS and its organisational context. The concepts of social and technical are however not found to be sufficient. The purpose of this chapter is to outline a theory appropriate for interpretation, description, explanation, and evaluation of the interaction between information systems and their organisational context. The developed theory involves not only the "social" and "technical" constructs but also other generic ones, namely "instrumental," "semiotic," and "pragmatic." As we shall see in the following text, these constructs are "generic" in the sense that they are not specific to any particular empirical setting but are high-level categories useful in describing and discussing social action in relation to information systems in general. We call this theory *socio-instrumental pragmatism,* aligning with the work of Goldkuhl and Ågerfalk (2002), Goldkuhl and Röstlinger (2003), Goldkuhl (2005), and Ågerfalk and Eriksson (2006).

The chapter proceeds as follows. In the next section, we briefly introduce some concepts of socio-instrumental pragmatism. To illustrate the use of socio-instrumental pragmatism as a theory of information systems, we use a simple example of an IS in the subsequent section. The example is brought from an extensive empirical study. This study involves an action research endeavour including development of an IS in an eldercare setting. The IS and its supported work practice were developed through a participatory design approach. We do not describe this case study in any detail but use part of the developed system and the work practice in order to illustrate our theoretical endeavour. We then condense our conceptualisation of the IS and its organisational context in the following section, where important concepts are clarified and related to each other. Our contribution should be understood as a way to conceptualise the information technology (IT) artefact and its context. Hence, this chapter can partly be seen as a response to the requests for theorising the IT artefact as espoused by Orlikowski and Iacono (2001) and Benbasat and Zmud (2003). Those papers have given rise to quite a debate (see, for example, Alter, 2003; Galliers, 2003). It is beyond the scope of our chapter to directly engage in this debate, although in the second to last section, we comment on our contribution as a response to these requests for theorising the IT artefact. Finally, this chapter concludes with a brief summary of the main points.

The Perspective of Socio-Instrumental Pragmatism

Every attempt to theorise on information systems and their organisational uses relies on some ontological assumptions. Are there any fundamental entities and processes in the social and artificial world that should direct our conceptualisations? The basic stance taken here is pragmatic. Blumer (1969, p. 71) states "that the essence of society lies in an ongoing process of action—not in posited structure of relations. Without action, any structure of relations between people is meaningless. To be understood, a society must be seen and grasped in terms of the action that comprises it." With inspiration from Blumer and his pragmatic forerunners Dewey (1931) and Mead (1934), we will let actions appear as the ontological core in our analysis. In the IS field, such a position has been argued by Goles and Hirschheim (2000) guided by discussions on the "new pragmatism" (Wicks & Freeman, 1998).

The kinds of actions we are interested in are social actions, for example, actions performed in a social context. Weber (1978, p. 4) made a classical definition of social action: "That action will be called 'social' which in its meaning as intended by the actor or actors, takes account of the behaviour of others and is thereby oriented in its course." Our interpretation of this definition is that a social action (performed by an actor) has *social grounds* ("takes account of the behaviour of others") and *social purposes* ("thereby oriented in its course"). In communication and other direct interaction between actors, the social character is obvious. A communicative act (e.g., a question) functions as an impulse or initiative for a subsequent act (presumably an answer) which then is seen as a response to the first act (Linell, 1998; Sacks, 1992). Talk and other social interaction are seen as such chains of initiatives and responses.

The social grounds do not only comprise the direct intended influence towards the actor. When acting, the actor may use immaterial and/or material instruments. These instruments have usually a social origin, and hence, the instrumental use in action implies a social influence on the actor (Vygotsky, 1962; Wertsh, 1998). This is obvious when people use language. All use of language is social in the sense that it uses the social instrument of language. The actor's thinking, speaking, and writing are shaped by the socially-constructed categories of the world manifested in language or other sign systems (Berger & Luckmann, 1966). This also means that the use of an IS must be social since there can be no such use without the exploitation of signs.

People intervene into the world through their actions. Actions are intended to make a difference (Dewey, 1931). When one usually talks about actions, such interventive actions are implied. However, all human action is not interventive and overt. There are covert actions, which are not intended as external changes. The perception and interpretation of the world is also seen as actions, although as covert ones (Schutz, 1970; Strauss, 1993). This also involves thought and conscious deliberation through reflection. Such covert actions (interpretation and reflection) do not aim at external change, rather a change to the actors themselves, in their knowledge about the world. Social interaction consists of related interventive and receptive actions. An ordinary communicative situation with a conversation between two actors consists of continual acts of speaking (i.e., intervening) and listening (i.e., receiving) (see, for example, Clark, 1996). The production of an utterance is followed by an interpretation of that utterance by the other actor. Conversation consists of such reciprocal pairs of intervention and interpretation (Goldkuhl, 2003), which are embedded in "adjacency pairs" of communicative actions (Sacks, 1992) as, for example, a question and a corresponding answer (which were mentioned earlier).

Such acts in communication processes are semiotic acts, since they specifically are dealing with signs (i.e., producing signs and interpreting signs). People perform other kinds of acts as well. They act towards material objects with the intent to accomplish material changes in the world. Most material actions are also social actions, in so far as they have social grounds and social purposes as stated earlier (confer also

Goldkuhl, 2003). Material actions are often parts of social interactions, and as such, they are intertwined with semiotic acts (ibid; Andersen, 1990). Vološinov (1985) expresses this in a clear way: "Verbal communication can never be understood and explained outside of this connection with a concrete situation... In its concrete connection to a situation, verbal communication is always accompanied by social acts of a nonverbal character, and is often only an accessory to these acts, merely carrying out an auxiliary role."

In material actions, people often use external instruments to enable or facilitate their actions. Also in communication, instruments are often used to improve the transfer of messages. Instruments, such as telephones, fax machines, and computers, make communication possible over time and distance. Instruments play different roles in action and interaction; they can also be more or less advanced. Goldkuhl and Ågerfalk (2002) and Goldkuhl and Röstlinger (2003) have distinguished three levels of instruments:

1.   **Static tool** (artefact-supported human action)

2.   **Dynamic tool** (human-artefact co-operative action)

3.   **Automaton** (human-defined artefact action)

A human must use a static tool directly in order to make a difference. For example, an axe is used to chop wood. A human uses a dynamic tool in a cooperative and interactive way. For example, a car must be maneuvred when driven. Automatic machines can perform work independently according to its program after being initiated by a human. When started, a washing machine works by itself. In actor-network theory—ANT (e.g., Latour, 1991)—artefacts are claimed to have action potential. We agree with this but maintain that different types of artefacts possess different types of action potential. A static tool (like an axe) does not have any independent action potential. It is just an instrument to be utilised by a human. A dynamic tool (like a car) has potential for certain actions but not independently of humans. The actions are performed in a cooperative way by the human and the dynamic artefact together. An automaton has the potential to perform actions independently. However, such an artefact must be arranged and initiated by humans, and so it can never be totally independent. These complementary claims imply that we reject a symmetric view on humans and artefacts as sometimes claimed in ANT; this discussion is furthered in the following text.

The most central of these socio-pragmatic preliminaries are summarised and visualised in the generic model of social action depicted in Figure 1. More elaborated descriptions can be found in Goldkuhl and Ågerfalk (2002), Goldkuhl and Röstlinger (2003), and Goldkuhl (2005). These references include also more elaborated descriptions of socio-instrumental pragmatism. The perspective elaborated here is a

Figure 1. A generic model of social action

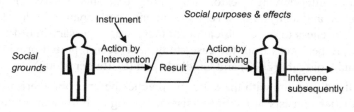

theoretical synthesis of different action-oriented theories from reference disciplines outside IS, mainly philosophy, sociology, psychology, linguistics, and organisation theory. Socio-instrumental pragmatism is especially adapted to features of the IS discipline. It is inspired and informed by action-oriented frameworks, such as, for example, American pragmatism (e.g., Dewey, 1931; Mead, 1934), symbolic interactionism (e.g., Blumer, 1969), social action theory (e.g., Weber, 1978), social phenomenology (e.g., Berger & Luckmann, 1966; Schutz, 1970) ethnomethodology/conversation analysis (e.g., Sacks, 1992), speech act theory (e.g., Habermas, 1984; Searle, 1969), activity theory (e.g., Wertsch, 1998), practice theory (e.g., Schatzki, Knorr Cetina, & von Savigny, 2001) and affordance theory (e.g., Gibson, 1979). As being a synthesis, socio-instrumental pragmatism does not try to make any complete integration of these diverse action theories. It picks different categories from these reference theories and integrates those into a coherent whole, tailored for IS studies (Goldkuhl, 2005).

When acting through and by means of an IS, the IS is used as the instrument by which interventive actions, and possibly also receptive actions, are performed. In the next section, this socio-pragmatic view of sociotechnical action is elaborated further by means of examples from a case study.

Actions and Instruments in Work Practices:
An Eldercare Case Study

For the purpose of illustration, we will use material from a case study on the development of a municipal eldercare unit—a longitudinal action research based case study. The action research project consisted of integrated work practice and information systems development. A new IS was developed in a participatory design setting, where researchers and eldercare personnel participated in a co-design endeavour.

Data generation in the case study has been pursued with different qualitative re-search methods: interviewing directors and nursing assistants, observations of their work, collection and analysis of several documents, participation in development seminars. A closeness to the empirical phenomena was necessary in order to gain reliable data. Experiences from the case study have been reported previously by Cronholm and Goldkuhl (2002) and Goldkuhl and Röstlinger (2002).

Let us start the discussion with the eldercare practice before computerisation. The eldercare practice consists of nursing assistants giving care to elderly people liv-ing in their own residences. The elderly people need assistance with ordinary tasks like hygiene, dressing, cleaning, and simple medical attention on a daily basis. A nursing assistant visits each client on one or more occasions each day. The visits are regulated by daily schedules, which inform the nursing assistant what tasks to perform. There exist different schedules depending on what kind of tasks to per-form and at what time of the day. There are typed contents on the schedules, but they also consist of hand-written annotations. Besides the schedules, there are also more informal communication between the nursing assistants, such as hand-written notes and verbal interaction. Quality assurance problems were encountered in the eldercare practice, which gave rise to the development of an IT system to support communication and documentation. Schedules are nowadays mediated by the IT system, and this has improved the quality assurance and the individualisation of the eldercare, which are important objectives of the work practice.

In order to understand what the new IT artefact does, we need to understand its role in the work practice. In order to do this, let us focus on three different types of actions in the work practice:

1.   Production/reproduction of daily schedules
2.   Reading of the schedules before home care visits
3.   Care service provided to the elderly clients

Based on the socio-pragmatic perspective outlined previously, we focus on actions as a kind of basic unit of analysis. A work practice consists of actions, actors, signs, and material artefacts related in meaningful ways (Goldkuhl & Röstlinger, 2002, 2003). The way social practices appear as meaningful to an inquirer is through mak-ing their constituent actions become visible; what people do in the work practice.

The first two kinds of action (creating and interpreting the schedule) are two inter-related parts of a communication process. One nursing assistant may, for example, annotate something to the schedule at one occasion as a message to her colleagues ("remember to take out the laundry"). Another nursing assistant reads the note when she is about to visit an elderly. And, she takes this into account during her visit to the elderly (taking care of the laundry). The first two actions are actions dealing with language (writing and reading) and are thus parts in a communication process. The last action is not a linguistic action. It is material action—changing physical objects in the world. This reasoning may be illustrated by the model of social action depicted in Figure 1.

We previously distinguished the difference between interventive and receptive actions. Actions 1 and 3 in the examples are interventive actions. The action 2 in the example is an interpretive action. All three actions are social actions, although they might all be performed in solitude without any direct interaction with another human. All actions described have social grounds and social effects. The first nursing assistant might write her note without any other colleague around her, but the communicative action is, of course, directed towards and intended for another human (for example, asking the (other) nursing assistant to visit the elder). The second nursing assistant may perform the second act—the reading of the schedule and the accessory note—in solitude. As an interpretive act, it is a typical social act. It certainly has social grounds through the written communication directed towards her. This act has also social purposes. The nursing assistant reads the message in order to arrive at an informed readiness on the eve of her visit to the elder. The third act—the material act of taking out the laundry at the elder's residence—may also be performed in solitude. This material act is, however, also a social act since there are obvious social grounds and social purposes. There was a request directed to her from her colleague (i.e., social grounds). She is taking out the laundry in order to help the elder and fulfil the obligations of the eldercare centre (social purposes).

All these genuinely social actions are performed by the use of different tools or instruments. The reading of the schedule requires the schedule being presented in a readable form, and annotating it requires a writable form. Both the "pen and paper" used initially and the subsequently-introduced computerised IS afford these actions. In both cases, the instrument is used for interpreting and expressing semiotic results as a basis for and as a result of social action. The first nursing assistant is guided by communicative intent. She wants to say something to her colleague on the next work shift. The computerised schedule is an instrument for her to perform this communicative action. The second nursing assistant wants to be informed before she embarks on her visits to the elderly people. She uses the computerised system comprising schedules in order to become informed. Thereby, she becomes capable of performing subsequent knowledgeable actions for the clients. The nursing assistant maneuvres the IT system in order to arrive at a specific schedule (a specific client at a specific date and work shift). This kind of maneuvring of the IT artefact implies both technical and semiotic knowledge. The nursing assistant must of course also have relevant organisational knowledge. She must be aware of the obligations of the eldercare centre and herself in her organisational role. She must know the institutionalised way of communicating expected tasks, for example, the work schedule, which now is comprised in the new IT system.

One of the main driving forces of this computerisation was to ensure the quality of the communication and documentation around the care of the elderly. The directors of the eldercare centre wanted the new IT system to be the main medium for communication. Earlier, there was a mixture of different communication media, such as different handmade forms, small handwritten messages, and oral communication. The idea was now to channel most of the communication through the IT system. The work schedule should describe all planned (desired) measures to be taken for a particular elder at one visit. This includes both standard measures generally performed for this elder and specific measures needed at one or a limited amount of occasions. This means that the work schedule in the IT system is a collection of several communicative acts performed by several persons in the eldercare staff. One role of the IT system is thus to collect and integrate these different communicative acts in a proper way, for example, to enable communications from many persons to the one nursing assistant to perform a particular visit.

Even if the IT system is considered to be the main medium for communication of work tasks, there will, of course, remain informal channels beside the system. There will be situations when it is more appropriate to still communicate in an informal way. The system will not hold a complete description of the elders and their different needs. Unanticipated discourses concerning the elders will be required, which are not suited for channelling through the IT system. Also, the system cannot communicate all necessary measures to be taken. The nursing assistants must, of course, be attentive during their visits and based on observations and demands from the elderly perform appropriate unplanned measures.

As shown earlier, the role of the IT system is to facilitate communication. The system must support and enable the eldercare staff to perform important communicative actions through the system, like work schedule planning. There are other communicative tasks not yet mentioned which are important in the work practice. Important incidents at the elderly must be reported into the care journal of each elder. The IT system supports the reporting of incidents into the care journal. The system must automatically manage the care journal and, on request, present parts of it to those privileged to read the journal. The organisational role of this care journal is to be part of a work practice or action memory. Actors in the work practice must be able to remember what has happened and what actions have been performed. The IT system gives institutionalised support for recollecting things that occurred and were performed.

In general, work practices are equipped with a diverse range of instruments for actors to use in their social endeavour. These are often technical instruments, such as computers and washing machines. The usefulness of these instruments within a practice is contingent upon the meaning attached to them by the actors. From this perspective, computers are mainly a means to improve communication (Flores, 1998). Indeed, IT artefacts are technical instruments. Their main functioning within a work practice, such as eldercare, however, is as instruments for social action.

This means that we can view IT artefacts in a work practice as: (a) technological artefacts with physical properties, (b) semiotic artefacts affording communication and interpretation, and (c) social instruments used to responsively express actors' beliefs, values, and intentions. These three aspects of IT artefacts may be analytically distinguished. It is important to see, though, that IT artefacts are not simply isolated technical systems related to a social practice, in whatever intricate way. Rather, their physical properties are what enable and restrict possible semiotic interpretations and expressions required to form the social practice at hand. To paraphrase the quotation from Mead (1934) earlier: they are not simply objects which are there—they make possible the existence or appearance of that situation, for they are part of the mechanism whereby that situation is created.

With this theoretical and empirical backdrop, the following two sections explore how information systems (as IT artefacts) can be conceptualised following socio-instrumental pragmatism and how such a conceptualisation contributes to our understanding of IS theory in general.

Conceptualising Socio-Instrumental Actions and Socio-Pragmatic Artefacts

Information systems (as IT artefacts) are technical systems. This is obvious. They consist of hardware and software. They are technical instruments, usually not aimed for direct support of material action. Instead, they support communication and other types of information handling. As such, they are communicative and semiotic devices. Information systems consist of representations, such as texts and other signs.

This means that an IS is not just a restricted technical tool. An information system is a *socio-pragmatic instrument*. As such an instrument, it is utilised to perform *social actions*. These social actions are communicative in nature. When we state that IT use involves communicative actions, this has certain implications. A communicative action is not only conveying information from one actor to another. To represent things in the world by use of signs is one function of communication. When performing a communicative action, the actor is also engaging in interpersonal relations with the addressee. The locutor does something in relation to the addressee. When a nursing assistant uses the IT system to state "remember to take out the laundry," she is talking about something in the world ("the laundry"), and, at the same time, she is requesting something to be performed by the other nursing assistant—a request to take out the laundry. This double nature of language (performative and referential functions) is well elaborated in speech act theory (e.g., Habermas, 1984; Searle, 1969).

As a socio-pragmatic instrument, an IS must thus be a semiotic instrument. It must have capabilities to process signs. In doing this in a sophisticated way, information systems rely on advanced technical equipment. This technical equipment needs to be managed by a human being who wants to utilise its semiotic capabilities. An IS is an instrument for producing messages to other people and an instrument to be informed by other people. The technicalities of an IS are necessary material bases of its functionality as a socio-pragmatic instrument. Without hardware and software, one could not write and read through an IS. The material nature of an IT artefact can make it instrumental for social purposes.

Usually, an IS has a pre-defined set of communicative possibilities as defined by its functionality and vocabulary (the latter usually defined by its database schema); not everything can be said. An IS is also an instrument for getting informed by others; otherwise, it would not be a communication instrument. It must support both parts of the communication process, for example, to express and to interpret. Information systems have the capability to execute communicative actions according to its pre-defined action repertoire (determined by its programmed software). The action repertoire includes affordances for communicating and interpreting. Affordances are such properties of an object which, through perception, makes the object actable for the actor (Gibson, 1979). An IT system as a communicative instrument supports writing and reading, that is, it is a mediator of communication. IT systems usually have advanced capabilities of mediating agency. Such a system does not only mediate one message from one person to another person. It has capabilities to mediate communication from many persons to many persons in intricate and sophisticated ways including the maintenance of an appropriate action memory (e.g., a database). An IS as part of an organisational context is depicted in Figure 2. This figure is based on the general model of social action (Figure 1). In this socio-pragmatic view of information systems, the most important property of such artefacts is referred to as their actability. In order to be socially useful, information systems must be actable for their users (Ågerfalk, 2004; Cronholm & Goldkuhl, 2002; Goldkuhl & Ågerfalk, 2002).

Such capabilities make the IT system an organisational agent. An agent is someone who does something on behalf of someone else. Humans working in an organisation are agents for that organisation. They act as representatives for that organisation, that is, on behalf of the organisation (Ahrne, 1994; Goldkuhl & Röstlinger, 2003; Taylor & Van Every, 2000). An IT artefact (being an organisational agent) does possess some action capabilities but lacks typical human attributes (consciousness, intention, emotion, social awareness, empathy). In some situations, it is appropriate to view the IT artefact as a mere instrument (a static or dynamic tool) to be used by humans. In other situations, it may be appropriate to bring its agent capabilities to the fore and, hence, its possibilities to interact with humans as other organisational agents.

Figure 2. An information system as a socio-pragmatic instrument in a work practice

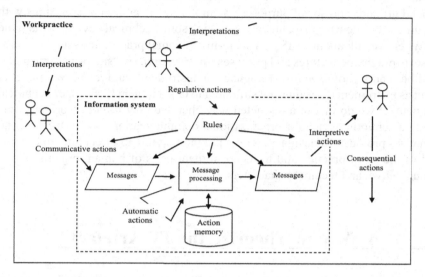

One key feature of this theory (socio-instrumental pragmatism) is that it should be used both for understanding the IT artefact and its human and organisational work practice of which it is part. This is a kind of *seamless theorising*, where we do not shift theoretical perspective when moving between the artefact and its human and organisational context (Goldkuhl, 2005; Goldkuhl & Röstlinger, 2003). According to this theory (ibid), actions are multi-functional; performing an action does several things. An action can, at the same time, be:

- a response to an action made by someone else (i.e., socially responsive);
- an expression of subjectivity, including a utilisation of immaterial instruments (such as knowledge and language);
- a utilisation of external instruments (e.g., technical artefacts);
- a compliance to organisational norms (e.g., role expectations);
- a production of action results (semiotic or material objects);
- a realisation of values and intentions; or
- an attempt to influence someone else (i.e., exerting power).

Being multi-functional, actions are also multi-dimensional. Actions performed by a human user when acting through an IT artefact can be described as social (having social grounds and social purposes), semiotic (using and producing signs with communicative intent), and technical (managing some technical device) at the same time. When we talk about an IS as a socio-instrumental pragmatic system, we emphasise its pragmatic features and purposes. *Instrumental* (in "socio-instrumental") should be read as both *semiotic* (language as instrument) and *technical* (material artefact as instrument). It is thus not sufficient to talk about an IS as a sociotechnical instrument. If we do that in a restricted way, then we may forget its primary role of being a semiotic device for organisational communication. Socio-instrumental pragmatism provides IS designers with a pragmatic view to direct attention to the whole of the work practice and to its constituent parts of human, organisational, communicative, and technical characters.

A Way to Theorise the IT Artefact

Based on a review of the complete set of 1990-1999 articles published in *Information Systems Research* (N = 188), one of the leading IS scholarly journals, Orlikowski and Iacono (2001) issued a general call to "theorising the IT artefact." The reason for taking such a measure was that a stunning 25% of the reviewed articles focused on other aspects than IT, referring to IT only incidentally or as background information. This should be understood in light of an ongoing quest for the identity and legitimacy of the field of information systems that started in the 1980s (see, for example, Banville & Landry, 1989) and recently culminated in a sometimes-heated debate caused by Benbasat and Zmud's (2003) already famous paper on "defining and communicating the discipline's core properties." The question underlying these efforts of organising the IS field seems to be three-fold. First, as pointed out by Benbasat and Zmud (2003), there is the issue of what to be included in IS research; that is, what are the core properties that must be considered in order to understand the role of IT in social settings? Second, the flip side of Benbasat and Zmud's (2003) coin is the question of what should be excluded from IS studies; that is, what properties of social life are not directly related to IT and thus better left to other disciplines to scrutinise? Finally, we need to understand the very concept of IT—to theorise the IT artefact. We must not regard IT as a technical black box but recognise what specific properties of this technology contribute to our understanding of its role in everyday life: "We will need to stop taking IT artefacts for granted and begin to take them seriously enough to theorise about them" (Orlikowski & Iacono, 2001).

It is generally believed that IT must be understood within a surrounding social context (e.g., Benbasat & Zmud, 2003). It is also generally believed that a fruitful analytic approach is to separate IT from non-IT, technical from social, and then to study how the two entities interact. This preferred separation of concerns is obvious from Benbasat and Zmud's (2003) model of the "IT artefact and its immediate nomological net" which includes the three core IS properties: the IT artefact, usage, and impact. It is also obvious from DeLone and McLean's (1992) IS Success Model, which includes the corresponding variables system/information quality, use, and impact.

We argue that, in order to seriously theorise the IT artefact, we need to develop theories that are useful in describing IT artefacts, IT artefacts' social context, and IT artefacts contextually. We need theories that let us see the social in the technical and the technical in the social. Obviously, this view is not too far from that of actor-network theory (e.g., Latour, 1991), where technology and people are both seen as social actants. However, as pointed out by Orlikowski and Iacono (2001), being concerned specifically with IT, we cannot accept general sweeping notions of technology. We must acknowledge the specific characters of IT, which include their symbol processing (semiotic) properties, their tool (instrumental) properties, and their social (agency) properties. The socio-instrumental theory of IT artefacts outlined in this chapter allows us to use one theoretical lens to study information systems in concert with humans, without losing our focus on core IS properties and without black-boxing technology, seen as something that is simply a cause or effect of something else. It enables us to view both humans and IT artefacts as organisational agents and to do this without losing sight of their fundamental differences in agency. This prevents us from falling into the trap of a too symmetrical view of humans and IT artefacts, which is one main criticism towards applications of actor-network theory within the field of IS (e.g., Walsham, 1997). The symmetrical view of ANT should thus not be confused with our ideal of seamless theorising mentioned earlier.

Orlikowski and Iacono (2001) conclude their research commentary by offering five premises for theorising IT artefacts. In short, they argue that:

1. IT artefacts are always value-based since they are designed and used by people with different interests, values, and assumptions.

2. IT artefacts are always embedded in a historical and cultural context.

3. IT artefacts are usually made up of several components and generic terms such as "the Internet" and "the Technology" should generally be avoided.

4. IT artefacts are not fixed and independent but co-evolve with the work practice in which they are embedded.

5. IT artefacts are subject to changes in technology.

Arguably, these premises go well with the proposed socio-instrumental pragmatism, which may thus be regarded as an instance of the sort of theorising called for by

Orlikowski and Iacono (2001). On the other hand, we think that Orlikowski and Iacono (2001) might be overly discouraging when stating that: "Given the context-specificity of IT artifacts, there is no single, one-size-fits-all conceptualisation of technology that will work for all studies." Indeed, any work practice-related theory is by definition localised to that specific work practice. On the other hand, we would like to argue that there are generic conceptualisations and units of analysis, such as those put forth in this chapter, that are general in nature but pragmatic enough to be applicable in most studies. There are a set of "core properties," or aspects, of IT in work practices that we should pay attention to in order to understand any IS in practice. We have termed these aspects the social, the technical, the instrumental, the semiotic, and the pragmatic. These properties, in turn, are by nature situational and can as such assist in eliciting important aspects embedded in particular research settings.

Conclusion

It is generally agreed that, in order to understand IT and its functioning in work practices, the surrounding social context must be seriously taken into account. A common view of conceptualising IT and its use is to make a sharp distinction between the technology as such on the one hand and social prerequisites and effects on the other. Contrary to this popular belief, we have articulated and illustrated a theoretical perspective that allows for conceiving of technological aspects and social aspects of work practices in an integrated way. The perspective, which we have termed socio-instrumental pragmatism, is founded in pragmatic theories of social action, and the main unit of analysis is that of mediated social action. By viewing the use of information systems as the performance of technologically-mediated social actions, we can distinguish between three important roles of IT: as an affordable technological base, as mediator of semiotic signs, and as a social instrument to responsively express actors' beliefs, values, and intentions. Instead of separating a social realm from a technical realm, we use "social" and "technical" as dimensions along which to study work practices. This way of reconciling the pragmatic, social, semiotic, and technical allows for a uniform approach to studying and understanding the relationship between IT and humans by directing attention to humans' social actions performed through and by means of IT. This approach goes beyond sweeping general notions of technology as part of socially-constructed reality and allows us to explore and exploit the genuine character of IT as part of an organisational agency.

Acknowledgments

This work has been financially supported by the Swedish Association for Local Authorities, the Swedish Agency for Innovation Systems (VINNOVA), the Science Foundation Ireland Investigator Programmes B4-STEP and Lero, and the Knowledge Foundation (KK-Foundation) through the programme for the promotion of research in IT at new universities and university colleges in Sweden (IT-Lyftet). The authors would like to thank Jack Downey for useful comments on a draft version of this chapter.

References

Ackerman, M. S. (2000). The intellectual challenge of CSCW: The gap between social requirements and technical feasibility. *Human-Computer Interaction, 15*(2/3), 179-203.

Ågerfalk, P. J. (2004). Investigating actability dimensions: A language/action perspective on criteria for information systems evaluation. *Interacting with Computers, 16*(5), 957-988.

Ågerfalk, P. J., & Eriksson, O. (2006). Socio-instrumental usability: IT is all about social action. *Journal of Information Technology, 21*(1), 24-39.

Ahrne, G. (1994). *Social organizations. Interaction inside, outside and between organization.* London: Sage.

Alter, S. (2003). 18 reasons why IT-reliant work systems should replace "the IT artifact" as the core subject matter of the IS field. *Communications of the Association for Information Systems, 12*, 366-395.

Andersen, P. B. (1990). *A theory of computer semiotics: Semiotic approaches to construction and assessment of computer systems.* Cambridge: Cambridge University Press.

Banville, C., & Landry, M. (1989). Can the field of MIS be disciplined. *Communications of the ACM, 32*(1), 48-60.

Benbasat, I., & Zmud, R. W. (2003). The identity crisis within the IS discipline: Defining and communicating the discipline's core properties. *MIS Quarterly, 27*(2), 183-194.

Berger, P. L., & Luckmann, T. (1966). *The social construction of reality.* Garden City: Doubleday & Co.

Blumer, H. (1969). *Symbolic interactionism: Perspective and method.* Berkeley: University of California Press.

Champion, D., & Stowell, F. (2002). Navigating the gap between action and a serving information system. *Information Systems Frontiers, 4*(3), 273-284.

Clark, H. H. (1996). *Using language.* Cambridge: Cambridge University Press.

Cronholm, S., & Goldkuhl, G. (2002). Actable information systems: Quality ideals put into practice. In M. Kirikowa, J. Grundspenkis, W. Wojtkowski, W. G. Wojtkowski, S. Wrycza, & Zupancic (Eds.), *Information systems development: Advances in methodologies, components, and management* (pp. 135-146). New York: Kluwer Academic/Plenum Publishers.

DeLone, W. H., & McLean, E. R. (1992). Information systems success: The quest for the dependent variable. *Information Systems Research, 3*(1), 60-95.

DeLone, W. H., & McLean, E. R. (2003). The DeLone and McLean model of information systems success: A ten-year update. *Journal of Management Information Systems, 19*(4), 9-30.

Dewey, J. (1931). *Philosophy and civilization.* New York: Minton, Balch & Co.

Flores, F. (1998). Information technology and the institution of identity: Reflections since understanding computers and cognition. *Information Technology & People, 11*(4), 352-372.

Galliers, R. D. (2003). Change as crisis or growth? Toward a trans-disciplinary view of information systems as a field of study. *Journal of the Association for Information Systems, 4*(6), 337-351.

Gibson, J. J. (1979). *The ecological approach to visual perception.* Boston: Houghton Mifflin.

Goldkuhl, G. (2003, July 1-2). Conversational analysis as a theoretical foundation for language action approaches? In *Proceedings of the 8th International Working Conference on the Language Action Perspective on Communication Modelling (LAP2003)*, Tilburg, The Netherlands (pp. 51-69).

Goldkuhl, G. (2005, March 15-16). Socio-instrumental pragmatism: A theoretical synthesis for pragmatic conceptualisation in information systems. In *Proceedings of the 3rd International Conference on Action in Language, Organisations and Information Systems (ALOIS*2005)*, Limerick, Ireland (pp. 148-165). University of Limerick.

Goldkuhl, G., & Ågerfalk, P. J. (2002). Actability: A way to understand information systems pragmatics. In K. Liu, R. J. Clarke, P. B. Andersen, & R. K. Stamper (Eds.), *Coordination and communication using signs: Studies in organisational semiotics 2* (pp. 85-113). Boston: Kluwer Academic Publishers.

Goldkuhl, G., & Lyytinen, K. (1982). A language action view of information systems. In M. Ginzberg & C. Ross (Eds.), *Proceedings of the 3rd International Conference on Information Systems (ICIS'82)* (pp. 13-29).

Goldkuhl, G., & Röstlinger, A. (2002, September 24-25). The practices of knowledge: Investigating functions and sources. In *Proceedings of the 3rd European Conference on Knowledge Management*, Trinity College Dublin, Ireland (pp. 262-273).

Goldkuhl, G., & Röstlinger, A. (2003) Towards an integral understanding of organisations and information systems: Convergence of three theories. In H. W. M. Gazendam, R. J. Jorna, & R. S. Cijsouw (Eds.), *Dynamics and change in organizations. Studies in organizational semiotics* (pp. 132-161). Boston: Kluwer.

Goles, T., & Hirschheim, R. (2000). The paradigm is dead, the paradigm is dead ... long live the paradigm: The legacy of Burrell and Morgan. *Omega—International Journal of Management Science, 28*(3), 249-268.

Habermas, J. (1984) *The theory of communicative action 1. Reason and the rationalization of society*. Cambridge: Polity Press.

Latour, B. (1991). Technology is society made durable. In J. Law (Ed.), *A sociology of monsters: Essays on power, technology and domination* (pp. 103-131). London: Routledge & Kegan Paul.

Linell, P. (1998). *Approaching dialogue. Talk, interaction and contexts in dialogical perspectives*. Amsterdam: John Benjamins Publ.

Mead, G. H. (1934). *Mind, self and society from the standpoint of a social behavorist*. Chicago: University of Chicago Press

Mumford, E., & Weir, M. (1979). *Computer systems in work design: The ETHICS method*. London: Associated Business Press.

Nurminen, M. (1988). *People or computers: Three ways of looking at information systems*. Lund: Studentlitteratur.

Orlikowski, W. J., & Iacono, S. (2001). Research commentary: Desperately seeking the "IT" in IT research—a call to theorizing the IT artifact. *Information Systems Research, 12*(2), 121-134.

Sacks, H. (1992). *Lectures on conversation*. Oxford: Blackwell.

Schatzki, T. R., Knorr Cetina, K., & von Savigny, E. (Eds.) (2001). *The practice turn in contemporary theory*. London: Routledge.

Schutz, A. (1970). *On phenomenology and social relations*. University of Chicago Press.

Searle, J. R. (1969). *Speech acts. An essay in the philosophy of language*. London: Cambridge University Press.

Strauss, A. (1993). *Continual permutations of action*. New York: Aldine de Gruyter.

Taylor, J., & Van Every, E. (2000). *The emergent organization. Communication at its site and surface*. London: Lawrence Erlbaum.

Vološinov, V. N. (1985). Verbal interaction. In R. E. Innis (Ed.), *Semiotics. An introductory anthology* (pp. 47-65). Bloomington: Indiana University Press.

Vygotsky, L. S. (1962). *Thought and language*. Cambridge: MIT Press.

Walsham, G. (1997). Actor-network theory: Current status and future prospects. In A. S. Lee, J. Liebenau, & J. I. DeGross (Eds), *Information systems and qualitative research* (pp. 466-480). London: Chapman & Hall.

Weber, M. (1978). *Economy and society*. Berkeley: University of California Press.

Wertsch, J. V. (1998). *Mind as action*. New York: Oxford University Press.

Wicks, A. C., & Freeman, R. E. (1998). Organization studies and the new pragmatism: Positivism, anti-positivism, and the search for ethics. *Organization Science, 9*(2), 123-140.

Winograd, T., & Flores, F. (1986). *Understanding computers and cognition: A new foundation for design*. Norwood: Ablex.

Chapter X

Sociotechnical Spaces:
Guiding Politics, Staging Design

Christian Clausen
IPL / Innovation and Sustainability,
Technical University of Denmark, Denmark

Yutaka Yoshinaka
IPL / Innovation and Sustainability,
Technical University of Denmark, Denmark

Abstract

The chapter addresses how insights from the social shaping tradition and political process theory may contribute to an understanding of the sociotechnical design and implementation of change. This idea is pursued through the notion of "sociotechnical spaces" and its delineation, with respect to the analysis of two distinct cases, namely, business process reengineering (BPR) and magnetic resonance imaging (MRI) in the light of "film-less" radiological practice, respectively. The chapter elaborates on sociotechnical space as being an occasioning as well as a result of sociotechnical choices and processes and points to how socio-material and discursive practices may render such spaces open to problematisation and action. It is suggested that the notion of sociotechnical spaces helps generate a sensitising guide for researchers and practitioners and, thus, may serve as a constructive means with which to localise potential political concerns in processes of change. This chapter tentatively points to some analytical implications and to challenges and possibilities for the "bridging" between spaces, which may otherwise be rendered analytically distinct.

Introduction

This chapter draws on recent concepts developed within the social shaping of technology (SST) tradition (Sørensen & Williams, 2002), combined with a political process analysis approach, and captured together in the notion of "sociotechnical spaces." A sociotechnical space for shaping implies a socio-material and discursive context (rather than a physical space alone) where sociotechnical ensembles can be analysed, addressed, and politicised (Clausen & Koch, 1999). "Space" is mainly an *occasioning* as well as a *result* of sociotechnical processes—taken to be heterogeneous processes of translation and displacement—in which social players interact with one another and with technological artefacts and programs for change.

The particular configuration of a space includes and sustains some actors, their agendas, and particular frameworks of action within it, while leaving others excluded. While the emergence and constitution of sociotechnical spaces are in no way to be taken as a priori givens, an analysis facilitated through the "spaces" notion may encompass any a priori demarcations, which some actors and their practices render as givens: this may include, for example, conceptions as to what is to be deemed (distinctly) social vis-à-vis technical in both problematisation and approaches to management and coordination. This chapter underscores such realities in its treatment of spaces and the selectivity they thereby manifest—a selectivity which the notion bears open to analysis. The authors believe this to be a particularly-pertinent challenge to organisational setups and concrete undertakings in sociotechnical change, interaction, and development.

Sociotechnical space is by no means intended as a well-delineated tool, but rather a sensitising concept. One implication of its approach is a greater attention towards the relational nature of what (and how) areas may be delimited vis-à-vis rendered open to negotiation and transformation. This may deal with technological design, implementation, and change processes, including the characterisation of the very artefacts or instruments involved or otherwise implicated in such change. This is particularly important from the vantage point of recognising the multiplicity in the complex of diverging set of issues, agendas, and practices that may be involved in the course of such processes of change.

The concept should help sensitise practitioners and analysts alike to these political dimensions and, in this sense, serve as a reference and guidance for sociotechnical action.[1] It should point to areas where reflexive approaches concerning involvement in "spacing" and "staging" of design activities and change processes might be helpful: these include the creation, configuration, and reconfiguration of actors and actants, the definition and redefinition of boundaries, and the bridging of diverse spaces as processes of translation and network building. A crucial dimension in design is the idea of differentiation, whether certain actors or aspects inevitably come to be included or excluded in the design process, and how problems and interests are mediated and, thus, defined as being relevant or not. In this chapter, we address—through the notion of "sociotechnical spaces"—how insights from the social shaping tradition and political process theory may contribute to an understanding of sociotechnical design and implementation of change. With this concept as a sensitising device, we explore some of the potential openings for design and social choice, indicate where such potential openings can be further explored, and, thus, stimulate a debate on viable strategies for the staging of sociotechnical action.

Sociotechnical Spaces

Space is a frequently-used metaphor to characterise changing relations between technology and society. The general idea is that different spaces configure technology differently. From a background in regional economics, Castells (1996) character-ises the "network society" as dominated by the logic of a global "space of flows" contesting or replacing the traditional "space of place." With this metaphorical expression is meant that people's individual spaces are invaded by non-traditional elements changing the distribution and construction of local and global phenomena. Castells (1996) views spaces as situated and contingent relations between material products—including people—who engage in historical-determined social relation-ships and practices that provide space with a form of function and a social meaning (Castells, 1996, p. 441). Such configurational spaces depict mainly geographical embedded and heterogeneous characterisations of industrial networks and chal-lenge generalised ideas of technological change. Also from industrial economics and innovation economics, space metaphors are used to address structural changes in sociotechnical relations often on a macro- or regional level. A major weakness in these approaches is the lack of interest in how networks, new structures, and posi-tions are constructed and maintained (Jørgensen & Sørensen, 2002, p. 202), and the focus is on companies and material objects where political differentiations and processes of meaning are left aside. From the social shaping of technology tradi-tion, a range of space metaphors like "laboratories," "ensembles," "development arenas," "niches," and so forth, have been presented (Sørensen & Williams, 2002). "Development arena" is a metaphor for the space where political, social, and technical performances related to a specific technological problem takes place. It is defined as "a spatial imagery that brings together heterogeneous elements that seem distant in geographical and conventional cultural space" (Jørgensen & Sørensen, 2002, p. 200). But, as with other metaphors in the social shaping tradition, it is focused on specific problems. In this case, it addresses the space that holds together settings and relations comprising the context and content of product and process development.

With the notion of sociotechnical spaces, we want to focus the attention towards socio-material, political and discursive practices, and emergent processes configuring the working of sociotechnical ensembles. The metaphor especially sensitises our attention to the inclusion and exclusion of actors, interests, and meaning as well as content in sociotechnical developments and design processes on project and organisational and interorganisational levels where programmed change is the typical case. In this sense, the metaphor has a different focus and goes beyond notions taking its departure in global, regional, geographic, or industrial change. By emphasising political processes in the creation of boundaries around the sociotechnical spaces, it builds on and provides a focusing instrument for studies and reflexive action in the social shaping tradition.

In keeping with the actor-network theory (ANT) and its principles of general symmetry and agnosticism as methodological guides to exploring sociotechnical action and phenomena of translation and displacement, actors anchored in technically-deterministic or generally-absolutist conceptions need to be explored and accounted for as well. Such conceptions are often reflected in management programs and agendas for courses of action for organisational development and embedded (pre)-established practices and norms of engagement (e.g., in professional interaction), as well as in the status and role of material and technical devices in the mediation of relations and tasks. ANT, especially in view of a political processes emphasis, must address this dimension, and the notion of "sociotechnical spaces" can be seen as a means to analytically deal with these issues of obduracy. The ambition is, thus, to address how such traditional (reductionist) conceptions are themselves also very much situated and partake in the mediation of roles and events, rather than to merely critically address them by way of debunking.[2] The sociotechnical spaces approach would treat and problematise the reductionist conceptions (and framework of action) as part and parcel of the qualification and elaboration of the spaces that is at hand. In so far as such conceptions too, enter into the active strategies and modes of engagement by *some* actors in their sociotechnical interaction, the resources being mobilised and articulated within such frames of interaction come to bear influence on the actor's specific room for manoeuvre.

The notion of "sociotechnical space" is, thus, intended as a contribution to understand the distributed character of sociotechnical complexity and its management. A sociotechnical space can, therefore, be seen as a target for political concern in organisations for technological change. Approaching sociotechnical issues and interaction involving actors through the notion of "spaces" allows for the staging, ordering, and localisation of change processes (their delimitation and opening) in an approach for focusing on intervention in and through design (Berg, 1998). A sociotechnical spaces approach allows not only for the potential opening of spaces for scrutiny and exploration, but also for the association of realms (a larger framework for the bridging of "spaces") otherwise rendered distinct and without immediate or obvious relevance to one another. In this light, the facilitation of particular views and combinations of knowledge and insight may lead to innovative processes in technology design, implementation, and change.

The notion of sociotechnical spaces draws from ANT and related social shaping approaches upon the understanding that the issue of "content" (e.g., technical content) and "context" (e.g., social context) are so strongly related as they necessarily go together as one common unit of analysis. In the most rudimentary of understandings, this would mean that content and context are inextricably interrelated and mutually constitutive, that is, that a phenomena or artefact only gives meaning as addressed in a concrete context.[3] In viewing the embedded (and configured) processes of sociotechnical change in this light, the focus of investigation falls then upon the heterogeneous (not distinctly technically- or socially-directed), negotiated (without distinct sets of a priori relations) and locally contingent (as to pre-conditions and effects entailed) characteristics of such change. By such, a focus is placed on the mediated nature of the processes and displacements entailed so these may be problematised with regard to the shifting contexts and content (Callon, 2002; Callon & Law, 1989).

The social and organisational arrangements are—like the technical elements in the sociotechnical spaces—not given a priori, but rather constituted through processes of inclusion, at the exclusion of others. The very nature of inclusion, and, as a consequence, how exclusion (however implicitly or explicitly) is being manifested, is problematic to be treated with the spaces approach. Sociotechnical ensembles are, thus, studied as part and parcel of the rationales or (political) programs for change. Such rationales, and the particular social actors and organisational arrangements, are taken to be results of, as well as the occasions for, the interaction which is rendered identifiable in such a space. The differentiation of actors and the means by which this is accomplished and manifested (in the form of who are included in versus who are excluded from the space) are, thereby, taken as elements suitable for analysis in the understanding of the problem (re-)definition and the mobilisation of resources with respect to the space.

In the following, we illustrate the notion of sociotechnical spaces through the analysis of how some concepts or technologies—in a pre-defined or pre-configured capacity—enter into the workings of diverse organisational and professional settings through a process of translation. Here, a framework of concepts or visions of sociotechnical change, stemming from outside the immediate contexts of their working, emerge as a relevant problematic into a concrete setting. Other spaces, thereby, influence the translation or appropriation of these elements into the settings in question, as the elements, in turn, are influenced through the process.

Our first illustration concerns the management concept of *business process reengineering* (BPR), analysed with regard to two different organisations, while the other deals with the development in medical practice toward *film-less* radiology. The latter illustration is examined specifically in relation to *magnetic resonance imaging* (MRI), in terms of this diagnostic imaging modality's set of knowledge practices as they are implicated in such a transition. The status of the workings of such change processes may be understood by making *visible* and open to problematisation the heterogeneous work and contingencies entailed (Suchman, 1995). The idea of "spaces" is, thus, a means to better understand the conditions amenable to the politicisation and staging of such change processes.

The Constitution of Sociotechnical Spaces: A Case of BPR

The constitution of spaces through a management concept is illustrated with cases of business process reengineering (BPR). This example is taken from a European study on the social shaping of BPR—a management concept (the PRECEPT project). It illustrates how sociotechnical change programs can be seen as constituting and framing specific sociotechnical spaces. The opening of new possibilities (and closing of others) for sociotechnical action with BPR is identified as part of the working of such a political program for change. This includes the translation of organisational external and internal conditions, recruitment strategies, mapping methods, the perception and use of ICT, and, more generally, the network building capacity of the "migrating" BPR program of change. The BPR concept is here seen as an actor network including the espoused programs, cases of practice, and the guru evangelists and consultants promoting it.

The present analysis draws on two original in-depth case studies of BPR projects from Denmark and Norway, respectively. The Danish study (labelled "DK Process plant") dealt with the implementation of BPR in a production facility (250 employees) belonging to a subsidiary of a large (foreign) multinational concern (Clausen & Busk Kofoed, 2002). The project emerged in response to shareholder demands calling for increased profits and more competitive performance while environmental regulatory demands also were being placed on the production facility. The Norwegian study ("NO Norwestoil") dealt with a relatively recent gas transport plant (from 1985, with 540 employees) under a Norwegian-based multinational concern (Clausen & Moltu, 2003; Moltu, 2002, 2004). BPR implementation was on the agenda here, as a result of dropping oil prices and perceived increase in market competition for gas on the home front and transfer of firm activities abroad.

It had been the case in both BPR projects that local top management grasped the signals from the central or concern management on cost cutting and organisational development and thus began organising their BPR projects with the aim of changing the internal plant organisation. As expected in the case of BPR according to consultants' offerings, the driving coalitions were found as a combination of management and consultants. But, as the following example from the NO Norwestoil will indicate, several organisational players through their interaction took part in the creation of this driving coalition. In this very process, the players interpreted a range of circumstances and contributed to the local translation of BPR, bringing in a diversity of ideas and offering their expertise.

The consultants from NO Norwestoil's R&D department were put in charge of the BPR project from the outset, and they suggested a BPR approach including a broad participation encompassing all employees. These consultants interpreted the BPR management concept as incommensurable to Norwegian work life traditions.[4] The unions were considered to be relatively strong in this company, and, for this reason, the consultants were keen to translate *orthodox* BPR into "BPR *with participation*." To avoid opposition from unions, a decision was made not to label the project as BPR, instead the neutral label "PA30" was used.

In the Danish BPR project, the management director (CEO) of the DK Process Plant hired an *international* consulting company (house consultant) to carry out the BPR analysis. A BPR project was set up as a consequence of the advice from these consultants with the declared goal of developing a modern, flexible organisation with increased delegation of responsibilities and competence. A detailed BPR project organisation was implemented including a "common team" (consultants and employees) with direct reference to the management directors as well as ad hoc groups with special analytical tasks. The driving coalition in the DK case centred around the local team of managers and the international consultants.

Subsequent coalition building processes around the organising of BPR projects went hand-in-hand with collecting, adopting, and transforming received[5] bits and pieces of BPR programs. Through the inclusion of certain groups and the exclusion of others, it became clearer to organisational members where the borderlines were drawn around the BPR spaces. The shaping of BPR concepts was in both examples inseparable from the coalition building process and should be seen as processes of mutual translation as indicated in Table 1. In the NO Norwestoil case, the BPR project was re-defined around a deep-rooted participative approach based on internal consultants, local management, and a tradition for union-supported collaborative TQM projects. In the DK Process Plant case, a more orthodox BPR concept (but nonetheless also including a group of employees selected by management) was adopted as a package emerging with the selection of international consultants, acting as house consultants for the concern together with the local team of managers.

During the process, participative mapping in both cases proved to be an effective tool in engaging organisational members—including shop floor workers—in the BPR project as well as in the securing acceptance toward the idea of organising work according to a process perspective. In both NO Norwestoil and DK Process Plant, the participative mapping activities gave positive outcomes for the participants in that they increased their knowledge on their work processes and became engaged in suggesting changes. In both cases, the mapping of work processes was used as strategic element by the driving coalition for controlling actors by enrolment and making workers accept the idea of process-oriented change. In the NO Norwestoil case, this strategy proved remarkably successful, and the BPR space was, in this respect, expanded to include almost all employees. BPR was increasingly seen by workers as a vehicle to gain influence on organisation and work. In the DK Process Plant, only a partial inclusion of employees took place signalling a more narrow creation of borders around the BPR space. As workers commented, participants in the project groups were "taken hostage" by the consultants.

But, in both cases, the broadening of the BPR space opened for more players and created expectations of being heard in the process. BPR projects in their attempt to enrol employees in the change process, at the same time, constitute a space for exchange of organisational debate where employees may develop their competences for participation in sociotechnical design.

As workers' design suggestions were rejected by the driving coalitions, the BPR spaces were narrowed down to fit with consultant's ideas of what would be expected and acceptable design solutions by industry standards. The implication of this being isolation of consultants in their role as the only drivers of the BPR projects and a destabilisation of the expanding BPR network. A coalition building in the DK

Table 1. Mutual translations of BPR concepts and political coalitions

BPR Cases	Coalition Partners	BPR Content
NO Norwestoil		
• constructing BPR project	local management internal consultants	union-supported, participative approach
• expanding BPR space	local management internal consultants unions, workers	broad participative process mapping methodology
• transforming BPR	local management international consultants	orthodox, top-down BPR
DK Process Plant		
• constructing BPR project	local team of managers international consultants	consultancy driven BPR with participation
• expanding BPR space	local team of managers international consultants employee representatives	limited participation in process mapping and "brown paper" drawing
• transforming BPR	local team of managers consultants (action researchers) broader teams of employees	broader participative approach with team building

Process Plant with university consultants launching a competing program based on ideas from the "learning organisation" and "developmental work" did not succeed in penetrating the boarders of the BPR space. A position outside the BPR space was established instead.

During the analysis and design phases, it became clear that the driving coalitions were pursuing BPR strategies within a framework of cost cutting. This definition of BPR—mirrored in workers and union responses to BPR—mounted to a confrontation of interests. But, the content of the responses developed differently in the two cases. The inclusion of international BPR consultants and the diminishing traditional union influence paved the way for a translation of BPR from a participative, continuous improvement-oriented BPR to a more orthodox BPR concept in the NO Norwestoil. An opposite development took place in the DK Process Plant, where the inclusion of university-based action researchers (after the international consultants had left) more or less dissolved the BPR project into a participative team building activity.

In this way, the BPR space is a contested terrain, where different competing ideas and interpretations of the content of BPR concepts, actor roles, the distribution of rights, and obligations in the projects are subject to controversial debate and politicising. Especially, the translation of process analysis to design solutions proved to be a contested terrain of organisational politics.

These BPR cases illustrate how the space metaphor can address the political dimensions and focus a case study on sociotechnical change. The cases illustrate how organisational players within a diversity of strategic options interact with and through a sociotechnical space where BPR projects and programs exist. While diverse players consider whether to join or fight the BPR space or whether to include or exclude others from the space, they negotiate the size and perimeter of the space in question. As part of the same processes of inclusion and exclusion, they negotiate the BPR project content, such as organisation and phases, mapping methods, and so forth, as well as the perspective and agenda for sociotechnical change. The most significant changes in the BPR spaces are illustrated through the exchange of consultants and the commitment or withdrawal of unions and worker groups. The sociotechnical spaces constituted by BPR programs and their actor networks are not spaces solely controlled by management and consultants. They, in turn, offer possibilities to politicise BPR and organisational change and reframe participatory practices from the perspective of broader organisational players. In this way, the outcome challenges pre-conceived and deep-seated notions held by management and consultants as well.

Sociotechnical Spaces in Technological Transition: A Case of MRI

The second case is based on a study of conventional (film-based) magnetic resonance imaging (MRI) practice in radiology, situating it within the context of a transition toward "film-less" and "paperless" practice relating to developments within "e-radiology" and, more generally, electronic patient records (EPR) in hospital practice.[6] The role and implication of sociotechnical spaces in MRI—where the imaging practice may be characterised as a knowledge practice particularly enmeshed in "film" as a medium for interdisciplinary exchange—is illustrated with the help of some contrasts afforded by the advent of "film-less" work practices.

Some advantages of electronically-based film-less practice have been pointed to as being helpful in reducing shortcomings in the use of film. These include the eventuality of relevant patient scans being unavailable (or lost) when/where they are actually needed (whether it be in radiology or in the clinic), as well as the task of having to maintain an otherwise enormous physical archive of "older" patient scans, and so forth. In some respects, the phasing-out of film and the seeming ubiquity of image accessibility through electronic venues do, indeed, suggest the meeting of such "programmatic" aspects of transformation to film-less practice. Yet, at the same time, the notion that otherwise *disparate* imaging modalities (such as the MRI, conventional x-rays, computed tomography (CT), and so forth,—albeit *within* the domain of radiological practice) may be grouped together into a unified archiving and communication system, gives occasion for problematising the drawing of boundaries of practice and knowledge—that such a vision of practice entails. The particular configuration of medical imaging into a film-less mode practice points to a different sort of sociotechnical space, into which the heretofore film-based practice of MRI becomes inscribed.

MRI is a digital imaging technique suited for rendering multiple sets of cross-sectional images of patients as a course of their diagnostic examination. The imaging process itself entails a complex and contingent set of translations across professional spaces of practice involving clinicians, radiologists, and technologists/radiographers to name a few. Their collaboration spans both fairly distributed settings (through the help of written exchanges of information and use of agreed-upon protocols), as well as more proximal situations (such as radiological *conferences*, where clinicians and radiologists are physically present). These exchanges of information are crucial in the processes not only of the interpreting of the pertinent images but the images' very "construction" itself (Yoshinaka, 2005).

While image acquisition in MRI is a digital process, the subsequent handling and interpreting of the acquired images have been through printing them onto "hardcopy" films, often viewed through a light-box display. Numerous sequential slices of images are taken along different angles of projection (mostly confined to a specific bodily region) in different types of images, revealing specific "traits" with regard to the morphology and pathology under scrutiny. For an individual patient's sitting for an MRI exam, this means that the total number of images may amount to numerous images. These images are assembled in sequence and image types onto hardcopy film for viewing and interpretation, and the manner of assembly is, to some degree, influenced by the specific practical and collaborative experiences involving the radiological department and the clinical departments, as well as the MRI scanner's particular make in terms of imaging characteristics.

In an MRI, the idea that images are circulated (on film) across various settings in and outside of the hospital (e.g., between radiology and clinical departments or incoming images through patient referrals) is nothing new. Yet, the move toward greater digitisation in medical practice, such as in the advent of film-less imaging practice, occasions inquiry as to the concrete knowledge and work practices entailed in the processes of scanning and interpreting these images in the immediate context of use. Particularly, the relation between the MRIs as digital versus printed images, and the very conditions which may have bearing on the (set of) images' scope of mobility in their capacity as film-based or film-less media, make the emphasis on the practices and concrete settings of work pertinent to address, not in the least, in the light electronically-mediated communication (ICT) through disjointed settings.

Along with a general move toward digitalisation in healthcare (with initiatives relating to the development of electronic forms of patient record keeping (EPR)), radiology has experienced a likewise trend toward digitalisation. The expectation in some departmental practices has hinged upon a makeshift practice of merging archived hardcopy (such as former MRI examinations of patients, pertinent to, and retrieved for the planning of, the periodic re-scanning of patients for monitoring, etc.), within the new digital framework, by way of simply scanning the analogue film "back-into" digital format, that is, in the digital archive.

In the concrete practice of MRI, however, the specificity of this imaging modality manifests pertinent problems in this regard. Namely, the MRI (as opposed to conventional x-ray or CT scans) loses much of its image quality in the process of being scanned from analogue hardcopy film back *into* digital display, where the contrast resolution that is so central to the interpretation of these images fails to be reproduced on screen.[7] While the back-catalogue of patient examinations are, in principle, also stored in their original (digital) format (as MRIs are digitally-acquired images), these lack the processing and assemblage of image sequences that takes place in their printing onto film. Thus, while such older MRI exams serve a function in the event of planning and comparing them to a patient's new scans, they are too numerous to systematically transfer into a new archiving and retrieval system developed for the digitalisation of the department.

Some departments experiencing a transition toward digitalised radiology may indeed take up a *hybrid* form of practice—albeit as a transitory measure—whereby new patient MRI exams are formatted for display, archived and communicated electronically, *while* old MRI exams are handled conventionally through film. The point with such practices is to avoid the loss of information that is brought about if the films are alternatively scanned into the electronic archiving system. This form of *mixed-use* practice[8] shifts the boundary drawn in the light of film-less imaging which particularly implicates the practice of MRI. That is to say, the configuration imposed by film-less imaging does not accommodate film-*based* practice well in the case of MRI. While older films figure centrally in the tasks of re-examining patients (in the scanning as well as interpretation), such a detail in the work processes are excluded. And, provisional attempts to re-scan films into digital format are (indirectly) excluded, in so far as such images miss the resolution otherwise so central to contrasts in MRIs.

Thus, while the particular configuration of film-less imaging links together disparate modalities into one system, it *excludes* salient aspects of MRI practice as a knowledge practice relevant for film-less imaging to give meaning in the first place. A common set of problem issues for the different imaging modalities, such as the practical management of the images for archiving and transition, is adopted and carried through. It, however, also illustrates an alternative space (re-opened) by practitioners themselves, namely in making use of such mixed-use practices, albeit as a provisional and temporary move.

Paradoxically, such a move has the effect of "facilitating" film-less practice, in so far as it amends the deficiencies entailed in solely relying on film-less imaging in the course of the transition. Active user strategies are, thus, at play in re-defining the space of interaction and material content envisaged through digitalisation. The setting reveals the actual contingencies of the specific knowledge practices and the delimitation and openings that avail themselves in relation to the particular programs of change in digitalisation.

Similarly, the space configured by film-less radiology bears influence on the particular practice of radiological conferences and radiologists' involvement in conferring findings of MRI examinations with the specific clinical departments they serve. While the idea of film-less practice suggests that communication and conferring on patient cases may take place in distinct locations between radiology and clinicians, many radiological departments in the Nordic countries have nevertheless held on to the need for mutual presence between the radiological and clinical parties in a common locale.[9] Radiological conferences, apart from the dialogue underscoring the immediate assessment of the patient status between the parties, also serve a role in (through dialogue) socialising the clinicians to the images and the radiologists to the clinical problem-issues of pertinence to the collaboration at hand.

Thus, while the rationale of film-less imaging and electronic communication support the idea of distributed access to images and communication among involved parties, this in no way dictates the most "effective" form of professional interaction that has been built up through film-based practice. And still, film-less practice as to the content of such communication does bear influence on the radiological conference itself. Whereas through film, the radiologists and the clinicians have been able to juxtapose different modalities, as well as specific differentiated images (in MRI) "at will" in the course of elaborating on the patient's case, in a shared space of interpretation and exchange (Kuutti & Karasti, 1995). Much work of "planning" the presentation of MRI findings at these film-less conferences has entailed having to delimit the number and type of MRI images that could be presented considerably. The constraints, which visual presentation on screens (as opposed to on film of the light-box display) bear upon the "content" of MRI exams in terms of attributing findings to specific images, can thus be said to be of consequence to the knowledge practice entailed.

The particular problem-definition as to image accessibility translated into such a system does not readily support other (perhaps more salient) issues of practical and epistemological bearing for some constellations of actors involved in the interpretation and use of MRIs. While the configuration of film-less imaging solves some problems (in its particular way), it thus leaves others unaddressed (and thus omitted). The metaphor of sociotechnical spaces sensitises to how programs of change selectively frame and prioritise particular issues, while effectively excluding others of potential concern for the success of the change processes in question.

Spaces: Some Strategic Implications and Ideas

Through the spaces notion, neither the occurrence nor sustenance of the spaces are taken as a priori givens; they are occasions as well as effects. The notion of sociotechnical spaces may help alert to the particularities (particular translations) of such a pre-constructed reality—constructed be it by omission or commission—and the extent to which subsequent translations are locked-in or maybe productively (re)-configured in the ensuing change programs through processes of problematisation and renegotiation.

Case studies from BPR illustrate how sociotechnical space is constituted as a contested terrain staging interactions among diverse players in debates of mapping and design of organisational solutions. The spaces approach keeps focus on the choices concerned with inclusion and exclusion of organisational players and the mutual translation of players and content of change. Similarly, the elaboration of film-less practice in MRI illustrates the nature of the delimitation such as a transition occasions for the existing knowledge practices in the course of change, while short of determining the nature of the change entirely. The metaphor of sociotechnical spaces sensitises to the priorities involved in particular socio-material practices, which are excluded by other forms of ordering. It, thus, opens up to multiplicities between sameness and difference (for example, in imaging modalities or problems associated with MRIs), and such boundary drawing (as to how modalities are rendered similar across the board or with specific, contingent needs for some) are of a political nature.

In projects of change involving multiple players and understandings of agendas and work practices, involved parties may have to deal with differing individual as well as collective resource constraints, such as time, conditions of involvement, and past experiences and competencies. These may influence how roles and identities are played out in the process of change. Spaces should be seen as a sensitising concept/framework and heuristic device, rather than a tool for identifying universally applicable objects and phenomena. The spaces notion sensitises the different spaces for negotiation that open up in the course of change, albeit calling for reflexivity on the part of the analyst as to the character of such interactions. The exchanges are contingent and partial, rather than all-encompassing, that is, rather than representing bits and pieces of a "coherent whole." Their seeming coherence is a result of a particular framing of the interactions, resultant of the temporal and delimited nature of their translations (Latour, 1999; Law, 2002).

The spaces approach may be used to analyse and re-address examples of sociotechnical design, such as that of the Scandinavian *UTOPIA*-project from the early 1980's (Ehn, 1988). UTOPIA pointed to the possibility of addressing design choices and strategies in the development, implementation, and use concerning text and graphic technology in the printing industry. The project opened up a space which, until then, had remained outside the realm of problematisation and politicisation, and thus unexplored and unarticulated, with regards to the involvement of the user-setting and its strategies in change processes. In particular, the project attempted at staging collaboration between, and thereby "bridging," otherwise distinct disciplinary traditions. Skilled workers, computer scientists, and engineers, as well as social scientists', involvement were thus framed within a new understanding as to the role of design and use for technological change.

The metaphorical notion of sociotechnical spaces enables us to analyse and understand complex contextual conditions for sociotechnical action. One important implication of this understanding could be an increased sensitivity *towards the selection* of issues to be opened for deconstruction *and subsequent politicisation* compared to issues that could be left as closed stable constructions (Latour, 2003). The notion of sociotechnical spaces can, in this way, contribute to a reflexive approach to design and change where constructions in the form of technology, programs, and taken-for-granted orders may be allowed to play their roles as a way of creating conditions for action. The difference compared to linear or rationalistic approaches would be the careful and conscious selection of the allowed constructions based on an explicit knowledge or expectation of the likely working of these constructions in the specific sociotechnical space.

References

Berg, M. (1998). The politics of technology: On bringing social theory into techno-logical design. *Science, Technology, & Human Values, 23*(4), 456-490.

Bijker, W. E. (1995). *Of bicycles, bakelites, and bulbs: Toward a theory of socio-technical change.* Cambridge, MA: The MIT Press.

Callon, M. (2002). Writing and (re)writing devices as tools for managing complex-ity. In J. Law, & A. Mol (Eds.), *Complexities: Social studies of knowledge practices* (pp. 191-217). Durham, NC: Duke University Press.

Callon, M., & Law, J. (1989). On the construction of sociotechnical networks: Con-tent and context revisited. In L. Hargens, R. A. Jones, & A. Pickering (Eds.), *Knowledge and society: Studies in the sociology of science, past and present* (Vol. 8, pp. 57-83). Stamford, CA: JAI Press.

Castells, M. (1996). *The rise of the network society.* Oxford: Blackwell Publish-ers.

Clausen, C., & Busk Kofoed, L. (2002). *BPR in the process plant—a case of BPR implementation in a Danish subsidiary plant of a multinational company* (PRECEPT Working Paper No. 10). Lyngby: Department of Manufacturing Engineering and Management, Technical University of Denmark.

Clausen, C., & Koch, C. (1999). The role of spaces and occasions in the social shaping of information technologies. *Technology Analysis & Strategic Man-agement, 11*(3), 463-482.

Clausen, C., & Moltu, B. (2003, July 3-5). *Socio-technical spaces: A new guide to organisational politics?* Presented at the 19th EGOS Colloquium, Copen-hagen.

Dawson, P., Clausen, C., & Nielsen, K. T. (2000). Political processes in manage-ment and the social shaping of technology. *Technology Analysis and Strategic Management, 12*(1), 5-16.

Ehn, P. (1988). *Work-oriented design of computer artifacts.* Stockholm: Almquist & Wiksell International.

Hatling, M., & Sørensen, K. H. (1998). Social constructions of user participation. In K. H. Sørensen (Ed.), *The spectre of participation: Technology and work in a welfare state* (pp. 171-188). Oslo: Scandinavian University Press.

Henderson, K. (1999). *On line and on paper: Visual representations, visual culture, and computer graphics in design engineering.* Cambridge, MA: The MIT Press.

Jørgensen, U., & Sørensen, O. H. (2002). Arenas of development: A space populated by actor worlds, artefacts and surprises. In K. H. Sørensen & R. Williams

(Eds.), *Shaping technology, guiding policy: Concepts, spaces and tools* (pp. 197-222). Cheltenham: Edward Elgar Publishing.

Kuutti, K., & Karasti, H. (1995, August 24-27). Supporting shared interpretation of a space of representations: A case of radiological conferences. In *Proceedings of the 1ˢᵗ Conference on Cognitive Technology*, City University of Hong Kong (pp. 75-85)

Latour, B. (1998). How to be iconophilic in art, science, and religion? In C. A. Jones & P. Galison (Eds.), *Picturing science, producing art* (pp. 418-440). London: Routledge.

Latour, B. (1999). On recalling ANT. In J. Law, & J. Hassard (Eds.), *Actor network theory and after* (pp. 15-25). Oxford: Blackwell.

Latour, B. (2003). The promises of constructivism. In D. Ihde, & E. Selinger (Eds.), *Chasing technoscience: Matrix for materiality* (pp. 27-46). Bloomington: Indiana University Press.

Law, J. (2002). *Aircraft stories: Decentering the object in technoscience*. Durham, NC: Duke University Press.

Moltu, B. (2002). *The social shaping of business process reengineering (BPR) in "Norwestoil"* (PRECEPT Working Paper No. 28). Lyngby: Department of Manufacturing Engineering and Management, Technical University of Denmark.

Moltu, B. (2004). *BPR på Norsk*. PhD dissertation. Trondheim: NTNU.

Sørensen, K. H., & Williams, R. (Eds.) (2002). *Shaping technology, guiding policy: Concepts, spaces and tools*. Cheltenham: Edward Elgar Publishing.

Star, S. L. (1992). The Trojan door: Organizations, work, and the "open black box." *Systems Practice, 5*(4), 395-410.

Suchman, L. (1995). Making work visible. *Communications of the ACM, 38*(9), 56-64.

Yoshinaka, Y. (2005). *Contrast in resonance: Knowledge processes and the sociotechnical articulation of magnetic resonance imaging (MRI) in interdisciplinary practice*. PhD dissertation. Lyngby: Technical University of Denmark.

Endnotes

[1]   In this chapter, we, thus, adopt a broad conception of politics, which "extends politics to include elements such as culture, the historical legacy of past events," and so forth (Dawson, Clausen, & Nielsen, 2000, p. 5). By explicitly taking up the political dimensions, we stress the entrenched, obdurate, and taken-for-granted nature of design and related processes, where players often

exercise programs of vested interests by their conceptual framing of a certain knowledge or problem definition. These aspects may have been somewhat downplayed in earlier constructivist-oriented STS concepts, even though they too have problematised the political tensions in knowledge claims and artefacts (Bijker, 1995).

[2]   Susan Leigh Star (1992, p. 398) has previously pointed to the need to problematise the very contextual and mediated nature of reductionist practices, in stating that "what we take to be the simplest of rational practices, in organisations and in everyday life, are in fact extremely problematic, negotiated and situated."

[3]   This relational approach to context and content does not necessarily suppose that the social constitutes the context and the technical the content. It may very well be that a technical problem setting frames the contours of the social content to be addressed. The point is that the social and the technical are inextricably intertwined and that the content cannot be de-contextualised.

[4]   According to Hatling and Sørensen (1998), the Norwegian working life tradition may have contributed to a participative practice, where it is assumed that employees expect to be invited to participate in organisational and technological change.

[5]   Especially, the internal consultants in the Norwegian case had gathered ideas and concepts form a diversity of sources including courses held by external consultants, newspaper articles, gurus, and prominent management figures. These ideas concerned issues as to whether or not to include participative elements, use of IT, mapping methods, and so forth (Moltu, 2004).

[6]   More specifically, attributions to film-less and paperless practices in the radiological domain entail systems for archiving and retrieving patient information, such as the picture archiving and communication system (PACS) for images and the more task-oriented radiology information system for patient flow and information management.

[7]   Bruno Latour (1998) makes a point of distinguishing information as "in-formation" whereby he underscores the understanding that information is always *put into form*, that is to say always *mediated*. The mobility which is granted information through the particularity of this mediation has consequences, also for its mobilisation. In-formation, and its receipt, can, thus, be said to be conditioned through the spaces of their making (design) and reproduction (use).

[8]   This notion is borrowed from Kathryn Henderson (1999) and stresses that such phenomena cannot be reduced to an issue of a merely-transitional nature with respect to problems encountered in the computer-aided transformation of work. Henderson underscores the epistemological underpinnings of user-strategies with respect to the socio-material anchoring of the transition and the way it is managed on a practical basis. These (paper-based) objects are indeed work objects that transcend a simple correspondence with the act of going over to screen-based practice, as these material objects are necessarily enmeshed in the very knowledge practices that get the work done.

[9]   Radiological conferences are a staple of the collaboration between radiology and clinical departments, particularly in the Nordic countries. While these conferences are kept brief, they are held at least weekly, where the individual clinical department (clinicians and trainees) meet up at the radiology department to review the individual patients that have been scanned during the time. The review of the individual cases may be brief or thorough depending on the need for further elaboration as to clinical information or radiological findings.

Chapter XI

Concerns with "Mutual Constitution":
A Critical Realist Commentary

Alistair Mutch
Nottingham Trent University, UK

Abstract

The case for "analytical dualism" as a means of approaching sociotechnical action is presented as an alternative to accounts which tend to conflate agency, structure, and technology. This is based on the work of Margaret Archer, whose work is, in turn, located in the traditions of critical realism. Her commitment to analytical dualism, which stresses both the importance of time in analysis and the emergent properties of structure, is argued to give a firmer purchase on the notion of context than the alternatives based on, for example, the work of Giddens and Latour.

Introduction

I want to start from the premise that what concerns many researchers in this area is how best to conceptualise the nature of "context." From the point of view of those researching information systems (broadly constituted), the concern is to avoid what they perceive as being, at best, an over-emphasis on technical factors and, at worst, the charge of technological determinism. They are keen, therefore, to emphasise the importance of the organisational, social, and cultural context in situating the development and use of technological artefacts. In this, they are joined by those studying information behaviour who are concerned to move away from a simple model of an "environment" in which behaviours are selected "rationally" toward the ongoing interaction of context and action. In this endeavour, the notion of "mutual constitution" is seductive, and the seduction is reinforced by those whose concepts are turned to for support. For some, this is the actor-network theory (ANT) of Bruno Latour and others, where there is a strong emphasis on action embedded in networks. For those working in this tradition, the removal of the hyphen from "socio-technical" is a deliberate act designed to stress the ineradicable coupling of the social and the technical. "Sociotechnical" action, therefore, represents the solution of the problem of context by its conflation into networks of actants. Not all analysts in this area, however, would wish to go so far and so, as in other areas of the study of organisation, the theorist of choice is often Anthony Giddens and his notion of "structuration." What is taken from this is the mutual constitution of structure and agency, where structures form the ever-present conditions for the production and reproduction of agency. The strength of such notions is their emphasis on the irrevocable interconnections between action and context, but their weakness, it will be argued, is a tendency to privilege action over context. That is, when we explore these approaches in a little more detail, we find that they do not help as much as we might like in the specification of context. These criticisms will be addressed briefly, but, as they have been considered elsewhere (Jones, 1999; Mutch, 2002), the main part of the argument will be devoted to the presentation of an alternative approach. The contention is that ideas drawn from the philosophical tradition of critical realism, and specifically from the application to social theory by the sociologist Margaret Archer, are of much more value both in specifying what we mean by context and in conceptualising the relationship between context and action. This is, therefore, an act of what Basil Bernstein (1996) calls "secondary recontextualisation." That is, the aim is to introduce some of the ideas and show how these can help existing approaches. Accordingly, after a brief introduction to some of the key tenets of critical realism, we look in a little more detail at what Archer has to say about the nature of structures (our "context") and the relationship of structure to agency (our "action"). The key argument is that, while there is no society (and, hence, no technology and no information) without people, the challenge is to examine the interaction between the structures which people create (including information and technology) and the subsequent action in which people engage. These more general ideas are then explored in the context of writings on organisations and technology. It is important to stress here that critical realism does not purport to be a substantive theory of either of these two domains; rather, it offers some conceptual clarity on ontological and epistemological issues which can further help the development of domain specific theories.

For Latour, the "classic" question of the relationship between agency and structure is a case of asking the wrong question. His focus is on the enrolment of a variety of actors (sometimes "actants," to distinguish non-humans from humans) in networks of greater or lesser scale and scope (Latour, 1993). The consequence is an extremely helpful language for describing processes that, in the hands of the adept, can be illuminating but can also lead simply to the production of more or less interesting stories. The particular value from ANT is the notion of "being specific about technology," but what we tend to get is an excellent language for describing process with the fading of context into the background (Monteiro & Hanseth, 1995). It may be for these reasons that rather more attention is paid to the work of Giddens (Walsham, 1992; Yates & Orlikowski, 1992). We need to be cautious here: it is not the purpose of this chapter to review the way in which Giddens has been employed, but we can take the comment of Hasselbladh and Kallinikos to stand in for many similar examples. "It is not our task," they argue, "to defend structuration theory. However, we would like to observe that the analysis undertaken by Barley and Tolbert … does not have much in common with Giddens' basic ideas" (Hasselbladh & Kallinikos, 2000, p. 716; cf. Phillips, 2003, p. 221). What is it, however, that people seem to be drawing from Giddens? It would appear to be the notion that structure is important in forming the context which both enables and constrains action. A series of concepts are provided (structures of signification, legitimation, and domination) which provide a more finely-grained conceptualisation of structure. However, whether what people take from Giddens and what is actually in Giddens are the same is open to some question. This revolves around Giddens' conception of structures as "memory traces" instantiated in action. This is a rather weak conceptualisation of structure, possibly weaker in practice than those who use it care to acknowledge (Jones, 1999). A rather large claim might be that, in practice, those who use Giddens are using the notion of structure in the rather stronger sense than Margaret Archer uses it. She has been one of Giddens' most trenchant critics, but, before turning to her work, we need to briefly explore some key tenets of critical realism, as this might be an unfamiliar set of ideas to many.

Critical Realism: An Introduction

We need to be clear at the outset that critical realism is a philosophical tradition that sees itself as "under-labouring" for other theories in both the natural and social sciences (Sayer, 1992). For these reasons, it is strictly speaking incorrect to talk about a critical realist analysis of organisations, technology, information, or any other phenomenon. Rather, substantive theories which address these domains can use the resources for conceptual clarity (Cruickshank, 2003b). At its heart, critical realism is an endeavour concerned with ontology. The realism indicates that the tradition asserts there is a reality independent of our knowing of it which has intransitive status. However, it rejects the notions drawn from what we might term scientific realism in the natural sciences, or positivism in the social sciences, that there is any direct access to this reality. Even in the natural sciences, where experimental closure can be reached in some cases, our knowledge of reality is not a reflection. Rather, it involves acts of interpretation at all stages, from observation to theory building. Much of our progress in the latter moves through the creative use of language, especially of metaphor (Lewis, 1999; Lopez, 2003). So critical realism makes bold claims about ontology but is altogether more relaxed about epistemology. Here, there can be multiple contending ways of knowing. Whether one is better than the other depends on its relation to what it is that we seek to know, not on its internal features. Within these basic conceptions, critical realism argues for an ontology of depth. That is, it pays due attention to the emergent nature of phenomena. Thus, in the work of Stephen Rose (1993) on the brain, memory is a system property of the brain which emerges from material substance but which is not reducible to particular parts of that material. Critical realism is, then, anti-reductionist in method and places emphasis on emergence and systemic properties at the relevant level of enquiry. It also suggests that we need to distinguish between the empirical, the actual, and the real. For critical realists, the empirical are simply surface sensations which are the product of deeper mechanisms. What actually happens may be disguised by these surface manifestations. However, the actual in its turn is produced by the real mechanism, and it is these mechanisms which analysts and scientists seek to explore. The object of study, therefore, should be the underlying mechanisms that produce surface manifestations—mechanisms which might not be apparent. They may, for example, only be activated in certain circumstances, or their impact may be confounded by the workings of counter-mechanisms (as noted later, we will often talk of "tendencies" rather than mechanisms in looking at the social world).

These propositions are derived in large part from the studies in the philosophy of science carried out by Roy Bhaskar (Collier, 1994). However, Bhaskar also has a considerable concern with human activity and developed a Transformational Model of Social Activity, which drew on the work of Giddens. This work has led to the emergence of an interest in his ideas in a number of domains in the social sciences with prominent figures being Andrew Sayer (2000) in geography and Tony Lawson (2003) in economics. In information systems research, John Mingers (2004) has worked with these ideas at a more philosophical level. However, this has led to de-bates which fail to focus on the development of these ideas on the terrain of social theory by Margaret Archer (Klein, 2004). Archer is a sociologist of education who, since the 1970s, has developed a set of rich and complex ideas which found their fullest expression in a series of (to date) four books (Archer, 1995, 1996, 2000a, 2003). These are closely interlinked but deal with separate aspects of the relation-ship between agency, structure, and culture. She terms this the "morphogenetic" approach—"morpho" being the element stressing change, "genetic" emphasising the importance of agency. There has been a move over the series toward a greater degree of concern with the nature of agency, but always with a strong focus on the objective characteristics of the context in which agency operates. In the following comments, I am forced to simplify what is a complex body of work with the twin aims of introducing the work (possibly sending people to the originals) and exploring how it might form a better set of concepts for the exploration of context than notions of mutual constitution.

Let us start with the nature of structures. Archer (1995) identifies two prevailing approaches to the nature of structure and agency. One is that which she terms "downward conflationism," which she finds in traditions such as structuralism, where social action is, as it were, simply "read off" the nature of structure. In such approaches, agency becomes a mere epiphenomenon with agents merely the bearers of structure. In such a situation, the task of analysts becomes simply to find the keys to unlock the code of structure, which once discovered will reveal all of the answers. Those approaches which deploy forms of technological determinism might exhibit some of these attributes, where social consequences are seen to flow inevitably from the fact of technical implementation. The other dominant approach, developed often in opposition to structuralist approaches, is one which places all of the attention on the interaction of agents and sees structures as either irrelevant or, again, a mere transient by-product of action. Her targets here are those who operate under the broad rubric of "methodological individualism," and she has been particularly concerned to counter the claims of rational choice theorists (Archer, 2000b). These she would term "upwards conflationists," and these approaches would, in their turn, be rejected by Giddens. His structuration theory is designed to avoid the false polarity engendered by either of the approaches we have outlined, but, Archer argues that in his formulations he falls into the trap of what she terms "central conflationism." The problem here is that in eliding the differences between agency and structure and in arguing for their mutual constitution, Giddens removes the analytical purchase which can be gained from holding the two terms apart (Emirbayer & Mische, 1998). Archer stresses the notions of emergent properties and temporality in arguing for a stronger conception of structure, which then leads to her argument for "analytical dualism." Her argument is that, while structures are created by people, those people are not "those here present now." That is, the structures that are produced by social interaction then take on objective status for future rounds of social interaction. Their emergent properties, emergent from but not reducible to the previous actions of social actors, have causal powers in shaping and enabling future projects. What do we mean here by "structure"? Archer suggests a number of components—roles, organisations, institutions, and systems—that are inter-related and have primacy depending on the context of analysis. This allows us some purchase on the relationship between the local and the global. Archer (1996) also further elaborates her account by considering the relationship between structure and culture. She is concerned in her account of culture to explode what she terms the "myth of cultural integration"—the notion that culture presupposes an integrated and necessarily harmonious set of relations—and suggests a need to analyse culture as a set of propositions about the world, some of which can be in logical contradiction with each other. We will take this notion of contradiction further in the following text, but, having presented an outline of the formation of structure (to use that as a shorthand just now for the combination of structure and culture), we have to consider the implications for agency.

Archer (1995) argues that, for the purpose of analysis, we need to hold agency and structure apart. This "analytical dualism" is quite clear in recognising that concrete situations will involve elements of agency and structure in complex interactions. She suggests that the way of getting at such situations is to engage in the production of analytical narratives that aim to tease out the relationship between agency and structure through a series of what she terms "morphogenetic" cycles (the "morpho" referring to the potential for change; the "genetic" referring to agential involvement). In each such cycle, we start with the prior structural conditioning, exploring how this shapes and enables social interaction. In turn, such interaction elaborates structures, either by changing them or, perhaps more frequently, reproducing and confirming them. In considering how structures form the context for action, we need to return to the logical relations of contradiction and complementarity. Such relations can exist within structures (such as within the institutions of law or the family), within cultures (such as contending ideas of the family) or between structures and cultures (such as when practices of family life are in distinction to theories about how that practice should be conducted). Archer is anxious to argue that the existence of logical contradictions does not necessarily mean a clash between social groups. Such contradictions may lie unnoticed and "unactivated" if there are no actors with the interest in deploying them. What such combinations of contradictions and complementarities give us (and Archer explores various combinations in considerable depth) are logics for situated action. Such logics may not be picked up upon, perhaps because social groups lack the weight to be able to deploy them. They may suggest logics of action, but there is no inevitability about them. However, actors who chose differently will have to pay opportunity costs, and their choices may bring them to accept other logical connections which they had not appreciated. So, for example, one argument might be that certain assumptions about how to go on are inscribed into software (Melucci, 1996). This inscription then confronts those who use the software with a "natural" and relatively easy path to follow. However, they may choose to do otherwise and create innovative uses. However, such uses have opportunity costs in terms of the effort needed to, say, customise the software. In turn, these innovative uses form the context for future rounds of social interaction. However, this is to make some assumptions about the nature of social action and those who participate in it, and so we need to consider what Archer has to say about agency.

A prime concern in Archer's work has been to counter both individualistic, rational choice models of agency and the over-socialised accounts that produce only "cultural dopes." Her argument is that we need to consider more carefully what we take agency to be, and she suggests a tripartite division into persons, agents, and actors. She starts with the embodied person, emergent from but not reducible to their biological constitution. These persons are strong evaluators, able to form and pursue value laden projects and to reflect on their progress towards them (Archer, 2000a). Such reflection, however, takes different forms—forms which Archer (2003) relates to modes of internal conversation. We all use, she argues, internal conversation to reflect on our projects but the forms that such conversations take differ and, in differing, affect our relations with the objective world of structure and culture that we face. This is to take a different line from Giddens (1991), whose emphasis is on the knowledgability of all actors, and from others, such as Bourdieu (1990), who places a stronger emphasis on the shaping of dispositions to act. Archer suggests that there are potentially three categories of reflexivity, all with different impacts on the degree to which persons will collide with structures. Some she terms "conversational reflexives." These rely on others to complete their internal conversations, and so they rely on a community of others who share their background assumptions. These people will avoid conflict with structures by seeking to steer away from it. Others are "autonomous reflexives," who conduct their conversations with themselves and take a strategic approach. These form the social actors whose pursuit of projects will lead them into collision with structures, leading to structural elaboration or change. The third category is that of the "meta-reflexive"—persons who reflect on their own reflexivity. They are, argues Archer, society's conscience, evaluating structure and culture against a moral yardstick and finding them wanting. (Archer recognises a fourth category, that of the "fractured reflexive," who for some reason is not able to conduct a satisfactory internal conversation and is so condemned to remain a passive primary agent at the mercy of buffeting forces.)

While these conversations and evaluations take place at the level of the person, they are clearly shaped by the category of agency. For Archer (1995), this is a collective category and is one partially constituted by involuntary positioning. By unequally distributed chance, persons are positioned in various categories of "primary agency"—as men or women, young or old, and so forth. In some cases, action is not needed to attribute primary agency—the simple fact, Archer argues, of an aging population has an influence on wider structures regardless of whether there are common bonds or perceptions of them among the elderly. However, of course, such bonds can emerge and can lead to "corporate agency," which is when a group of agents perceives a shared interest in joint action to further what they seem to have in common. Such agency then shapes the persons who engage in it by, for example, giving them access to differential resources of language with which to conduct their internal conversations (Mutch, 2004). It also forms the preconditions for the role of the actor. This is the individual engaged in social action, shaped and enabled by objective constraints. This could be the occupation of a particular role, the expectations for behaviour in which have been shaped by previous occupants and by the emerging body of knowledge and ideas about how to go on in such a role. These suggest ways in which the actor should go on. The person is, of course, free to do differently but only if the costs for so doing are paid.

This, then, is a broad sketch of Archer's bold and sophisticated arguments about the relationship between agency and structure. To recap, they make strong claims about the nature of both structure and agency. They posit the existence of structures as possessing emergent properties which have causal powers. Such structures form the context in which action takes place. That action is undertaken by strong evaluators with intentions to act formed by their value laden moral projects. Such projects may cause them to collide with existing structures, reproducing them or challenging them in the process. Structures provide strong situational logics of action, but the simple existence of either contradiction or complementarity in these logics has no necessary consequence for action. While such an approach still insists on the "mutual constitution" of "the parts and the people," it suggests that we need to hold them apart in order to explore the inter-relationship between them over time. The stress is on the construction of analytical narratives that pay attention to the unfolding of cycles of interaction between agency and structure over time. It should be clear that this is a different perspective on "mutual constitution," but what implications does this have for the study of organisations, information, and technology?

Critical Realism: Implications

We need to repeat again the warning that critical realism is not about replacing or creating anew substantive theories of particular social domains. It is entirely compatible with the reworking of existing theories, using the ontological clarity that critical realism claims to offer. We also need to recognise that Archer's work is a work of social theory, in which the objects of attention are societies in the process of change over large tracts of time and space. However, she would claim that her approach could be deployed at a number of levels of analysis; part of the challenge for those interested in the analysis of organisations, information, and technology is to show how this might be done. It starts, argues Cruickshank (2003b), through the construction of domain specific meta-concepts through the immanent critique of existing bodies of work. It is not the purpose of the present argument to construct such concepts, nor is there the space for such an endeavour. However, it is possible to point to some avenues for exploration. There have already been some rather limited initial forays, but it should be clear from them that the enterprise is in its infancy (Ackroyd & Fleetwood, 2000; Cruickshank, 2003a; Lopez & Potter, 2001). Two substantial bodies of work, which offer material for these endeavours that are worthy of further review, are labour process theory and the new institutionalism. A wide body of work has been produced under the stimulus of labour process theory, initially inspired by Braverman's (1974) deskilling thesis but often departing far from his original concerns. From this work has emerged the current focus on critical management studies, as well as much other valuable work on the nature of organisations. What unites much of this otherwise very disparate work is the focus on conflict and power in organisations. In recent years, much of this perspective has been brought to bear on the expanding area of "knowledge management" (Prichard, Hull, Chumer, & Willmott, 2000). An example which has considerable relevance for those exploring information and technology in organisations is the careful exploration of the impact of organisational politics on the deployment of Lotus Notes™ in a pharmaceutical company presented by Hayes and Walsham (2000). This is of importance when set against much of the literature on information use in organisations, when the context, as in Choo (1998), is only lightly sketched in and is simply seen as the placeholder for individual behaviour. However, for many of the excellent empirical studies emerging out of this critical tradition, the context is largely confined to organisational boundaries with the broader social and cultural context being little explored. If we wish to seek examples of bodies of work that could potentially tie organisations more tightly into their broader context, then the work of the new institutionalists might be of some interest.

The new institutionalism in organisational analysis is a broadly North American phenomenon with its roots in the rejection of rational choice models (Powell & DiMaggio, 1991; Scott, 2001). This gives it something of a shared agenda with some of Archer's (2000b) concerns. What is also interesting is the way that, in some incarnations, it is concerned to relate what happens in organisations to broader forces, particularly in situating action in the context of taken-for-granted understanding about appropriate forms for action and structure. The problem is that, in this endeavour, such forces become all powerful and the organisation becomes reified into a unitary body whose actions are largely determined by these taken-for-granted assumptions (DiMaggio, 1998). From the perspective of Archer's morphogenetic approach, the problem is an excessive focus on culture with institutions being conceived of as cognitive constructions shorn of their material and social dimensions. These forces are then given excessive weight in an example of what she would term "downwards conflationism." The space for agency, both within organisations and on behalf of organisations, is radically reduced. Such criticisms are articulated by many who work within the parameters laid down by the tradition, notably in recent years by Lounsbury and Ventresca (2003) in their calls for a "new structuralism." While we might argue that any form of structuralism is a dangerous path to follow, the resources presented by Archer would seem to be valuable for these internal critics; in turn, the arguments presented by these critics are of value in suggesting some elements of a distinctly critical realist approach.

One concern is that, broadly speaking, these approaches give relatively little weight to the inter-twined problematic of information and technology. Archer, for example, has barely anything to say about technology save for a brief mention in considering theories of post-industrial society (Archer, 1990). However, her approach of analytical dualism based on emergent properties seems to fit well with the perspective elaborated by Andrew Feenberg (2001) in his *Questioning Technology*. Feenberg's work appears to have little impact in our domain, judging by the paucity of citations, but he too starts by recognising the merits of accounts based on constructivist approaches. However, these, he argues, neglect to place their findings in a broader political context. Feenberg, as a political philosopher working in the tradition of critical theory, is anxious to provide an account which situates technology in a broader context in order to further a project of democratising communicative practices (Feenberg, 1991). Now, we might recognise a wide range of problems with this project, particularly its reliance on Habermasian idealism, but for our current purposes the interest is in Feenberg's account of the nature of technology, in which he argues for a two-level model, which can be recast in the form of analytical dualism. In this case, what is important is to pay equal attention to the constitution of technologies and their implementation in practice, which can be best done by holding the two apart. For Feenberg, the two moments are "primary instrumentalisation," which is to do with the constitution of the artefact, and "secondary instrumentalisation," which is to do with realisation. For each, Feenberg suggests a number of attributes.

For the process of constitution, Feenberg suggests that there is a process of the decontextualisation of some features from their original context so that they can be integrated into a technical system. This depends in turn on reductionism, in which "de-worlded things are simplified, stripped of technically useless qualities, and reduced to those aspects through which they can be enrolled in a technical network" (Feenberg, 2001, p. 203). This then enables the object to be considered as an autonomous one, subject to technical laws. This then gives the artefact its seemingly purely technical quality; it has been rendered as such by a process which then returns it back to the world as seemingly being not of it. However, in order to be part of that world again, the artefact has to be part of a social process that is more familiar to accounts given from, for example, actor-network theory, with Feenberg using terms such as "enrolment" to construct his account of realisation. For example, he notes that, "To function as an actual device, isolated, decontextualised technical objects must be combined with each other and re-embedded in the natural environment. Systematisation is the process of making these combinations and connections, in Latour's terms, of 'enrolling' objects in a network" (Feenberg, 2001, p. 205). He also suggests moments in this process of mediation and concretisation. In mediation, ethical and aesthetic considerations supply new qualities to the technology which help to accommodate it to the new context. In concretisation, the technologies are combined with working practices to form new ways of working, which are clearly a prime concern of those working in this domain. Feenberg's approach is, then, an attempt to combine what we have learned through processual views of technology and a concern with the broader context. From the perspective of critical realism, the concern is not with the account of technology, which seems helpful, but with the legacy of critical theory. Here again, the ideas of Archer can form a more robust view of structure, but Feenberg's work provides resources which could help to repair the gap caused by the lack of consideration of technology. The importance here is in the emphasis on both the objective character of the technology as it appears to the user and the potential for re-interpretation in the course of social action.

Conclusion

I have argued that ideas derived from critical realism, and in particular the morphogenetic approach of Margaret Archer, have a considerable amount to offer students of organisation, information, and technology. While such ideas start from the premise that it is human activity which is central to the creation of society, they offer a better approach to the intertwined relationship of information and technology than rather vaguer notions of "mutual constitution." They do so by offering a stronger conception of structure than, for example, Giddens. By using the notion of emergent powers and stress the centrality of time, they draw a stronger picture of structure and culture forming an objective context which humans face in their engagement in social action. However, persons can choose, based on their strong evaluation of their personal projects as value laden to confront or shy away from such structures, although they cannot avoid their implications entirely. As agents, such persons are placed involuntarily in particular positions, which shape their interests and resources. Deploying these resources as social actors, they can act in ways other than their interests and the logic of their situated action would suggest, but only if they are prepared to incur the opportunity costs of their actions. Such is only a brief sketch of the richness and complexity of these ideas. It needs to be stressed that ideas such as these are still under development and elaboration in their home domain of social theory. Their application in the realm of organisations is in its infancy, but such an application is not a question of starting from scratch. Rather, I have tried to point to some existing ideas and approaches which would form a part of any more fully formulated perspective. The work of formulating such a perspective continues, but what can we say at this stage that it offers students of information and technology?

At a very simple level, we could argue that more attention to these ideas would help in sensitising researchers to certain aspects of context that they ought to be aware of. The conceptual clarity offered by the stronger sense of structure would seem to gel better with the way that researchers seem to conceive of structure in practice than notions drawn from Giddens. However, theories also carry with them logical entailments that go further than sensitisation (Stones, 1996). For critical realism, the aim of research is the uncovering of the causal powers that are in operation, albeit that in the human domain we would express these as tendencies rather than as laws. We would also be tentative in our approach, recognising that our conclusions, in open systems, can only be corrigible and provisional. However, we would lay a particular stress on the importance of time. To construct an analytical narrative which seeks to explain the tendencies at work, we need to explore a sufficient stretch of time (D'Adderio, 2004). A criticism of much work that focuses on implementation would be the timescale of the research. This would be in two aspects. One would be that the period examined before the particular focus of the research is relatively short. From the earlier discussion, it is clear that this period needs to be long enough to be able to appreciate the shaping of the context that action takes place in. Secondly, insufficient attention is often paid to the period of social action itself and to the subsequent structural elaboration. Often this is because the pace of change at different levels of analysis is compressed, with the impression being given that taken-for-granted social practices change at the same pace as organisational routines (Barley & Tolbert, 1997). Social realism can help us here with its notions of stratified reality and careful attention to definitions. However, even at the level of situated action at the micro level, our analyses are often too quick to conclude that a particular instantiation is a "success" or a "failure" when we are only looking at a brief snapshot. Given that we are aware of the plasticity of technology and the creative ability of users, albeit within more or less strong contexts, we need to allow time to unfold to be able to see if what we are recording are durable effects or mere growing pains.

References

Ackroyd, S., & Fleetwood, S. (2000). *Realist perspectives on management and organisations*. London: Routledge.

Archer, M. (1990). Theory, culture and post-industrial society. In M. Featherstone (Ed.), *Global culture* (pp. 97-119). London: Sage.

Archer, M. (1995). *Realist social theory: The morphogenetic approach*. Cambridge: Cambridge University Press.

Archer, M. (1996). *Culture and agency. The place of culture in social theory*. Cambridge: Cambridge University Press.

Archer, M. (2000a). *Being human: The problem of agency*. Cambridge: Cambridge University Press.

Archer, M. (2000b). Home economicus, Homo sociologicus and Homo sentiens. In M. Archer & J. Tritter (Eds.), *Rational choice theory* (pp. 36-56). London: Routledge.

Archer, M. (2003). *Structure, agency and the internal conversation.* Cambridge: Cambridge University Press.

Barley, S., & Tolbert, P. (1997). Institutionalization and structuration: Studying the links between action and institution. *Organization Studies, 18*(1), 93-117.

Bernstein, B. (1996). *Pedagogy, symbolic control and identity: Theory, research, critique.* London: Taylor & Francis.

Bourdieu, P. (1990). *The logic of practice.* Cambridge: Polity.

Braverman, H. (1974). *Labour and monopoly capital: The degradation of work in the twentieth century.* New York: Monthly Review Press.

Choo, C. W. (1998). *The knowing organization: How organizations use information to construct meaning, create knowledge and make decisions.* New York: Oxford University Press.

Collier, A. (1994). *Critical realism: An introduction to the philosophy of Roy Bhaskar.* London: Verso.

Cruickshank, J. (2003a). *Critical realism: The difference it makes.* London: Routledge.

Cruickshank, J. (2003b). *Realism and sociology: Anti-foundationalism, ontology, and social research.* London: Routledge.

D'Adderio, L. (2004). *Inside the virtual product: How organizations create knowledge through software.* Cheltenham: Edward Elgar.

DiMaggio, P. (1988). Interest and agency in institutional theory. In L. Zucker (Ed.), *Institutional patterns and organizations: Culture and environment* (pp. 3-19). Cambridge: MA: Ballinger.

Emirbayer, M., & Mische, A. (1998). What is agency? *American Journal of Sociology, 103*(4), 962-1023.

Feenberg, A. (1991). *Critical theory of technology.* New York: Oxford University Press.

Feenberg, A. (2001). *Questioning technology.* London: Routledge.

Giddens, A. (1991). *Modernity and self-identity: Self and society in the late modern age.* Cambridge: Polity.

Hasselbladh, H., & Kallinikos, J. (2000). The project of rationalization: A critique and reappraisal of neo-institutionalisation in organization studies. *Organization Studies, 21*(4), 697-720.

Hayes, N., & Walsham, G. (2000). Safe enclaves, political enclaves and knowledge working. In C. Pritchard, R. Hull, M. Chumer, & H. Willmott (Eds.), *Managing knowledge* (pp. 69-87). Basingstoke: Macmillan.

Jones, M. (1999). Structuration theory. In W. Currie, & B. Galliers (Eds.), *Rethinking management information systems* (pp. 103-135). Oxford: Oxford University Press.

Klein, H. (2004) Seeking the new and the critical in critical realism: Déjà vu? *Information and Organization, 14*, 123-144.

Latour, B. (1993). *We have never been modern*. Hemel Hempstead: Harvester Wheatsheaf.

Lawson, T. (2003). *Reorienting economics*. London: Routledge.

Lewis, P. (1999). Metaphor and critical realism. In S. Fleetwood (Ed.), *Critical realism in economics: Development and debate* (pp. 83-101). London: Routledge.

Lopez, J. (2003). *Society and its metaphors: Language, social theory and social structure*. London: Continuum.

Lopez, J., & Potter, G. (2001). *After postmodernism: An introduction to critical realism*. London: The Athlone Press.

Lounsbury, M., & Ventresca, M. (2003). The new structuralism in organizational theory. *Organization, 10*(3), 457-480.

Melucci, A. (1996). *Challenging codes: Collective action in the information age*. Cambridge: Cambridge University Press.

Mingers, J. (2004). Real-izing information systems: Critical realism as an underpinning philosophy for information systems. *Information and Organization, 14*, 87-103

Monteiro, E., & Hanseth, O. (1995). Social shaping of information infrastructure: On being specific about the technology. In Orlikowski et al. (Eds.) (1996), *Information technology and changes in organizational work* (pp. 325-343). London: Chapman Hall.

Mutch, A. (2002). Actors and networks or agents and structures: A critical realist critique of actor-network theory. *Organization, 9*(3), 477-496.

Mutch, A. (2004). Constraints on the internal conversation: Margaret Archer and the structural shaping of thought. *Journal for the Theory of Social Behaviour, 34*(4), 429-445.

Phillips, N. (2003). Discourse or institution? Institutional theory and the challenge of critical discourse theory. In R. Westwood, & S. Clegg (Eds.), *Debating organization* (pp. 220-231). Oxford: Blackwell.

Powell, W. W., & DiMaggio, P. (1991). *The new institutionalism in organizational analysis*. Chicago: University of Chicago.

Prichard, C., Hull, R., Chumer, M., & Willmott, H. (2000). *Managing knowledge: Critical investigations of work and learning*. Basingstoke: Macmillan.

Rose, S. (1993). *The making of memory. From molecules to mind.* London: Bantam.

Sayer, A. (1992). *Method in social science: A realist approach.* London: Routledge.

Sayer, A. (2000). *Realism and social science.* London: Sage.

Scott, W. R. (2001). *Institutions and organization.* London: Sage.

Stones, R. (1996). *Sociological reasoning: Towards a past-modern sociology.* Basingstoke: Macmillan.

Walsham, G. (1992). *Interpreting information systems in organizations.* Chichester: Wiley.

Yates, J., & Orlikowski, W. (1992). Genres of organizational communication—a structurational approach to studying communication and media. *Academy of Management Review, 17*(2), 299-326.

Chapter XII

A Framework for Monitoring User Involvement and Participation in ERP Implementation Projects

José Esteves
Instituto de Empresa, Spain

Joan Pastor
Universitat Politècnica de Catalunya, Spain

Josep Casanovas
Universitat Politècnica de Catalunya, Spain

Abstract

In this chapter, a framework for monitoring user involvement and participation within ERP implementation projects is proposed by using the goals/questions/metrics method. The results of this work are three-fold. First, a literature review is presented on the topic of user involvement and participation as related with ERP implementation projects. Second, a framework for monitoring user involvement and

participation in ERP implementation projects is proposed. And third, a goals/ques-
tions/metrics preliminary plan is proposed to monitor and control user involvement
and participation within ERP implementation projects.

Introduction

Enterprise resource planning (ERP) systems are large and complex systems, and their implementation often requires fundamental changes in the way organizations perform their business processes. Introducing and integrating these systems into an organization is not only a significant financial investment but also a significant risk, which requires skills in change management, process redesign, and business project management. ERP implementation success is influenced by a large number of factors, and, most of the time, it is difficult to measure them objectively. Usually, the metrics proposed within ERP implementation methodologies are related with milestones and costs aspects. This is particularly due to the fact that these methodologies follow the common definition of project success—basically to have full functionality delivered on time and on budget. User involvement and participation is one of the most cited critical success factors (CSFs) in ERP implementation projects (e.g., Bancroft, Seip, & Sprengel, 1998; Bingi, Sharma, & Godla, 1999; Esteves & Pastor, 2000; Kale, 2000; Kawalek & Wood-Harper, 2002; Nah, Lau, & Kuang, 2001). User involvement and participation results in a better fit of user requirements achieving better system quality, use, and acceptance (Esteves & Pastor, 2000).

However, during the initial phases—ERP acquisition and early stages of ERP implementation—end-user involvement is not mandatory but a personal decision to get involved or not. Surveys such as that reported in Wilson, Bekker, Johnson, and Johnson (1996) suggest that user involvement is largely confined to analysis and evaluation activities at present with users tending to be passive rather than active participants. In more conventional bespoke development of information systems, the involvement of users is seen as critical to successful implementation (Markus, 1983). However, despite the popularity of user participation, an obvious anomaly is that, even with user participation, resistance still occurs and systems fail (Cavaye, 1995; Olson & Ives, 1981). In the ERP context, Howcroft and Light (2002, p. 75) mention that "end users are crucial in terms of understanding the operational aspects of the tasks performed and as a result their opinion as to the suitability of a product should at least carry equal weight with the opinions of senior management and systems developers." They also suggest that ignoring their wishes could have potentially disastrous consequences.

The terms *user involvement* and *user participation* have been commonly used interchangeably in information systems (IS) literature (Barki & Hartwick, 1994), but they are not the same and here we attempt to clarify both concepts. Kappelman and McLean (1991) hypothesized that IS success is indirectly influenced by user participation and mediated by user involvement. The most accepted model of user involvement, user participation, and system use was developed and tested by Barki and Hartwick (1994, 2001). This study attempts to provide a set of metrics to help control and monitor user involvement and participation in ERP implementation projects in order to help managers achieve success in their projects. The derived set of metrics is the initial one from which particularly an ERP implementation may start its own specialized set. According to Jurison (1999, p. 28), the purpose of project control is "to keep the project on course and as close to the plan as possible, to identify problems before they happen and, implement recovery plans before unrecoverable damage is done." In our survey for prior research, we have found that the extensive literature on user involvement and participation is basically related to software development. Thus, there is the need to adapt and/or extend previous work to ERP implementation projects, which have their own characteristics and life cycle. As a result of this study, we are interested in a combined set of metrics to help managers understand the situation of the ERP implementation project. We have used the goals/questions/metrics (GQM) method to develop this set metrics. The result of the application of this method is a GQM plan. The GQM plan is a document that contains the goals, questions, and metrics for a measurement program (Solingen & Berghout, 1999)—in this case, an ERP implementation project. The first phase of the study focuses on the definition of a set of metrics for user involvement and participation. This chapter proceeds as follows. First, we present background in user involvement and participation and the GQM method. Next, we describe the research methodology used. Then, we present the GQM plan proposed. Finally, we present some conclusions and issues for further work.

Background on User Involvement and Participation

In IS literature, the terms *user involvement* and *user participation* have frequently been used to mean the same thing. However, Barki and Hartwick (1989, 1994) claimed that the two concepts are different and thus need to be defined separately:

- **User involvement:** is defined as "a psychological stage of the individual, and defined as the importance and personal relevance of a system to a user" (Hartwick & Barki, 1994, p. 441), for example, their attitude toward the development process and its product (the IS itself).

- **User participation:** is defined as the observable behavior of users in IS development and implementation, for example, the set of operations and activities performed by users or their representatives during the IS development process (Hartwick & Barki, 1994) or activities during the system implementation (Kappelman & McLean, 1991).

Barki and Hartwick (1989, 1994) argued that the earlier-mentioned interpretation of involvement would be consistent with how that term is used in the fields of psychology, marketing, and organizational behavior. Kappelman and McLean (1991) introduce the term *user engagement* to include both user participation (the behavior) and user involvement (the attitude). Thus, according to their account, user engagement is "used to refer the total set of user relationships toward IS and their development."

User Involvement

Many reasons have been given to involve users in IS implementation projects. User involvement is predicted to increase user satisfaction and acceptance (Ives & Olson, 1984) by: developing realistic expectations about system capabilities; providing an arena for bargaining and conflict resolution about design issues; leading to system ownership by users; decreasing user resistance to change; and committing users to the system. Kappelman and McLean (1991) suggested that user involvement is something distinct from, although associated with, user participation, and that the psychological state of user involvement may be more important than user participation in understanding IS success. An important aspect related with user involvement is *user perceived control*. Baronas and Louis (1988, p. 114) stated that, "by involving end user in decisions relating to implementation, workers may become more invested in the success of the implementation and more satisfied with the system through the social-psychological mechanism of perceived control." *Personal control* has been defined in terms of choice, predictability, responsibility, and ability to reduce or get relief from an unpleasant condition. Baronas and Louis (1988) suggested that:

- Systems implementation is likely to be experienced by non-technical users as a period of transition during which users make sense of, and cope with, various differences between old and new systems and their anticipations of these differences.
- Systems implementation is likely to represent a threat to user's perceptions of control over work.

Traditionally, the assumption in terms of user involvement is that if the organizational structure of an IS project is in place and appropriate committee meetings attended, their integration and coordination will occur. However, as Amoako and White (1997, p. 41) state that "unlike the technical side of project management, these activities are very loosely defined, and very often include no mechanisms for the integration that will achieve the desired results." Therefore, there is the need for the distinction between structural integration and effective management of the involvement process. Characteristics such as user expertise, degree of organizational decentralization, project complexity, users' previous experience with IS, could determine the degree of their involvement. Barki and Hartwick (1994) differentiated user involvement from other psychological states particularly attitude. While the term *user attitude* "should be used to refer to a psychological state reflecting the affective or evaluative feelings concerning a new system" (p. 62), user involvement refers to "a belief—the extent to which a user believes that a new system is both important and personally relevant" (p. 62). Kappelman (1995) divides user involvement in two types: user process involvement and user system involvement. User process involvement refers to the psychological identification of users with the process of IS development (i.e., their subjective attitude toward the IS development task). In addition, user system involvement refers to the psychological identification of users with respect to IS itself (i.e., their subjective attitude toward the product of development).

User Participation

According to Briolat and Pogman (2000), "user participation is advocated in order to discover users' needs and points of view, validate specifications, and hence build better IS for the organization." Participation reflects what specific behaviors are performed, how many of these behaviors are performed, and how often they are performed (Barki & Hartwick, 2001). The role of user participation in organizational activity can be viewed from the perspective of two different behavioral theories (Ives & Olson, 1984). These theories are *planned organizational change* and *participative decision making*. The implementation of a new IS often implies a planned change in the way that an organizational unit pursues its objectives. Participative decision making emphasizes the role of individuals in working groups. Ives and Olson (1984) also outlined how user participation (at that time, they named it user involvement) can improve system quality by: providing a more complete assessment of user information requirements; providing expertise about the organization the system is to support; avoiding development of unacceptable or unimportant features; and improving user understanding of the system. Mckeen and Guimarães (1994) showed that user participation has a positive relationship with user satisfaction. They also argued that four factors affect this relationship: task complexity, system complexity, user influence, and user-developer communication. Barki and Hartwick (2001) define four dimensions of user participation:

- **Responsibility:** The performance of activities and assignments reflecting overall leadership or accountability for the project.

- **User-IS relationship:** The performance of development activities reflecting users' formal review, evaluation, and approval of work done by the IS staff.

- **Hands-on-activity:** The performance of specific physical design and implementation tasks.

- **Communication activity:** Activities involving formal or informal exchanges of facts, needs, opinions, visions, and concerns regarding the project among the users and between users and other project stakeholders.

Based in a meta-analysis study, Pettingell, Marshall, and Remington (1988) concluded that the inclusion of users in definition and design stages is the best way to

Figure 1. Constructs proposed by different authors for user involvement and user participation

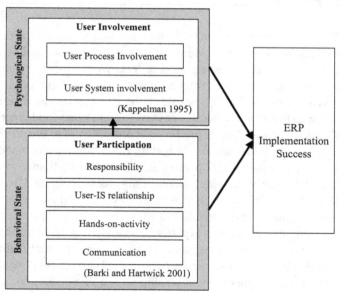

increase their perception of the value of the system. Jiang, Chen, and Klein (2002) suggest that pre-project partnering helps to involve users during the project and to motivate them in order to achieve project success. Pre-project partnering refers to a work philosophy in which system stakeholders work together before the project begins (Cowan, Gray, & Larson, 1992). The purpose of pre-project partnering is to build a foundation among stakeholders for collaboration. In addition to identifying key stakeholders and their objectives, partnering emphasizes the activities of identifying potential conflict areas, providing a process for resolution of conflict, and incorporating a continuous improvement component in the project process. These results show the importance of involving users before the project starts and then in all the implementation phases. Figure 1 presents a summary of the constructs proposed by different authors for user involvement and participation. These constructs are the basis for the development of our metrics program.

User Involvement/Participation in the Context of ERP Implementations

In this section, we present our understanding of user involvement and participation in an ERP implementation context. We focus on why user involvement and participation is important and how it could be better done. Among the main reasons to involve users in ERP implementations, we have: to maximize user acceptance; to improve system functionality; and to improve ERP configuration. User involvement and participation provides with an intelligent function in aid of project management (Kawalek & Wood-Harper, 2002). Organizations intending to implement an ERP system must be willing to dedicate some of their best employees to the project for a successful implementation, according to Bingi et al. (1999), who mention that these employees should not only be experts in the relevant business processes of the organization but also be aware of the best business practices in the industry. They should exhibit the ability to understand the overall needs of the company and should play an important role in guiding the project efforts in the right direction. These employees can play different roles in the project. Some will integrate the project team, others will be key-users, and some others will be end users who will help in specific moments according to the project needs. As Baronas and Louis (1988) mentioned, users perceived IS implementations as a period of transition during which personal control is threatened. This aspect is often detected in ERP implementation projects since in most cases these implementations are associated to significant changes in their working routines. This threat may cause conflicts during the ERP implementation project and resistance to ERP system acceptance.

According to Amoako and White (1997), the management of user involvement and participation requires at least two forms of two-way communication: communication between the various team members (inwards communication) and communication between the project team and the user groups on one side and the management groups on the other (outwards communication). Not surprisingly, strong communication inwards and outwards is found to be as another critical success factor in ERP implementation projects (Esteves & Pastor, 2000; Nah et al., 2001). This two-way communication must inform users of project changes that might affect their activities, and users must get adequate feedback on their concerns. It requires also telling and showing users that their input is valued, used, and will be sought constantly, that is, that they must be committed with the project. Amoako and White (1997) also suggest a set of guidelines in order to manage user involvement and participation. User participation deals with the topics related to the management of their time and activities within the organization, and managers must decide how much effort these users dedicate to their usual activities and to the project and when they do both things. Most organizations cannot afford the effort of completely dedicating these users towards ERP project needs. In contrast, some project managers argue that the involvement and participation of users delay the accomplishment of task schedules. Therefore, and due to time pressures, they decide to avoid the involvement of users. Esteves and Pastor (2001) studied the relevance of user involvement and participation along the phases of SAP® implementation projects with the ASAP® methodology, and their conclusion is that user involvement and participation is more critical in design, realization, and preparation phases. These are the phases where their know-how is very important to achieve a good fit of the ERP system to organizational needs. A detailed task where users must be especially involved is in the definition of forms and reports. Project team members must get end-user requirements, then customize forms and reports, and finally get user acceptance (Welti, 1999). As Welti (1999) says, this is a time-consuming task but most of those documents represent the company image to the customer. He suggests that forms and reports should be discussed and settled with the user in the realization phase.

User Role-Based Concept and Activities in ERP Implementation Projects

In IS research, much interest has been directed at the role of users in the development and implementation of IS. User roles are used to manage resources or skill sets as they pertain to tasks and deliverables that are done on projects. User roles can be thought of as the types of skill or people needed in order to complete a project. As Terry and Standing (2004) mention, the term "user" is open to ambiguity. Land and Hirschheim (1983) acknowledge the existence of different types of users: senior management who bear ultimate responsibility for the organization's well-being and who may use outputs of IS developments; middle management who are responsible for the management control staff using the IS; and finally those operational staff who regularly interact with the system. From project conception throughout the development life cycle, each of these users may contribute or participate in IS development activities. In order to understand the involvement and participation of users in ERP implementation projects, we analyzed a typical ERP implementation methodology. The objectives of this analysis were two-fold. First, we attempted to identify the different user roles in a typical ERP implementation project. Second, we attempted to identify and analyze the different activities that users play in a typical ERP implementation. In this case, we used the Accelerated SAP® methodology (ASAP®) and its related processes.

ASAP® is the implementation methodology that is used to perform a rapid implementation of the SAP® R/3® system. The ASAP® implementation methodology

Table 1. Roles used along a SAP® implementation project

SAP® implementation project roles	Project Preparation (5 wp)	Business Blueprint (7 wp)	Realization (17 wp)	Final Preparation (6 wp)	Go & Live (2 wp)
Project manager	4	6	11	5	2
Project sponsor	2	2	2	1	2
Steering committee	2	3	4	1	
Project team	2	2	7	3	1
Business team leader	3	4	13	4	1
Technical team leader	4	4	11	5	
Consultants		4	11	4	1
IT professional (different functions)		2	11	2	
End user					
Key user		1	7	3	1
Business process owner		1	8	1	
Key site sponsors		1	1		
Line manager		1			
Core change team	3	3	2	1	1
Extended core change team		2	1		1
Project risk manager					
ABAP developer			4		
Development manager			4		
SAP® reviewer		2	1	1	1
SAP® project manager	2				
Help desk provider			1	1	1
Documentation and training developers			1	1	

is structured in phases, work packages, activities, and tasks. ASAP® distributes all work packages across the individual phases according to activity areas and user roles. The user role-based concept ensures redundancy-free, goal-oriented work according to the task at hand and enables the synchronization of all activities. Table 1 represents the different stakeholder roles in a typical SAP® implementation project and the five ASAP® implementation phases. For each role, we quantified the number of work packages (wp) for which that role is defined as "involved" in each phase. In none of the phases, end users are directly expressed as "needed," except the role of the business process owner. Power users (a.k.a., key users) are involved in all phases except on the project preparation phase. The purpose of this phase is to provide initial planning and preparation of the SAP® implementation project. The steps of this phase help identify and plan the primary focus areas to be considered such as: objectives, scope, plan, and definition of project team. Both business process owners and power users are more involved in the third and fourth phases, when the system is parameterized and tested, whereas in the second phase their role is to help in business process modeling and redesign.

Paradoxically, the lack of proposed direct involvement of end users in ASAP® implementation projects, especially in the project preparation and the business blueprint phases, contradicts the need to ensure that users participate in these tasks in order to improve user acceptance and to achieve project success. Usually, ERP implementation methodologies sound more worried with the system implementation, and they pre-suppose that end users will accept the ERP system. The rest should be provided by implementation consulting methodologies.

Research Methodology

As we have mentioned, we have used the GQM method to develop a metrics plan. The steps of our research study have been the following:

- literature review related with the user involvement and user participation topic;
- definition of goals related with user involvement and participation in erp implementation projects;
- definition of questions associated for each goal;
- definition of metrics associated to each question; and
- definition of the preliminary GQM plan.

The information provided by the literature review was our main source of knowledge. We used the concept of a preliminary GQM plan due to the fact that any final GQM plan must be specific to the given real situation and thus validated by the project team that is going to use it. Here, we only provide a starting and thus tentative generic proposal for this plan.

A GQM Preliminary Plan for User Involvement and Participation within ERP Implementations

The measurement framework has been defined in terms of metrics, mechanisms of data collection, and guidelines to use the collected data. It has been defined on the basis of the GQM paradigm (Basili, Caldera, & Rombach, 1994; Solingen & Berghout, 1999) that considers a conceptual level referred to the definition of the GOALS, an operational level consisting of a set of QUESTIONS regarding the specific goals, and a quantitative level identifying a set of METRICS to be associated to each QUESTION. We next present an overview of the GQM approach, and then we describe each of the components of the GQM preliminary plan: measurement goals, questions, and metrics. For each measurement goal defined, the following aspects are described: goal description and its refinement into questions and, finally, refinement from questions into metrics.

Overview of the GQM Method

The GQM approach is a mechanism that provides a framework for developing a metrics program. It was developed at the University of Maryland as a mechanism for formalizing the tasks of characterization, planning, construction, analysis, learning, and feedback. GQM does not provide specific goals but rather a framework for stating measurement goals and refining them into questions to provide a specification for the data needed to help achieve the goals (Basili et al., 1994). The GQM method contains four phases: the planning phase, the definition phase, the data collection phase, and the interpretation phase (for more details, see Solingen & Berghout, 1999). The definition phase is the second phase of the GQM process and concerns all activities that should be performed to formally define a measurement program. By using a GQM, a certain goal is defined, this goal is refined into questions, and, subsequently, metrics are defined that should provide the information to answer these questions. By answering the questions, the measured data can be analyzed to identify if the goals are attained.

One of the most important outcomes of this phase is the GQM plan. A GQM plan (a.k.a., GQM model) documents the refinement of a precisely specified measurement goal via a set of questions into a set of metrics. Thus, a GQM plan documents which metrics are used to achieve a measurement goal and why these are used—the questions provide the rationale underlying the selection of the metrics.

Goals of the GQM Preliminary Plan

In our case of user involvement and participation, the definition of the measurement goals was made using the template provided by Basili et al. (1994). A GQM goal is described according to a template with five dimensions that express the object to be measured, the purpose of measurement, the measured property of the object (quality focus), the subject of measurement (viewpoint), and the context of the measurement (environment). We defined two measurement goals based in our CSF, user involvement, and user participation (see Table 2).

Questions and Metrics

For each measurement goal, we defined a set of questions and related metrics (see Table 3). To define these questions, we made an extensive literature review on user involvement and participation topic (see the previous background section). The questions of our user participation measurement goal are based in the Hartwick and

Table 2. Goals for user involvement and user participation

Goal 1

Analyze:	User participation
For the purpose of	Monitoring
With respect to	ERP implementation project
From the viewpoint of	Project team
In the context of	ERP implementation project

Goal 2

Analyze:	User involvement
For the purpose of	Monitoring
With respect to	ERP implementation project
From the viewpoint of	Project team
In the context of	ERP implementation project

Table 3. Questions for user participation goal

	Questions
Responsibility	1. How much responsibility did you have as a user for estimating project and systems costs? 2. How much responsibility did you have as a user for requesting additional funds to cover unforeseen time/costs overruns? 3. How much responsibility did you have as a user for managing the project (e.g., staffing the project team, calling and running meetings, report to senior manager, etc.)? 4. How much responsibility did you have as a user for overall success of the project and the system? 5. How much responsibility did you have as a user for initiating the project? 6. How much responsibility did you have as a user for determining system objectives? 7. How much responsibility did you have as a user for estimating project and system benefits? 8. What specific behaviors are performed? 9. How many of these behaviors are performed? 10. How often they are performed?
User-project team relationship	11. Did the project team draw up a formal agreement of work to be done during the project? 12. Were you able as a user to make changes to the formal agreement concerning work to be done by the project team during the project? 13. Did you sign off as a user the formal agreement concerning work to be done by the project team during the project? 14. Did you formally evaluate as a user an information requirements analysis developed by the project team concerning the system? 15. Did you as a user formally review work done by the project team concerning the system? 16. Did you as a user formally accept and sign off work done by the project team concerning the system? 17. Did you as a user formally review an information requirements analysis developed by the project team concerning the system? 18. Did you as a user formally evaluate work done by project team concerning the system? 19. Did you as a user approve project timetables? 20. Did you as a user prepare project progress reports?
Hands-on activities	21. Did you as a user [design; help to design; have nothing to do with designing] input/output forms? 22. Did you as a user [design; help to design; have nothing to do with designing] screen layouts? 23. Did you as a user [design; help to design; have nothing to do with designing] report formats? 24. Did you as a user [prepare; help prepare; have nothing to do with preparing] users manuals? 25. Did you as a user [design; help to design; have nothing to do with designing] the user-training program? 26. Did you as a user [train; help train; have nothing to do with training] other users to use the system? 27. Did you as a user [design; help to design; have nothing to do with designing] system security procedures? 28. Did you as a user [set; help set; have nothing to do with setting] system access priorities? 29. Did you as a user [determine; help determine; have nothing to do with determining] data access privileges? 30. Did you as a user participate in testing activities?

Table 3. continued

Communication activities	31. How often did you communicate informally with other users concerning the project? 32. How often did you exchange facts, opinions, and visions concerning the project with other users? 33. How often did you discuss your reservations and concerns regarding the project with other users? 34. How often did you communicate informally with the project team concerning the project? 35. How often did you exchange facts, opinions, and visions concerning the project with project team? 36. How often did you discuss your reservations and concerns regarding the project with the project team? 37. How often did the project team discuss their reservations and concerns regarding the project with you? 38. How often did you communicate informally with senior management concerning the project? 39. How often did you exchange facts, opinions, and visions concerning the project with senior management? 40. How often did you discuss your reservations and concerns regarding the project with senior management? 41. How often did senior management discuss their reservations and concerns regarding the project with you?

Barki (2001) survey. This survey has been used and validated in several IS research studies. We adapted this survey to the context of an ERP implementation project.

The questions (see Table 4) for measurement goal two are related with user involvement, and they arose from the literature review we made on the topic and especially on the "personal involvement inventory" instrument presented by Zaichowsky (1985). This instrument was developed "to measure a person's involvement with products"

Table 4. Questions for user involvement goal

	Questions
User involvement	42. Did you think as a user that the ERP system was essential for your work? 43. Did you think as a user that the ERP system was trivial? 44. What was the level of the ERP system significance? 45. Did you think that the ERP system was important for you as a user? 46. Did you think that you needed the ERP system to perform your job? 47. What was the level of the ERP system relevance to you as a user? 48. Did you think that the ERP concerns to you as a user? 49. Did the ERP system matter to you as a user? 50. Did the ERP system mean something to you? 51. Did you feel excited with the ERP system? 52. What is the level of the ERP system interest to you?

(Zaichowsky, 1985, p. 349). As suggested by Barki and Hartwick (1994), we have eliminated the constructs related to user attitude, focusing only on user involvement constructs. With regard to Kappelman's (1995) constructs on user process involvement and user product involvement, since they are variations of the larger concept called user involvement, we have considered them minor variations of Zaichowsky's (1985) constructs. Thus, here we only present the questions for the general concept—user involvement.

Metrics Identification

For each question, we defined metrics in order to answer the respective question. Tables 5 and 6 show the metrics and the respective relationship between the questions defined earlier and the metrics.

For each metric, we defined the following aspects: what they are measuring, when they must be measured, what possible values they could have, who will measure them, what medium is used for data collection. We created a special form for the metrics description. Most of the metrics proposed are direct measurements except the metrics related with percentages.

Table 5. The set of metrics for user participation goal

Dimension	Metrics	Questions
Responsibility	Responsibility for project estimation	1
	Responsibility for estimating costs	1
	Responsibility for requesting additional funds to cover unforeseen time/costs overruns	2
	Responsibility for managing the project	3
	Responsibility for overall success of the project	4
	Responsibility for initiating the project	5
	Responsibility for determining system objectives	6
	Responsibility for estimating project and systems benefits	7
	Types of behaviors performed	8,9
	Estimated duration of behavior	10
User-project team relationship	User's participation in project plan	11
	Changes made by users to project plan	12
	Participation in project sign off	13
	Participation in evaluation of information requirements analysis	14
	Participation in sign off of information requirements analysis	16
	Participation in review meetings	17,18,19
	Participation in support meetings	15,20

Table 5. continued

	Participation in forms design	21
	Participation in screens layout	22
	Participation in reports format	23
	Participation in user manuals preparation	24
Hands-on activities	Participation in training plan	25
	Participation as trainer	26
	Participation in systems security procedures	27
	Participation in system access priorities	28
	Participation in data access privileges	29
	Participation in testing activities	30
Communication activities	Communication between users	31,32,33
	Communication between users and project team	34,35,36, 37
	Communication with senior managers	38,39,40,41

Table 6. The set of metrics for user involvement goal

Dimension	Metrics	Questions
	Essential	42
	Trivial	43
	Significance	44
	Importance	45
	Necessary	46
User involvement	Relevance	47
	Concerns	48
	Matters	49
	Means	50
	Excitement	51
	Interest	52

Toward a Framework for Monitoring
User Involvement and Participation

Based on the literature review on user involvement and participation and on our prior research on ERP implementations, we propose a framework for monitoring user involvement and participation within ERP implementation projects (see Figure 2). The framework takes into account the ERP implementation phases, user involvement and participation dimensions (see Figure 1), and the different user roles in an ERP project. This framework is adapted from the framework proposed by Olson and Ives (1980) for specifying types of user involvement. In an ERP implementation project, these user roles are quite well typified in the ERP implementation methodologies.

We propose that user involvement and participation metrics should be interpreted, taking into consideration three dimensions: user involvement and participation, ERP user roles, and ERP implementation phases. Users play different roles and have different relevance along the ERP implementation according to their roles (Esteves & Pastor, 2001). Hartwick and Barki (2001) analyzed the questions in terms of the different user roles in a project. They concluded that the role that users play on a team was found to have a strong impact on overall participation, as well as on each of the four participation dimensions. It is expected that users that are members of the project team have more participation than non-members, both overall and on each of the four dimensions. Users that become the project managers are expected to have more participation than members overall, but not similarly to other dimensions. For the responsibility dimension, the difference between managers and team members was much greater than the difference observed for the other three dimensions.

The literature on user involvement and participation identifies diverse dimensions that should be taken into account for measuring and monitoring this issue. Finally, previous research (e.g., Barki & Hartwick, 1994, 2001; Kappelman, 1995) has shown that the construct of user involvement and participation in the development/implementation of an IS must be measured at different stages of the process. Furthermore, Esteves and Pastor (2001) showed that user involvement and participation relevance varies along the ERP implementation phases. For instance, according to Esteves and Pastor (2001), it is expected that key users involvement participation will be higher in design, realization, and preparation phases.

Therefore, the values for metrics are affected by the relationship between these three dimensions. We have defined five types of users: top management, team members, key users, IS personnel, and end users. Users can also be categorized by their different levels (Olson & Yves, 1980): executive management (top level), operational management (middle level), supervisory personnel, and operating personnel. Although we did not mention before, other stakeholders like the ERP vendor play an

Figure 2. A framework for monitoring user involvement and participation in ERP implementation projects

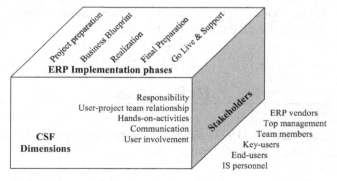

important role in an ERP implementation project, and it would also be desirable to analyze their involvement in the ERP implementation project. There is evidence that some ERP projects failed to achieve good levels of involvement of some or all types of stakeholders. Regarding users activities, instead of defining them in another dimension, as in the Olson and Ives (1980) framework, we consider them as part of the ERP implementation phases. We prefer this option because all of the ERP implementation methodologies provide a detailed explanation of work packages, activities, and tasks by user role along the different ERP implementation phases.

Conclusion and Future Work

This study presents a set of metrics for user involvement and participation within ERP implementation projects. User involvement and participation is cited as one of the most relevant critical success factors in ERP implementation projects. The set of metrics is based on the existing knowledge on user involvement and participation in the IS field in general and in the ERP topic in particular. This fact is very important since organizations do not seem to have this internal knowledge prior to the ERP implementations. Thus, one of the contributions of this study is that of bringing into public attention those issues related with user involvement and participation that require active management, yet they may not normally be treated as important issues until they become critical.

We think these metrics have two important pro-active characteristics: (1) metrics help to detect deviations from the project plan and to act before damage is made, and (2) these metrics can have the effect of motivating and encouraging top managers in the general involvement and commitment with the ERP project. The results of this work are two-fold. First, a GQM plan to monitor and control ERP implementation projects is presented and, second, a literature review on user involvement and participation on ERP implementation projects. The purpose of this study is not to describe an exhaustive list of metrics. Instead, we intended to present a rational way to develop these metrics in future ERP implementation projects and to provide the first set of metrics that should be extended and adapted according to the specific needs of each particular ERP implementation project.

References

Amoako, K., & White, K. (1997). When is user involvement not user involvement? *The Executive's Journal*, *13*(4), 40-46.

Bancroft, N., Seip H., & Sprengel, A. (1998). *Implementing SAP R/3* (2nd ed.). Manning Publications.

Barki, H., & Hartwick, J. (1989). Rethinking the concept of user involvement. *MIS Quarterly, 13*(1), 53-63.

Barki, H., & Hartwick, J. (1994). Measuring user participation, user involvement, and user attitude. *MIS Quarterly, 18*(1), 59-82.

Barki, H., & Hartwick, J. (2001). Communications as a dimension of user participation. *IEEE Transactions on Professional Communication, 44*(1), 21-35.

Baronas, A., & Louis, M. (1988). Restoring a sense of control during implementation: How user involvement leads to system acceptance. *MIS Quarterly, 12*(1), 111-124.

Basili, V., Caldera, C., & Rombach, H. (1994). Goal question metric paradigm. In J. Marciniak (Ed.), *Encyclopedia of software engineering* (Vol. 1, pp. 528-532). John Wiley & Sons.

Bingi, P., Sharma, M., & Godla, J. (1999). Critical issues affecting an ERP implementation. *Information Systems Management, 16*(3), 7-14.

Briolat, D., & Pogman, J. (2000). *User involvement influence on project productivity in a rad environment: A quasi-experiment.* European Software Control and Metrics Conference, Munich.

Cavaye, A. (1995). User participation in system development revisited. *Information & Management Journal,*(28), 311-323.

Cowan, C., Gray, C., & Larson, L. (1992). Project partnering. *Project Management Journal, 22*(4), 5-11.

Esteves, J., & Pastor, J. (2000). *Towards the unification of critical success factors for ERP implementations.* Presented at the 10th Annual BIT Conference, Manchester.

Esteves, J., & Pastor, J. (2001). *Analysis of critical success factors relevance along SAP implementation phases.* Americas Conference on Information Systems.

Hartwick, J., & Barki, H. (1994). Explaining the role of user participation in information system use. *Management Science, 40*(4), 440-465

Ives, B., & Olson, M. (1984). User involvement and MIS success: A review of research. *Management Science, 30*(5), 586-603.

Jiang, J., Chen, E., & Klein, G. (2002). The importance of building a foundation for user involvement in information system projects. *Project Management Journal, 33*(1), 20-26.

Jurison, J. (1999). Software project management: The manager's view. *Communications of the Association for Information Systems, 2*(17).

Kale, V. (2000). *Implementing SAP R/3: The guide for business and technology managers.* Sams Publishing.

Kappelman, L. (1995). Measuring user involvement: A diffusion of innovation perspective. *The Data Base for Advances in Information Systems, 26*(2/3), 65-86.

Kappelman, L., & McLean, E. (1991). The respective roles of user participation and user involvement in information systems implementation success. *International Conference on Information Systems* (pp. 339-348).

Kawalek, P., & Wood-Harper, T. (2002). The finding of thorns: User participation in enterprise system implementation. *The Data Base for advances in information systems, 33*(1), 13-22.

Land, F., & Hirschheim, R. (1983). Participative systems design: Rationale, tools and techniques. *Journal of Applied Systems Analysis, 10*, 91-107.

Markus, M. (1983). Power, politics, and MIS implementation. *Communications of the ACM, 26*(6), 430-444.

Mckeen, J., & Guimarães, T. (1994). The relationship between user participation and user satisfaction: An investigation of four contingency factors. *MIS Quarterly, 18*(4), 427-452.

Nah, F., Lau, J., & Kuang, J. (2001). Critical factors for successful implementation of enterprise systems. *Business Process Management Journal, 7*(3), 285-296.

Olson, M., & Ives, B. (1980). Measuring user involvement in information system development. *International Conference on Information Systems* (pp. 130-143).

Olson, M., & Ives, B. (1981). User involvement in systems design: An empirical test of alternative approaches. *Information & Management Journal, 4*(4), 183-196.

Pettingell, K., Marshall, T., & Remington, W. (1988). A review of the influence of user involvement on system success. In *Proceedings of the 9th International Conference on Information Systems* (pp. 227-236).

Solingen, R., & Berghout, E. (1999). *The goals/question/metric method: A practical guide for quality improvement of software development.* McGraw-Hill.

Terry, J., & Standing, C. (2004). The value of user participation in e-commerce systems development. *Inform Science Journal, 7*, 31-45.

Welti, N. (1999). *Successful SAP R/3 implementation: Practical management of ERP projects.* Addison-Wesley.

Wilson, S., Bekker, M., Johnson, H., & Johnson, P. (1996). Costs and benefits of user involvement in design: Practitioners views. In *People and Computers XI Proceedings of HCI '96* (pp. 221-240).

Zaichowsky, J. (1985). Measuring the involvement construct. *Journal of Consumer Research, 12*, 341-352.

Chapter XIII

Investigating the Interdependence of Organisations and Information Systems

Laurence Brooks
Brunel University, UK

Christopher J. Davis
University of South Florida, St. Petersburg, USA

Mark Lycett
Brunel University, UK

Abstract

Using the personal construct theory (PCT) as an underlying conceptual frame, this chapter explores the interdependence of organisations and information systems. Two PCT-related techniques—repertory grid analysis (RepGrid) and cognitive mapping (CM)—were used to investigate the dynamics of this interaction. Changing business models and information technologies were investigated in two distinct work settings: in each case, the technique contributed substantial insight into the role of information systems in that context. The analysis shows that the techniques have matured to a stage where they provide a basis for improved understanding of the organisational complexities related to information technologies. The techniques focus on the social construction of meaning by articulating and interpreting the discourse that surrounds the development, implementation, and use of information technology in organisations. It is these ongoing discourses that create the dynamic complexities in the organisations, as they "play" themselves out, and develop, over time. Current research has articulated and improved awareness of the issues and concerns that surround computer-based information systems (CBIS). Despite the differing contexts and work processes, the findings from each case suggest that the techniques facilitated social construction and increased the conceptual agility of managers, leading to improved integration of organisational processes and technology. The chapter concludes by drawing out the idea of the development of a conceptual model to act as a framework for the analysis of cognitive schema and shared understanding. In developing and participating in this shared understanding, both organisational and technological communities could increase their awareness of each other's issues and concerns, thereby enabling them to improve the conceptual agility of the organisation.

Introduction

This chapter explores the significance of the social construction of meaning within communities of discourse (Orr, 1996) that surround information technology and organisational management. Organisational discourse is central to the communication of concepts and ideas that enable individuals and groups to: (a) make sense of the world in which they work and (b) understand the changes to work brought about by new technologies, such as information systems (IS). The advantages of focusing research on work processes rather than either technology or the organisation itself has been established in the literature (Orlikowski & Barley, 2001) and adopted in this research. Therefore, this chapter's focus is on the reciprocal influences of computer-based information systems (CBIS) and organisations on one another.

Technological change, such as that involving CBIS, involves developers, workers, and managers in a complex and extended dialogue. This dialogue is characterised by two important dimensions. First, the level (detail) of design activity ranges widely during the evolution of a CBIS. Second, and perhaps consequentially, responsibility for activity surrounding the CBIS is shared between a number of individuals; such sharing could be simultaneous—in committee, team, or group activities—or sequential. Sequential sharing arises from the episodic nature of project phases. Although formal role assignments might be in place throughout the life of a project, changing responsibilities and work assignments mean that the relationships are constantly re-negotiated as the project progresses. Project phases are characterised by the evolution of new channels of communication that supersede previously existing ones. This chapter explores the dynamics of this evolutionary dialogue and the extent to which it can be related to the ability to manage change.

In the research discussed here, both organisation and technology were conceived of as processes. In order to explore the complex interactions and dialogue among the various communities involved in a CBIS project, both investigations sought to avoid the limitations of taking a "snapshot" of a specific project. Our research interest is in the social construction of the technology through the development of specifications, documents, and other communications that contributed to the dialogue surrounding a CBIS. Our investigations sought to explore the processes that sustained the discourse about the CBIS and the organisation. The social construction of meaning that takes place as technology and organisation simultaneously evolve or unfold over time provides the locus from which the significance of the issues and concerns faced by those involved can be presented and interpreted, that is, to make the relevant parties aware of the dynamic complexities in their organisations. However, articulating and monitoring this dialogue is not a trivial task. In this chapter, we describe two alternative, but related, approaches. These were used in independent organisational settings. Our aim in this chapter is not to demonstrate inter-case generalisability *per se*, rather to demonstrate the value of the process perspective, the complementarity of the data gathering and analysis techniques employed, and their capacity to elicit shared mental models. The two approaches to the development of shared mental models show that they can be used to: (1) improve conceptual agility (that is, the ease with which issues, concerns, and values from one community of practice [for instance, software developers] can be brought to mind in another community [for instance, organisational managers]) and (2) to demonstrate that the constructs and concepts that comprise the shared mental model—and thus provide the improved conceptual agility—are an essential foundation to building the bridge between business and information systems at the worker, management, and strategy levels.

The research techniques used were repertory grid analysis (RepGrid) and cognitive mapping (CM). They were used to address the problem of providing a forum or a medium for the exchange of ideas and concerns between the technological and organisational communities. Although by no means comparable in terms of the work they undertake, the organisations studied faced similar issues in articulating and addressing the concerns surrounding the management of large-scale CBIS on which their organisation is increasingly dependent.

The remainder of this chapter explores the capability of both RepGrid and CM to enhance understanding and appreciation of the complex interactions that occur as CBIS are developed, implemented, and used in their organisational setting. The concluding sections explore commonalities in the nature of the constructs elicited by the two techniques. Despite the fact that the techniques and the work context in which they were applied differed, some content and representational similarities suggest the existence of higher-level cognitive artefacts (which we refer to as "super constructs"). These, we suggest, represent components of the shared mental models articulated during the research. Although the research data are directly relevant only in their specific contexts, re-analysis and reflection suggests that the complementarity of the RepGrid and CM techniques and their outputs could be exploited to substantially improve researchers', users', and managers' understanding and appreciation of the issues surrounding the design, implementation, and use of CBIS.

The super constructs represent shared cognitive schemata or mental models of the organisational complexities related to CBIS and the work processes they support. The super constructs are important components of the dialogue that facilitate the interaction of the technology and organisation processes through the CBIS project phases. Their importance emerged over time: iterations of RepGrid and CM articulated and clarified the super constructs. This process enabled the participants in our original research to identify, appreciate, and prioritise the issues that affected their work, specifically reducing misinterpretation and misattribution. This proved invaluable as they prepared for or managed changes brought about by the introduction of CBIS.

Many of these changes were planned and well prepared for, whereas others were not, especially as not all the impacts of a CBIS can be anticipated. Such unanticipated impacts give rise to issues and concerns that, although significant to the workers involved, are frequently difficult for them or their organisational managers to explain. As the studies show, the techniques used in this research enabled these emergent concerns to be articulated and discussed within both the user and managerial communities. The techniques provide powerful support for the process of learning: participants in this research frequently reported that their understanding of their role/work and its relation to both the CBIS they used and the wider enterprise of the organisation had increased. This suggests that shared cognitive schemata are an important contributor to organisational effectiveness, through better understanding of the issues surrounding the workers (people in the organisation) and their interactions with the CBIS.

Following an overview of discussion of the personal construct theory (PCT) in the next section, we introduce the two techniques that share its theoretic base. First, we discuss our use of RepGrid to articulate constructs surrounding a large scale forensic CBIS. We then discuss our use of CM to investigate the change processes experienced by CBIS specialists in a large financial institution. The fifth section of the chapter discusses the major findings from the research, highlighting the similarity of the research outcomes despite the disparity of the work settings. The chapter concludes with some proposals for further research to explore the extent to which PCT-derived super constructs provide empirical data that can be used to assess and compare complex interactions arising from the use of CBIS in other organisational contexts.

Personal Construct Theory (PCT)

The personal construct theory (PCT) (Kelly, 1955a, 1955b) provides the common theoretical foundation for both repertory grid analysis (RepGrid) and cognitive mapping (CM). PCT was originally developed for use in psychology, principally in clinical therapeutic contexts. Three key assertions are seen to underlie PCT:

1. that people make sense of their world through contrast and similarity;
2. that people seek to explain their world (why is it so? what made it so?); and
3. that people seek to understand the significance of their world by organising concepts hierarchically.

In the traditional application of PCT, individuals are asked to express their view of the world in terms of constructs, each having a positive and negative pole (expressing the concept and its perceived opposite). The relationship between the constructs is then evaluated through an exhaustive paired or three-way comparison to develop what are known as repertory grids, which can then be subject to analysis (RepGrid). Equally, the relationships between the constructs may be reflected in a more visual approach, as developed in a related technique known as cognitive mapping (CM). The individual techniques are described in more detail in the following sections.

Both RepGrid and CM can be used inductively to investigate situations, where the nature and significance of the issues is not known in advance. Given that some consequences of using CBIS are unanticipated, the techniques provide a major advantage over questionnaires and similar research instruments that rely solely on pre-defined investigatory criteria. Equally, the strength of PCT's theoretical base and the structure provided by the RepGrid and CM techniques contrast with the more unstructured and debated nature of emergent techniques, such as the grounded theory (Glaser & Strauss, 1967). The following sections explain how we set out to exploit the particular strengths of these PCT-based techniques.

NAFIS and Repertory Grid Analysis (RepGrid)

The National Automated Fingerprint Information System (NAFIS) is a large-scale distributed information system which became operational in all 43 police forces in England and Wales in July 2001. RepGrid was one of four techniques (the others were observation, interview, and document analysis) used to assess the impacts of NAFIS on the process and organisation of fingerprint work. The NAFIS database, located in West London, holds the national fingerprint collection of some 50 million fingerprint images. It also holds a database of outstanding (latent) finger marks from crime scenes. NAFIS interfaces directly with the Police National Computer (PNC) that holds descriptive (alphanumeric) data about convicted offenders. Together, the alphanumeric data held on PNC and the corresponding fingerprint images (called "ten-prints") held on NAFIS comprise the National Criminal Justice Record System (NCJRS).

NAFIS uses Automated Fingerprint Recognition (AFR) protocols to provide a comprehensive information system supporting two distinct processes: (1) the verification of the identity of individuals arrested and (2) the identification of those responsible for crime. Historically, identity verification has been: (a) the responsibility of the National Identification Service (NIS) at New Scotland Yard in London, whereas identification of (latent) marks left at the scene of a crime, and (b) a local (police force) responsibility. NAFIS brought these two processes together: since each process depends on the comparison of fingerprint images, NAFIS removes the need for both national (to support (a)) and local (to support (b)) collections. The devolution of the ten-print verification process to the 43 forces brought with it responsibilities previously held by staff at the NIS. Although the ten-print process was familiar to provincial fingerprint officers, its management and resource implications were not.

RepGrid was used in the research to articulate the experience and expertise of fingerprint workers in order interpret the issues and concerns that faced them and their colleagues as NAFIS was introduced into operational use. The specialty of the work, the peculiarity of the task environment, and the complexity of the organisational structure presented significant research challenges. RepGrid was chosen as a data gathering technique since it provided an epistemologically neutral medium. That is to say, although offering a robust structure for dialogue between researcher and participant, the RepGrid imposed no predetermined content or direction. The "agenda" for the RepGrid conversations with fingerprint workers were set by them rather than us.

The RepGrid conversations with members of the fingerprint community gave rise to the negotiation of shared meaning and heightened awareness of the inter-subjectivity of the perception and significance of issues and concerns surrounding the use of NAFIS. During the course of the NAFIS study, 56 RepGrid analyses were carried out with 24 participants.

The initial phase of each RepGrid analysis followed the conventional pattern (as described by Fransella, 2003). Each participant was asked, "What tasks are involved in fingerprint identification?" This question defined the "universe of discourse," ensuring that the scope of each conversation was the same but without directing its content. The selection of an appropriate opening question is the key to fully exploring the richness of the system of personal constructs. However, experience and practice are essential in order to balance the openness and flexibility of RepGrid and simultaneously minimise the risk of interviewer bias. This balance was achieved by adopting the research protocol developed by Thomas and Harri-Augstein (1985) whereby the interviewer acts as "teacher-consultant," explaining the phases and outcomes of the techniques to participants but simultaneously encouraging them at all times to use their own words as verbal representations of their experience.

Participants' responses to the initiating (universe of discourse) question were verbal descriptions of their experience of fingerprint work, which were recorded. These verbal task descriptors included both current manual tasks and tasks supported by NAFIS. Typically, participants named tasks in the sequence of their execution: the completeness of the list was intuitively clear to the participant. When a comprehensive list of tasks had been compiled, they were differentiated by a process called triadic elicitation. The list was presented back to the participant three tasks at a time. For each group of three (triad), the participant explained which task, if any, differed from the other two and how it did so. Participants also explained what made the non-differentiated tasks similar (Thomas & Harri-Augstein, 1985). In this way, the task list enabled the development of a series of bi-polar constructs, unique to each participant, capable of differentiating the tasks. The task descriptions provided the column headings and the bi-polar constructs the headings for the two "poles" of the rows in the repertory grid. Participants then rated each task in turn against the constructs using a 5-point Likert scale. The example in Figure 1 shows the task

Figure 1. A "raw" repertory grid

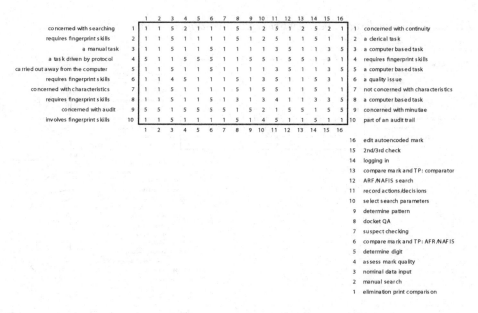

		1	2	3	4	5	6	7	8	9	10	11	12	13	14	15	16		
concerned with searching	1	1	1	5	2	1	1	1	5	1	2	5	1	2	5	2	1	1	concerned with continuity
requires fingerprint skills	2	1	1	5	1	1	1	1	5	1	2	5	1	1	5	1	1	2	a clerical task
a manual task	3	1	1	5	1	1	5	1	1	1	1	3	5	1	1	3	5	3	a computer based task
a task driven by protocol	4	5	1	1	5	5	5	1	1	5	5	1	5	5	1	3	1	4	requires fingerprint skills
carried out away from the computer	5	1	1	5	1	1	5	1	1	1	1	3	5	1	1	3	5	5	a computer based task
requires fingerprint skills	6	1	1	4	5	1	1	1	5	1	3	5	1	1	5	3	1	6	a quality issue
concerned with characteristics	7	1	1	5	1	1	1	1	5	1	5	5	1	1	5	1	1	7	not concerned with characteristics
requires fingerprint skills	8	1	1	5	1	1	5	1	3	1	3	4	1	1	3	3	5	8	a computer based task
concerned with audit	9	5	5	1	5	5	5	5	1	5	2	1	5	5	1	5	5	9	concerned with minutiae
involves fingerprint skills	10	1	1	5	1	1	1	1	5	1	4	5	1	1	5	1	1	10	part of an audit trail
		1	2	3	4	5	6	7	8	9	10	11	12	13	14	15	16		

16 edit autoencoded mark
15 2nd/3rd check
14 logging in
13 compare mark and TP: comparator
12 ARF/NAFIS search
11 record actions/decisions
10 select search parameters
9 determine pattern
8 docket QA
7 suspect checking
6 compare mark and TP: AFR/NAFIS
5 determine digit
4 assess mark quality
3 nominal data input
2 manual search
1 elimination print comparison

descriptors or elements as column headings and the constructs used to differentiate them as labels at the end of each row. The numbers indicate the ratings applied to each of the element and construct combinations.

Each completed grid was analysed on-site using a two-dimensional cluster analysis that re-ordered both the task elements (columns) and constructs (rows) according to the correspondence of their numeric ratings to re-order the rows and columns. We used the RepGridII software provided by Shaw and Gaines (1990). The content of individual cells remains exactly as they were completed by the user. However, in order to highlight the statistical associations the order of the rows and columns is changed so as to juxtapose the most similar ones. The associations are represented by adding a simple hierarchical structure to the grid: an example is shown in Figure 2. The scales are simply an indication, in percentage terms, of the alignment of the rows or columns spanned by the branches of the hierarchical "tree."

No further statistical analysis of the data was carried out at this time: such analyses tend to usurp the processes of analysis and interpretation from the user (Hufnagel & Conca, 1994). Rather than successively summarising or abstracting the participants' responses, we sought to re-immerse the data into the task context. This preservation of ownership of the research process further reduced the likelihood of misinterpretation, further decreased the likelihood of interviewer bias, and reinforced the integrity and validity of the data.

Instead of further statistical analysis, the re-ordered grid was presented to the participant, who was asked to explain what the clusters meant in the context of their

Figure 2. A re-ordered repertory grid after two-dimensional cluster analysis

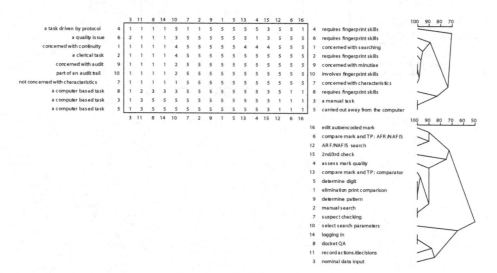

work. This process, called talkback (Thomas & Harri-Augstein, 1985), diverges significantly from the conventional statistical analysis of repertory grid data used, for instance, by Hunter (1997). For our research, RepGrid provided a conversational technology (Thomas & Harri-Augstein, 1985) that strives to adhere to the fundamental principles of PCT. By fulfilling a role as teacher-consultant, the interviewer offered RepGrid to the participants as a medium for reflection on their own experience. This further minimised the likelihood of interviewer bias and maintained ownership and direction of the conversation by the participant. RepGrid provided a powerful medium for the organisational discourse, enabling participants to articulate their experience of fingerprint work and the values that they used to judge it.

Each analysis, or conversation, started from scratch with the same question. Most participants took part in three analyses during the study, which spanned development, implementation, and use of the system over a total of seven years. During the talkback phase, the spaced-focused grid was annotated to indicate the meaning attributed to the clusters. Additionally, following the second and third RepGrid analyses, participants were asked to compare the most recent grid with the previous grid(s). This provided a substantial extension of the talkback protocol, enabling change in both working practices and interpretations of those changes to be monitored and discussed as utilisation and understanding of NAFIS increased.

In these analyses, the participants were responsible for interpretation of the repertory grid and the data that it contained. The RepGrid process gave rise to substantial learning at a number of levels. Individual participants increased the repertoire of language used to describe and explain their work: many remarked that they had not thought of or would have described fingerprint work "in that way" before. This is an example of what Thomas and Harri-Augstein (1985) call self-organised learning. The value of RepGrid to this study did not lie either in the quantity or quality of the numeric data contained in the grids, nor in the rigour or reliability of the statistical protocols underpinning the FOCUS analysis. Rather, the value of RepGrid arose from the dialogue that it supported and the articulation of a number of super constructs (these can also be thought of as "work motifs" as explained more fully in Davis & Hufnagel, 2004). Super constructs are used to indicate the context specificity of the shared constructs that represent the cognitive schemata used by the participants to explain their very specialist work.

The utility of the super constructs that arose from our inductive use of RepGrid arose from the mutual understanding of the issues and concerns that gave rise to them. By relying on RepGrid to provide structure and form to the narrative but without dictating content, the outcome was a series of super constructs that used language readily meaningful in the task context, enabling fingerprint workers' concerns to be appreciated within the wider police community. The utility of the super constructs was further demonstrated during later phases of the research. Observation of fingerprint work and interviews with supervisors, organisational managers, and others involved in the wider investigative process were guided by the super constructs.

These research interventions enabled the issues and concerns articulated by the fingerprint workers to be addressed. For instance, the devolution of ten-print processing had a variety of impacts in each of the police forces studied, all of which had different internal structures and processes. On one occasion, a research-led seminar enabled senior managers in one force to reallocate people between tasks and departments to overcome a significant operational problem that had arisen as a result of a misapprehension of NAFIS functionality among workers and managers in another department.

This brief example shows how the super constructs articulated using RepGrid were used by organisational managers to discuss and address the concerns of the fingerprint workers as the impacts of NAFIS "unfolded" in the work setting. Use of the super constructs by fingerprint workers and their managers demonstrates their contextual validity and fidelity. Articulation of the super constructs using RepGrid enriched and improved communication, enabling workers and managers to more fully appreciate the others' concerns about operational issues that arose during implementation and operational use of NAFIS. In this way, the super constructs helped to inform and guide organisational managers' decision making in directions that improved the process and organisation of fingerprint work.

In addition to such valuable practical outcomes, our use of RepGrid also shows how the interpretation of empirical field study data itself can be enriched by retrospective analysis within the work context. This suggests that in addition to providing the basis for a cycle of learning and organisational development, RepGrid data could be combined with materials from interviews, observation, CM, and other sources. Such combination would increase the likelihood that data analysis is "anchored" in the conceptual structure of the research context, thereby increasing the reliability and validity of the findings derived from the empirical data set.

UKFI and Cognitive Mapping

Technology Group (TG) is the division of a large UK Financial Institution (UKFI), which has evolved from a building society to a financial group of 10 strategic business units that service both corporate and personal banking and investment needs. TG is responsible for the development, implementation, and day-to-day operations of information systems of business-to-customer (B2C) and business-to-business (B2B) business streams. TG consists of about 90 information systems specialists distributed in three locations within the UK, handling the information systems of the financial institution nationally, including its Web and call centre services.

Despite the group's diversification, retail banking is still the core business unit of the group. It serves approximately 15 million customers through approximately

714 branches, 3,180 ATMs. The group launched e-banking in May 2000, aiming to provide access to customer services through the Internet, telephone, digital TV and WAP mobile phones. The centrality of the retail banking for the financial health of the group, along with its reliance on information systems, triggered the need for this study.

This study focuses on the relationship between TG and the retail banking business unit. The aim was to facilitate information systems development and implementation for retail banking by improving collaboration. The primary objective was to uncover the root causes of existing barriers to collaborate and define a solutions space that would enable negotiation and action taking (for an alternative view on this case and further information see Hatzakis, Lycett, Macredie, & Martin, 2005).

During the course of the study, over 30 semi-structured interviews were held with board and top-level managers within TG and the retail business. Within this context, CM was used to: (a) interpret and represent individual perspectives of those involved in the study in order to (b) synthesise in a group representation an inter-subjective view of corporate reality. This inter-subjective view aimed to highlight the differences and similarities of individual perspectives and issues and concerns discussed.

CM was originally developed by Eden (1988) as a technique for use in strategic decision making in organisations. It adopts Kelly's concept of constructs, but uses them in a much less rigid way than RepGrid (see the third section). Constructs are identified from the statements individuals use in describing a situation during an interview and are represented as brief phrases in natural language. Sometimes, the negative pole will be given, but often it is assumed to be implicit. Rather than carry out the repertory grid comparison, the links between constructs are identified from the chain of argument employed in describing the situation. The relationship between constructs is assumed to take the form of explanations and consequences as shown in Figure 3. The relationship may be positive (i.e., construct A reinforces construct B), negative (construct A operates in the opposite direction to construct B—reinforcing the negative pole), or connotative (implying a relationship between the constructs, but of unknown or neutral effect).

Figure 3. Basic mapping convention for representing relationships between constructs

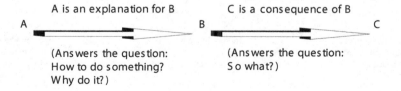

The product of a CM exercise is, therefore, a map (in the style of a directed network) made up of nodes (consisting of phrases used by the individual to describe the situation) and arcs (links identified from the individual's description of the situation). Discussing it with the interviewee validates the structure and content of the map.

The mapping is initially carried out with pencil and paper during a normal interview. The large number of constructs generated in a one-hour interview (100 or more) often results in a very "messy" picture/map being generated. This then needs to be "tidied-up" both for analysis and feedback to the interviewee. As part of this tidying process, the map can be transferred to a specific computer application (Decision Explorer™),[1] which has been developed to operationalise cognitive mapping. Note that this study used CM in the general style of Eden (Eden & Ackerman, 2001), from which was developed the specific Decision Explorer™ tool. Decision Explorer™ enables much easier handling of large numbers of constructs and introduces a much higher degree of flexibility in manipulation of the maps. In addition, it provides a degree of CM appropriate analysis, which would not be found in other concept mapping tools (e.g., Thinkmap®, IHMC-CMap™), that deal with information visualisations and knowledge modelling.

Following this tidying of the map, the information is generally presented back to the interviewee for amendment and/or confirmation that it is an appropriate representation of their viewpoint (an example is shown in Figure 4). Rather than working with

Figure 4. Example of section of a cognitive map used in a feedback session

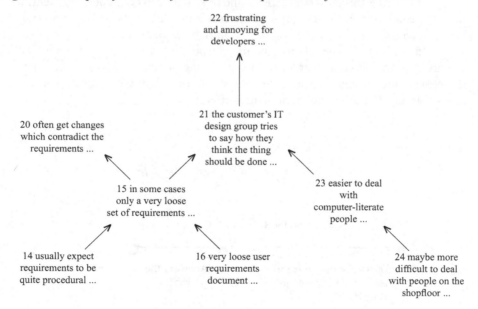

the whole map, particular chains of argument can be separated out and are much easier to examine. At this point, there is wide scope for negotiation over the content and structure of the map, using the physical map (whether working directly with the software or on printed output) as the negotiative object. As already noted, the mapping process (including the feedback to the interviewees) allows for learning to occur, in that the process of reflecting on work practices, and deciphering their rationale, allowed for insights by the individual participants that might not otherwise have been made.

Having established some agreement over the basic outline for the map, the next step is to begin to make use of it. In practical terms, maps of more than about 30 concepts are too difficult to deal with as a whole and Decision Explorer™ includes analytical routines which can aid the identification of: clustering of concepts; the beginnings and ends of chains of arguments (often described as assertions and goals); constructs which have many others associated with them (described as issues); or which are branching points in a chain of argument (option points). This analysis can help to guide in the validation and interpretation of the map.

In its application in strategic decision making, cognitive mapping can be used as part of a more general method known as strategic options development and analysis (SODA). In this approach, different stakeholders whose views have been individually mapped are brought together in a meeting (a SODA workshop). The individual maps are compared and a collective map is negotiated which seeks to merge those of the individuals. Where there is uncertainty or different views about the meaning of constructs, this can be examined in the individual maps and debated among the meeting participants. By retaining elements of the original (individual) maps in the collective map, the stakeholders' sense of ownership of the group viewpoint is encouraged. By providing a rich representation of individual viewpoints, the similarities and differences between different stakeholders can be studied and debated. Apart from the process and affective benefits of such negotiation, the collective map can serve as an agenda for strategic action by identifying shared goals, problems, and options.

Cognitive mapping is an established technique in strategic consultancy (Brooks & Jones, 1996), but it has not been widely applied in the information systems field (although there has been a recent attempt to bring CM into the IS context (see Nakayama & Armstrong, 2005). It may be argued, however, to have many characteristics which would commend it for use in information systems development (Clarke, Horita, & Mackaness, 2000). These include:

- **Simple to use/non-intrusive:** pen and chapter recording during a "normal" interview.
- **Easily comprehensible:** uses interviewees own words.

- **Emphasis on negotiation of viewpoints:** validation of maps allows exploration/clarification of viewpoints and explicit debate in group sessions.
- **Computer-based support:** therefore it may be more acceptable/interesting to IS professionals.

The study within UKFI used interviews, based on a three-section interview schedule, that aimed to explore perceptions of: (1) the current situation and interviewees' experience with TG or Retail Banking; (2) issues of collaboration between the two groups and definition of a potential solutions space; and finally, (3) relationship management and attitudes toward it. Each interview lasted between 20 minutes and one hour and was tape-recorded and transcribed.

Cognitive mapping was used as analytical, rather than data collection, technique. Therefore, mapping was carried out based on the interview transcripts, rather than the "live" interviews. While this is not an ideal situation, the argument is that it does provide a degree of efficacy within this type of more constrained context.

Since the interviews were fully transcribed, the individuals' own words were used to form the map constructs as much as possible. Each map consisted of 100-300 constructs depending on the interview duration, along with the detail and conciseness of individuals' discourse. Maps were "tidied-up" using Decision Explorer™, in order to present a more orderly representation. Due to the very large level of detail contained within these maps, a "stripped" set version of each map was derived, in

Figure 5. Schematic representation of bridging links to produce an aggregate map

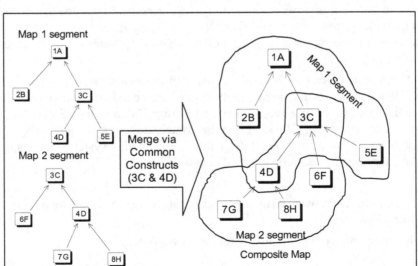

which the essential part of the map could be viewed in a more manageable sense as a type of summary of the wider picture. Given the amount of information contained in each map, insights were more easily drawn, and the wider set of issues was more easily identified.

Following the tidying of individual maps, a collective (or "composite") map was created by aggregating and linking individual maps based on common themes to highlight similarities (see Figure 5). Linking was based on researchers' reflections regarding commonalities across different maps (Hodgkinson, Maule, & Bown, 2004). These links were denoted with a different notation to highlight the type of imposed link. This map was presented to representatives of the organisation for identifying shared goals, problems, and options. Used in conjunction with other analysis techniques, this can be used to set the agenda for strategic action.

The value of presenting the aggregate cognitive map to UKFI company representatives arose from its conciseness in representing and maintaining the multiplicity of individual perspectives. This provides the basis for further exploration of conflicting issues surrounding the process of information systems development within UKFI. As noted already, the main aim for this study was to investigate the different perspectives held by TG and retail banking, in order to identify and remove possible barriers. The result of the map analysis was a set of 6 "goal" concepts and 16 "key issue" concepts. These were then translated into five main problem areas and used in the feedback to the main members of UKFI.

1. **Collaboration:** Issues include inconsistent ways of working, entangled organisational structure, and "over-the-wall" mentality between TG and retail banking.

2. **Communication:** Across the business/TG "gap," for example, the range of communications issues that do not occur in a clear/timely manner.

3. **Focus:** Need for a clear focus and delivery of business priorities between retail banking and TG.

4. **Recognition:** Issues related to the recognition of TG contribution and inequality of status within the company.

5. **Trust:** Underlying mistrust between aspects of the business.

As with the RepGrid and NAFIS, these problem areas are expressed in language that is compatible with the UKFI context and could be used as points of discussion to bridge understanding between the diverse areas of the business. As with RepGrid, the advantage of CM in this type of context is that the issues/problem areas arise directly from the map analysis, which was based on maps taken directly from the interviews with members of the organisation. In this way, the issues can be seen to arise directly out from the interviewees' understandings of the situation (as mediated by the mapping process) and, therefore, be directly relevant and significant to them (and the organisation).

Discussion

Although the contexts in which they were used differed, the outcomes of the RepGrid and CM processes were similar in terms of the nature and utility of the constructs that they identified. Comparing RepGrid and CM directly, while both techniques are well suited to the articulation and exploration of constructs used to explain organisational change (Cropper, Eden, & Ackermann, 1990), CM has an advantage over RepGrid since the latter can be argued to lack a "propositional" structure (Pidd, 1996). Pidd also compares the techniques, highlighting the ability of CM to help people understand and interpret other people's view of reality (Orlikowski, 2002). Through the use of the shared maps, it is possible for each person in a group to gain a clearer understanding of another's position (and rationale behind that position) without giving up their own. Through negotiation, it is possible to come to a group view, using the group map as a negotiative focus (or artefact). Use of the talkback protocol enables RepGrid to make a similar contribution. Consequently, each technique provided similarly deep insights into issues and concerns that emerged in their respective organisational contexts.

The crucial point here is that, despite their disparity, the organisational contexts studied shared elements common to many CBIS, particularly that of organisations (and the people that constitute them) feeling that the "technology" is in the driving seat, and that they are in danger of losing control over the situation. In the case of NAFIS, the changes in the organisation were seen as being driven by the resource changes brought about by the ability of the technology to do what could not have been done before (i.e., the combination of the verification/identification processes). In the case of UKFI, the scenario was more dispersed, with the general feeling of separation between the TG and the Retail Bank, resulting in a lack of communication and shared common goals. While no specific technology was involved here, it is a more generalised version of the NAFIS scenario, whereby, the perception that the technology and hence the technology group (TG) were driving the organisation.

In the same way that the RepGrid allowed the police participants to re-conceptualise the role and usefulness of NAFIS, the introduction of a relationship manager role in UKFI was beginning to increase understanding between the TG (information systems) people and the user communities they served. In each case, the research outcomes increased understanding of the contextually specific issues by supporting the development of shared cognitive schemata that facilitated discussion, explanation, and action. In this way, both RepGrid and CM, using their personal construct roots, were tapping into the subtleties of individual perception and the problems encountered when these emerge into the intra-group and inter-group contexts. As both these organisations were beginning to realise, the introduction of ever-increasing technological complexity brought an equal and important level of organisational complexity. Where, at one point in time, it might have been assumed that a technology slows down and allows for some adjustment period to occur (a sort of "breathing space" for the organisation), it has now been recognised that organisations are having to live in this continual state of flux and change—what this chapter has termed dynamic complexity.

Comparing the two approaches used in the studies, it can be seen that whereas RepGrid is constrained and well bounded, CM is more open and free flowing. However, both produce representations of the more sensitive aspects of the complex organisational settings. As such, the complementarity of the two PCT approaches provides insights that are often difficult to otherwise uncover and, more importantly, to clearly demonstrate to the appropriate stakeholder groups. In this way, both the approaches provide insights into the dynamic complexities faced by organisations, which can be argued to be the first step in taking better control over themselves.

Conclusion

In addition to sharing a common theoretical foundation, it can be argued that CM and RepGrid produce complementary outcomes, since each supports the natural flow of the individual and collective narrative (in general, although not in the specific CM case reported here). Both techniques provide the basis for context specific self-organised learning (Thomas & Harri-Augstein, 1985) through the development of shared conceptual schemata or mental models. Although the NAFIS and UKFI studies differ substantially in terms of the types of work undertaken, they exhibited surprisingly similar characteristics in terms of the communication issues faced by workers and organisational managers making changes in response to the development, implementation, and use of large scale CBIS. Our research suggests that shared mental models provide significant insight into the processes of individual and collaborative learning, change management, and organisational development.

By allowing the narrative to be presented in a diagrammatic form (as shown in Figures 2 and 4), both techniques enabled the modelled constructs to inform later phases of the organisational discourse. Whereas RepGrid enables a smaller set of constructs to be exhaustively explored and elaborated, CM allows the wider view (scenario) to be represented and multiple perspectives to be drawn together. This suggests that, if deployed together in the same organisational setting, additional analytic insight might be gained from reconciliation of these bottom-up and top-down modelling perspectives. Without pre-determining content, these techniques effectively exploit the theoretic foundation of PCT to provide a common basis for the representation of a hierarchical structure or schema of constructs. The techniques articulated and facilitated the use of language and terms that provided a shared understanding between the business and technology communities. We took care to ensure that the analytic protocols, tools, and techniques we used produced a hierarchy of constructs that not only faithfully represented participants' issues and concerns, but enabled the significance or priority of those issues and concerns to be inferred from the hierarchy.

Additionally, since both techniques are value-free in the sense that they provide structure and form to the organisational discourse but without determining content, they were well suited to the investigation of the interdependence of information systems and organisations. This quality is particularly useful since many of the impacts of information systems are not and cannot be known in advance or anticipated. Both techniques facilitate the free flow of ideas from the dialogue with the participants to be represented and analysed using language that is firmly anchored in the conceptual structure of the work context. Our experience and findings to date show that the super constructs articulated using these techniques provide a powerful medium for the identification and resolution of issues and concerns that arise as CBIS are assimilated into work. The brief examples discussed in this chapter show how RepGrid and CM can elaborate organisational discourse in ways that make it more consensual and, therefore, capable of bridging the conceptual and linguistic "gap" between organisational managers responsible for mainstream business and technical staff responsible for the development and implementation of information systems. As discussed previously, this, in turn, allows the organisation to begin to gain more control over the dynamic complexities inherent in modern technological organisations.

Although the outcomes of the CM and RepGrid processes differ substantially in their appearance and presentation, it is our view that their common foundation in personal construct theory demonstrates a substantial opportunity to further explore their complementarity. Our research to date has shown that the techniques provide substantial insight into the dynamic interplay of the technology and organisation processes. The interaction of technologies such as NAFIS and the human experts who use them will, we believe, become an increasingly important area of research. As technological functionality and performance increase and the range of applications widen, the repertoire of issues and concerns arising through technology and human interaction will increase. Equally, UKFI was seeking ways/approaches to bring closer together the core business and technology groups to facilitate much greater effective working patterns.

We anticipate that further work will enable us to develop a model that provides a framework for the analysis of cognitive schema and shared understanding, or super constructs, in a range of organisational settings. We also anticipate that such a model will increase awareness of issues that concern both organisational and technology communities and, perhaps most importantly, enable the conceptual agility of developers, organisational managers, and workers (their ability to appreciate one another's issues, concerns, and values) to be improved. This chapter contends that such conceptual agility is an essential pre-requisite for the full exploitation of newer information technologies such as enterprise resource planning systems, computer-supported collaborative work systems (CSCW), and knowledge management systems. Such agility is also essential for optimising the interaction of technology and human workers in a range of scenarios, in order for organisations to be more effective in areas such as information systems outsourcing and component-based software development (CBSD).

References

Brooks, L., & Jones, M. (1996). CSCW and requirement analysis: Requirements as cooperation/requirements for collaboration. In P. Thomas (Ed.), *CSCW requirements and evaluation* (pp. 10-20). New York: Springer Verlag.

Clarke, I., Horita, M., & Mackaness, W. (2000). The spatial knowledge of retail decision makers: Capturing and interpreting group insight using a composite cognitive map. *The International Review of Retail, Distribution and Consumer Research, 10*(3), 265-285.

Cropper, S., Eden, C., & Ackermann, F. (1990). Keeping sense of accounts using computer-based cognitive maps. *Social Science Computer Review, 8*(3), 345-366.

Davis, C., & Hufnagel, M. (2004). Implementeing information systems to support knowledge work: An exploration of work motifs. In *Proceedings of the Twelfth European Conference on Information Systems (ECIS 2004),* Turku, Finland.

Eden, C. (1988). Cognitive mapping. *European Journal of Operational Research, 36*(1), 1-13.

Eden, C. (2004). Analyzing cognitive maps to help structure issues or problems. *European Journal of Operational Research, 159*(3), 673-686.

Eden, C., & Ackerman, F. (2001). *Making strategy: The journey of strategic management*. London: Sage.

Fransella, F. (Ed.). (2003). *International handbook of personal construct psychology*. Chichester, UK: John Wiley and Sons.

Glaser, B., & Strauss, A. (1967). *The discovery of grounded theory: Strategies for qualitative research*. London: Weidenfeld & Nicolson.

Hatzakis, T., Lycett, M., Macredie, R. D., & Martin, V. A. (2005). Towards the development of a social capital approach to evaluating change management interventions. *European Journal of Information Systems, 14*(1), 60-74.

Hodgkinson, G., Maule, A., & Bown, N. (2004). Causal cognitive mapping in the organizational strategy field: A comparison of alternative elicitation procedures. *Organizational Research Methods, 7*(1), 3-26.

Hufnagel, E. M., & Conca, C. (1994). User response data: The potential for errors and biases. *Information Systems Research, 5*(1), 48-73.

Hunter, M. G. (1997). The use of rep grids to gather interview data about information systems analysts. *Information Systems Journal, 7*(1), 67-81.

Kelly, G. (1955a). *The psychology of personal constructs, volume 1: A theory of personality*. New York: Norton & Co.

Kelly, G. (1955b). *The psychology of personal constructs, volume 2: Clinical diagnosis and psychotherapy*. New York: Norton & Co.

Nakayama, V. K., & Armstrong, D. J. (2005). *Causal mapping for research in information technology*. Hershey, PA: Idea Group Publishing.

Orlikowski, W. (2002). Knowing in practice: Enacting a collective capability in distributed organizing. *Organization Science, 13*(3), 249-273.

Orlikowski, W., & Barley, S. (2001). Technology and institutions: What can research on information technology and research on organizations learn from each other? *MIS Quarterly, 25*(2), 145-165.

Orr, J. (1996). *Talking about machines*. New York: Cornell University Press.

Pidd, M. (1996). *Tools for thinking*. Chichester: John Wiley and Sons.

Shaw, M., & Gaines, B. (1990). *RepGrid II manual*. Calgary: Centre for Person-Computer Studies.

Thomas, L., & Harri-Augstein, E. S. (1985). *Self organised learning—foundations of a conversational science of psychology*. London: Routledge and Kegan Paul.

Endnote

[1]   A software package, Decision Explorer™, has been developed for the purposes of problem structuring using cause or cognitive maps. The software enables visual interactive modelling in which concepts can be entered, edited, and moved around a computer screen. It also allows a range of analyses to be carried out on the maps. The software has been used across the globe by business consultants, strategy consultants, group decision support facilitators, and others for about 10 years. Information about suppliers can be obtained from Banxia Software Ltd in the UK at www.banxia.com (Eden, 2004).

Chapter XIV

USE IT to Create Patient Relation Management for Multiple Sclerosis Patients

Margreet B. Michel-Verkerke
Trivium zorggroep Twente, The Netherlands

Roel W. Schuring
Reinier de Graaf Groep, The Netherlands

Ton A. M. Spil
University of Twente, The Netherlands

Abstract

Patients with Multiple Sclerosis (MS) visit various healthcare providers during the course of their disease. It was suggested that information and communication technology (ICT) might help to orchestrate their care provision. We have applied the USE IT-tool to get insight in the relevant problems, solutions, and constraints of the MS care both in the organizational and the information technological area. There is hardly a chain of healthcare, but rather, a network in which informal communication plays an important role. This informal network worked reasonably effective but inefficient and slow. MS patients-count is only small for most care providers.

Patients thought that lack of experience caused their major problems: insufficient and inadequate care. To improve care, we proposed a solution that combines an "MS protocol," the introduction of a central coordinator of care and a patient relation management (PRM) system. This is a simple Web-based application based on agreement by the caregivers that supports routing, tracking, and tracing for an MS patient and supplies the caregivers with professional guidelines. It is likely that we would have suggested a far more complicated ICT-solution if we had only analyzed the MS care process as such, without specific consideration of the dimensions in the USE IT-tool.

Introduction

Research in human-computer interaction (HCI) has been spectacularly successful and has fundamentally changed computing (Myers, 1998). The adoption of information technology has changed less dramatically and is a major problem in healthcare today (Berg, 2001). The HCI community has tended to portray the average user as someone who knows how to deal with IT and who willingly participates in this interaction (Marsden & Hollnagel, 1996). The average user does not exist in healthcare; they range from laggards to innovators (Rogers, 1995), and, most times, HCI is designed to address the innovators (Spil, Schuring, & Michel-Verkerke, 2004). This means that highly-complex systems are designed that have to be used by people that have limited capacity to deal with computers. Interaction design, a newly-coined discipline (Coiera, 2003), believes that information systems design should include the people who will use them. We developed an interview model, called USE IT, that includes the end user in the IS design process by determining his or her user characteristics before the actual system design process starts.

In this chapter, the USE IT model (Spil, Schuring, & Michel-Verkerke, 2004) is applied to define what use of information and communication technology (ICT) would support healthcare professionals in providing care to patients suffering from Multiple Sclerosis (MS). Two aspects of the relation between technology and human interaction will be discussed in this research: first, technology—partly—replacing human interaction, and second, factors that influence the success of human interaction with technology, in respect to actual use.

The next section, *Background and Motivation*, describes what problems in the MS healthcare chain motivated us to conduct the research. In the *Methodology* section, it is discussed why the USE IT-model is the appropriate methodology for this research. The complete research design is given in the *Research Design* section. After that, the results of the case study are presented in the *Results* section. The discussion of the findings in the following section, *Discussion*, will lead to the presentation of patient relation management (PRM), as a solution for the problem. In the final section, overall conclusions will be drawn.

Background and Motivation

A rehabilitation hospital asked us to study the healthcare chain of MS in a Dutch region which serves about 500 MS patients and includes three large hospitals (with a total of about 1,800 beds) in order to know what ICT-solution could improve MS care. In this research, a healthcare chain is defined as follows: *The healthcare chain is constituted of all care providers involved in the care for a particular group of patients* (Michel-Verkerke, Schuring, Spil, & Hummel, 2003). In the ideal situation, a healthcare chain is designed and implemented and not a randomly-originated collection of care providers. To make a healthcare chain a chain, the care providers should be linked by binding engagements concerning the care to provide to the particular patient group. These engagements comprise agreement on: (a) what care should be provided by whom in what way for how long in what place; (b) how and when patients are transferred from one care provider to another; and (c) how patient information is communicated. Since healthcare is organized in a functional way (i.e., wards and practices are grouped by the profession or specialty of the care provider) and not in a process-oriented or product-oriented way, it is hard to organize and implement healthcare chains cross-organizationally (i.e., across the healthcare institutions). For the same reason, and because the level of ICT-resources in healthcare is low—none of the participants used an electronic patient record (EPR)—many healthcare professionals consider implementing a cross-organizational EPR to support the care processes in a healthcare chain to be utopian at the moment. Still, a strong desire to improve MS care and the awareness of the potential benefits of the use of ICT in healthcare were the motivation to start this research.

The challenge of this research-project was to find a solution that, on the one hand, is locally and practically applicable and, on the other hand, can serve as a base for a more general, broader solution like an electronic patient record (EPR). Since it was not clear as to what kind of ICT-solution the research would lead, the second challenge was to find an appropriate methodology to perform the research. As will be explained in the next section, we considered a methodology for requirements analysis not adequate to comply with the explorative aspects of our research. Based on the results of previous research, we decided to use this research to investigate whether the USE IT methodology developed from an evaluation study on IS success is also suitable for revealing the factors that determine IS success in this particular case (Spil, Schuring, & Michel-Verkerke, 2004).

Multiple Sclerosis

Multiple Sclerosis (MS) is a disease that affects the central nervous system. Due to causes that are not entirely understood, the sheaths of the nerves change, which reduces the ability to transmit signals. Patients may suffer from tiredness, have difficulty moving, may have reduced sight, and a range of other problems. There is no cure available for MS; treatment may be able to relieve the patients' symptoms and, by that, extend the period that the patient is able to function independently.

Patients with MS visit various healthcare providers during the course of their disease. A general practitioner (GP) might be their first contact, but, as the disease progresses, a neurologist, urologist, rehabilitation hospital, homecare, home-adaptation, and many other types of support are normally needed. In a perfect world, all of these types of care are delivered in an orchestrated way. However, reality is different. Each care provider uses his or her own patient records and working method. The patient needs to be self-managing. Based on the formal documents we studied, we were able to model the formal referral model through the MS chain (Figure 1) (Michel-Verkerke, Schuring, Spil, & Hummel, 2003).

Methodology

As was stated in the introduction, the attitude of healthcare professionals toward the use of computers varies from innovators to laggards (Rogers, 1995). Because of this, the actual use of available computers cannot be taken for granted, and we consider an information system only successful when it is actually used in practice as part of the care process. In order to discover what factors make care providers to use an information system, we reviewed papers on tools to reveal the user's requirements or tools to stimulate user participation in the development of information systems in healthcare which have been published in previous years (e.g., Beuscart-Zephir, Anceaux, Crinquette, & Renard, 2001; Brender & McNair, 2001; Meijden, Tange, Troost, & Hasman, 2001; Staccini, Joubert, Quaranta, Fieschi, & Fieschi, 2001). These tools usually focus on a fit between the developed system and the user on one aspect of innovation-diffusion. The USE IT tool is built on a large number of such publications and assists in obtaining insight into the nature and relevance of problems and of possible solutions. Thus, the papers consider all of these aspects of the problem. It considers constraints and pre-requisites, which are particularly relevant when resources are limited and choices have to be made as to which problems will be solved and which will not. The USE IT tool also demonstrates that the requirements-determinant is not *the only* determinant of user adoption. Proposed

Figure 1. The formal referral model of the MS healthcare chain

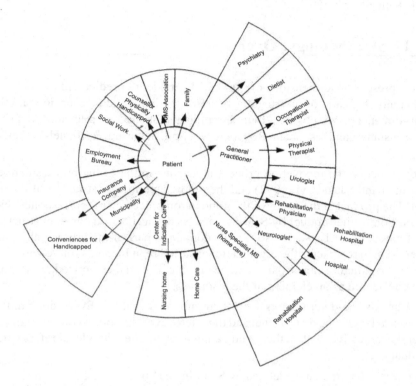

Referral takes place from the inside to the outside. The patient does not need any official referral to go to the GP, Center for Indicating Care (CIZ), municipality, insurance company, employment bureau, social work, counselor PH, and the MS association. The CIZ (Centrum Indicatiestelling Zorg in Dutch) is an organ independent of healthcare organizations, subsidized by the national authority. Its task is to indicate and allocate home care, admission to a nursing-home, and old-people's home. Adapted conveniences are available through the healthcare insurance company or the municipality, i.e., the WVG-authority; WVG stands for the Dutch Wet Voorzieningen Gehandicapten, which can be translated as Law Facilities Handicapped.

The CIZ decides on admission to a nursing home or whether the patient is eligible for home care. The latter may concern nursing or general care. Advice, information, or instruction by home care is available without intervention of the primary physician or the CIZ. This is the type of home care that is given by a nurse specialist that is specialized in MS patients. Referral by the GP is needed to get access to treatment by other physicians or paramedics. The star in the boxes of physicians indicates that physicians may generate referrals to the same paramedical healthcare workers as the GP. The rehabilitation physician serves as the gate to other healthcare providers in the rehabilitation hospital. The neurologist decides on admission to the hospital and is also the person who refers to a nursing specialist in the outpatient clinic. In one part of the area that was studied, these two specialized nurses are, in fact, the same person.

solutions that come to mind after the analysis can be organizational changes, IT-related changes, or both.

USE IT Methodology: Overview

First, we present the dimensions of the USE IT model to predict and evaluate innovation and diffusion of information systems: the innovation-dimension and the domain-dimension, which make four determinants for success: relevance, requirements, resistance, and resources (Rogers, 1995; Spil, Schuring, & Michel-Verkerke, 2004).

With the process, the innovation process is meant, similar to the process defined by Saarinen and Sääksjärvi (1992) and the innovation process structure of Larsen (1998). The product is the result of this innovation process. This corresponds with the definition of the product by Saarinen and Sääksjärvi and the artifact structure in the framework of Larsen. Also, the IT domain is part of the artifact structure; the user domain represents the organizational structure in Larsen's framework. The time horizon structure can be part of the requirements, and the knowledge structure can be considered as an element of the resources.

Table 2 shows the determinants with their sub-determinants. Every determinant comprises to levels: the macro level and the micro level. The macro level represents a general perspective, that is, the organizational level. The micro level refers to the individual user.

The *relevance* determinant is defined by Schuring & Spil (2003) as: *"the degree to which the user expects that the IT-system will solve his problems or help to realize his actually relevant goals."* The word "expects" expresses that relevance is a factor that is important in the course of the adoption process, not only in evaluation. The word "actually" is crucial in their view of relevance. Relevance is not to be confused with the degree to which the user considers outcomes as being positive. The set of outcome-dimensions that someone considers "positive" is larger than the set of outcome-dimensions that are relevant. Imagine a physician, who basically considers IT-outcomes of a computer decision support system, such as, assistance in diagnosis, disease prevention, or more appropriate dosing of drugs, as "positive." This does not automatically imply that the IT-adoption is relevant to him; it is only relevant if these dimensions are high on his "goal agenda."

Table 1. The USE IT model (from Michel-Verkerke, Schuring, & Spil, 2003)

USE IT Model	User Domain	Information Technology Domain
Product	Relevance	Requirements
Process	Resistance	Resources

Table 2. The USE IT determinants (based on Spil, Schuring & Michel-Verkerke, 2004)

Determinant	Level	Sub-determinants
Relevance	Macro-relevance:	Economic improvements Social improvements Functional improvements Saving time and effort
	Micro-relevance:	Solve here-and-now problems Compatibility with working process
Resistance	Macro-resistance:	Lack of opportunity to change
	Micro-resistance:	Inability to change Bad attitude
Requirements	Macro-requirements:	Strategic general requirements Tactical approach
	Micro-requirements:	Functional requirements Performance requirements
Resources	Material:	Hardware & Software Time Money
	Immaterial:	Adaptability Capabilities Reliability

Relevance defined in this way comprises relative advantage (Rogers, 1995), net benefits (DeLone & McLean, 2002), perceived usefulness (Davis, 1989), and job relevance (Chismar & Wiley-Patton, 2003), and results in task support satisfaction, which is a criterion for user satisfaction (Garrity & Sanders, 1998).

In their study on the implementation of an electronic prescription system, Schuring and Spil found that lack of relevance was the major determinant that explained the failure of the implementation (Spil, Schuring, & Michel-Verkerke, 2004).

Resistance is the personal attitude of all stakeholder groups towards the introduction of an information system (Spil, Schuring, & Katsma, 2002). The main IS-quality aspect of resistance is the attitude and the willingness to change. Pare and Elam (1999) also focus on the attitude of the professional when they assess clinical information systems. The end users have an important role because their norms and values determine the effectiveness of the information system. Resistance was found to be the cumulative effect of the other three determinants (Spil, Schuring, & Michel-Verkerke, 2004).

Expectance of reduced quality of work life satisfaction, high complexity, and the lack of trialability can result in resistance (Garrity & Sanders, 1998; Rogers, 1995). Observability reduces resistance (Rogers, 1995). Offenbeek and Koopman (1996) connect people with resistance potential because they can feel that the quality of their working life will be decreased. Mumford (1995) observed that user participation contributes to effective organizational change. Wissema (1987) defines resistance as willingness to change and the difference between results and expectations.

Resources are defined as the degree to which material and immaterial goods are available to design, operate and maintain the information system (Spil, Schuring, & Michel-Verkerke, 2004). The main focus of the determinant resources will be on the people and on the costs these people cause. Next to that, the reliability of the information technology and the information systems are considered. Resources defined in this way refer to service and system quality (DeLone & McLean, 2002), management support, and mature IS function (Saarinen & Sääksjärvi, 1992). Resources (human, physical, and monetary components [Ansoff, 1965]) are needed to implement the new information system into the organization. The human resources can both be insufficient in time and in experience (risk of technology). Insufficient material resources (Offenbeek & Koopman, 1996) will have a limiting influence on the other three risk domains.

The *requirements* determinant evaluates the meaning of the information system. *Requirements are defined as the degree to which the user needs are satisfied with the product quality of the innovation* (Spil, Schuring, & Michel-Verkerke, 2004). This includes such aspects as the functional capability, the ease of start-up, and the ease of use. Meeting the end-user's requirements results in high information quality, system quality (DeLone & McLean, 2002), high interface satisfaction (Garrity & Sanders, 1998), and high compatibility (Rogers, 1995).

USE IT Methodology: Strategy

To measure the determinants the USE IT tool consists of structured interviews. In this way, a more precise insight can be obtained in the nature and relevance of problems and solutions before implementation, and this insight can be tested with

Table 3. The USE IT—interview protocol for patients

MS Patient	
Pat.1	Would you be so kind to describe the course of your illness to me, and especially your route through healthcare?
Pat.2	What care do you receive at the moment?
Pat.3	Do you experience bottlenecks in the care delivered?
Pat.4	What role does MS play in your life?
Pat.5	How do you experience the cooperation between care providers or institutions?
Pat.6	How do you experience the supply of information on MS?
Pat.7	How do you experience the way care providers deal with the information about you?

the same tool during the evaluation of the implementation. For the interviews with patients, we used a much shorter questionnaire, which is listed in Table 3.

Research Design

From the literature review, it can be learned that the successful implementation of an information system depends on the degree to which the characteristics of the intended end users—being relevance, requirements, resistance, and resources—are taken into consideration. This knowledge together with the purpose of the research as described in the second section lead to the formulation of the following research-questions:

1.   In what way does an improvement of the information-services in the healthcare chain contribute to the improvement of the quality of care for patients with Multiple Sclerosis?

2.   What should a solution look like that solves the local problem but that also aligns with knowledge and standards on EPR and serves as a first step or building block of an EPR?

3.   What user characteristics of care providers will influence the successful imple-mentation of a proposed solution?

4.   Is the USE IT tool an adequate tool to reveal these user characteristics?

So, could ICT help to coordinate the workflow for MS patients and does the USE IT tool help to find out?

At the start of the research project, a workshop is organized to generate commit-ment for the research. Of each institution or profession involved with MS care in

Table 4. Interview-protocol

Category	Explanation
Primary process	Given care, co-operation, referrals
Information	Information-needs, communication, desired and available services
Relevance	Relevance of MS care compared with other groups of patients
Resistance	Resistance to change and resistance to ICT
Resources	Available ICT-services, available time for change
Priority	Other projects, innovations
Local system	Political forces

Table 5. Professions and institutions of the interviewees

Institution	Profession	Number
MS patient-association	Counselor (volunteer)	2
Regional hospital 1	Nurse-specialist	1
Regional hospital 1	Neurologist	1
Co-operation of the regional hospital 2 and home-care 1	Nurse-specialist	1
Rehabilitation hospital	Physiotherapist	1
Rehabilitation hospital	Medical doctor	1
Home-care 1	Manager Care	1
Home-care 1	Nurse	1
Psychiatry	Manager ambulant care	1
Regional Indication Organ	Counselor	1
Insurance company	Medical adviser	1
Municipality (WVG)	Counselor	1
Center for Occupational Therapy	Occupational therapist	1
Nursing-home	Medical doctor	1
Social Pedagogic Service	Counselor Physically Handicapped	1

the region, those care providers with a special interest in treating MS and who are actually involved in providing care to MS patients were invited to be interviewed. This resulted in 17 USE IT interviews. Each interview took about one and a half hours. Table 4 gives an overview of the categories of the interview questions. Table 5 shows the professions and institutions of the interviewees.

Also six of the approximately 500 patients were interviewed to get an impression of how they experienced the provided care (see Table 3). These interviews took about one hour. A report is made of each interview and all reports are analyzed. The results are presented in the next section.

Results

Studying the communication patterns, as reported by the care providers in the interviews, showed the lack of orchestration of patient-flow or workflow in MS care. Actual communication between care providers does not at all match the formal referral pattern. Depicting the actual communication in Figure 1 would give a tangle of dozens of arrows. Table 6 is a cross-table of information flows between the parties involved. From this, it can be learned that there is hardly a chain of healthcare—rather, a complex network with many cross-relations exists.

Table 6. Patient-related contacts between care providers

Interviewed (number) Reported contacts and referrals	MS Association (2)	Nurse-specialist MS (2)	Rehabilitation-Hospital (2)	Neurologist	Home care (2)	Regional Indication Organ	Social Counselor Physically Handicapped	Municipality (Conveniences)	Occupational Therapist	Nursing Home	*total*
MS Association	1	1		1			1				*4*
Nurse-specialist MS	1				1			1	1		*4*
Rehabilitation Hospital	1	1	1	1	1		1	1	1	1	*9*
Neurologist	1	1	1						1	1	*5*
Home Care	1	1	1		1	1	1		1		*7*
Psychiatry		1	1								*2*
Regional Indication Organ	1	1			1		1	1		1	*6*
Insurance company	1										*1*
Municipality (Conveniences)	1				1	1					*3*
Occupational Therapist	1	1			1						*3*
Nursing Home		1				1		1	1		*5*
Physical Therapist		1	1	1	1						*4*
General Practitioner		1	1	1	1	1	1			1	*7*
Family	1	1			1	1			1		*5*
Hospital ward	1		1		1						*2*
Urologist	1	1	1	1							*4*
Dietician						1					*1*
Social Work	1						1				*2*
Counselor Physically Handicapped		1									*1*
Employment Bureau		1						1			*2*
Others	1					2	5	1			*10*
total	*15*	*14*	*8*	*5*	*11*	*7*	*12*	*5*	*6*	*4*	*87*

Horizontally: positions or institutions that were interviewed. Vertically: positions or institutions with whom they have patient-related contacts are marked with number "1." Grey boxes indicate that formal referral is possible.

The two coordination mechanisms that could be found were: the official referral system and informal communication (mutual adjustment) (Mintzberg, 1979). The formal communication did not suffice for two reasons: not all information needs were covered and the GP cannot fulfill his formal role as central coordinator of care because he is too busy with other tasks. The informal network between care providers seemed reasonably effective, but inefficient and often slow. Within this network, we found hand-overs between caregivers that were executed by the patient himself. Six care providers indicated that the patient is the major source of information. A survey of the care provided and the progress of the care process was missed by both the patient and the care provider. Electronic records, when in use, only contain administrative information. Care-related information was only recorded in local paper patient records.

It is not a great surprise that patients and caregivers sometimes get lost or stuck in the jumble of MS care, although patients felt these problems to a lesser extent than caregivers. All in all, patients seemed satisfied about the provided care, although they consider it very fatiguing to arrange new facilities or access to "new" caregivers, since a very pro-active role of the patient is necessary; the patient needs to be his own case-manager. This is especially bothersome because MS patients get less energetic when the disease develops. The patients had little complaints about the low level of contacts that had been noticed to exist between caregivers. The relation with each caregiver may continue for years, so, they saw little need for intensive contact between these caregivers. Table 7 gives an overview of the bottlenecks and disturbances, as reported by care providers.

The USE IT interviews also made clear that MS care is not very relevant for most care providers. That is to say, caregivers have high compassion to MS patients, but most caregivers only occasionally saw MS patients. The only notable exceptions to this were the specialized MS nurse and some of the caregivers in the rehabilitation

Table 7. Bottlenecks and disturbances (care providers)

Bottlenecks and Disturbances	Total
Waiting-lists for conveniences, nursing home and psychologist	9
Coordination, communication, working according to plan	9
Double work, fragmentation and lack of survey, due to lack of coordination	5
Care providers do not know each others' possibilities in care	5
Care providers do not know about each others' progress according to the patient	5
Limited time for providing care	4
Insurance companies, municipality, and GP are unfamiliar with MS	3
Care provider only listens to the patient and ignores advise of other care providers	3
The patient does not have survey of who is treating him	2
The MS association behaves as being a professional care provider	2
Patients wait too long before requesting a convenience	2
General Practitioner should be coordinator, not just referrer	2

hospital. But even in this group, the maximum percentage of patient-time spent on MS patients does not exceed 40%. The neurologist in the largest hospital in the area is specialized in MS. However, also for him, MS patients create just above 10% of his work.

Because of this infrequent contact with MS patients, the knowledge of caregivers about MS care seemed to be lacking at times. All interviewed patients said this lack of knowledge was the reason for one of the major problems reported: incidents of insufficient and inadequate care. It should be noted that none of the care providers mentioned this theme. Not all healthcare providers were aware of the service that other caregivers could provide in general and do provide for a specific patient. Another consequence of the rather low prevalence of MS is the lack of knowledge present at municipality, RIO, and insurance companies about the urge and specifications of needed conveniences.

The low relevance of MS care for care providers also caused resistance toward a specific solution for the MS care. Care providers feared the situation, where each patient group has its own computer-based record. They feared to be loaded with separate solutions for every separate chronic disease. Little or no resistance toward the use of ICT as such is reported. The reported lack of time to provide proper care and long waiting lists for nursing homes are general healthcare problems and not specific for MS care.

Discussion

The interview results clearly show that the formal referral is not the backbone of the healthcare chain, and the GP and neurologist do not play a central role in MS care. Since referrals not only comprise the transfer of the patient to another care provider, but also the transfer of the patient data, the failure of the formal referral tree has major consequences for the transfer of patient information. The many communications between care providers proved to be a very inefficient and slow compensation for the lack of information "flow" through the healthcare chain. The hampering information flow caused a reduced quality of provided care: the patients do not receive all the care they need at the moment they need it. This leads to the answer of the first research question: To improve the quality of care for MS patients, the information services should be improved in such a way that all care providers have all relevant patient data available at the time they see the patient, know what care is provided already, and what care they themselves should provide to the patient. They also need to know to whom they should or could refer the patient when they have finished their treatment. This means that the information services should support the transfer of relevant patient data, provide relevant up-to-date medical knowledge about MS to each care provider, and expose knowledge about the structure of the MS healthcare chain.

The interview data did not result in a straightforward answer to the second research question, that is, a clear design of the best solution, but gave the constraints and pre-requisites, which have to be taken into account when designing a solution. These constraints and pre-requisites follow from the user characteristics as described in the results: low relevance of MS care, low resistance to ICT, but high resistance to a specific solution, little resources, and a desire for good coordinated care and good communication. This means that a solution to the problems in MS care has to meet the following constraints:

1.   No isolated solution for MS care: a specific solution must be expandable for other diseases.

2.   Implementation and maintenance must take very little effort and costs; and

3.   The solution must adhere to the present conditions.

Since the future users of the solution can be characterized as care providers with little to no resistance to the use of ICT as such and in favor of innovations as long as it is clear what benefits these will bring to the patient, implementation of a solution that meets the constraints and pre-requisites is expected to be successful. What this solution could look like is further described in the next section.

The USE IT tool proved to be very helpful in revealing the user characteristics. The interviewed care providers appreciated having a chance to express themselves, but, at the same time, the interview questions did not provoke the interviewees to exaggerate nor to trivialize. Information on all determinants was gained, but, before designing an information system, a requirements' analysis on a detailed level should be performed.

Patient Relation Management

The discussion of the results revealed the objectives a solution has to achieve. First of all, care for MS patients must be orchestrated in order to improve the "flow" of patients and related information through the healthcare chain. The second purpose of the solution is to raise the level of knowledge about MS, its treatment, and the way MS care is organized. To accomplish these results, it is crucial that care providers actually use the solution and comply to the agreed way to provide care to patients with MS.

Several interviewed caregivers considered a regional cross-functional and cross-organizational EPR as *the* solution to the problems in MS care, although many did not consider this a realistic solution, since no regional electronic patient record or likewise ICT facility that could serve as a basis for a solution, existed in the area studied. The main benefits of an EPR would be to know who is involved with what patient and to have access to the necessary information without being dependent of other caregivers such as the GP as "pass on-desk" of information. An EPR could help to make clear among care providers what each of them does for an individual patient. However, both the realization and the use of a regional EPR for *all* patients (not just people suffering of MS) and *all* care providers (and not just involved in MS care) demand much more effort, time, and expenses than is available for improving MS care. Also, the condition that MS patients make up a small percentage of the total patient population for most healthcare professionals is unaffected. As a consequence, patients will retain the problem that healthcare providers do not give adequate care, nor is it sure that referral patterns will improve.

That is why we suggest a solution that combines three elements. First, we suggest orchestration of MS care by an "MS protocol" that lists the options of care that each of the care providers offers and in which agreement is accomplished about the routing of a patient through the healthcare chain when the patient is diagnosed with MS.

Second, we suggest that the nurse specialist should play a central role as coordinator of care. But to fulfill this coordinating, role support is needed. So, the third element is to build a patient relation management (PRM) system. Since almost all care providers had (or would have in short notice) access to e-mail or the Internet, this PRM will consist of a Web-based patient routing system, based on an agreement of the caregivers in the region on patient flow (cf. the MS protocol). When a patient is reported to the system, a message will be send automatically to those caregivers, which should be informed. The information in the system comprises the names of the reported patients and the names and functions of the caregivers that are or have been involved with the treatment of the patient and the likely next steps (caregivers) in the treatment. PRM does not substitute the patient records from the various caregivers. PRM also does not contain any medical data of the patient in its simplest version, but it could be considered to expand PRM with two options: (1) composing structured notes about the patient contacts, and (2) composing referral or transfer letters or messages. Both options are meant to support the information flow through the healthcare chain. The composed notes and messages should be structured and standardized, for example, by using HL7, in such a way that they can be received and processed by linking healthcare information systems, like a hospital information system (HIS) and EPR. The system is accessible via a Web site that contains general information on MS and medical guidelines for caregivers.

PRM is based on both work flow management and customer relationship management. The MS protocol is incorporated in PRM and serves as the workflow definition (Reijers, 2003, p. 18). In this way, PRM steers the care processes; care providers are alerted when a patient is referred to them and are advised to whom they should refer the patient. In this way, PRM acts as a workflow management system (WfMS): PRM "delivers the right piece of work to the right resource at the right time" (Reijers, 2003, p. 18). Since care providers have their professional responsibility, they are free to ignore the given advice. PRM users can also track and trace the patient's contacts with healthcare professionals. Although PRM lightens the task of the coordinator of care, a human coordinator is still required to evaluate and to update the MS protocol and the system.

Improving communication and cooperation in healthcare by linking care providers of different professions can cause communication problems of a different nature. Each profession uses its own terminology, and the same terms can have different meanings and trigger different actions. Although the care providers only mentioned the lack of communication and information and did not complain about mis-interpretation of information, the risk of semantic problems is real when human communication is partly replaced by information systems, especially when information systems are linked to create a WfMS (Cardoso & Sheth, 2003). When creating PRM, it is important to manage the risk of semantic heterogeneity from the start, that is, the compilation of the MS protocol. All professional terms and actions should be clearly defined and agreed upon by the participating care providers. Using a standard like HL7 when designing and implementing PRM can be very helpful to prevent semantic problems.

The CRM-aspect of PRM helps to create an overview of the nature and progress of patient contacts (Peppers & Rogers, 1999; Scheers, 2001). In contrast with the application of CRM in commerce, PRM is not intended to raise the number of client (i.e., patient) contacts, but to raise the satisfaction of the client and the efficiency and effectiveness of the patient contacts. PRM supplies patients and care providers with a survey of patient contacts that occurred, and the option of making notes can serve as a record of agreed arrangements and actions. The information in PRM can also be used to evaluate the MS protocol and PRM.

PRM supports the organizational solution of the main problem of the caregivers by making the agreed guidelines and patient flow available, easy to maintain, and enriching it with knowledge caregivers need. They know to whom they should refer the patient and which caregivers can be asked for more information about the patient. From the USE IT model, we can learn that an information system is only actually used when it is relevant to the end users. The interview results showed us that relevance for a specific MS solution is low, and any solution will only be used when use takes little effort. The motivation to use PRM originates from the high compassion care providers have with patients suffering from MS and their desire to provide good care. We expect that the effort to report a patient to the system is rewarded by the more efficient communication that results and the information the caregiver can retrieve about the treatment of the patient. Many caregivers, who seldom see an MS patient, lack this knowledge.

Eventually, PRM could serve as a first step to accomplish a cross-functional, cross-organizational regional EPR. During the interviews, it became clear that other chronic diseases have similar problems (Michel-Verkerke, Schuring, & Spil, 2005). So, PRM could be expanded to healthcare chains for other chronic diseases.

To be a building block of an EPR, PRM must be designed and built according to international standards. Its architecture has to be open and transparent to make linking possible to different information systems, such as an EPR or an HIS in different institutions. Since PRM contains information of patients and caregivers, security is important and should conform to the security code for healthcare.

A major advantage of PRM is that it is a simple, inexpensive solution to actual problems experienced by local caregivers, which does not create a new island of automation. Neither does PRM prohibit the development and implementation of an EPR. On the contrary, we think that PRM can pave its way. The success of an electronic patient records (EPR) is determined by several conditions. When looking at physicians, an EPR has to meet three requirements to be successful: (1) the EPR must expose all relevant date and functions, anywhere, anytime; (2) using the EPR must be compatible with the medical process of each individual physician; and (3) the EPR must allow different levels of authorization to protect professional autonomy (Michel-Verkerke, 2003). According to several authors, an EPR should also contain active elements (Dick, Steen, & Detmer, 1997; Ginneken & Moorman, 1997). To meet these four criteria of success, an EPR must cross the borders of its orientation (Michel-Verkerke & Spil, 2002). The importance of a well-designed architecture and the use of standards are stressed by Van Ginneken (2002) and Stegwee (1999).

PRM does not offer all this. PRM stems from the care process orientation but could also be applied in the medical technology or administration orientation (Michel-Verkerke, Schuring, & Spil, 2003). PRM fails on the first EPR criterion, and its activity is limited to notifying caregivers that a patient, whom should be seen, is reported. Further analysis would be needed after the introduction of PRM to clarify which design of a regional EPR could have added value.

Conclusion

Existing tools to identify processes and interviews with future users are common ways to map the conditions where IT solutions can be applied in healthcare. We learned from this research that the USE IT analysis of the characteristics of the end user helps to provide a more appropriate picture of the problem and the constraints and pre-requisites for solving it. It is likely that we would have suggested a far more complicated ICT solution if we had only analyzed the MS care process as such, without specific consideration of the USE IT dimensions. When communication and information exchange fail, quality of care is sub-optimal, and the healthcare chain is rather a collection of islands without bridges or ferries instead of a railway network with stations and a timetable, it is more than natural to see "a complete overhaul as the only way to address a potentially failing system" (Adis, 2005). As was stated in the previous section, several interviewed caregivers considered a cross-functional and cross-organizational EPR as *the* solution to the problems in MS care. But the development of such a solution requires not only resources that by far exceed the available resources for MS care, but also an authority that is able to impose the EPR to all involved healthcare institutions. Although the Dutch government tries to accelerate the development of a national EPR by the foundation and designation of the National ICT Institution in Care (www.NICTIZ.nl) as the director of information and communication technology in healthcare, such authority that can enforce the implementation of a national EPR in organizations does not exist. And in "a nonhierarchical organization no one entity can exert control over the whole system" (Lafky, 2005). This does not mean that a national or regional EPR will never be established, but it will take several years, perhaps decades. In the mean time, patients long for a solution to their problems, and care providers wish to improve the quality of care. The USE IT analysis revealed the constraints and pre-requisites in this case and helped us to balance the breadth of the proposed solution with the nature of the situation the future users of the system are in. The use of IT does not automatically mean that an EPR is needed.

This chapter gave an example of a thorough analysis of problems of workflow management in a healthcare setting. The solution we suggest is specifically geared for this type of care (i.e., network rather than chain, chronic, low relevance for most care providers). It is a complex solution in the sense that it combines the creation of a protocol with the introduction of a new organization form (the coordinator) and with the introduction of the PRM. It is a simple solution in the sense that none of these three elements is on itself complex or difficult to realize. Each of these three elements is equally important, as only the introduction of all three elements will lead to improved workflow management. When we particularly focus on the role of IT for the workflow management in the healthcare network, it is once again an essential enabler for new organizational forms. We have tried to find solutions that were entirely organizational or IT-related, but we have not managed to design one that could work. So, in line with what many thought when we started the project, IT was essential to create a solution, although it could not bring a solution on its own.

References

Adis, W. (2005). Discussion A on Article 4: Rethinking healthcare. *International Journal of Technology and Human Interaction, 1*(4), 76-77.

Ansoff, I. (1965). *Corporate strategy.* New York: McGraw-Hill.

Berg, M. (2001). Implementing information systems in health care organizations: Myths and challenges. *International Journal of Medical Informatics, 64*(2-3), 143-156.

Beuscart-Zephir, M. C., Anceaux, F., Crinquette, V., & Renard, J. M. (2001). Integrating users' activity modeling in the design and assessment of hospital electronic patient records: the example of anesthesia. *International Journal of Medical Informatics, 64*(2-3), 157-171.

Brender, J., & McNair, P. (2001). User requirements specifications: A hierarchical structure covering strategical, tactical and operational requirements. *International Journal of Medical Informatics, 64*(2-3), 83-98.

Cardoso, J., & Sheth, A. (2003). Semantic e-workflow composition. *Journal of Intelligent Information Systems, 21*(3), 191-225.

Chismar, W. G., & Wiley-Patton, S. (2003, January 6-9). *Does the extended technology acceptance model apply to physicians.* Paper presented at the 36th Hawaii International Conference on System Sciences, Hawaii.

Coiera, E. (2003). Interaction design theory. *International Journal of Medical Informatics, 69*(2-3), 205-222.

Davis, F. D. (1989, September). Perceived usefulness, perceived ease of use, and user acceptance of information technology. *MIS Quarterly,* 319-340.

DeLone, W. H., & McLean, E. R. (2002, January 7-10). *Information systems success revisited.* Paper presented at the 35th Hawaii International Conference on System Sciences.

Dick, R. S., Steen, E. B., & Detmer, D. E. (1997). *The computer-based patient record: An essential technology for health care* (Revised ed.). Washington, DC: National Academy Press.

Garrity, E. J., & Sanders, G. L. (1998). Dimensions of information success. In E. J. Garrity & G. L. Sanders (Eds.), *Information systems success measurement* (pp. 13-45). Hershey, PA: Idea Group Publishing.

Ginneken, A. M. v. (2002). The computerized patient record: Balancing effort and benefit. *International Journal of Medical Informatics, 64*(2-3), 97-119.

Ginneken, A. M. v., & Moorman, P. W. (1997). The patient record. In J. H. v. Bemmel & M. A. Musen (Eds.), *Handbook of medical informatics* (pp. 97-119). Houten, The Netherlands: Bohn, Stafleu, Van Loghum.

Lafky, D. (2005). Discussion B on Article 4: Healthcare IT—do all roads lead to a bridge? *International Journal of Technology and Human Interaction, 1*(4), 78-79.

Larsen, T. J. (1998). Information systems innovation: A framework for research and practice. In T. J. Larsen & E. McGuires (Eds.), *Information systems innovation and diffusion: Issues and directions* (pp. 411-434). Hershey, PA: Idea Group Publishing.

Marsden, P., & Hollnagel, E. (1996). Human interaction with technology: The accidental user. *Acta Psychologica, 91*, 345-358.

Meijden, M. J. v. d., Tange, H. J., Troost, J., & Hasman, A. (2001). Development and implementation of an EPR: How to encourage the user. *International Journal of Medical Informatics, 64*(2-3), 173-185.

Michel-Verkerke, M. B. (2003). *What makes doctors use the electronic patient record?* Enschede: University of Twente.

Michel-Verkerke, M. B., Schuring, R. W., & Spil, T. A. M. (2003, September 3-9). *Use IT or leave IT: A model to reveal user satisfaction of ICT-support in health care processes ex ante and ex post.* Paper presented at the 3rd International Conference of the Hospital of the Future, Warwick, UK. Warwick: Association for Healthcare Technology and Management.

Michel-Verkerke, M. B., Schuring, R. W., & Spil, T. A. M. (2005). The USE IT model case studies: IT perceptions in the Multiple Sclerosis, Rheumatism and stroke healthcare chains. In T. A. M. Spil & R. W. Schuring (Eds.), *E-health systems diffusion and use: The innovation, the user and the USE IT model* (pp. 177-191). Hershey, PA: Idea Group Publishing.

Michel-Verkerke, M. B., Schuring, R. W., Spil, T. A. M., & Hummel, M. (2003). *De MS-zorgketen in Twente: Eindverslag van het onderzoek naar de informatiestromen in de MS-zorgketen.* Enschede: University of Twente.

Michel-Verkerke, M. B., & Spil, T. A. M. (2002, June 6-8). *Electronic patient records in the Netherlands, Luctor et Emergo; But who is struggling and what will emerge?* Paper presented at the 10th European Conference on Information Systems, Gdansk, Poland.

Mintzberg, H. (1979). *The structuring of organizations: A synthesis of the research.* Englewood Cliffs, NJ: Prentice-Hall.

Mumford, E. (1995). *Effective systems design and requirements analysis.* London: MacMillan.

Myers, B. (1998). A brief history of human computer interaction technology. *ACM Interactions, 5*(2), 44-54.

Offenbeek, M. v., & Koopman, P. (1996). Interaction and decision making in project teams. In M. A. West (Ed.), *Handbook of work group psychology* (pp. 159-187). Chichester, UK: John Wiley & Sons, Ltd.

Pare, G., & Elam, J. (1999). Physicians' acceptance of clinical information systems: An empirical look at attitudes expectations and skills. *International journal of Healthcare Technology and Management, 1*(1), 46-61.

Peppers, D., & Rogers, M. (1999). *One to one manager: Real-world lessons in customer relationship management*. New York: Currency.

Reijers, H. A. (2003). *Design and control of workflow processes* (Vol. 2617). Berlin: Springer.

Rogers, E. M. (1995). *Diffusions of innovations*. New York: The Free Press.

Saarinen, T., & Sääksjärvi, M. (1992). Process and product success in information systems development. *Journal of Strategic Information Systems, 1*(5), 266-277.

Scheers, D. (2001). *Netwerken aan ketens* (Vol. 10). Deventer: Kluwer.

Schuring, R. W., & Spil, T. A. M. (2003). Relevance and micro-relevance for the professionals as determinants of IT diffusion and IT-use in healthcare. In G. Grant (Ed.), *ERP & datawarehousing in organizations: Issues and challenges* (pp. 219-232). Hershey, PA: IRM Press.

Spil, T. A. M., Schuring, R. W., & Katsma, C. (2002, July 15-16). *Assessing resistance of professional users as a determinant of IT-diffusion and IT-use in healthcare*. Paper presented at the 9th European Conference on Information Technology Evaluation, Paris.

Spil, T. A. M., Schuring, R. W., & Michel-Verkerke, M. B. (2004). Electronic prescription system: Do the professionals use it? *International Journal of Healthcare Technology and Management, 6*(1), 32-55.

Staccini, P., Joubert, M., Quaranta, J.-F., Fieschi, D., & Fieschi, M. (2001). Modelling health care processes for eliciting user requirements: A way to link a quality paradigm and clinical information system design. *International Journal of Medical Informatics, 64*(2-3), 129-142.

Stegwee, R. A. (1999). The electronic patient record, An architecture for successful introduction. In *Proceedings: Toward an Electronic Health Record Europe,* November 14-17 (pp. 58-63). London: Centre for Advancement of Electronic Health Records.

Wissema, J. G. (1987). *Angst om te veranderen? Een mythe!* Assen: Van Gorcum.

Chapter XV

Contextual Characteristics of Creativity:

Effects on IT-Supported Organisational Brainstorming

Dick Stenmark
The Viktoria Institute, Sweden

Abstract

As a much needed quality in today's businesses, creativity is an important area of research. Creativity is a complex and multi-faceted concept and can thus be studied from a variety of perspectives. In this chapter, we describe an attempt to support organisational creativity with information technology—in this case, an electronic brainstorming device. While implementing and evaluating this prototype, it was noticed that the sheer presence of technology did neither guarantee usage nor success. Contextual factors such as organisational culture and attitudes seem to have an equally important role, and this observation called for a more focused analysis of the motivational aspects of creativity management. Based on the empirical data from the electronic brainstorming system evaluation and literature on organisational creativity, three general pieces of managerial advice to promote corporate creativity are suggested: reconsider the use of extrinsic rewards; recognise creative initiatives; and allow redundancy.

A Need for Creativity

As noted by many commentators, the importance of creativity in industry has risen dramatically during the last few decades. During the peak of the industrial era, a company could prosper from slowly developing and refining one single product or service. The increasing pace with which business now reshapes itself—propelled by the new capabilities offered by information technology (IT)—places higher demand on the organisational members to be able to see and grasp new opportunities. Globalisation, and the competition that accompanies it, further adds to the need for creativity in an entrepreneurial way, and it is argued that employees of tomorrow will be valued more for their ability to create new knowledge than for being able to manage known facts (Carr, 1994; di Sessa, 1988; Drucker, 1993; Reich, 2002). Successful handling of creativity is, therefore, a factor of increasing importance and should be considered a vital aspect of (knowledge) management.

Creativity is typically defined as the development of ideas that are (1) novel or original, and (2) useful (or potentially so) (Amabile et al., 1996b; Oldham & Cummings, 1996; Paulus, 2000), and creativity is seen as a pre-requisite for innovation (e.g., the implementation of useful ideas in the organisation). An important part of the creative process is, therefore, to support and enhance idea generation (Paulus, 2000), and a traditional approach has been to encourage employees to submit their ideas to a suggestion system. This approach has been used in U.S. and European companies since at least 1880 (Robinson & Stern, 1997), and companies with suggestion systems have shown that this leads to production improvements. The ideas submitted are typically attended to and reviewed by a proposal-handling committee (PHC). Good suggestions are usually rewarded in some way, while not so good proposals are rejected.

Although being a well-known approach in practice, relative little research exists on suggestion systems (Frese, Teng, & Wijnen, 1999). Nonetheless, a number of serious shortcomings with the suggestion system approach have been identified (Frese et al., 1999; Stenmark, 2001b). First, there is a problem of communication. Suggestions are seldom shared with the entire organisation. Good ideas may be implemented locally but remain unheard of in other parts of the organisation, resulting in the "reinventing-the-wheel" syndrome. Other ideas may be prematurely rejected due to the user's inability to accurately communicate the vision that he or she has, or the PHC's limited capacity to understand and appreciate the quality of a perhaps innovative—and thus unconventional—suggestion. Had these ideas only been made public, they could have started other creative ideas elsewhere in the organisation (Stenmark, 2001b). Second, many ideas are never proposed at all—for several reasons. One thing generally recognised as a serious performance blocker is evaluation apprehension: the fear of being measured by ones' peers. We are reluctant to present tentative and immature ideas if we risk losing face in front of our colleagues.

Instead, we keep our potentially revolutionary ideas to ourselves, again missing an opportunity for organisational benefit (Diehl & Stroebe, 1987; Stenmark, 2001b). Another reason is the threshold an official suggestion system constitutes: we may feel that our idea is not worthy of being submitted as an official proposal or we may lack the ability or motivation to write-up our proposal in the form required for a suggestion to be accepted (Frese et al., 1999). These problems threaten to undermine the system since Diehl and Stroebe (1987) has shown a high correlation between quantity and quality. Receiving many ideas is thus a fundamental principle if you want good ideas (Frese et al., 1999).

To address these shortcomings, this action-oriented study aimed to promote the idea generation phase by pairing the suggestion system approach with the principles underpinning brainstorming as posited by Osborn—for example, large quantities, elaboration on others' ideas, and absence of criticism (Osborn, 1953). This hybrid approach resulted in the implementation of an online suggestion system prototype called Mindpool. The technical features of this prototype have been described in detail elsewhere (Stenmark, 2001b, 2002) and shall only briefly be accounted for in the section, *The Mindpool Prototype*. Technology is known to affect organisations—sometimes positively, sometimes negatively. We acknowledge that creativity is a highly-human aspect and do not suggest that it can be "outsourced" to computers, but it seems plausible that IT-support, if wisely applied, can support creativity, and the focus in this chapter is on the organisational implications derived from the evaluation of such an attempt.

Next, we are going to look at existing theories on creativity before describing the site and the research methodology used in this work in the section, *Site and Methodology*. The following section briefly describes some of the fundamental features of the Mindpool system. Thereafter, the results are accounted for in the section, *Empirical Results*, and discussed in detail in the following section. The chapter finishes with conclusions and managerial implications in the final section.

Theories on Organisational Creativity

Much has been written on creativity and from many different perspectives. As noted by Oldham and Cummings (1996), a large body of literature has been concerned with the *individual* aspects of creativity, and this line of primarily psychology-related work has dominated the creativity research for decades. Although this work has its merits, creativity depends also on *contextual* factors such as management style and work climate (Agrell & Gustafson, 1996). During the last 10 or so years, research that focuses on contextual factors has become more substantiated, and organisational creativity has been defined as a function of individual abilities, group norms, and organisational culture (Paulus, 2000). In this chapter, we focus on this emerging area.

Amabile's work on the social psychology of creativity (cf. Amabile, 1983; Amabile et al., 1996a) is generally regarded as a classic in the empirical study of creativity. One fundamental principle for creative work identified by Amabile is the importance of intrinsic motivation. Intrinsic motivation is defined as "motivation that arises from the individual's positive reaction to qualities of the task itself; this reaction can be experienced as interests, involvement, curiosity, satisfaction, or positive challenge" (Amabile et al., 1996a, p. 115). Extrinsic motivation, in contrast, is defined as "motivation that arises from sources outside the task itself; these sources include expected evaluation, contracted-for reward, external directives, or any other similar source" (Amabile et al., 1996a, p. 115). Strong evidence exists showing that the use of rewards in creative work has a detrimental effect on performance (Frese et al., 1999), especially if the reward is used to induce people to do things they otherwise would not (Amabile et al., 1996a). Amabile and colleagues continue to define control (ability to influence one's work conditions), playfulness (opportunity and resources to experiment freely), organisational climate (attitudes towards change, failure, and risk taking), work settings (degree of surveillance), and individual differences as major social factors influencing creativity (Amabile, 1983; Amabile et al., 1996a, 1996b).

Working explicitly with suggestion systems, Frese et al. (1999) suggest a set of contextual factors including system responsiveness, suggestion inhibitors, supervisor support, self-efficacy, and rewards. Paulus (2000) has a similar model where he refers to social as well as cognitive stimulation. He concludes that challenging goals, structured interactions, autonomy, supportive management, and, perhaps most important, cognitive diversity are the factors that best seem to facilitate creativity in groups. Oldham and Cunnings (1996) emphasise motivation, complexity of work, management style, and the individual style of creativity (incremental or radical) to be the most vital aspects of organisational creativity. Finally, Shalley, Zhou, and Oldham (2004) have identified job complexity, relationship with supervisors and co-workers, rewards, job evaluation, deadlines, and spatial configuration of the workplace to affect creativity. Although commentators have pointed to the need of a comprehensive set of creativity indicators, no such schema has emerged. Oldham and Cummings (1996) suggest that perhaps too little research is devoted to the study of creativity in organisational settings. Nonetheless, a core of common elements can be identified in the earlier-mentioned work and these have been gathered in Table 1. I shall elaborate further on the four strongest themes and use them in the subsequent analysis.

Table 1. Factors enhancing organisational creativity as reported in the literature

Theme	Amabile et al., 1996a	Frese et al., 1999	Paulus, 2000	Oldham & Cummings, 1996	Shalley et al., 2004
Motivation	Intrinsic vs. extrinsic motivation	Quality of work, financial rewards	Challenging goals, accountability	Motivation, job satisfaction	Monetary incentives and recognition
Autonomy	Influence on work	Job control	Self-managed teams	Absence of external control	Absence of (critical) evaluation
Work settings	Supportive evaluation, collaborative flow	Job complexity	Cognitive diversity, structured interaction	Job complexity	Job complexity, low spatial density
Climate	Attitudes towards change, risk taking	Management support	Supportive environment	Management style	Relationship with mgmt and co-workers
Additional aspects	Work load, slack, time to experiment		Cognitive style	Creative style	Creative style

Motivation

Reward has long since been the main motivation for work, and most adults would not engage in their profession without monetary compensation. When it comes to the effect of rewards on creativity, there is little agreement among scholars (Shalley et al., 2004). Financial rewards may indeed be a factor for employees' willingness to develop and submit ideas (Frese et al., 1999), and this is also the assumption underpinning many companies' suggestion system policies (Robinson & Stern, 1997). However, consistent reports show that working primarily for extrinsic motivation has, counter to what most practitioners seem to assume, a negative impact on creativity (Amabile et al., 1996a; Frese et al., 1999; Robinson & Stern, 1997). Instead, one should focus on, and try to stimulate, *intrinsic* motivation. Frese and colleagues note that people are motivated to develop ideas when they feel they thereby can positively impact their work situation, and found that the prospect of better work, that is, easier or safer, predicted submitting suggestions (Frese et al., 1999). Paulus (2000) finds that challenging goals paired with accountability of performances also help raise motivation and that being motivated is an important social stimulation for group creativity. Although acknowledging the importance of motivation, Oldham and Cummings (1996) understand motivation as an umbrella concept linked to job satisfaction and identify significant relations between motivation and the other aspects described next.

Autonomy

Control from administrative superiors, both financial and conceptual, typically affects creativity negatively (Deci, Connell, & Ryan, 1989; Oldham & Cummings, 1996). The same is true for anticipated judgmental evaluation, for example, when the creativity of an individual is contrasted to some standard (Shalley et al., 2004). In contrast, a higher degree of self-control over one's work—including both choice of task and method for completing task—stimulates and enhances creativity. This sort of self-organising is referred to as individual autonomy (Amabile et al., 1996a; Nonaka & Takeuchi, 1995; Paulus, 2000). Being in control of one's work makes possible the kind of experimentation that stimulates the generation of new ideas (Amabile et al., 1996b; Frese et al., 1999). While acknowledging that autonomy facilitates group creativity, Paulus (2000) notes that self-management often is related to and often confounded with other organisational factors such as motivation and work settings and points out that it is, therefore, difficult to correctly measure the impact of autonomy on group effectiveness.

Work Settings

Amabile et al. (1996b) stress the importance of work group support, for instance, through a free and collaborative flow of ideas and a fair and supportive evaluation of suggestions. Allowing ideas to flow across the organisation increases the probability of creative idea generation as the exposure to other stimuli increases (Amabile et al., 1996b; Nagasundaram & Dennis, 1993). Paulus (2000), arguing in the same vein, emphasises the fact the cognitive diversity (in groups) increases the number of potentially novel combinations that can arise and claim that diverse, but overlapping, knowledge is a primary basis for idea generation. A similar and related aspect is job complexity. It has been noted that complex and challenging jobs that require a variety of skills are more likely to motivate and promote creativity than are simple and routine jobs (Oldham & Cummings, 1996). Higher complexity of work also means that employees must further develop their skills, which, in turn, leads to more learning and increases the chance of thinking of new ideas (Amabile et al., 1996b; Frese et al., 1999). Also, physical aspects of the work setting may affect creativity. In their review, Shalley and colleagues (2004) point out that low spatial density may help boost creativity by reducing distractions.

Climate

Organisational climate can include inhibiting factors such as fear of failure, pre-occupation with routines and traditions, excessive reliance on salient rewards, suspicion toward new ideas, lack of management support for innovations, or a too rigid organisational structure that cannot adjust to the changes innovation may bring. It may also contain the exact opposite (Amabile et al., 1996a).

For creativity to flourish, a certain level of risk taking must be allowed (Amabile et al., 1996b). Research has shown that when people feel free to suggest unusual ideas without having to worry about reprimands, they are likely to be more innovative. This suggests the organisation be flexible enough to encompass whatever unexpected innovations that may surface (Amabile et al., 1996a). Management obviously play an important part in this. Oldham and Cummings' (1996) review of management style shows that support rather than control from supervisors helps foster creativity, although an individualised or selective approach is warranted. Also, Frese et al. (1999) and Paulus (2000) comment on the importance of a supportive environment. While Frese and colleagues find no relation between submitting ideas to a suggestion system and supervisor support, they instead suggest that supervisors may be more important in shaping the quality of the ideas rather than in generating them. Paulus, finally, stresses the need to overcome social inhibitors such as evaluation apprehension and free riding by implementing and nursing a supportive environment. In other words, not only does management need to be supportive, but the environment as a whole. This obviously also includes co-workers (Shalley et al., 2004).

Additional Aspects

Trying to find common patterns and themes in the literature, it is important to acknowledge that the earlier-mentioned themes are somewhat overlapping, and the boundaries between them are blurred. In addition, there are great individual differences to creativity that obviously also are important to understand. For example, people have different cognitive and creative styles. Paulus (2000) reminds us that while some prefer surroundings where stimuli are similar, others actively seek cognitively dissimilar domains. In any given group, there will be cognitive differences, and individuals will thus not be equally stimulated. Having examined both suggestion systems submissions and patent disclosures written, Oldham and Cummings (1996) further point out that there are also differences in creative styles, ranging from adaptive, that is, striving to "do things better" by incrementally improving current activities, to innovative, for example, wanting to "do things differently" by radically changing the current practice (p. 628). Traditional suggestion systems typically seem to fit the first category of adaptive creativity.

Other issues not covered in the previous categories include the work load, the amount of slack time, and the opportunity to experiment. Amabile and colleagues speak of playfulness. Play at work occurs when people have enough time and freedom to constructively experiment with ideas not immediately useful from a business perspective. Though not all play is creative, all creative acts include an element of play (Amabile et al., 1996a). Enabling this at an organisational level requires an amount of redundancy not often seen in today's slim organisations (Nonaka & Takeuchi, 1995).

When presenting and discussing the empirical data in the sections, *Empirical Results* and *Discussion*, we shall return to and use these themes. Before starting with the data, however, we need to learn more about the setting of this research and how the investigation was carried out, and go through a quick explanation of the electronic brainstorming system used.

Site and Methodology

We shall briefly describe here the research setting where the study was carried out and account for the methodological approach taken.

Research Setting

This research was carried out at Volvo Information Technology's Headquarters in Göteborg, Sweden. Volvo IT is an IT service providing a company within the Volvo group, and at the time for the research, they had approximately 2,500 employees worldwide. Roughly 900 of these worked at the head office.

Despite being an IT service company, Volvo IT was heavily influenced by the industry legacy from its manufacturing siblings. Volvo IT had a process-oriented organisation, arranged to meet the business requirements of the other corporate companies, which for many years had been the only customers. Volvo IT tried to maintain a governance function for IT solutions, assuring that synergies between the various companies within the group were exploited. A high degree of standardisation was thus hailed as the optimal situation, and Volvo IT's centralised mainframe operation, which had received several international awards for high efficiency and cost-effectiveness, had always been the backbone of the company's business. Volvo IT was, however, not the exclusive provider of IT services within the group, and the other companies could purchase their services also from external providers. As long as mainframe processing was the core of the business, Volvo IT was on top of the competition, but the shift towards more Web-enabled solutions opened the field for new and smaller players. This put new demands on creativity and the ability to quickly produce new business solutions.

Although not institutionalised, brainstorming as a method for idea generation and problem-solving was widely adopted within the company and had been used for many years. Brainstorming should not be understood here in the strict Osbornian sense but rather as an unprejudiced and informal meeting where also "wild" and tentative ideas were allowed and encouraged. In the 1980's, the Volvo School—the group's internal provider of courses and seminars—regularly gave courses in *lateral thinking*, a method for enhancing creativity developed by de Bono, and *mind-mapping*, a technique for developing a more creative and innovative approach to thinking introduced by Buzan. Such non-IT-related topics were removed from the menu during the recession in the early 90's, and, although the school eventually recovered from the cut backs, courses targeted at enhancing creativity are no longer available.

Volvo IT maintained a traditional box-on-the-wall suggestion system. Employees were supposed to submit ideas and suggestions for improvement to a proposal-handling committee (PHC), which would honour the proposer of a good idea with a financial remuneration. The policy was to let half of the company's first year's savings, which might come to a substantial amount of money, go to the proposer. During 1999, the PHC received 226 proposals and spent a sum of approximately US$ 45,000 on individual rewards. The numbers for the following years are of the same magnitude. Even if proposals could be sent collectively by a group of people, most of them where submitted by individuals, and it was more usual to see several submissions from the same individual than group submissions.

Research Method

Reviewing the text on electronic brainstorming (EBS), we find that much of the research carried out in the 1980s and early 1990s were laboratory experiments with students as subjects. In a review from 1994, Pervan (1994) reports that 172 out of 203 investigated cases were carried out in research environments and not in business environments. This is understandable, since it is much easier to allocate a group of students than to persuade business executives to invest their time and efforts in research activities. Nevertheless, the use of students is highly problematic for a number of reasons: student groups are formed solely for the experimental task and thus have no history (Pinsonneault & Kraemer, 1990); students show substantially other reasons for and reactions to participation than do the business people they are substituting (Dennis, Valacich, & Nunamaker, 1990). Unfortunately, this problem extends to studies of creativity at large (Paulus, 2000), and too little work has been focusing on real organisational conditions (Oldham & Cummings, 1996). Acknowledging this critique, this research takes place in a real-world industry setting. Having a desire not only to study and understand but also to intervene in and influence the processes under study, this research approach may be described as an action case (Braa & Vidgen, 1999). This hybrid is a mix of understanding and change, designed to balance the trade-offs between being an observer capable of making interpretations and a researcher involved in creating change in practice. Instrumental in this research was the Web-based brainstorming application prototype—Mindpool—developed by the author to act as a change agent. The Mindpool prototype system, designed to address and potentially eliminate the production losses typically seen in electronic brainstorming, was made generally available to all employees on the corporate intranet. The system has been presented in detail elsewhere (Stenmark, 2001b, 2002) and is only briefly described in the next section.

Before installing and evaluating Mindpool, a base line was established by having a masters' student conduct 10 semi-structured interviews with employees about their views on creativity, suggestion systems, and management. These interviews, lasting approximately 40 minutes, included both members of the proposal-handling committee (PHC), that is, the people responsible for evaluating submitted ideas, and ordinary office workers. In addition, we explicitly invited 32 users to test the application. Among these 32 were the 10 people interviewed earlier. Not all invited users took the opportunity to try the application, but the log files revealed that 52 different users accessed the application, indicating that it was instead found and used also by people other than only those initially invited. Most people did only read the suggestions without making suggestions of their own, and this sort of "lurking" was an expected behaviour. During the three-week test period, Mindpool received 22 suggestions submitted by eight different users and 14 of these were submitted the very first week. After the test period, the application log files were used to randomly select eight users who were interviewed concerning their views of the application. Finally, the result of the masters' thesis work was presented and discussed at a workshop, which the masters' student, the author, and some 20 organisational members attended. The notes from this discussion and the interview transcripts were thereafter analysed by the author.

Initially, this research set entirely within the electronic brainstorming discourse and, therefore, relied exclusively on (technical) EBS literature for design, data interpretation, and analysis. Turning out to be a failure, we turned to a broader set of literature, realising we had to analyse not only technology itself but also structural and cognitive factors such as culture, motivation, trust, and mindset (Orlikowski, 1992). For this chapter, the empirical data has been reinterpreted using a different theoretical framework, consisting of text on organisational creativity in a much broader sense as presented earlier. The distillation of the four central aspects of organisational creativity accounted for this and the analysis of the data was not a sequential process but an iterative one where both the data and the literature was re-read and re-analysed a number of times. Following Orlikowski's (1993) advice, the progress of the data analysis work thus took place on several levels in a comparative fashion, going from broader to narrower and more focused concepts. This process was continued until a satisfactory explanation and stability had been reached.

The Mindpool Prototype

Mindpool is an intranet electronic brainstorming system (EBS) prototype, available to the entire organisation. The idea is to mimic the creative atmosphere found in brainstorm sessions, where no suggestions are turned down but instead are used to spawn new and possibly even better ideas (Osborn, 1953). Mindpool is based on three fundamental design principles: asynchronicity, anonymity, and accessibility. Unlike ordinary EBS, Mindpool supports asynchronous brainstorming, which means that users do not have to be active simultaneously. This removes the temporal restriction present in other media, for example, chat forums. The system further allows the proposer to be anonymous while yet providing a mechanism for letting people contact them. The reasons for anonymity are two; first, it eliminates evaluation apprehension and thus enables users to submit proposals without risking making fools of themselves—a fact known to have a positive effect on the amount of ideas (Diehl

Figure 1. The visualisation of ideas in Mindpool, which shows the date and time: (1) of the submission, the subject (2) of the submission, the identification number (3) of the submitter, and the actual content (4) of the suggestion.

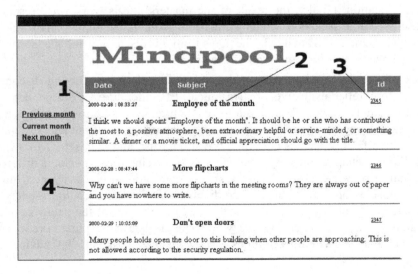

& Stroebe, 1987). Second, not revealing the contributor helps separating personalities from the issues, thus promoting a more objective evaluation—especially so when power differences exist among the participants (Nunamaker, Dennis, Valacich, & Vogel, 1991). Accessibility is achieved by the Web interface allowing access to all organisational members from their ordinary work places, thereby inviting the entire organisation to be part of the process rather than just a group of a selected few.

Suggestions are submitted as e-mails and automatically added to a Web page. The Web is accessible from all platforms, and the persistent nature allows the idea to linger long enough for it to be found by many different people in different locations and contexts, thereby allowing ideas to develop long after the point of introduction. The possibility to add comments directly to the proposal, as is the case in news groups, is absent in Mindpool. This helps shielding the new idea from public negative critique. Still, a mechanism that made it possible to contact the proposer either to ask for or to provide more information was provided. Though the latter may contain criticism, the original idea remains publicly available and can serve as a seed for others, while the critique is not displayed. The fact that each contributor can be traced also enables individual recognition, which is otherwise a problem in anonymous EBS. For details about Mindpool and the design rationale, see Stenmark (2001b).

Mindpool was intended to be a hybrid system, pairing the principles underpinning brainstorming with the suggestion system approach. The rationale was that: (1) lowering the threshold would increase the number of submissions (and submitters); (2) all submissions would be exposed on the corporate intranet; (3) the multitude and diversity of ideas would stimulate to new ideas; and (4) useful suggestions would eventually emerge out of this cumulative process. Assessing the quality and potential value of each suggestion would still be a task for the proposal handling committee, but more people would be engaged in the process and ideas that were not good enough to be implemented organisation-wide could still be picked up and applied locally.

Empirical Results

When interviewed about their view on creativity, many respondents expressed it in terms of problem solving. To illustrate, one respondent defined creativity as "[…] the ability to recognise and solve a specific problem." Most respondents also stressed the importance of stimuli of some kind to spark creativity, and mentioned the interaction with other people as an important source. Aside from the shared view of "input from people" as being an important stimuli, a diversity of other situations were mentioned during the interviews: facing a challenging task; going to conferences; visiting other companies; looking at different applications; or doing physical workout. These activities sparked creativity by mentally taking the user somewhere else. Many of the respondents also claimed the characteristics of the work tasks to be important for creativity. Particularly important was if the task was challenging and non-routine:

> *I improvise a lot in my work. I get new ideas while doing things [...].If a task is challenging and fun, you become creative [...]. When I'm focused on a thing or on a work process, I get ideas related to that task. I think it's difficult to just sit down and put on the thinking hat [and produce ideas]; ideas pop up while working.*

This quote also illustrates the opinion shared by all respondents that creativity could not be ordered about. "It's more difficult to be creative when you really have to" is an utterance that well depicts the common view of the interviewees; creativity is highly-situated and spontaneous. Management's role, as the respondents saw it, was to create a positive atmosphere of openness and trust, where there was a high tolerance for dissentient opinions.

> *It's important to have a positive atmosphere, since it makes people bootstrap themselves. Encouragement is thus very important… that and what sort of manager you have. After all, he's the one who has the final say.*

New ideas were not always welcomed though, and, in particular, the respondents commented negatively on the tinkering often associated with creativity. Experimenting, they argued, can sometimes be a source of trouble if not carried out in controlled test environments. Several of the respondents actually expressed reluctance for trying out new ideas at work. One network operator explained:

> *Creativity can cause problems, too. In a production environment that has to work… well, if it is working, you'd better leave it alone and not try to fix it up, because then you create problems."*

The saying "If it ain't broke, don't fix it" applied here, according to the informant. However, even had there been an interest in testing new things and had an environment in which experiments could safely be carried out existed, the organisational members were simply too busy to engage in tinkering, they claimed. Several respondents explained that they had no time for extraordinary activities, or to do things outside their immediate duties:

You [...] don't have time to speculate, or be creative in a general sort of way. We're too tightly governed by budgets and deadlines.

Another interviewee pointed out:

Not only does it require time but it also takes energy to be creative. [...] If you have too much to do you can't be creative any more.

Sending ideas to the suggestion system was one such activity that became down-prioritised due to the workload. Only two of the interviewees had ever submitted anything to the suggestion system, and in both cases it was several years ago. Another reason to withhold ideas brought up by the respondents was the perceived risk of having to implement the idea yourself, thereby further adding to your workload. One interviewee frankly admitted:

Should I come up with an idea that would help the company but not give me anything tangible in return, I wouldn't mention it. I mean, should I suggest it to my manager he would probably want me to take care of it. That's how they thank you for being smart: you get more work!

Although admitting they did not know much about the suggestion system, all respondents believed that a suggestion submitted had to be both concrete and well thought-through to be considered by the PHC. This resulted in the threshold for participating becoming too high. One respondent's comment illustrates this opinion:

It has to be serious stuff, which makes you a bit reluctant to submit. I mean, it has to be something really worthwhile. Much of what I do is part of my daily work and it's not something you would submit—it's part of my ordinary tasks.

The fact that the suggestion system was a black box underpinned these beliefs since the employees could not see the suggestions submitted by others. This also resulted in some users conveying it as meaningless to submit suggestions since they figured somebody else had probably already thought of the same idea and already suggested it.

Mindpool, in contrast, offered full insight into the suggestion database, which the respondents saw as useful. They commented on this as a quick and easy way to get your view out in the open for others to be inspired by. In particular, they appreciated the fact that ideas were exposed to Volvo as a whole and that the application protected the identity of the proposer. Anonymity was considered an important feature since it would eliminate evaluation apprehension. "People are afraid one would laugh at or ridicule their ideas otherwise, so this is a much needed feature," said one informant. Although the users thought of Mindpool as "potentially useful," the prototype application was no immediate success, and usage after three weeks was still rather low. The respondents commented this in terms of the critical mass problem:

> *I think this is good, if only you get going and get it up to speed, sort of. [...] There's too little content at the moment—you don't want to be the first one to contribute.*

Another reason given for not having tried the Mindpool application was the respondents again did not have the time. According to the interviewees, this sort of pro-active creativity was not explicitly encouraged by management and hence received low priority:

> *I haven't got round to it. If you don't do it right away, you forget about it. We haven't time to be creative on pure speculation.*

Among the informants who had used Mindpool, there were complaints about the lack of structure and order in the system. One user suggested the introduction of an administrator or a moderator whose job would be to screen, sort, and categorise the suggestions:

> *There should be someone to make sure that there is some order to it and that the suggestions are serious. You know—weed out the crap [...]. That person could perhaps also direct certain ideas to the right place in the organisation...*

Another hampering circumstance was the fact that several interviewees saw Mindpool and the traditional suggestion system as competitors:

> *If you have a good idea, why post it here [in Mindpool] instead of submitting it to the PHC? There you might get a reward and you know you'll get a response. In this system [Mindpool] you just post things and you'll never know whether someone uses it.*

A similar comment was:

> *If I post [my idea] on this web site, someone might take it and send it to the*
> *suggestion system, and if it turns out to be useful and rewarded, I don't get*
> *a thing. You don't want that to happen.*

The fear of being robbed of a good idea that these quotes illustrate could be traced back to the reward system in place. The possibility of tangible remuneration that the reward system represented was perceived as a motivating factor and the respondents clearly testified that without such a construct there would be no reason to participate:

> *If you come up with something useful from a financial point of view, and*
> *you know you can get a part of it, you get motivated by the money. It can*
> *often be the triggering factor that gets things out in the open.*

The respondents considered creativity and inventiveness to be outside their ordinary work tasks, and Mindpool was, therefore, an application that received marginal interests. Unless you received some extra benefit, it did not pay off to be creative, and the employees did not bother to engage in creativity that only the company would benefit from.

> *The person who suggests something that gets implemented should obviously*
> *have a part of it [the profit/savings], not the least so considering that he or*
> *she would otherwise not do anything about it.*

The interviewees did mention alternatives to monetary compensations, albeit implicitly. They indicated that they were willing to develop their ideas as long as the ideas were in line with their own interests and provided that they were given adequate time. They, therefore, advocated the introduction of a "creativity forum," separate from the suggestion system, where creative people would be "allowed to spend time" trying to develop ideas they have. To be recognised as a creative person and officially allowed entry to such a group would be like becoming one of the "Knights of the Round Table," as one respondent put it, and that was to be seen as a reward in itself.

Discussion

The design of Mindpool, with its distributed and asynchronous nature, enabled company-wide brainstorming by using Web technology. Mindpool eliminated the need of large facilities and simultaneous sessions, thereby, in theory, allowing company-wide continuous brainstorming. This novel blurring of boundaries between electronic brainstorming and ordinary work activities should, according to theory, have a positive effect on creativity. Although receiving 22 ideas during the three-week test period meant that we outperformed the suggestion system quantitatively, the creativity-boosting effect was less than anticipated, and even though the prototype worked well technically, we considered usage a failure. By including insights from social psychology, we embrace a multi-disciplinary approach to IS use in organisations. To analyse the reasons for this unsuccessful intervention and derive managerial implications, we focus the discussion on the contextual factors synthesised earlier: motivation, autonomy, work settings, and climate.

Motivation

It was very obvious from the interviews that the organisational members had financial reward in mind when discussing creativity. The practical experiences with Mindpool confirm the findings derived from the previous work at the same site (Stenmark, 2001b) that organisational members express a concern for not receiving recognition and reward for their contributions. The introduction of Mindpool—which had no such reward mechanisms implemented—made this concern very obvious. The suggestion system in use remunerates the proposer of a good idea with financial compensation corresponding to half of the company's first year's savings. Although explicitly claiming the reward mechanism to have an encouraging effect, the low usage of both the suggestion system and the Mindpool prototype suggests otherwise. During 1999, the PHC received suggestions from 226 of the 2,500+ employees, which means that less than 10% of the organisational members participated actively. This testifies that even though the employees believed that money would work as a motivator, they were wrong. The discrepancy between the espoused and the actual behaviour observed at Volvo is consistent with the literature (cf. Amabile et al., 1996a, 1996b; Frese et al., 1999). Research on suggestion systems shows that the reliance on extrinsic motivation limits participation to typically 10 to 15% of the employees, as opposed to 70 to 80% when no reward system is used, or when recognition is kept to a symbolic level (Robinson & Stern, 1997). Instead, when being truly interested in a task, the opportunity to indulge in and develop such a task was tacitly conceived as a reward in it self. Being able to do so seems to create an intrinsic motivation less likely to affect creativity negatively, and it, therefore, appears that motivation should be catered for not by relying on large sums of money—despite the respondents testimonies—but on interests, involvement, curiosity, satisfaction, and positive challenges, such as suggested by the literature (Amabile et al., 1996a).

Autonomy

One respondent told us that he often improvised during his work. This may suggest that the employees had certain control over their work and the autonomy to take initiatives and attend to tasks in a non-routine way. Such autonomous and self-initiated activities are powerful because they are driven primarily by intrinsic motivation. Research in a corporate setting has shown that professional interest rather than espoused theory is what motivates people (Stenmark, 2001a). When employees are allowed, and in fact encouraged, to pick and pursue their own projects, they are driven by their personal interests. Although Volvo IT employees were allowed to improvise, it was tacitly assumed that improvisation should be limited to problem-solving or other reactive situations only. Time constraints and lack of funds hindered the employees from being creative *proactively*. The documented reluctance to change working, albeit not necessarily optimal, procedures suggests possibly also mental restrictions to certain types of creativity. The testimonies given earlier suggest that employees were activity driven rather than goal driven (cf. Arbaoui & Oquendo, 1994), and that their degree of autonomy was de facto limited.

Literature stresses the need to go beyond the obvious since planned actions can only take an organisation in directions already anticipated. To reach the unexpected (and innovative), the company must go beyond what is scheduled and put its trust in the unplanned actions that often are the result of user initiatives (Robinson & Stern, 1997). Often, if not always, these unanticipated and unofficial activities are indeed also user initiated and propelled by the users' intrinsic motivation. The expression "skunk works" was coined during the Second World War by the aircraft manufacturer Lockheed Martins to describe a situation where a small group of technicians were allowed to work outside the established bureaucracy and with minimal management control (Mischi, 1999). It has been shown that creativity and innovation are aided by low formalisation and large degrees of freedom, especially during the initial stages (Kanter, 1988). It is also recognised that creativity often requires extra-ordinary dedication and commitment and that most employees would willingly do far more than the company could possibly ask of them if only they were allowed to work with things in which they were really interested. The "creative forum" suggested by one respondent where ideas could be tested and developed could be seen as a way to institutionalise skunk work. However, allowing a group of employees to be creative would have little effect on Volvo's performance as compared to if the entire workforce was encouraged to act more autonomously.

Work Settings

To reduce evaluation apprehension, the setting offered by Mindpool was based on anonymity. While at the same time being supportive verbally of this feature, the participants reacted negatively in action to this arrangement as they felt their contributions were neither recognised nor rewarded. The participants were all used to open office landscapes with only a minimum of sound-insulating screen separating the desks. These acoustic walls were low enough for employees to talk to their neighbours and overlook the entire building floor, and collaboration—both formal and informal—occurred regularly. In such an environment, anonymity is not the attribute one would first think of. Instead, the organisational members seemed to be well aware of each others' merits and competencies, and in such a setting increased accountability may have worked better (cf. Paulus, 2000).

The openness and free exchange of ideas that Amabile et al. (1996b) found characterise a creative environment that could not be identified at our site. Instead, we witnessed competitiveness causing employees to hide ideas from one another. Competitiveness can indeed stimulate creativity (cf. Paulus, 2000) but, in combination with anonymity and salient rewards, it did not have that effect at Volvo. We saw two different reasons for not sharing ideas; one was to avoid being robbed and thus miss out on the reward; a second was not to generate additional workload. As to the first, the reward-based suggestion system had been in place for decades but was, as we have seen, not much used. The employees probably thought that they eventually would have time and opportunity to develop their idea to reward-deserving suggestions but apparently this never did happen. Whatever embryonic figments they may have had remained silently in their minds failing to generate either personal or organisational gain. It seems that removing the money at stake would have eliminated much of this problem. As to the second, the employees were afraid to suggest changes that would increase their workload. Their current assignments kept them more than busy and when suggestions are not rooted in a personal commitment, having to implement them is conceived as a punishment. Hence, management should primarily encourage employees to develop their areas of interests. Furthermore, it is possible that tasks that one individual finds unattractive, may appeal strongly to someone else in the organisation.

Finally, Mindpool's ability to make visual ideas to the entire organisation was acknowledged by the respondents. The implications are that suggestions should always be made salient, and time should be allocated for those interested in developing the ideas further.

Climate

Face-to-face brainstorming has been used at Volvo for many years without causing conflicts regarding rewards or recognition. This fact suggests that it is not the brainstorming process *per se* that causes Mindpool to fail but some other, contextual factor. One possible reason may be found in the observation that group work, such as brainstorming, often is carried out locally, with participants from the same department or organisational unit. It can be assumed that people who know and trust one another have higher levels of reciprocity and therefore are more willing to share ideas and information. Under such conditions, for example, when users are likely to meet one another repeatedly, favours are eventually returned. Mindpool, in contrast, begged users to share their insights with anonymous strangers without guarantee for reciprocity. However, it is a documented fact that the sharing of advice among perfect strangers occurs rather regularly on the Internet. Why would these people take the effort to help unknown and distant others solve their problems? Regardless of why, these interactions, although they occurred with no physical contact and without the true identity of the other participants necessarily being revealed, have been shown to give rise to group identity and create a sense of community (Constant, Kiesler, & Sproull, 1996). It is clear that Mindpool did not establish this.

The employees stated that they were more creative when having fun and when being challenged by non-routine work, but their accounts also suggested that their tasks in reality were mostly carried out in a rather controlled environment where spontaneous experimentation were unlikely to occur. Risk taking—identified in the literature as an important aspect of creativity—was not viewed positively. The respondents also acknowledged that management attitudes greatly influenced the creative climate but they did not say much about to what extent they thought this influence was positive or negative in their particular case. Indirectly, however, the statements about tight budgets, heavy work-load, and reluctance to change suggest no active management support; nor did we find any evidence of support on a peer-to-peer level.

Additional Aspects

Differences in preferences between individuals are obvious and inescapable. This means that there is no magic formula that can be applied to all situations. Many different managerial approaches should be applied simultaneously to cater for the differences among the co-workers; the literature has pointed to differences in both cognitive style and creative style, and the previously-mentioned accounts verify this. We have further seen that our respondents contradict themselves. They all seem to believe that rewards would help them be more creative, and yet they testify that the reward system makes them reluctant to share ideas with one another, thereby effectively reducing creativity.

Appreciation of creative work requires a delicate balancing between intrinsic and extrinsic motivation and must be done skilfully. Whatever reward is chosen, it should be used to recognise the expertise or ability of the group or individual, and the reward should be used to motivate further work and not act as a bribe. Encouraging work-focused feedback (as opposed to person-focused feedback) and discouraging excessive initial critique of new ideas foster a positive attitude towards creativity. By demonstrating that innovations and creativity are valued by communicating the potential of the work and accomplishments that have been made, intrinsically-motivated employee initiatives could be further propelled.

In modern society, play and work are tacitly assumed to be mutually exclusive—it is perceived "unprofessional" to play. From a creativity perspective, however, this separation is unfortunate since many important discoveries have been made while playing. Hence, more resources should be allocated for experimenting. Although it is not desirable to reinvent the wheel from scratch, thereby repeating all of the errors previously made, it is often necessary to allow every one to build their own wheel. This is due to the strong relationship between knowledge and action. Learning-by-doing is the only way to acquire certain knowledge, and this suggests that enough redundancy should be allocated to allow for the experimenting that leads to this experience. The desire to be taken up among the "Knights of the Round Table" that one respondent expressed can be seen as an illustration of the need for time to elaborate on one's own ideas.

However, activity-oriented organisations do seldom allow for much spontaneous self-initiated activities, as testified by the quoted respondent earlier. Tight budgets and deadlines are denying the employees the ability to follow-up on the hunches they get, or to be "creative on speculation" as one respondent put it. In a goal-oriented setting, members have more freedom to take whatever approaches they see fit to reach the goal. It seems Volvo IT has cut down the redundancy that, according to Nonaka and Takeuchi (1995), is so vital to knowledge creation. To set free the desire to initiate creative acts that already exists within most people, the company must take appropriate actions. For example, Toshiba and 3M allow their employees to devote 15% of their time to self-initiated activities (Robinson & Stern, 1997). At Volvo IT, no such time is allocated.

Limitations and Suggestions for Future Research

This study was originally designed as an action case project, and the introduction of Mindpool was intended to boost idea generation and creativity within the company under study. The design of the Mindpool prototype was based on the electronic brainstorming literature, and no particular attention was paid to the contextual factors. When the project turned out to be unsuccessful, we searched the literature to find plausible explanations for this failure. The analysis presented herein is thus applied in retrospect; had the study been designed to test the effect of contextual factors, we would probably have used another set of questions and interviewed another set of respondents. However, as with creativity, many good research results come out of the unexpected and, as pointed out by Blythin and colleagues (1997), failures often offer good opportunities for new insights.

Our research was carried out in one Swedish organisation. Contextual factors, including norms and culture, are likely to differ significantly between and even within organisations and countries, and one must ask oneself to what extent these results can be generalised. Brainstorming is a well-known and widely applied technique, and reward-based suggestion systems have long since been used in both Europe and the U.S. From a practitioners' point of view, it, therefore, seems likely that the lessons learned here can be applied to organisations other than the one studied. Further, suggestion systems and electronic brainstorming systems have been developed in parallel and seemingly without sharing results and experiences. Although this chapter describes a failing attempt to marry the two streams, we continue to believe such a cross-fertilisation has great potentials and would, therefore, like to see more academic work in this area.

The literature on electronic brainstorming teaches us that such tools may be used to enhance group creativity—in particular, if the group is larger than 15 individuals. However, most research behind such findings has been carried out in research settings or using students to substitute for real business people. It has yet to be shown that these findings can be replicated in work settings, such as the one described in this chapter. More research on creativity is, therefore, needed in organisational contexts and not only in labs.

The work presented in this chapter indicates that anonymity is a coin with two sides. While anonymity has been shown to eliminate evaluation apprehension and thereby contribute to increased participation, we found it reducing accountability and thus having a negative effect in participation. Future research should try to find means to preserve and make salient the contribution of each individual while protecting them from critique.

Conclusion

In this work, we intended to improve organisational creativity at Volvo IT by marrying electronic brainstorming and a traditional suggestion system. The action case project turned out to be unsuccessful, but a number of interesting findings could be recorded—findings that may prove useful to both practitioners and scholars.

First, we observed that when (a large sum of) money is at stake, employees are discouraged from sharing thoughts and ideas with their peers. Instead, individuals are keeping their tentative thoughts to themselves, trying to work out something really rewarding. This situation causes a focus on the reward rather than on being innovative. Further, the obvious risk is that the employee may never arrive at the groundbreaking conclusion on her own, without interaction and dialogue with other humans, and we, therefore, suggest that organisations should reconsider extrinsic motivation in the form of (large) financial compensation.

Second, although salient rewards seem to have a negative impact on creativity, people in general need to be appreciated, and organisations should, therefore, officially recognise creative initiatives and achievements. This suggests that IT tools intended to support creativity must make salient whoever contributes to the system—without necessarily revealing every link between proposals and proposers; anonymity is still an aspect that has to be balanced in.

Third, it seems lack of time has a negative impact on creativity. When deadlines and budgets are cut so tight that the employees barely manage to do what is expected, they have very small chances to practice the playfulness that is a pre-requirement for creativity. Organisations should, therefore, consider allowing redundancy in the form of slack time for the employees to be creative. While waiting for that to happen, IT tools for creativity may need to be more unobtrusive and more embedded in day to day routines.

References

Agrell, A., & Gustafson, R. (1996) Innovation and creativity in work groups. In M. A. West (Ed.) *Handbook of work group psychology* (pp. 317-343). Chichester: John Wiley.

Amabile, T. M. (1983). *The social psychology of creativity*. New York: Springer-Verlag.

Amabile, T. M., Collins, M. A., Conti, R., Phillips, M., Picariello, M., Ruscio, J., & Whitney, D. (1996a). *Creativity in context: Update to the psychology of creativity*. Boulder: Westview Press.

Amabile, T. M., Conti, R., Coon, H., Collins, M. A., Lazenby, J., & Herron, M. (1996b). Assessing the work environment for creativity. *Academy of Management Journal, 39*, 1154-1184.

Arbaoui, S., & Oquendo, F. (1994, February 7-9). Goal oriented vs. activity oriented process modelling and enactment: Issues and perspectives. In B. C. Warboys (Ed.), *Proceedings of the Third European Workshop on Software Process Technology,* Villard de Lans, France (pp. 171-176). Berlin: Springer.

Blythin, S., Hughes, J. A., Kristoffersen, S., Rodden, T., & Rouncefield, M. (1997, November 16-19). Recognising "success" and "failure": Evaluating groupware in a commercial context. In *Proceedings of GROUP '97*, Phoenix, AZ (pp. 39-46). New York: ACM Press.

Braa, K., & Vidgen, R. (1999). Interpretation, intervention, and reduction in the organizational laboratory: A framework for in-context information system research. *Accounting, Management, and Information Technologies, 9*, 25-47.

Carr, C. (1994). *The competitive power of constant creativity*. New York: American Management Association.

Constant, D., Kiesler, S., & Sproull, L. (1996). The kindness of strangers: On the usefulness of weak ties for technical advice. *Organizational Science, 7*, 119-135.

Deci, E., Connell, J., & Ryan, R. (1989). Self-determination in a work organization. *Journal of Applied Psychology, 74*, 580-590.

Dennis, A. R., Valacich, J. S., & Nunamaker, J. F. (1990). An experimental investigation of the effects of group size in an electronic meeting environment. *IEEE Transactions on Systems, Man and Cybernetics, 25*(5), 1049-1057.

Diehl, M., & Stroebe, W. (1987). Productivity loss in brainstorming groups: Towards the solution of a riddle. *Journal of Personality and Social Psychology, 53*, 497-509.

di Sessa, A. (1988). What will it mean to be "educated" in 2020? In R. S. Nickerson, & P. P. Zodhiates (Eds.), *Technology in education: Looking toward 2020* (pp. 43-66). Hillsdale, NJ: Erlbaum.

Drucker, P. (1993). *Post-capitalist society*. New York: Harper Collins.

Frese, M., Teng, E., & Wijnen, C. J. D. (1999). Helping to improve suggestion systems: Predictors of making suggestions in companies. *Journal of Organisational Behaviour, 20*, 1139-1155.

Kanter, R. M. (1988). When a thousand flowers bloom: Structural, collective and social conditions for innovation in organizations. *Research in Organizational Behavior, 10*, 169-211.

Mischi, V. (1999, October 11-13). Skunk works: "Speciation" strategies for creativity. In *Proceedings of Creativity and Cognition '99*, Loughborough, UK (pp. 101-107). New York: ACM Press.

Nagasundaram, M., & Dennis, A. R. (1993). When a group is not a group. *Small Group Research, 24*, 4, 463-489.

Nonaka, I., & Takeuchi, H. (1995). *The knowledge-creating company*. London: Oxford University Press.

Nunamaker, Jr., J. F., Dennis, A. R., Valacich, J. S., & Vogel, D. R. (1991). Information technology for negotiating groups: Generating options for mutual gain. *Management Science, 37*(10), 1325-1346.

Oldham, G. R., & Cummings, A. (1996). Employee creativity: Personal and contextual factors at work. *The Academy of Management Journal, 39*(3), 607-634.

Orlikowski, W. J. (1992, November 1-4). Learning from notes: Organizational issues in groupware implementation. In *Proceedings of CSCW '92*, Toronto, Canada (pp. 362-369). New York: ACM Press.

Orlikowski, W. J. (1993). CASE tools as organizational change: Investigating incremental and radical changes in systems development. *MIS Quarterly, 17*(3), 309-340.

Osborn, A. F. (1953). *Applied imagination*. New York: Scribner's.

Paulus, P. (2000). Groups, teams and creativity: The creative potential of idea generating groups. *Applied Psychology, 49*(2), 237-262

Pervan, G. P. (1994, May 8-11). A case for more case study research in group support systems. In *Proceedings of TC8 AUS IFIP Conference*, Bond University, Gold Coast, Queensland (pp. 485-496).

Pinsonneault, A., & Kraemer, K. L. (1990). The effects of electronic meetings on group processes and outcomes: An assessment of the empirical research. *European Journal of Operational Research, 46*(2), 143-161.

Reich, R. B. (2002). *The future of success. Working and living in the new economy* (revised ed.). New York: Vintage Books.

Robinson, A. G., & Stern, S. (1997). *Corporate creativity: How innovation and improvement actually happen*. San Francisco: Berrett-Koehler.

Shalley, C. E., Zhou, J., & Oldham, G. R. (2004). The effects of personal and contextual characteristics on creativity: Where should we go from here? *Journal of Management, 30*(6), 933-958.

Stenmark, D. (2001a). Leveraging tacit organizational knowledge. *Journal of Management Information Systems, 17*(3), 9-24.

Stenmark, D. (2001b, January 3-6). The mindpool hybrid: Theorising a new angle on EBS and suggestion systems. In *Proceedings of HICSS-34*, Maui, HI. IEEE Press.

Stenmark, D. (2002, January 7-10). Group cohesiveness in face-to-face and electronic brainstorming: Lessons from an action case study. In *Proceedings of HICSS-35*, Hawaii. IEEE Press.

About the Editor

Bernd Carsten Stahl is a reader in critical research in technology of the School of Computing and a research associate at the Centre for Computing and Social Responsibility of De Montfort University, Leicester, UK. His interests cover philosophical issues arising from the intersections of business, technology, and information. This includes the ethics of computing and critical approaches to information systems. He is the editor-in-chief of the *International Journal of Technology and Human Interaction*. More information can be found under: http://www.cse.dmu.ac.uk/~bstahl/

About the Authors

Pär J. Ågerfalk, PhD, is a postdoctoral research fellow at the University of Limerick, Ireland, and an assistant professor (universitetslektor) in informatics at Örebro University, Sweden. His current research centres on open source software development in the secondary software sector, globally-distributed and flexible software development methods, and how information systems development approaches can be informed by language/action theory. His over 40 peer-reviewed publications have appeared in a variety of international journals, books, and conference proceedings, and he is an associate editor of the *European Journal of Information Systems* and *Systems, Signs & Actions*. He is currently a guest editor of *Communications of the ACM* and *Software Process: Improvement and Practice*.

Ian F. Alexander is an independent consultant specialising in requirements engineering. He is also an experienced instructor and has written training courses for a range of organizations. He is the author of the Scenario Plus! toolkits. His principal research interest is in improving the requirements' engineering process through scenarios and other people-centred techniques. He is currently exploring the use of scenarios on a technology project to investigate the reuse of specifications for control systems in the German automobile industry. His book, *Writing Better Requirements*, was published by Addison-Wesley in 2002, and another book, *Scenarios, Stories, Use Cases*, was published by John Wiley in 2004. He has published numerous technical papers and is on the Program Committee of the Requirements Engineering 2004 Conference. He helps to run the BCS Requirements Engineering Specialist Group and the IEE Professional Network for Systems Engineering. He is a chartered engineer.

Laurence Brooks is a lecturer in the School of Information Systems, Computing and Mathematics at Brunel University, UK. Previously, he was a lecturer in the Department of Computer Science, University of York, and held a research position in the Judge Institute of Management Studies, University of Cambridge. Dr. Brooks has a PhD in industrial management (University of Liverpool) and a BSc in Psychology (University of Bristol). His research interests include: techniques for better knowledge elicitation in the early systems development and for bringing together the business and technological areas of an organization; the role that social theory might play in contributing to our understanding of information systems in areas such as health information systems and collaborative work support systems. He is a member of the national boards of the UK Academy for Information Systems (UKAIS) and the UK Systems Society (UKSS). He has published in journals such as the *Information Systems Journal*, *The Information Society* and the *European Journal of Information Systems*. He can be reached at laurence.brooks@brunel.ac.uk.

Josep Casanovas is a professor at the Technical University of Catalonia in Barcelona, in the Statistics and Operational Department. During his career, he has combined teaching, research, and several management education roles. He has published several articles in top academic journals and conferences in the areas of simulation, operational research, and information technology. He can be reached at josepk@fib.upc.edu.

Charlie C. Chen is an assistant professor in the Department of Computer Information Systems at Appalachian State University, USA. His research areas are e-learning effectiveness, mobile commerce, and knowledge management. Prior to this position, he taught at California State University, Northridge. He has authored more than 12 referred articles and proceedings, and presented at many professional conferences and venues. He has published in the *Communications of AIS*, *Knowledge Management Research and Practice*, and the *Journal of Information Systems Education*. He has authored a chapter on global information systems in the *Encyclopedia of Information Systems* and a chapter on traditional versus Internet EDI in the *Encyclopedia of E-Commerce, E-Government, and Mobile Commerce*. Dr. Chen received his PhD from the Claremont Graduate University and an MBA from the American Graduate School of International Management (Thunderbird)

Christian Clausen is an associate professor with a MSc (Eng.) with specialisation in production management. Previously, he was a consultant and contract researcher at the Danish Technological Institute, Department for Industrial Psychology from 1978 to 1986, an associate professor at the Technical University of Denmark (DTU), Unit of Technology Assessment from 1987 to 1994, and Department of Technology and Social Sciences from 1995 to 2000. Since 2001, he has been an associate professor at the Department of Manufacturing Engineering and Management, as head of the Section of Innovation and Sustainability. His current research interests and teaching include social shaping of technology, technology management, and sociotechnical dimensions of design and innovation.

Christopher Davis is an assistant professor of information systems at the University of South Florida, St. Petersburg, USA. He has held faculty positions at a number of universities in the UK. His current research explores the impact of information systems on knowledge workers, in particular the training challenges presented by increasingly sophisticated and specialist information systems. He has carried out research in the healthcare, financial services, criminal justice, and defence sectors. He is a member of the British Computer Society, the Association for Information Systems, the ACM and was recently elected to senior membership of the Institute of Electrical and Electronics Engineers (IEEE). He can be contacted at davisc@stpt.usf.edu.

José Esteves has been a professor and chair of the information systems area at the Instituto de Empresa, Madrid, Spain, since 2004. He is also the chair of the Software AG-Alianza Sumaq Research Center in E-Government. He received his PhD in information systems from the Universidad Politécnica de Catalunya (UPC), Barcelona, a master's and engineering degrees in information systems from the Universidade do Minho (UM), Portugal, and a diploma in business administration from the Instituto Superior de Tecnología Empresarial, Porto, Portugal. He is the author of many articles about ERP systems published in international conferences, books, and journals. His research interests focus on the implementation and use of enterprise systems, ERP, impact of information systems on organizations, user satisfaction, benefits of information systems, e-government, knowledge management, and its use at organizational level. He can be reached at jose.esteves@ie.edu.

Susan E. George received her BSc and PhD in computer science from the University of Reading, UK, and MSc in knowledge-based systems from Edinburgh University, UK. Dr. George has undertaken post-doctoral research at both the Department of Optometry and Vision Sciences, University of Wales, and the School of Computer and Information Science, University of South Australia. Her research interests lie within the field of artificial intelligence, especially the theology of intelligent technology, artificial neural networks and pattern recognition, with applications in a variety of fields.

Göran Goldkuhl, PhD, is a professor of information systems at Linköping University and Jönköping International Business School, Sweden. He is the director of the Swedish research network VITS, consisting of 40 researchers at six Swedish universities. He has published several books and more than 80 research papers at conferences, in journals, and as book chapters. He is currently developing a family of theories, which all are founded on socio-instrumental pragmatism: Workpractice Theory, Business Action Theory, Information Systems Actability Theory. He has a great interest in interpretive and qualitative research methods, and he has contributed to the development of Multi-Grounded Theory (a modified version of Grounded Theory). He is editor-in-chief for the journal *Systems, Signs & Actions* (www.sysiac.org).

Anita Greenhill serves as a lecturer in Accounting & Finance at the University of Manchester. She received her PhD from the Engineering and Information Technology Faculty, Griffith University. Anita has over 50 published articles in various fields of interest and expertise: information systems; virtual communities; sociology; skills acquisition in information technology; gender and information technology; information technology policy and education; and qualitative research methods. Her research has appeared in the *International Journal of Technology and Human Interaction*, the *Journal of Information and Society,* and the *Journal of New Technology, Work and Employment.*

Albert L. Harris is a professor in the Department of Computer Information Systems at Appalachian State University, USA, and is editor-in-chief of the *Journal of Information Systems Education*. He received his PhD in MIS from Georgia State University, his MS in systems management from the George Washington University, and his BS in quantitative business analysis from Indiana University. Dr. Harris teaches a variety of graduate and undergraduate classes in information systems. He is a member of the Board of Directors for the Education Special Interest Group (EDSIG) of AITP, served for three years as treasurer of EDSIG and is a member of the Board of Directors of the International Association of Information Management (IAIM). His research interests include: IS education effectiveness, IS ethics, and international IS. He has published extensively in refereed journals and international, national, and regional conference proceedings and has written chapters in several books.

Lynette Kvasny serves as an assistant professor of information sciences and technology, and a founding member of the Center for the Information Society at The Pennsylvania State University, USA. She earned a PhD in computer information systems from the Robinson College of Business, Georgia State University. She is the recipient of the National Science Foundation CAREER award. Her research interests include the digital divide, IT workforce diversity, and community informatics. Her research has appeared in the *Data Base for Advances in Information Systems, Information Systems Journal*, the *Journal of Computer Mediated Communication, International Journal of Technology and Human Interaction,* and *Information, Communication and Society.*

Mark Lycett has a BSc in computing and business management (Oxford Brookes), an MSc in information systems (Brunel University, UK) and a PhD in information systems (Brunel University). Prior to returning to education, he spent a number of years in industry and has both worked on and managed a number of national and international business change/development projects. His research concentrates on all aspects of organisational and information systems development and he has a number of publications in these areas. He can be contacted at mark.lycett@brunel.ac.uk.

John McCarthy is a psychologist whose research is concerned with conceptualising aesthetic and experiential perspectives on technology and teasing out the implications for theories of design and use of interactive systems. He is a senior lecturer in the Department of Applied Psychology, University College Cork, Ireland.

Lisa Meekison has a doctorate in cultural anthropology and has worked as a brand researcher and strategist in the UK and Canada for four years. She currently resides in Toronto.

Margreet B. Michel-Verkerke spent thirteen years with teaching nurses and doctors-assistants after her graduation as a physician. During this period, she developed an interest in the application of information and communication technology in education. She started to study computer science at the Open University. In 2000, she continued her studies at the University of Twente, The Netherlands, which resulted in her graduation with an MSc in business information technology in November of 2003. From 1998, she worked as a project manager in the area of e-learning in vocational education. She decided to switch to the application of ICT in healthcare in 2001, when she became a research assistant at the University of Twente. Her main fields of interest are the improvement of care processes by the enhancement of cooperation and coordination by use of ICT and the electronic patient record. In 2004, she started to put her knowledge in practice as senior staff in Trivium zorggroep Twente, an organization specialized in complex care for the elderly.

Alistair Mutch is a professor of information and learning at Nottingham Trent University, UK. He has published widely on aspects of managerial information use in addition to interests in the history of management and the development of critical realist approaches to the study of organizations. He recently published *Strategic and Organizational Change: From Production to Retailing in UK Brewing 1950-1990* (Routledge, 2005), which explores the application of critical realist ideas in a little more depth. He is currently working on the notion of "practical reasoning" in the context of applications such as data warehouses. He is a member of the editorial board of the journal *Organization*.

Loren Olfman is the dean of the School of Information Science and a professor of information science at Claremont Graduate University, USA, and Fletcher Jones chair in Technology Management. He came to Claremont in 1987 after graduating with a PhD in business (management information systems) from Indiana University. His research interests include: how software can be learned and used in organizations, the impact of computer-based systems on knowledge management, and the design and adoption of systems used for group work. A key component of Dr. Olfman's teaching is his involvement with doctoral students; he has supervised 36 students to completion. He is an active member of the information systems community.

Joan A. Pastor is a professor at the Technical University of Catalonia in Barcelona, Spain, who is currently leading the Twist Group on IS qualitative research, addressing topics such as ERP procurement and ERP implementation issues by applying IS qualitative research methods. He holds a degree in computer science and a PhD in information systems engineering, both from the Technical University of Catalonia in Barcelona, Spain. He can be reached at pastor@lsi.upc.es.

Giuseppina Pellegrino is currently a Postdoc fellow at the Department of Sociology and Political Science, University of Calabria, Italy. She received a PhD in science, technology and society from the same department. As part of her doctoral dissertation, she carried out an ethnographic study of intranet technology in an Italian and a British company. She published a book and several articles in international journals and conference proceedings. Her research interests concern: the intersections between sociology of technology and organization studies; new media and everyday life; ethnographic and narrative approaches. She is currently investigating mobile technologies in everyday life at individual and organizational level.

Steve Sawyer is a founding member and associate professor at The Pennsylvania State University's School of Information Sciences and Technology, USA. He holds affiliate appointments in Management and Organizations; Labor Studies and Industrial Relations; and the Science, Technology and Society. Steve does social and organizational informatics research with a particular focus on people working together using information and communication technologies. He can be reached at sawyer@ist.psu.edu.

Roel W. Schuring is interested in the effects of organization on processes of work and the effectiveness of technology. He started in Geneva at the International Labour Office in 1987, where he studied the effects of assembly automation on the occupational structure of assembly work. During the nineties, he mainly worked on the effective organization and introduction of programs for continuous improvement in organizations. From 1998 to 2004, he led the research of the Healthcare Management Department of the University of Twente. He currently is the manager at the Reinier de Graaf Group Hospitals in Delft, The Netherlands.

Sarah Spiekermann is an assistant professor at the Institute of Information Systems at Humboldt University Berlin, Germany, where she is doing research in the fields of technology acceptance (especially e-privacy), knowledge management and electronic commerce. Besides science and teaching, she serves as the director of InterVal, The Berlin Research Centre on Internet Economics. InterVal is concerned with the impacts of information technology on markets and proposes new solutions to fulfill market requirements. Furthermore, she is leading the TAUCIS project which looks into future implications of ubiquitous computing for our society. Dr. Spiekermann received her PhD in computer science from Humboldt University Berlin. Before that, she worked as a strategy consultant for A.T. Kearney and as a strategic marketing manager for the EMEA for Mobile Internet inventor, Openwave Systems (Redwood City, CA). She studied business and economics at the University of Passau and at the European School of Management (ESCP-EAP) in Paris, Oxford, and Berlin, and holds a MSc degree from Aston University (Birmingham, UK).

Ton A. M. Spil is teaching in the area of business information systems at the University of Twente, The Netherlands. In 1988, he finished his master's in computer science and started his own company consulting big firms on strategic information systems planning. In 1996, he finished his PhD thesis on the effectiveness of these plans, after which he specialized in the application area healthcare and professional organizations. In 2000, he was project manager on a big e-health research project on electronic prescription systems for general practitioners. He edited a book called, *Strategies for Healthcare Information Systems*, published by Idea Group Inc. in 2001. He chaired and organized many healthcare tracks on many conferences (ECIS, HICSS, & IRMA). His main subject of research in 2006 is the governance and inter-organizational aspects of information strategy and user satisfaction of IT in healthcare (USE IT).

Dick Stenmark is a senior lecturer at the Department of Applied IT at the IT University of Göteborg, Sweden. His teaching and research interests include information seeking behaviour, search engines, and knowledge management systems. Dr. Stenmark also has more than 17 years of experience from industry, where he worked as an information architect and intranet consultant. His work is published in the *Scandinavian Journal of Information Systems*, the *European Journal of Information Systems, Knowledge and Process Management*, the *Journal of Management Information Systems*, and he serves as an editorial member for the *International Journal of Knowledge Management*.

Andrea Tapia is an assistant professor of information sciences and technology at The Pennsylvania State University, USA. Prior to her arrival at Penn State, she completed a National Science Foundation funded post-doctoral fellowship at the University of Arizona entitled *Universities in the Information Age*. Her PhD is in the area of sociology and focuses on the study of technology, culture, and workplace organizations. Her most recent work examines the nature of computer-centered, high-tech industry. She is particularly interested in the how the workplace and employer-employee relations change when in a high-tech environment. At the core of her research is her interest in the social values attributed to technology and the power structures that arise within organizations due to the manipulation and use of those techno-values—in other words, techno-social capital. She can be reached by email at atapia@ist.psu.edu.

Eileen M. Trauth serves as a professor of information sciences and technology and as the director of the Center for the Information Society at The Pennsylvania State University, USA. She received her PhD in information science from the University of Pittsburgh. She has received several scholarly awards including the Fulbright Scholar Award, the E.T.S. Walton Visitor Awards from Science Foundation Ireland, and a National Science Foundation IT Workforce Grant. Her research has appeared in *MIS Quarterly, Telecommunications Policy, ACM Transactions on Office Information Systems, Information and Management, and Information Technology and People*. She has also published a book, *The Culture of an Information Economy: Influences and Impacts in the Republic of Ireland*.

Peter Wright is a cognitive scientist with an interest in the experiential, social, and cultural aspects of the design and use of interactive technologies and with developing theory and tools for experience-centred design. He is a reader in human-computer interaction in the Department of Computer Science, University of York, UK.

Yutaka Yoshinaka is an associate professor with a PhD and an AB from Cornell University (1988), and an MSc (Eng.) from the Technical University of Denmark (DTU, 1998) with specialisation in planning and technology management. His research experience includes developing tools for health services quality assessment in Japan (Instructor, Nippon Medical School, Tokyo). From 1999 to 2002, he was a PhD scholar at DTU's Department of Manufacturing Engineering and Management. His dissertation topic was titled, *Knowledge Processes and the Sociotechnical Articulation of Magnetic Resonance Imaging in Interdisciplinary Practice*. His current teaching and research at DTU concerns sociotechnical dimensions of innovation and design practices.

Index

K

kit 29, 31–32, 51–52
KMS 172–174, 177, 180, 187; see also *intranet-based knowledge management system*
knowledge management 172–178, 180, 185–188; see also *intranet, power, practice, rhetoric, technology*
system (KMS) 172–174, 177, 180, 187

L

labour process theory 237
laggards 286, 288
language 195, 197, 203, 205–206
Latour, Bruno 230–232, 239; see also *actor-network theory*
learning
asynchronous 128, 149
styles 129, 130–131, 134, 138, 140–141
life cycle 40–41, 48, 68
localisation 113, 118; see also *location*
local context 173
location 113, 116; see also *localisation*

M

magnetic resonance imaging (MRI) 213, 217, 222
maintenance operator 33
management concept 217–219
Management Science Journal 4
material action 197–198, 201, 203
medical imaging 222
mental models 267–268, 281
metaphor 32, 60, 66–67
visual 66
metrics identification 259
middle-class 8–9
Midgley's onion 52
military enemy 36
Mindpool 308, 315–317, 319–322, 324–326; see also *electronic brainstorming*
mis-use 183
MISQ 4
misunderstanding 172–175, 178–181, 186, 188; see also *ambiguity, interpretive flexibility, failure, multiplicity, negotiation*

mobile computing 152–154
work 152
morphogenetic approach 238, 240; see also *Margaret Archer*
motivation 306, 308–311, 322; see also *incentives, Mindpool, rewards*
extrinsic 309–310, 322, 326, 328
intrinsic 309–310, 322–323
MRI 213, 217, 222; see also *magnetic resonance imaging*
MS 285–286, 288, 293; see also *Multiple Sclerosis*
care 285–287, 293–294, 296–299, 301–302
Multiple Sclerosis (MS) 285–286, 288, 293; see also *chronic disease*
definition 288
multiplicity 173, 176, 179, 187–190; see also *misunderstanding*
multiview 56
mutual constitution 230–231, 234, 237, 240; see also *agency and structure, context, sociotechnical action, structure and agency*

N

narratives 103–104, 106, 120, 173, 183–185, 189
near-knowledge transfer (NKT) 135, 138, 140–141, 144, 146
negative
roles 36
stakeholders 36
negotiation 172, 174, 178–181, 188–189; see also *misunderstanding*
network
building 214, 218
society 215
wireless 152, 154, 159, 161, 171
new institutionalism 237, 238
NKT 135, 138, 140, 141, 144, 146; see also *near-knowledge transfer*
non-use 173, 183–184, 189
normal operator 33

O

OAL 128–134, 137, 140, 145, 147–149; see also *online asynchronous learning*
OAL environment 128–134, 137, 140, 145, 147–148

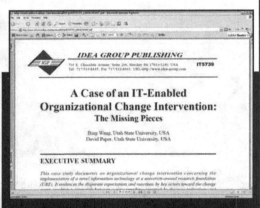